Build the Ultimate Home Theater PC

Build the Ultimate Home Theater PC

Ed Tittel
Mike Chin

Wiley Publishing, Inc.

Build the Ultimate Home Theater PC

Published by
Wiley Publishing, Inc.
10475 Crosspoint Boulevard   OCT 1 2 2006
Indianapolis, IN 46256
www.wiley.com

Published simultaneously in Canada

ISBN-13: 978-0-471-75549-4
ISBN-10: 0-471-75549-4

Manufactured in the United States of America

10 9 8 7 6 5 4 3 2 1

1B/SS/RR/QV/IN

For general information on our other products and services or to obtain technical support, please contact our Customer Care Department within the U.S. at (800) 762-2974, outside the U.S. at (317) 572-3993 or fax (317) 572-4002.

Wiley also publishes its books in a variety of electronic formats. Some content that appears in print may not be available in electronic books.

Library of Congress Cataloging-in-Publication Data

Tittel, Ed.
  Build the ultimate home theater PC / Ed Tittel, Mike Chin.
    p. cm.
  Includes index.
  ISBN-13: 978-0-471-75549-4 (paper/website)
  ISBN-10: 0-471-75549-4 (paper/website)
  1. Home entertainment systems--Amateurs' manuals. 2. Microcomputers--Design and construction--Amateurs' manuals. I. Chin, Mike, 1984- II. Title.
  TK9961.T56 2006
  621.388--dc22
                    2005026455

I dedicate this book to my family. My wife, Dina, and nearly two-year-old son, Gregory, were both inspiration for and victims of this book. I'm grateful for the inspiration and sorry for the lost hours. I'd also like to thank my Mom and Dad for cultivating my love of language and tolerating the curiosity that continues to lead me into new projects and tomfoolery to this very day!

—*Ed Tittel*

Credits

Contributors
Matt Wright
Devon Cooke

Executive Editor
Chris Webb

Senior Development Editor
Kevin Kent

Technical Editor
Loyd Case

Production Editors
Michael Koch
Angela Smith

Copy Editor
Kim Cofer

Editorial Manager
Mary Beth Wakefield

Production Manager
Tim Tate

Vice President and Executive Group Publisher
Richard Swadley

Vice President and Executive Publisher
Joseph B. Wikert

Project Coordinator
Michael Kruzil

Graphics and Production Specialists
Denny Hager
Joyce Haughey
Stephanie D. Jumper
Barbara Moore
Lynsey Osborn
Julie Trippetti

Quality Control Technicians
John Greenough
Leeann Harney
Jessica Kramer
Carl William Pierce

Proofreading and Indexing
TECHBOOKS Production Services

About the Authors

Ed Tittel is a full-time freelance writer and consultant with an interesting background. A former anthropologist by academic training, Ed switched into computing in 1979 and has been working full-time in the field since 1981. Ed's filled a lot of different jobs in various aspects of high-tech including stints as a manager and individual contributor in software development, field applications engineering, network consulting, training, and technical marketing. During his early years in the industry Ed worked for companies like Information Research Associates, Burroughs, Schlumberger, and Excelan. He capped off his corporate tenure with a 7-year stint at Novell, which he ended in 1994 as that company's director of technical marketing when Novell decided to leave his beloved adopted hometown of Austin, Texas.

Ed started writing freelance part-time in 1986 and has been writing full-time since 1994. He's worked on more than 130 books (including more than 60 titles for John Wiley & Sons), and has written thousands of Web and magazine articles. Ed's currently Technology Editor for *Certification Magazine*, and a regular contributor to numerous Web sites, including several TechTarget.com venues, TechBuilder.org, CramSession.com, and others. He also writes for Tom's Hardware and translates articles from German into English for them as well. Ed's most recent book project (not counting this one) is the *PC Magazine Fighting Spyware, Viruses and Malware* (Wiley 2004). Ed's been fooling around with PCs since 1984, when he bought his first one: a giant, cantankerous 80286 PC/AT he'll never forget. While working on this book, the number of PCs Ed has built topped the 40 mark (but the authors did build more than 10 for this project). For more information about Ed, or to contact him by e-mail, visit his Web page at www.edtittel.com.

Mike Chin has been scribbling and messing with gadgets since before dropping out of kindergarten. Korean by birth, Mike bounced between Thailand and Boston, and between arts and sciences, getting a degree in modern history with a minor in physics before his first real job as a business journalist in Bangkok. Canada beckoned in the '80s, and Mike spent a decade in the high-end home audio business, even getting into designing and building custom audio gear.

Since the early 1990s, Mike has worked as a technical writer in hardware development, documentation, and technical marketing. He became a freelance writer/consultant in 1999 and worked on numerous documentation projects for companies in Canada, the U.S., and Taiwan. Mike's main project for the past 4 years has been the Web site he created, www.silentpcreview.com (SPCR), which has become *the* Web authority regarding all things related to acoustics in computers. Over three quarters of the voluminous content of the site bears his byline. "Silent Mike" travels extensively to PC industry events, provides noise-related design consulting for PC companies, and maintains a test lab for acoustic and thermal analysis of the countless PC hardware sent to him for review. SPCR is the closest Mike has come to reaching that elusive equilibrium between science and art, left and right brain.

Contents at a Glance

Contents

• •

Part I: Meet the Modern Multimedia PC

Part II: PC Pieces and Parts

Part III: Planning and Building Your Media Center PC

Part IV: Media Center PC Projects

Acknowledgments

Three different cadres deserve recognition for their parts in this book:

First, there's the bold team of engineers and geeks at IBM in Boca Raton, who not only came up with the PC in 1980–81, but who also did more than anyone might believe to turn it into a genuinely open, industry-wide, non-proprietary phenomenon. Without them, books like this one would simply be impossible.

Second, there's a whole raft of people who helped me work on this book in lots of ways. I can't thank all of them by name, so please accept my thanks in general. Those who I must recognize include Justin Korelc, who helped me put together an amazing number of PCs in few weeks; Richard Bird, who provided insight, experience, advice and more and started me on this project so well; Susan Austin of nVidia, who totally blew me away with her quick and informative responses to some truly odd queries; Greg Messmer of PC Alchemy, who helped me understand the HTPC business; Damon Muzny of AMD who provided great feedback and evaluations; and Vivian Lien of Corsair, who not only offered us RAM for our builds, but lots of news, information, and friendly advice. Thanks also to John Swinimer (ATI), Kevin Tu (Shuttle), Han Liu (Antec), Karen Mazzei (Western Digital), Phil O'Shaughenessy (Creative Labs), Cyrus Cha (Ahanix), Sam Harmer (Micron), Heather Skinner (Kingston), Julie Smith (Edelman/Microsoft), Ming Jeng and Jacky Huang (DFI), Michele Sun and Marti Miernik (AOpen), Tony Ou (Silverstone), Dominic Wong (Avermedia), and a whole slew of folks at Logitech.

Third, there are my colleagues and co-authors. Mike Chin was a great source of information, insight, and advice throughout the writing of this book, as well as taking on several chapters. Matt Wright of HTPCnews.com not only wrote a couple of chapters, but was the ultimate fountain of HTPC knowledge and experience behind this book. Devon Cooke did a great job on the sound cards chapter and provided audio insight for other chapters, as well.

Introduction

Windows Media Center Edition represents a major rethinking and reworking of what an operating system is, what kinds of activities it should support, and how it looks and works. While Media Center Edition 2005 is indeed based on Windows XP post Service Pack 2, it has been rearranged and changed to aim itself squarely at the living room rather than the office, and more for entertainment and less for work. We believe it represents a first big step toward the proliferation of special computer operating environments so that instead of a desktop OS and a server OS we're moving toward more specialized roles and capabilities, of which media center is a first instance of that kind.

In this vein, a Media Center PC (a PC that meets Microsoft's hardware and component requirements to run Windows Media Center Edition, usually abbreviated as MCE) is also somewhat different from a typical desktop or notebook PC. It's got to have a remote control, for one thing, and it's got to be able to handle and manage TV signals, play music and DVDs, and make a place for itself in a typical home entertainment center.

What's a Home Theater PC (HTPC)?

In the most general sense, a Home Theater PC (HTPC) is a personal computer that can acquire, store, manage, and play all kinds of entertainment material. By consensus, this includes television, music, DVD movies, and digital photos. Some HTPCs even provide access to radio transmissions over the air. But because Internet access (a key source of program guides, broadcast/play schedules, and descriptive information about music, movies, TV shows, and other programming material) is *de rigeur* for any HTPC, it's easy to select and listen to any of the thousands of radio stations that stream onto the Internet without a radio receiver of any kind present.

There's no requirement that an HTPC run MCE nor any other Windows operating system (though plenty of them do). Enthusiasts of different stripes will argue with equal vehemence that Linux or the Mac OS (a variant of Unix itself these days) work as well or better than any flavor of Windows you might care to name in an HTPC. But, just as the majority of desktops worldwide run Windows, so do the majority of HTPCs as well. That's why we focus our coverage in this book on Windows Media Center Edition, rather than trying to cover all the possible bases when it comes to building one's own HTPC. While this is in part a function of our own knowledge and experience, having worked with and around Windows more or less exclusively for almost 15 years, it's also a nod in the direction of what's practical—namely, that the vast majority of hardware and software components and products needed to put a fully functional HTPC together are available first and foremost (and often, only) for Windows PCs.

Why Build Your Own HTPC?

This really is a question you'll want to answer before buying this book, and again, before beginning the build process for your own HTPC. At one time, you could have answered "to save money." But today, with some HTPCs available for under $1,000—albeit in tower cases and not terribly well suited for the kind of quiet operation a home entertainment center sometimes demands—you probably won't be able to save that much money by doing it yourself.

To us (and we hope to the majority of readers of this book) the best answers to this question are:

- To learn and understand more about how HTPCs work in general, and how MCE-based HTPCs work in particular

- To invest the care, time, and effort necessary to construct a quiet, good-looking HTPC with the functionality that's right for you

- Because you like to do things yourself, and don't mind spending time, money, and energy on what you do

Certainly for us all of these factors came into play, as well as one other burning desire: to reduce the number of remote controls cluttering our living room coffee tables. At one point, one of the authors of this book had no less than six remotes to deal with for his entertainment center; now, with a sleek, quiet Media Center PC at the heart of that system he need use only one remote regularly (the MCE remote), and another only from time to time (the TV remote to switch video signals so he can watch satellite HDTV—but more on that subject later).

What's in This Book

This book is the result of two years of playing around with Windows Media Center, followed by six intense months of building, tweaking, and taking care of up to half a dozen home-built Media Center PCs. You'll find that the book falls into five parts, each of which addresses part of the HTPC equation:

- Part I introduces the concept of the Home Theater PC, and explains how a basic PC works and what must be added or changed to turn it into an HTPC instead.

- Part II deals with the components that go into a typical HTPC, with a chapter for each of the major components or subsystems involved. Thus, you'll find the case and power supply covered up front, followed by the motherboard, the CPU, memory, hard disks, optical storage/playback, graphics and video, sound cards and audio, loudspeakers, displays, an Internet link, and the remote control all covered in chapters of their own.

- Part III deals with planning, purchasing, assembling, and testing the parts that go into an HTPC, followed by installing MCE 2005 to get the whole system up and running. This is where all the previous parts of the book come together, as you explore the processes involved in putting a system together, then making it work.

- Part IV takes you through three separate HTPC build projects, each with its own case, motherboard, CPU, and so forth. You'll get a detailed bill of materials, walk through construction step-by-step, read about problems encountered and solved, and see photos of the construction process followed by a tour of the finished system.

- Part V comprises supplementary appendixes and includes information and pointers to all kinds of additional detail, news, information, tutorials, and other resources available online. Topics covered include MCE itself, PC hardware information, DVD and movie information, music information and download sources, plus similar coverage of radio, TV, home video, and audio for MCE-based HTPCs.

This book is best read from start to finish in order. However, it was also written so that it can be used as a reference manual for the various components and subsystems in an HTPC, and to document the HTPC build and install processes. Feel free to skip around if you don't want to take each step in the complete journey involved in selecting, purchasing, assembling, testing, and installing all the software and components that go into building a modern Home Theater PC. After an initial read-through, we expect the book will serve best as a reference as and when you go through the steps involved in constructing your own HTPC.

Who This Book Is For

This book is aimed at the intermediate to advanced computer user, preferably one who knows how to use a screwdriver and insert and remove PC components. If you are a beginner or a PC hardware novice, then this book may not be for you. If you understand the basic pieces and parts in a modern PC and aren't afraid to take one apart or (more important) put one together, please dive right in.

You will need to purchase at least $1,000 worth of components and software to put a workable HTPC together(preferably $1,400 or more. If you can't afford that kind of money, it's better to wait until you've got enough funds to start building, though that shouldn't stop you from reading as much as you want in this book or from other sources.

How To Use This Book

You'll want to begin by reading as much of this book in the order in which chapters are presented as you can (if you're already familiar with a topic in Part I or Part II, feel free to skip over those parts). You'll definitely want to read all of Parts III and IV, to get a sense of what's involved in planning, purchasing, assembling, installing, and testing an HTPC system.

Once you start you own construction process, you'll want to return to the chapters in Part II to bone up on the components you'll be selecting and buying. Then you'll want to refer regularly to Part III to help you plan and implement the build process. And of course, if you use one of the three examples presented in Part IV as the blueprint for your own system, you'll want to refer regularly to that chapter as you go through the various steps involved in putting that system together and making it work.

All along the way, you should find the information, references, and resources in Part V at least of interest, if not of definite and immediate help. We tried throughout to include numerous sources for community input, Q&A, and outright support to help you over such rough spots as you may encounter.

Conventions Used in This Book

In this book you will find several notification icons that will point out important information. Specifically, four types of icons will appear:

 Provides valuable information that will help you avoid a disaster.

 Pointers to other parts of the book, or to Internet sites, where you can find more information about whatever subject is at hand.

 Provides extra information to which you need to pay special attention.

 Recommendations to save time, reduce cost, or ensure the best possible results for your HTPC.

Companion Web Site

For links, updates, and news about recent developments, product, or software releases, and other stuff relevant to building an HTPC please visit this book's companion Web site at www.wiley.com/go/extremetech. We're asking readers to share their favorite resources with us and promise to include the best of those in updates to the book's companion site on a timely basis.

If You Build It, They Will Come . . .

We sincerely hope the final result of reading this book is the construction of a fair number of HTPCs. If you build one, we think you'll find (as we have) that a nice, quiet HTPC makes a great addition to (and replacement for) numerous components in a typical home entertainment center. If you plan a good machine, and buy quality components, there's no reason why the ultimate Home Theater PC can't find a home in your entertainment center. Enjoy!

Build the Ultimate Home Theater PC

Meet the Modern Multimedia PC

Basic PC Components and Elements

Before you can build a PC properly, it's important to understand the pieces and parts that go into creating a working personal computer. It's also important to understand the roles that components play, and how various factors in one component can impose requirements and trade-offs on selection of other components. In part, you can understand what's inside a PC (and by extension, what's needed when putting a PC together) by cracking open the case and inspecting its contents. Though the actual components themselves may vary, here's a list of the kinds of things you will always find in or around a PC:

➤ The PC case or enclosure

➤ The PC electrical system, including power supply and cabling

➤ The CPU

➤ Various forms of storage that vary in speed and capacity, including:

  ▪ RAM

  ▪ Hard disks

  ▪ Optical drives, including CD and DVD drives

  ▪ Floppy disk drives (these are uncommon on many PCs nowadays, especially Home Theater PCs)

➤ A motherboard

➤ One or more interface cards that plug into the motherboard (At a minimum this usually includes a graphics card — and at least a TV tuner card — on a Home Theater PC.)

➤ Input devices, such as a keyboard and a mouse

➤ Output devices — for example, a monitor, speakers for sound, a printer for printed output, and so forth

➤ Cooling and ventilation elements

All kinds of other elements appear in many computer systems, but this chapter describes a minimal set of PC components at a basic level of detail. Chapters in Part II of this book cover these same items in detail and tackle only one or two of them in any given chapter. That's where you'll find the most information, vital statistics, tips, and suggestions for researching, selecting, purchasing, installing, and troubleshooting PC components.

Here, you're looking at a fairly generic homebrew desktop PC. In other words, it's stocked with the basic components that any PC typically includes but not the full complement of components that some PCs could include. In the next chapter, you'll see what kinds of components must be added to a generic PC to turn it into a Home Theater PC (HTPC). To facilitate this process, you'll see photos intended to illuminate the discussion of PC component elements, and to illustrate the current focus.

Before Taking a PC System Tour

If you want to take a tour of your own PC, you're certainly welcome to do so. But before you start, you'll want to complete the following steps:

1. Save any work in progress, close all open applications, and then shut down your PC.

2. If the Windows shutdown doesn't turn off the power to your PC (it will on newer systems, but not on older ones), turn off the power yourself. This means finding the power switch for the power supply, which is normally a rocker switch somewhere on the front or back of the unit.

3. Disconnect all cables attached to the PC. If you're not sure you can put things back where you found them later on, draw a diagram that shows where cables go and then label the cables to match that diagram.

Tip

A piece of tape secures a small piece of paper to each cable, if you like (we like 3M invisible tape for this job because it's easy to remove and leaves no sticky residue). When labeling lots of cables, however, we like to use Post-It Flags for this purpose — indeed, 3M even makes Durable Tabs that "are made to last and easy to write on" that are perfect for labeling cables and leaving those labels attached. You can buy Post-It Flags (including Durable Tabs) at most office supply stores like Office Depot or OfficeMax.

4. Examine the PC case to determine what kind of tool(s) you'll need to open it up. Most cases — like the example used in this chapter to illustrate PC components and internals — use machine screws of some kind. Some require a flat head screwdriver, others a Phillips head screwdriver, and still others are best handled with hex drivers or small wrenches. See what you've got, and then pick the best tool for the job. Remove the screws that hold the case together (and re-apply the diagramming advice from the previous step if needed). Slide the case shell off, and you're ready to tour your own system while reading about and looking at the one depicted in this book.

Tip

Whenever you remove screws or other small items from a case, or other computer assembly, store them temporarily in a paper cup, an envelope, or other small container so you can find them when you need to put things back together. If you're taking several things apart (or have small parts from several disassembled components to deal with), be sure to label what's what.

Of course, if you're an experienced PC veteran and have already seen enough PC innards to identify what you see and to know what's where, simply follow along without taking anything apart. There will be plenty of opportunities to take things apart and put them back together later in this book!

After you've cracked the case and removed the shell, don't be surprised if you find some dust and dirt inside the case along with the components you're about to survey. If you want to clean up, you might want to equip yourself with a can of compressed air to blow things clean before you put them back together. You can find single cans and multi-packs at most computer stores (such as Fry's or CompUSA) for $3 or so and up per can.

Caution

Be sure that the power to your PC is completely off before disconnecting any cables. Unplug the power cable from the wall socket before unplugging it from your computer case, just to make doubly sure you're not risking an unpleasant shock or worse. Exercise caution when working inside your PC; although you'd have to work at it to expose yourself to outright hazard, such hazards are there and are best avoided. Don't touch anything you don't have to or aren't instructed to as you follow along in this book.

Figure 1-1 shows the insides of a generic homebrew PC right after the case was opened (and the inside cleaned). Note how the ribbon cables that attach various drives to the motherboard and a SCSI controller obscure much of the inside view. This is typical inside many PCs so don't be surprised if the inside view into your own PC is likewise obstructed.

After removing the cables from the two CD players (one SCSI, the other IDE), the floppy drive, and the hard disk, the PC's innards are much easier to see, as shown in Figure 1-2. This figure serves as the basis for the rest of the tour, with callouts to help you identify various pieces and parts.

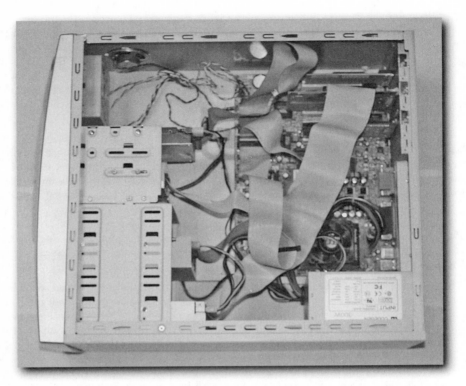

FIGURE 1-1: A first look inside the case shows mostly cables, plus glimpses of other odds and ends.

Unless you're sure you can put things back exactly the way you found them, you might want to label your cables as you remove them. Pay attention to how and where they hook up, so you can replace them correctly. Most drive cable connectors use slots or guides so that connections seat properly only when inserted with the right orientation. But you must pay attention and be gentle when removing or reinserting cable connectors: excess force can damage the connectors on a drive, a controller, or your motherboard. Take our word for it: although it's easy and cheap to replace a cable, you don't want to replace any of those other items (none of them costs less than $25 or $30; some can cost hundreds of dollars).

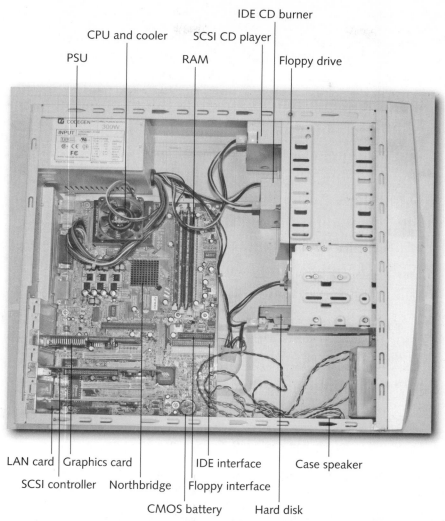

FIGURE 1-2: Once the ribbon cables are out of the way, you can see more of the PC's innards.

First Tour Stop: The Big Picture

Please take another look at Figure 1-2. Careful examination reveals the following:

- The power supply at the upper left, with typical red, yellow, and black wires in bundles that attach to the drives and the motherboard. Notice that the power supply is clearly rated at 300 watts at the upper right of its enclosure.

- The motherboard sits beneath the power supply and extends all the way down to the bottom of the case. A large black plastic fan assembly atop the CPU cooler covers the CPU, and three vertically aligned memory sockets appear to its right. Though you can't see one in this view, the power supply also has its own built-in fan.

- A whole series of connectors that service devices built into the motherboard appear in an integrated block at the upper left, immediately to the left of the CPU cooler. Here's where you'll find USB and DIN-9 connectors for keyboard, mouse, and other devices, as well as serial, parallel, and audio ports.

- The interface cards (and various empty card slots) appear in the lower half of the motherboard, on the left (this lets connectors fit into standard spacers at the back of the case so as to accommodate external cables where needed). There are three interface cards emplaced. From top to bottom they are: a graphics card, a SCSI controller, and a network interface card.

- From the upper-right corner to down below the middle of the case, you see two sets of drive bays. On top, there's room for up to four standard 5.25" devices (of which two slots are occupied with CD drives: player above, burner below; the other two slots are empty). Underneath, there's room for two 3.5" devices: the floppy drive is above, a hard disk below (no empty 3.5" slots, in other words).

- The drive cables connect into rectangular pin blocks at the motherboard's right center, just to the right of the topmost interface card (SCSI controller). The shorter block on top is where the floppy drive's cable plugs in; the two longer blocks beneath it are IDE (integrated drive electronics) connectors. All three of these sockets can support one or two devices, so although this PC uses only one device for each one, the number of devices could double were that necessary or desirable. The ribbon cable for the SCSI CD-ROM player at the very top of the 5.25" drive bay attaches to the SCSI controller card at the lower left, as shown in Figure 1-1.

- The various fine wires at the lower right hook up to controls on the front of the case, including an on-off switch and the reset button, but also to a small loudspeaker mounted in the case at the very bottom beneath the (empty) fan housing.

Notice that all items mentioned at the outset of this chapter in the first recitation of PC components are shown in Figure 1-2, or their presence is indicated by ancillary equipment (as with the CPU cooler, which indicates the presence of a CPU at the same time it hides the CPU from direct view). All of them are also mentioned in one way or another in the preceding list that calls out various elements of the figure. The sections that follow take a closer look at these various elements and give you a chance to understand what role they play in a PC and its operation.

The Case Is Home Base

A recurring question on quiz shows is "What's the largest organ in the human body?" The answer to that question is "the skin," and that's both as obvious and hard to notice as the case is for a PC. Nevertheless, as the outer shell that protects a PC from dirt and jostling, and its users from the sharp points and shock hazards that PC innards present, the case is a key component in any computer. If you look very carefully at Figure 1-2 at the area above the motherboard connector block, you'll see a series of small holes drilled into the plastic housing. That's one of two air vents on the case depicted. The other is at the lower right, where the empty fan housing is situated. In a hotter running PC, it would be a good idea to install a fan there as well. This particular PC contains few enough components that extra cooling isn't necessary.

As we cleaned this case to photograph it, the vent near the CPU cooler was covered in dust, indicating strong air intake (and the CPU cooler's fan is the obvious culprit here). Proper ventilation and sufficient room for a PC's components are the only inarguable must-haves in a PC case. But as you learn in the next chapter (which deals with HTPC requirements) and in Chapter 3 (which covers cases and power supplies), aesthetics, form, materials, extras, and layout can all be important when choosing the right case for any PC — but especially for an HTPC.

Power Makes the PC Go

Many but not all PC cases are sold with power supplies already installed. The power supply is a key PC component because it converts alternating current from the wall socket into direct current (using a transformer) and also delivers various voltage levels to PC devices (common voltage levels inside PCs include 3.3 V, 5 V, and 12 V, among others).

A power supply must be able to provide sufficient power to handle all devices at peak load. Each device on a PC is rated in terms of peak wattage. What's most desirable is that the sum of all device peaks be less than the peak wattage rating for the power supply. What's absolutely mandatory for the PC to work properly is that the sum of all device peaks be no more than the peak wattage rating for the power supply. On the PC depicted in Figures 1-1 and 1-2, total peak wattage for all devices is about 180 watts, or 40 percent lower than the peak wattage for the power supply. That's a comfortable and workable margin and leaves room to add one or two more devices without cause for concern.

When a system vendor or aftermarket system builder puts a PC together, they'll routinely create a power budget for all of the devices that the unit includes (and if there are empty bays or unused interface card or memory sockets, devices that the unit *could* include as well). That's how they make sure the power supply is adequate for the PC they sell. If you build your own PC, this kind of planning becomes your responsibility. That said, you'll find plenty of information in this book to help you plan adequately and to help you stay within your power budget through add-ons and upgrades.

The CPU Does All the Real Computing

A PC's central processing unit, or CPU, is where actual computation takes place in a PC. Though there are plenty of smart chips elsewhere on the motherboard, on interface cards, and even built into storage devices, when you run a program on your PC, it loads and executes on the CPU. That explains why CPU speed and power ratings are so important, and why those who build computers often spend hundreds of dollars on such chips. It also explains why they're willing to spend between $50 and $100 for the best available chip coolers to keep CPUs working at optimal performance levels. The laws of physics and solid state devices pretty much decree that the faster and more powerful a CPU, the more heat it will produce — and hence, the more important cooling becomes.

Beneath the fan and the Thermaltake cooler you can see in Figures 1-1 and 1-2 (it's hard to miss) you'll find a 32-bit Socket A Athlon CPU that runs at 1 GHz. Those in the know can recognize a vintage 2002 CPU from this description, one that today is pretty much obsolete and more deserving of pity than respect. Windows XP Professional requires only a 300 MHz CPU or better, but even so this relative old-timer pokes along as compared to its more modern brethren.

CPU issues are raised again in the next chapter, when important trade-offs between quiet operation and performance are covered. They also provide a key focus in Chapter 5, which takes CPUs as its primary subject (and keeping them cool as a secondary subject).

Everything Lives in Storage

PCs come equipped with many and varied forms of storage. Even CPUs incorporate some relatively small amounts of storage where they keep upcoming data and instructions close at hand so they can grab and use them quickly, and as a place to store the results of current computations or operations. On a computer, storage may be organized into a hierarchy by speed and size, where items that persist over time reside primarily in bigger but much slower storage devices. While programs are executing or data is being processed, however, it tends to flow through smaller, faster elements in the hierarchy at extremely rapid rates (see Table 1-1).

Table 1-1	**Elements in a Computer Storage Hierarchy**	
Speed/Size	*Type/Name*	*Description*
Fastest/ Smallest	CPU registers	Where instructions and data that the CPU will use next or is using now reside, and where immediate results of computation are deposited.
	CPU caches: L1 cache L2 cache	Storage space built onto the CPU chip. Pre-fetched instructions and read-ahead data stored for imminent use. Local data and operating context maintained here.
	RAM	Where programs that are running and data being used reside, sometimes in whole, often in part (other parts may be on disk, particularly large programs or data sets too big to fit into RAM).
	Disk	Where programs reside when not running, and where data, documents, and other items reside when not in use.
	Optical media	Where programs or data reside when not stored on disk, or as archived for protection, distribution, or playback (as with music CDs or movies on DVD).
Slowest/ Largest	Tape	Archival medium designed for backup, long-term storage, or to meet records retention requirements. Seldom, if ever, used on most PCs.

Drives also form their own subhierarchy within this larger hierarchy. Disk drives are faster than optical or floppy drives, so the former are used for active data storage, whereas the latter tend to be used for archiving, program or data distribution, and playback of large recorded works (such as music on CD or movies on DVD).

Storage essentially provides room for computers to work in at the smaller, faster end of the hierarchy and room for computers to store programs and data in at the bigger, slower end of the hierarchy. But nearly all elements in the hierarchy are important (the advent of very large, cheap disk and optical drives is slowly but surely pushing tape out of this picture) and hence nearly all of them get significant coverage in this book.

A typical home user Windows XP PC is perfectly adequate with 512MB to 1GB of RAM, 80 to 120GB of hard disk space, and a CD or DVD burner or player (note: if you buy a burner, you automatically get a player as well). In the next chaper, you'll learn more about how these requirements change in the face of large digital media collections on an HTPC. In Chapters 6, 7, and 8 you'll learn more about what that means for RAM, hard disks, and optical storage devices, respectively.

Everything Plugs Into the Motherboard

If the CPU is the brains of a PC (as the analogy so often goes) the motherboard is its Grand Central Station. Everything on its way into or out of the PC travels through the motherboard at some point or another. It's also where most devices ultimately attach and it provides the sockets or connections where RAM, interface cards, and the CPU all plug themselves in, as well as home to the connectors for user input devices such as a mouse and keyboard.

These days, more and more functions that used to require interface cards are built into motherboards. This doesn't mean you can't elect to use a higher quality, more capable interface card to perform some task or deliver a specific capability, but it certainly makes it cheaper and easier to use plain-vanilla built-in implementations where quality and performance may not be terribly important.

Three common examples of built-in functionality on modern motherboards include the following:

- **Audio:** What used to require installing a sound card is now part and parcel of most modern motherboards. Users with special audio requirements or who want the highest possible fidelity may still elect to disable onboard sound and install a high-end sound card instead.

- **Graphics:** Most motherboards include basic built-in graphics, on a level with what you'd get from a $40 PCI graphics card with 64MB of video RAM. That's not good enough for HTPC use, though it is adequate for people who don't play animated games, watch DVDs, or do other things on their PCs that require more graphics "oomph."

■ **Network access:** Most motherboards include one or more network interfaces these days; often this means two 10/100 Ethernet links, or a 10/100 and Gigabit Ethernet, or some combination of wired and wireless Ethernet connections. Except for servers or other PCs that require lots of network links or extremely high performance, hardly anybody installs network interfaces in PCs any more.

For typical desktop use at home or in the office, PC buyers are happy to save money and use built-in capabilities instead of buying additional interface cards. For a Home Theater PC, this certainly applies to networking (if the right kind is available), but it may not apply to sound, depending on how the HTPC will be used. Graphics and video cards are covered in Chapter 9, sound cards in Chapter 10, and network connections in Chapter 13.

User Input: Keyboard, Mouse, and . . .

For most home and office desktop users, a keyboard and a mouse are the only user input devices needed. Today, an emerging question for how these devices connect to the PC then becomes "Stay wired or go wireless?" But because the built-in connectors required for a Windows mouse and keyboard are built into all PCs, only the type, look and feel, and cost of these devices typically come into play. Gamers may also add a game controller to their user input device collection, but that's usually about it.

This changes dramatically when you're considering an HTPC, as you learn in the next chapter. That Chapter 14 devotes itself in part to infrared remote controls should tell you something about what's involved in that change!

Computer Output: Monitor, Printer, and . . .

For all computer users some kind of display is essential to tell them what their computer is doing and also what they're doing with their computers (as the characters popping up on my own monitor as I type this and every sentence for this book continually remind me). For most home and office desktop users a 15- or 17-inch cathode-ray tube (CRT) or liquid crystal display (LCD) is adequate; power users may up the size of the display to 19 inches or beyond. Some gonzo types may even elect to use multiple monitors so they can multitask more effectively, or simply because modern Windows versions let them do so.

Many computer users also have at least one printer available to them, often attached using the universal serial bus (USB) or perhaps a parallel printer port (although this is less common nowadays, even modern PCs still include parallel ports in the battery of standard connectors). Whether that printer is a laser or an inkjet or prints in color or monochrome, most offices and households keep at least one printer around.

Things change on an HTPC, as you learn in the next chapter, both in terms of displays (think TV and home theater) and in the lesser likelihood that a printer is attached to such a PC (although there may be one attached to another PC somewhere else on the network).

Cool Runnings

No PC will work without some cooling and ventilation. Even the relatively old model photographed for Figures 1-1 and 1-2 requires airflow of 50 cubic feet per minute (cfm) over its poky CPU. More modern CPUs require even more airflow, as do the bigger power supplies necessary to feed them the electricity they consume. The same is true for more powerful graphics cards, which now include fans to cool their fast and powerful GPUs (graphics processing units) as a matter of course.

In general, the more stuff you have inside your PC, the more important cooling becomes. It's not unthinkable that added ventilation would be needed in the PC depicted earlier in this chapter were it to house an additional hard disk or two, more memory, and a high-end graphics card, all of which it could accommodate with relative ease.

Cooling deserves even more attention in HTPCs than in ordinary desktops for all kinds of reasons. That's why the topic of cooling is revisited in the next chapter, and covered in Chapters 3 (cases and power supplies), 5 (CPUs), and 9 (graphics cards) as well.

Putting All the PC's Pieces to Work

In the conclusion to this introductory chapter, we want to follow what happens to the various parts of a PC as you turn the power on, and the machine starts up. This will allow you to understand how and when the various parts of the PC come into play. It will also provide an opportunity to introduce other parts of the system, including some items on the motherboard to which you've not yet been introduced. So buckle up, don your hardhat and safety goggles, and let's walk through what happens during initial startup on a PC.

Step 1: Turn On the Power

Many modern PCs have two power switches: one on the front and one on the back. Either way, when you first switch on the power, the power supply comes up and begins to feed voltage into the rest of the system — in fact, as you look at the insides of your PC you can see exactly where that power goes by following the wire bundles from the power supply to their destinations. In the machine depicted in Figures 1-1 and 1-2, power goes to four places: the motherboard, the CD-ROM drive, the floppy drive, and the hard disk. The interface cards draw power from the motherboard, which delivers power through its onboard circuitry to the interface card sockets. Likewise, the CPU and RAM also draw power from the motherboard, as do all other devices built into or mounted onto the motherboard.

Tip If your PC has two power switches, it's for a good reason. The one on the back is usually built right into the power supply, whereas the one on the front is controlled through the motherboard. In that case, the switch on the front lets you turn the machine on when you want. But after Windows starts, such PCs usually turn control of that switch over to the motherboard, which in turn grants control to Windows. That explains how and why some machines can power themselves off when you perform a Windows shutdown. The switch on the back lets you turn the PC off even when it's hung or crashed because it basically controls access to A/C power directly. Thus, it's smart to think of (and use) the switch on the back only in cases of dire emergency, when you're sure you'll need to reboot in any case.

Step 2: Power-On Self-Test Routines

You've probably noticed that when you turn your PC on, several sequences of character text parade across the screen before the actual operating system boot-up begins. What's going on is that all those interface cards and the motherboard that come equipped with a basic input/output system, or BIOS, run a set of diagnostic routines to make sure they're working okay and that all parts are functional and accessible. These are known as Power-On Self-Test or POST routines and serve to prevent a PC from hurting itself (or its data) by trying to operate when the system doesn't check out properly. If it helps you to think of POST routines as a mandatory pre–boot-up check, feel free to look at them that way.

During the POST phase the little speaker you saw attached to motherboard and the bottom right of the case in Figures 1-1 and 1-2 really comes into its own. Though it can be forced to play real audio, its primary job is to make "beep codes" audible. Different BIOSes have different beep codes, so if you'd like to know more about how to interpret them, check the Cross Reference later in this section. Here and now, it suffices to say that when something goes wrong during the POST sequence, beep codes permit the PC to inform you about its status and provide clues as to the source of the problem(s) involved.

A more detailed look at the POST sequence runs as follows:

1. Test the power supply to make sure it's turned on and has released its reset signal (indicates proper operation: no beep means power supply OK).

2. CPU exits its reset status mode and confirms that it can execute instructions (no beep means CPU OK).

3. BIOS performs self-test to make sure it's readable and that its checksum is valid (calculated value matches stored value, indicating no corruption or damage; no beep means BIOS OK).

4. A special form of computer memory called CMOS performs a self-test to make sure it's readable and that its checksum is also valid (no beep means CMOS OK). (CMOS stands for complementary metal-oxide semiconductor, but what's important about this battery-powered memory is that it contains the current and correct configuration information that the PC needs to identify all installed devices, interface cards, and so forth.) Note: You can see the CMOS battery in Figure 1-2 at the bottom right of the motherboard; it's the circular metal disk that looks like a coin. Its job is to provide continuous power to the CMOS even when the PC is shut down, to keep current configuration data available for the next boot-up.

5. CPU performs a memory check on the motherboard, and checks its memory controller, the memory bus, and all installed memory modules (no beep means memory hardware checks out OK).

6. The first 64K of memory is checked for read/write capability; if it checks out OK, it will have the remaining POST code copied to it, and will run from that memory afterward (no beep means memory read/write check is OK).

7. The I/O bus and controller are checked to make sure they're accessible and working properly. (This is what the computer uses to communicate with other devices in the PC, including interface cards, storage devices, and so forth; no beep means I/O hardware check is OK.)

8. The I/O bus must be able to read/write from the video subsystem and be able to read video RAM (this is when the BIOS on a graphic card will perform its own POST, if applicable) and when actual screen output during the boot process can begin (no beep means video subsystem checks out OK).

Only if your PC reports OK status on all checks mentioned here will it actually begin the boot process. But first, if other interface cards have BIOSes on board, their POST routines must also complete successfully. Hopefully, it's also obvious that if you hear no beeps but your PC does nothing that something is wrong with delivery of power to the motherboard, making some kind of power supply problem the most likely culprit.

 Cross-Reference Lots of potential sources about POST beep codes are available online. One especially good one is at www.computerhope.com/beep.htm. You'll find a complete explanation of the POST process there, plus pointers to beep codes for major varieties of PC BIOS (and the Macintosh).

Step 3: The Boot Load Process

When the POST completes succesfully on any Intel *x*86-compatible computer (which includes pretty much anything that identifies itself as a PC nowadays), the CPU reads the CMOS to identify a boot drive. The first sector on this drive (cylinder 0, head 0, sector 1) includes two very special items of information:

■ A small but very special program called a *boot loader*, which seeks the bootable partition on the boot drive and loads the first sector of that partition into memory to continue the boot process

■ The *partition table* for the boot drive, which indicates how the drive is divided up into one or more independent group of sectors called partitions

Together, these items comprise the first sector of the boot drive, which is often called the Master Boot Record, or MBR. It's one of the most important keys to a successful system boot on a PC.

When the boot loader executes, it checks the partition table to look for an entry with the "bootable" or "active" flag set to identify where the next program to control the booting process is located. The boot loader reads the first sector of the boot partition into memory (which is known as the Boot Sector, not to be confused with the MBR) and then turns control over to the program that begins there.

The program in the Boot Sector looks for the operating system kernel, loads it into memory, and starts it running. This is the point at which the real software boot process begins, and the boot loader ceases operation. On modern Windows operating systems (Windows NT Workstation, Windows 2000 or XP Professional, Windows XP Home, and all related Server versions, plus Windows 2003 Server) a program named NTLDR takes over for the operating system boot.

Step 4: (Windows) Operating System Boot-Up

NTLDR reads a special data file called `boot.ini`. If multiple operating systems are present on the PC, it offers a menu that allows users to select the operating system they'd like to boot (but defaults to a specific item after a timeout period expires). It's also possible to force Windows to boot into one of various modes at this point (Safe mode, Safe mode with networking, Last Known Good Configuration, and so on) to override normal boot behavior.

After those selections are made or a timeout expires, operating system boot-up begins in earnest. Windows then begins to load and execute operating system kernel files, which make up the core of the operating system. Next, NTLDR causes a program named NTDETECT.COM to execute. It probes the system completely to build a list of all installed hardware components found. After this, NTLDR loads the CPU-specific portion of the operating system kernel along with device drivers for all devices marked as boot devices. After these processes complete successfully, NTLDR turns control over to the primary Windows kernel program NTOSKRNL.EXE, which in turn completes loading basic services needed for minimal operation. At this point, Windows switches from character mode (only text characters show on screen, as in the command window) to graphics mode and displays a graphical screen with a status bar to show load progress.

When the final operating system load completes, Windows displays a login window. Only after a user logs in to the system successfully is Windows boot-up considered complete. After that, the PC is yours to do whatever you want it to, subject only to the limits of your imagination, the Windows operating system, and the programs at your disposal.

Cross-Reference The best and most comprehensive description of the Windows XP boot process resides on the dotnetjunkies Web site at `http://dotnetjunkies.com/WebLog/unknownreference/articles/12284.aspx`. It's cited as having been copied from a course handout at Quinebaug Valley Community College in Connecticut, but because the original is no longer available, this copy will have to suffice. If you want to know more you should definitely read this run-through.

Wrapping Up

Although Home Theater PCs and more ordinary PCs — like the ones you've read about in this chapter — have a lot in common, numerous and important differences exist between an ordinary home or office desktop and a Home Theater PC. In this chapter, you learned what kinds of parts and components the two types of PCs share; in the next chapter, you learn how the components in an HTPC can differ from their more ordinary counterparts, as well as what kinds of parts an HTPC is likely to incorporate that an ordinary PC might not.

Bringing Media to the PC

A simple equation can help illuminate this chapter and the primary subject of this book. Let's write it as PC + media = Home Theater PC (HTPC), and restate it in a sentence as "Adding entertainment and other media to a PC produces a Home Theater PC." Although this may not be literally true, it's certainly true enough to explain much of what makes a Home Theater PC so different from a typical desktop PC. This chapter explores those differences in more detail, and this should help you understand why a typical HTPC has more components than a desktop PC, and why so many of its requirements diverge from those for desktop PCs as well.

Though the actual home theater components in an HTPC will vary, here's a list of the kinds of things you will find in many Home Theater PCs that you may or may not find in most desktop PCs. Remember also that everything mentioned in Chapter 1 as a basic PC component is needed in an HTPC, though some component choices will differ from what you'd buy for a desktop PC:

➤ A combination CD/DVD player that can play music CDs and movie DVDs, as well as read computer media in each format.

➤ A sound card with multichannel audio capabilities, which might be attached to a home entertainment system (a receiver or home theater unit) or directly to a set of loudspeakers.

➤ A television interface, often called a TV card. These include one or two TV tuners, and might be attached to a computer monitor, a conventional TV, or a High Definition TV (HDTV). Some TV cards also include FM receivers and can play radio stations as well.

➤ A remote control, suitable for managing content and program selection without requiring use of mouse or keyboard.

These are just the items that are more or less typical in an HTPC that appear less frequently in desktop PCs (if at all). In the next section, you can get a sense of how HTPC requirements can influence the selection of other items that are common or required in any PC.

What's Different About an HTPC?

Many of the conventional PC components mentioned in Chapter 1 are subject to a different set of selection criteria when they're destined for use in a Home Theater PC. Here's a brief rundown of some considerations that differ between desktop and Home Theater PCs:

- Because cases and power supplies are bundled so often, both elements become subject to special needs in an HTPC. Most HTPC buyers prefer horizontal cases to match the other components in their entertainment systems — not to mention problems inherent in shoehorning a tower case into a typical entertainment center. Home theater use also demands a degree of quiet in the living or family room that's seldom necessary in an office, whether it be at home or at work. This means power supplies and other cooling gear inside the case become subject to substantial noise constraints.

- Graphics cards must be able to drive television sets as well as computer monitors. A living or family room situation and entertainment use argues that a TV set is the most likely display that an HTPC will drive. This means that if the TV set can't accommodate a digital video input (DVI, increasingly common on newer TVs), the graphics card must offer some kind of video output suitable for a TV set. In this case, component video outputs deliver the best results, with S-Video in second place.

- Requirements for quiet operation also impact selection of other PC components, especially those with fans or other moving parts. This means CPU coolers and other fans must be as quiet as possible. It also means that storage devices such as hard disks and optical drives must be selected not just by type or capacity, but also by the amount of noise they produce.

- The large collections of files and large file sizes associated with digital computer media — including digital photos, music, recorded television programs, DVDs, and so forth — mean that HTPCs must provide large amounts of storage space to accommodate typical and sizable media collections. 200GB is a bare minimum; 500GB to 1TB (1,000GB) is probably more workable. (Note: Although this storage should be available, it doesn't have to be housed inside the HTPC itself.)

- A mouse and keyboard are helpful at times on an HTPC, but the typical operating scenario — user on the couch, HTPC in the entertainment center — makes wireless versions of these devices more practical and usable than wired ones.

- HTPCs need Internet access every bit as much as desktop PCs. But if a network connection isn't handy (available on the wall behind the entertainment center, in other words), a wireless network link is more practical and easier to install and manage.

- An HTPC is likely to spend lots of time crunching on big digital media files. Some of the processing involved requires substantial CPU and memory resources, which in turn suggests that more powerful CPUs and more memory are preferable. This requires making trade-offs between power and noise, because more power produces more heat and requires more cooling, which in turn inevitably causes more noise.

- An HTPC requires specialized software to handle the many and varied forms of digital media that such PCs store, organize, and play back or display on demand. This book focuses on a special version of Windows XP called Microsoft Windows XP Media Center Edition 2005. It incorporates all kinds of special features and functions, from an interface designed to look good on a TV set and work well with a remote control to a set of capabilities designed to handle digital music, photos, movies, TV, and radio with ease and simplicity.

 Cross-Reference You learn more about Windows XP Media Center Edition (MCE) 2005 later in this chapter, but it's discussed further throughout this book. In particular, Chapter 14 deals with MCE-compatible remote controls, and Chapter 17 covers installing and configuring MCE on a newly built Media Center PC.

Although the foregoing information suggests a set of design considerations for HTPCs, it's probably a good idea to state them explicitly and directly. In the section that follows, you find a set of HTPC design elements that we've elicited from reading just about every resource we can find on the subject, our own experience with HTPCs, and reading about the many pre-fab Media Center PC offerings available around the world.

Elements of HTPC Design

To understand an HTPC it's important to approach its design from numerous perspectives. The following list of items derives from an appreciation of where an HTPC is likely to be situated as much as it does from a technical analysis of the kinds of things it must do. That said, here's a handful of considerations you'd be wise to keep in mind at all times as you decide what components should go into your HTPC (or as you evaluate the components in somebody else's design, should you decide to buy a pre-fab unit instead):

- Horizontal cases fit entertainment centers better than vertical ones do (it's not advisable in many cases to turn vertical cases on their sides as a quick-and-dirty fix). State this design guide as "Horizontal is better than vertical."

- Quiet operation is essential if you want to use your HTPC for movies and music. Both have quiet passages in which the noise from a typical desktop PC can be noticeable, if not distracting or downright objectionable. State this design guide as "Keep it quiet!"

- When it comes to memory, storage, and CPU power, more is almost always better on an HTPC. Though this will clash with the preceding design guide, it's also important to build enough of all three components into your HTPC to do the job adequately, if not extremely well. State this design guide as "Build in ample storage, memory, and CPU power."

- Standard televisions use analog signals, but computers use digital data representations. The best-looking TV uses as much digital technology as possible. This may mean older TV sets should be replaced with newer ones that handle digital and analog inputs with equal facility. State this design guide as "Do it in digital if you can."

- The home theater experience is more enjoyable and authentic on larger displays, and you can get more from DVD movies and modern High Definition TV on displays that work more like movie screens than conventional TVs. This might mean switching from an older CRT (tube) based TV set to a bigger, wider, flat screen or (rear) projection TV setup. State this design guide as "Wide screen displays make better home theater."

- The home theater experience is also more enjoyable and authentic when accompanied by multichannel sound systems. If you're still listening to two-channel hi-fi, you might want to consider moving to five or more channels, with speakers and output to match. Many users simply connect their HTPCs to multichannel home entertainment systems; others simply attach multichannel speaker systems to their HTPCs and do away with the other stuff. State this design guide as "Multichannel sound delivers better home theater."

Use these design guides to help you decide what you need in your HTPC, and to help you trade off what you want versus what you can afford. If you do, you'll be able to assemble components that will help you not only get your entertainment media organized and under control, but also make it enjoyable to view and share with others.

Making Trade-Offs

It's essential to understand the principle of an engineering trade-off so you can build an HTPC that you can live with, but one that also does the things you want it to do. The notion of a trade-off means that you must trade one thing against another. The concept of an engineering trade-off means you must sacrifice one thing to gain another any time you select the elements in a real solution. Where HTPCs are concerned, one such trade-off pits computing power and capability against noise. You must balance things like total CPU power, memory and storage capacity, computer graphics handling capability, and the addition of more bells and whistles to your system against the increases in noise that they bring to your listening or viewing experience.

Most experts appear to value quiet over raw power. Our own experience has been that a quieter (but less powerful) HTPC produces a more positive listening or viewing experience as well. Only you can decide how to balance this particular trade-off for yourself.

Other trade-offs you'll inevitably tackle include cost versus function and cost versus quiet. This is a polite way of warning you that building a more powerful, capable system costs more than building a less powerful and capable one. Interestingly, a deliberate choice of the quietest components across the board will also cost more than buying plain-vanilla components, even though it may result in an HTPC that's less powerful and capable than a noisier system would be.

Taking an HTPC System Tour

This part of the chapter shows some photographs of the innards of two different Media Center PCs:

- **An HP Media Center m7070n Photosmart PC** (see Figure 2-1). This is a moderately priced unit (about $1,200 with applicable discounts) from a well-known global PC vendor. It uses a tower case and offers a middle-of-the-road collection of components and capabilities.

FIGURE 2-1: Inside the case of the HP m7070n Photosmart PC.

■ **A Hush Technologies Media Center Edition 2005 PC** (see Figure 2-2). This is a higher-priced unit (about $2,500) from a boutique designer and builder of silent, fanless PCs. It's built using a heavy-duty, solid, horizontal, low-profile aluminum case with components on a par with those found in the HP in terms of capability, but quieter than those in the HP unit.

FIGURE 2-2: Inside the case of the Hush MCE 2005 PC.

In the sections that follow, you find separate discussions of each system, followed by a concluding section that compares (primarily in Table 2-1, which lists their components side by side) and contrasts these two offerings (in the discussion that follows the table).

Touring the HP m7070n

Before you read about what you see in Figure 2-1, here's a list of the typical components inside an HP m7070n:

■ **CPU:** Intel Pentium 4 640 (3.2 GHz) with hyperthreading technology

■ **Memory:** 1GB DDR PC3200 RAM (up to 4GB max)

- **Graphics card:** ATI Radeon X300 SE PCI-E 128MB video RAM and TV output
- **Hard drive:** 250GB 7200 RPM SATA hard disk
- **Optical drives:** LightScribe Double Layer DVD±R/RW (also CD burner), 24x DVD ROM player (2 total)
- **TV card:** Hardware encoder with personal video recorder (PVR) capability, single TV tuner, FM tuner (with antenna), works with cable, digital cable, satellite TV, and antenna
- **Front access ports:** 9-in-1 memory card reader, HP Personal Media drive bay, 2 USB 2.0, 1 FireWire (IEEE 1394), microphone/headphone
- **Rear access ports:** 4 USB 2.0, 1 FireWire (IEEE 1394), composite video, S-Video, and Audio inputs, serial, parallel, mouse, and keyboard ports
- **Networking:** 10/100 Base-T network interface
- **Sound:** Intel High Definition Audio (up to 7.1 surround sound)
- **Remote:** HP MCE remote with IR receiver
- **Peripherals:** HP multimedia keyboard and optical mouse (wired), 56K modem
- **Case:** Standard PC tower with 300 W fan-cooled power supply
- **Dimensions:** 15.16" × 7.6" × 16.54" (vertical tower)

In reexamining Figure 2-1, please notice the following. First, you can see two unused PCI slots at the lower left (beneath the graphics card and above the TV card). Second, you can see one unused 3.5" drive bay if you look carefully at the right center part of the figure (one is for the 250GB hard disk; the other is for a removable HP Personal Media Drive). Notice all the individual cables you can see snaking out of the power supply, down the rear of the drive bays, and at the bottom of the case. Finally, check out the enormous fan on top of the CPU cooler. Big is better when it comes to fans, because they can move more air when turning more slowly (and slower rotation means less noise). This is a decent-looking PC inside, and the tower case does leave plenty of room for air to circulate and for other components to be added later on.

Touring the Hush MCE 2005 PC

Before you read about what you see in Figure 2-2, here's a list of the components inside a baseline Hush MCE 2005 PC (upgrades for most components are available from the vendor at extra cost; a totally maxed-out system would cost about $3,700):

- **CPU:** Intel Pentium 4 (2.8 GHz, Socket 478, 800 MHz FSB) with hyperthreading technology
- **Memory:** 512MB DDR PC3200 RAM (up to 4GB max)
- **Graphics card:** ATI Radeon 9600 128MB video RAM and TV output
- **Hard drive:** 200GB 7200 RPM Seagate Barracuda SATA hard disk

- **Optical drive:** TEAC DV-W24E Slimline DVD±R/RW (also CD burner)
- **TV card:** Hauppauge WinTV-PVR-150MCE includes PVR, hardware encoder, single TV and FM tuner
- **Front access ports:** 2 USB 2.0, 2 FireWire (IEEE 1394), microphone/headphone
- **Rear access ports:** 4 USB 2.0, composite video, S-Video, and audio inputs, serial, parallel, mouse, and keyboard ports
- **Networking:** 10/100 Base-T network interface
- **Sound:** High Definition Audio (up to 8-channel surround sound, including SPDIF and RCA audio outputs for integration with entertainment systems)
- **Remote:** Microsoft MCE remote with IR receiver
- **Peripherals:** None included
- **Case:** Heavy custom aluminum case with 240 W Hush silent power supply
- **Dimensions:** 14.9" × 4" × 17" (horizontal slimline case)

There's a lot less room inside the Hush case than inside the HP case so things are a lot more crammed together. The first thing that jumps out is the total absence of fans; instead, a heat pipe conducts heat from the CPU just below center in the photo to the right-hand edge of the case, where it can dissipate through the unit's enormous external heat sink. The unit accommodates only two interface cards in a riser from the motherboard at the lower right. Both expansion slots are taken: one for the graphics card, the other for the TV card. There's no room to grow in this PC, making remove and replace the only options for changes or upgrades.

Finally, notice the total absence of loose wire bundles. All wires are neatly enclosed in nylon mesh sleeves, no bare wires anywhere are longer than they need to be. This is a highly sophisticated build-out, and probably the nicest looking set of purchased PC innards we have ever seen. Only a serious case modder would care enough to create a better looking layout than this!

HP and Hush: Compared and Contrasted

As Table 2-1 illustrates, you pay slightly more than twice as much for the Hush PC, and get slightly less for your money. Why then would anybody want to double their outlay? The company name, Hush Technologies, says it all: this PC is as close to silent as any device with one or more disk drives can get. Although you can occasionally hear a drive working (both optical and hard disk drives make some noise), there's no constant white noise from any fan to interfere with listening to music or watching movies. Apparently, for some media fans this degree of quiet is worth paying a hefty premium to obtain.

Table 2-1   HP and Hush PCs Side-by-Side

Feature/function	HP	Hush	Difference
CPU	P4 3.2 GHz	P4 2.8 GHz	HP uses newer socket type, faster CPU
Memory	1GB PC3200	512MB PC3200	Both have same max RAM capacity; HP doubles Hush
Graphics card	ATI Radeon X300 PCI-E	ATI Radeon 9600 AGP 8x	Both comparable; HP's is newer, faster
Hard drive	250GB 7200 RPM	200GB 7200 RPM	HP offers 50GB more storage on a noisier drive
Optical drive(s)	DVD±R/RW, DVD-ROM	DVD±R/RW	HP includes second read-only DVD drive
TV card	Single TV/FM tuner, PVR	Single TV/FM tuner, PVR	Both nearly identical
Front access ports	9-in-1 memory card reader, 2 USB 2.0, FireWire, microphone/ headphone	2 USB 2.0, 2 FireWire, microphone/ headphone	Hush has no card reader; HP has only 1 FireWire
Rear access ports	4 USB 2.0, FireWire, etc.	4 USB 2.0, etc.	Both nearly identical; Hush puts all FireWire on front
Networking	10/100 Base-T interface	10/100 Base-T interface	Both identical
Sound	Intel High Definition up to 7.1	High Definition up to 7.1	Both nearly identical
Remote	HP MCE remote	Microsoft MCE remote	Both nearly identical
Peripherals	Keyboard, mouse	None included	HP yes, Hush no
Case	Vertical tower	Heavy aluminum horizontal	HP offers a PC; Hush a work of art
Dimensions	15.16" × 7.60" × 16.54"	14.9" × 4" × 17"	Hush case smaller and sleeker; HP bigger and roomier

Given the price points for the two machines, it's likely that HP will sell a great many more m7070n units than Hush will sell MCE 2005 PCs. But given that the Hush unit offers only half as much RAM, a slower CPU, and 50GB less disk space, lacks a second optical drive, and includes neither mouse nor keyboard, it's a testament to the appeal of quiet computing that the company sells any at all. And sell them they do indeed (and according to several dealers in the United States, most buyers add more memory, disk space, and dual tuner TV cards to their machines, and pay around $3,100 for a typical Hush MCE 2005 PC purchase).

Windows Media Center Edition Basics

The version of Windows you most often see called MCE or MCE 2005 in this book is formally known as "Microsoft Windows XP Media Center Edition 2005." It's essentially a heavily modified and extended version of Windows XP Home Edition with Service Pack 2 (SP2) applied. Those modifications and extensions are what make MCE different from plain-vanilla Windows XP, so that's what's covered in this basic introduction and overview. Right now, if you think of MCE as a version of XP designed to look good on a TV set, to work well with a multibutton remote control, and to handle media of all kinds, you're starting to catch on.

The best way to appreciate the differences between ordinary Windows XP and MCE is to compare MCE's start-up screen to XP's Start menu. These are depicted in Figures 2-3 and 2-4 and show that whereas XP offers a standard "tell me what to do" type of selection menu, MCE offers access to various types of media for viewing or playback instead.

There's actually more going on in the MCE interface than a printed screen shot can illustrate. What the screen can't show is that it was captured on a television screen, not a computer monitor. There's no real sense of scale from the image, but it reads very well from across the room. A typical computer user sits no more than 30 inches away from most monitors and is often closer; a typical entertainment center user sits at least 48 inches away from most TV sets and is often further away. Microsoft uses very large characters and created a special font to make MCE menus and selections as easy as possible to read.

On MCE-compatible remote controls the green button is one that triggers the MCE interface to open (in fact, the same green icon that appears in the upper right of the screen in Figure 2-3 matches the green button on Microsoft's own MCE remote control device, and the button on OEM versions like the HP remote). It's easy to change the highlighted item in the pick list using up or down buttons on the remote, and a click of the OK button triggers a subsidiary menu display that uses the same large fonts and easy-to-navigate layouts.

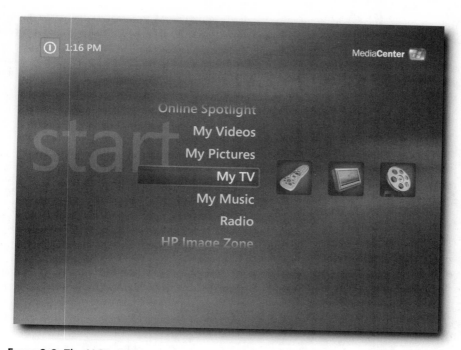

FIGURE 2-3: The MCE start-up screen aims straight at media: videos, pictures, TV, music, and radio are the primary choices.

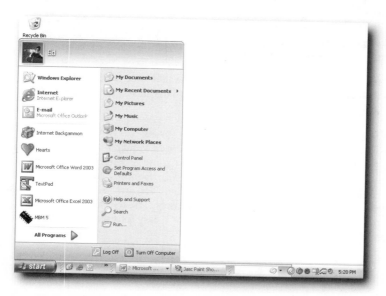

FIGURE 2-4: The Windows XP Start menu lets you pick among tasks, applications, and data collections, organized in various ways.

MCE also presents screens of information designed to be easy to interpret and understand. One of the underpinnings of MCE's handling of TV listings is called the electronic program guide, or EPG. A sample listing appears in Figure 2-5 and shows six channels' worth of programs across a 3-hour time slot. Selecting a program to watch is as easy as using up and down, right and left buttons to land on the right item, and then pressing OK. It's just as easy to record a program by pushing the record button on the remote instead.

FIGURE 2-5: The EPG makes it easy to pick programs by channel, time slot, or program name (note how the remote uses Rewind and Fast Forward buttons to jump the whole window forward or backward in time).

Lest you be tempted to think such capability only works for TV, take a look at the My Music screen in Figure 2-6. The default selection is what's shown, and lists items in the digital music collection by album/CD title, along with thumbnails of corresponding cover art. MCE uses the Internet automatically to retrieve the metadata (titles, album art, artist information, and so forth) and constructs these listings automatically for its users. The left-hand menu controls what information is displayed; the right-hand grid makes it easy for users to pick individual entries to play, record, or dig into further.

FIGURE 2-6: My Music can list music collections by album, artist, playlists, and so forth and makes it easy to choose items for listening, copying, or other activities.

In fact, MCE setup and configuration is itself designed to work by remote control. Figure 2-7 shows one of many TV settings that users click through when they set up their systems for initial use (or make configuration changes later). The green selection indicates the action to be taken. If the user clicks OK, it affects TV signal setup in MCE; if the user clicks an arrow key, it highlights the No option in green instead. All of MCE's many settings and preferences can be accessed and managed using the remote control, if users so choose. It's a remarkable extension of the graphical user interface to a different paradigm, based on the wireless remote and a living or family room setting, and it works pretty much across the board.

Those who wish to use a keyboard and mouse can do so inside MCE to employ shortcut keys or cursor selections to drive the interface. Those who wish to interact with the conventional Windows XP interface can minimize MCE into a window on the XP desktop or switch over to Windows XP. But those users intent on using a Media Center PC only for media need never interact directly with conventional Windows.

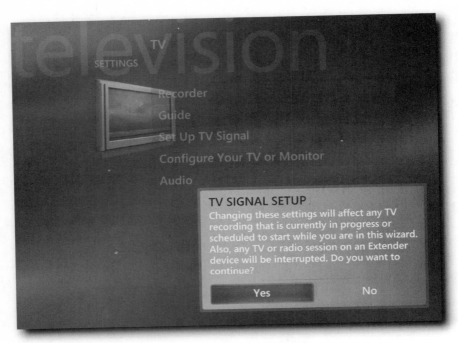

Figure 2-7: All the elements and settings involved in MCE configuration and setup are designed to work well by remote control.

HTPC: At Home in the Entertainment Center

In discussing HTPC components throughout this book, and in selecting components for the three system build projects that cap off its contents, the focus remained set on the HTPC design elements enunciated earlier in this chapter. As the budgets for the three projects will attest, these build projects cover a range of costs from the low end of the price range to its middle. But the principles that guided component selection favored quieter operation versus more raw computing power, but also favored mid-range prices rather than always seeking the quietest (and more expensive) options.

Perhaps the most important factors that drove the selection of components for coverage in Chapters 3 through 14 and inclusion in the build projects in Chapters 18 through 20 were the following:

- HTPC cases should fit into entertainment center furniture and look good amidst receivers, DVD players, and other audio and video equipment components. This calls for horizontal cases 19" wide or narrower. This is the standard width for rack-mounted audio and video equipment and has been the benchmark for designing equipment components and the furniture that houses them for years. Where possible, smaller cases were favored over larger ones. To meet the needs of "one PC fits all uses" we did include a tower case build as well.

■ Wherever possible, quieter components were selected rather than more powerful ones, particularly where fans come into play. When quieter options are available, they are also discussed in this book where and when it makes sense to do so.

■ All components and equipment referenced in this book are fairly easy to find on the Web, but there's a companion Web site that includes a comprehensive alphabetized directory of all items mentioned. This also means that information can be kept current online, though it will slowly but surely change over time making the print version less and less accurate. We also tried to pick items that were available from multiple sources so that competition could help keep prices under control. Nevertheless, HTPC is a specialty area and some HTPC-specific items (cases, TV cards, fanless graphics cards, and remote controls are all pretty good examples) are more costly than more typical mass-market components (CPUs, memory, disk drives, and so forth) and less subject to declining prices over time.

Cross-Reference   Don't forget to consult the various appendixes at the end of this book for pointers to more information and resources online. Appendixes A and B are particularly germane to the subjects covered in this chapter.

Wrapping Up

As we said before, although Home Theater PCs — like the ones you've read about in this chapter — and more ordinary PCs have a lot in common, numerous and important differences exist between an ordinary home or office desktop model and an HTPC. In this chapter, you learned about the components that are more or less required on an HTCP, such as a TV card and TV display capability, large amounts of memory and storage, and a remote control, as well as how requirements for components can change between the desktop and the home theater. For the former, price and power are often most important; for the latter, quiet is a key consideration, as is the ability to blend into and work well in a living or family room setting.

PC Pieces and Parts

part

The HTPC Case and Power Supply

Some people believe that the PC case is just an enclosure for the PC's contents, and others believe that the case sets the stage for everything else inside. Whether it's just the skin around the package or it makes the package be what it is, the case is undoubtedly a key component in an HTPC. We are inclined to put a lot of weight behind and thought into the selection process for an HTPC case, particularly because looks, layout, and functionality matter more for such cases than they do for ordinary desktop PCs. Our thinking is that the case must not only provide desirable technical characteristics — and this chapter digs into them deeply, never fear — but also that it must fit into a typical entertainment center both physically and visually.

Power supplies aren't thrown into this chapter randomly, just to give them a place to go. Most PC cases, including those designed specifically for HTPC use, include a power supply. That's why we discuss them in this chapter, where we explain their purposes along with potential problems they can pose for HTPCs and how proper selection helps to mitigate or sidestep those problems.

In this chapter, you get a detailed look at several HTPC cases and at some power supplies. You also tour a couple of cases and power supplies, to establish what some of these things look like (and because of our own selection process in deciding what to show you, how we think they should look). Along the way you learn about the following items, all of which are worthy of investigation and consideration when evaluating or selecting a case or a power supply for your HTPC:

> **Form factor:** Computer cases come in many shapes and sizes in general, as do the cases chosen for commercially available Media Center PCs. That only more expensive Media Center PCs use cases designed specifically for HTPC use says a lot about what buyers are willing to pay and where system vendors often choose to cut costs. Other issues related to form factor include what types of motherboard and power supply they can (or do) accommodate and how much room they provide for interface cards, drives, and other components.

➤ **Ventilation:** Computer cases provide various mechanisms to enable airflow and also include fan housings (and sometimes fans as well) to increase airflow and cooling. Proper ventilation is essential, yet selection of ventilation components, especially fans, is crucial to the kind of quiet operation that an HTPC demands. In general HTPC cases require larger, less restricted airflow vents than ordinary desktops, along with well-directed airflow inside the case.

Ventilation is also mandatory for certain specific modern PC components, especially CPUs and certain chipsets. Chapter 4 briefly addresses how motherboards offer fan sensors and speed controls; Chapter 5 deals directly with CPU coolers and provides instructions on how to select them for HTPC use.

➤ **Noise control:** Proper design and sound dampening techniques can keep sounds from traveling far from a PC case. It's important to think about what makes and causes noise inside a PC and then to make sure the case helps to prevent or block such noise as does occur. Even the quietest components can sometimes make small amounts of noise, but the case can keep that noise from reaching anyone's ears. In part this means that noise must be able to escape from inside the HTPC case only through indirect paths, so as to give noise dampening the opportunity to deaden and diminish what sounds do emerge from that case.

➤ **Materials and construction:** Case construction must emphasize low resonance (to keep the effects of vibration to a minimum), sturdy materials (to provide minimal sources for vibration), and good sound insulation and isolation (to minimize noise conduction and production) as well.

➤ **Appearance:** Because HTPCs must generally make themselves at home in entertainment centers and even present themselves to polite company from time to time, the overall appearance of an HTPC case is more important than for ordinary desktop PCs. Considerations like color, size, fit, and finish are all more critical when it comes to selecting an HTPC case than finding a box for your workaday workhorse.

By considering each of these factors when evaluating any case you might use for an HTPC, you can quickly separate what's suitable from what's not. As far as HTPCs go, it's reasonable to consider any case that looks good, offers good ventilation, is well built and sturdy, and that addresses noise effectively. You'll have the chance to inspect some good examples in this chapter.

As for power supplies, concerns about noise and ventilation apply equally but are inextricably intertwined. That's because modern PCs, including Media Center PCs, can require sufficient wattage so that the power supplies that drive them require at least occasional active ventilation (in other words, a fan) to stay cool. If you purchase a power supply separately from a PC case, other considerations also come into play. Here's a list of important points to ponder when considering any power supply, whether on its own or as part of what's included with so many PC cases:

■ **Total electrical output:** Power supplies are rated by maximum wattage; most HTPCs require somewhere between 240- and 350-watt power supplies.

Tip

Power supplies are also known as power supply units, and are often abbreviated as PSUs. That's how we refer to them throughout the rest of this chapter.

■ **Cooling approach:** Some PSUs, mostly lower-cost items designed for ordinary desktop use, employ high-speed fans that run whenever the power supply does. Quieter, more expensive PSUs employ sensors to turn the fan on or off in response to internal temperature, and regulate fan speed by temperature as well. Intermediate models use fans that run all the time, but that lower fan speeds when lightly loaded and run at maximum fan speeds only when heavily loaded.

■ **Noise output:** The primary source of noise on most PSUs is the fan (or multiple fans, in some cases), but other sources of electromechanical noise (such as humming or buzzing) sometimes occur in some PSUs as well. Careful consideration of PSU noise ratings is an important criterion when selecting one for HTPC use.

■ **Power connections:** PSUs are built to support specific types of motherboards, so that you'll buy a PSU to match the power connector on your motherboard. The vast majority of motherboards and PSUs available these days adhere to the ATX standards for form factor and power connectors (and regular ATX, mini-ATX, FlexATX, and micro-ATX motherboards all use the same 24-pin power connector). That said, Intel offers numerous variations on this theme aimed at PSU makers at its Desktop Form Factors site. The company has published guidelines for at least five variants there — namely, ATX12V, SFX12V, TFX12V, LFX12V, and CFX12V PSU Design Guides.

Cross-Reference

The Intel Desktop Form Factors page is available online at www.formfactors.org. This is where you'll find information about PSUs that address needs for modern devices like SATA drives, PCI-Express interfaces, and more. The most relevant specifications are ATX12V and SFX12V, unless you plan to implement an extremely compact HTPC system.

■ **Electrical efficiency:** Although not all PSU vendors publish efficiency stats for their products, this measures how much energy the PSU turns into DC voltage and how much gets turned into heat. A 70-percent efficient PSU turns 30 percent of the energy it consumes into heat. In HTPCs where cooling and ventilation are so important, this metric means more than it does in many other circumstances and is worth researching.

The sections that follow look at some cases and power supplies so you can understand the various considerations already mentioned and understand the impact of price on performance and functionality.

A Tour of Two Cases

Before you look at and dig into some photos, be ready for some interesting discussions as you examine these photos. It's especially important to be sensitive to air flow, fans or fan housings, pathways for noise, and sound dampening approaches implemented in these cases. By way of comparison, we also observe that although it's easy to find a decent tower case for a desktop PC for under $50 without factoring noise and looks into search criteria, most decent HTPC cases cost at least $100, and many cost $150 to as much as $300 depending on bells and whistles. Whereas one of your authors prefers horizontal or cube cases that tend to fit inside home entertainment centers more readily, the other has no inclination to bypass more conventional-looking tower cases (and in fact has worked as a consultant with one case manufacturer to design such a case).

Silverstone LaScala LC14 HTPC Case

Figure 3-1 shows a three-quarter profile view of the Silverstone LaScala LC14 case. This view is chosen deliberately to depict the large air vents on the side of the case that is showing (there's a matching set on the other side, too). The front features two doors that cover 5.5" drive bays, for one or two optical drives, plus a set of control buttons on the left, with power and reset buttons to the right. The case includes no power supply, and cleverly hides four USB ports, two audio ports, and one FireWire port around the upper left corner. The LC14M includes a vacuum fluorescent display in the front center; the LC14B (which costs about $100 less) does not. Otherwise, both models are identical.

FIGURE 3-1: Silverstone LaScala LC14M has clean lines with a VFD at front center, two optical drive doors to the right, and ample vents on the unit's side.

Table 3-1 summarizes the rest of this case's features and functions.

Table 3-1   Silverstone LaScala LC14 Features and Functions

Item	Details
Type	Horizontal ATX desktop/HTPC case
Case material	Steel and plastic
Dimensions	H 172 mm x W 437 mm x D 434 mm (6.77" x 17.20" x 17.09")

Item	Details
Ventilation	Vents on both sides and rear of case, fan mount on left side
PSU	240 W 12VTFX with power factor correction (PFC), no SATA power connectors
Drive bays	Internal 3.5" (2), External 5.5" (2 accessible through front panel; see Figure 3-2)
Suspension	Four aluminum/rubber feet, good match to AV components
Expansion slots	Seven expansion slots, including one for AGP/PCI-E at far left, with six more to the right
Connectors/ Indicators	Power (on/off), Power LED, HDD Activity LED, front-side panel ports (USB, audio, FireWire), multimedia control buttons
Roominess	Case is reasonably roomy, easy access for motherboard installation, no instructions provided, some issues with 3.5" drive cable clearance
Noise dampening	Hard disk bolts directly to case with no provision for noise dampening (user can drill new mount holes, but increases drive heat). No additional noise dampening panels or materials
Cooling	92 mm fan at front of case, with 2 60mm fans at read of case provide ample ventilation with CPU cooler fan (stock fans somewhat noisy)

FIGURE 3-2: The Silverstone LC14 case has two 5.5" pop-open doors at right.

FIGURE 3-3: Rear view of Silverstone LC14 case showing 60 mm fans at top center, PSU space at left, and 7 expansion slots at right.

Although this case is attractive (the photos show a black model, but it also comes in silver) and well built, it does have some minor issues. Because the 3.5" drive cage is positioned over the top center of the case, it also is positioned right over the IDE connectors on many typical motherboards. Those using IDE drives may have a little trouble routing the IDE cable from one or two drives to the corresponding motherboard connector, and should experiment with alignment and arrangement before tacking down the motherboard. Those using SATA drives may find that cables with a right-angle connector on one end are a little easier to work into the SATA port on the drives as well. On the plus side, the left-hand side (facing the case front) of the case is open, so it's very easy to slide the motherboard in from that side instead of dropping it in from the top.

Tip

Whenever you build a PC it's important to check the internal case temperature, the CPU temperature, and at least the PSU exhaust temperature (most motherboards support checking the first two, but for most you'll need a thermometer or temperature sensor to check the third value). If you can't check these temperatures with built-in sensors in your system, you should purchase and use a temperature sensor of your own during system testing. CPUs and PSUs can fail if their temperatures run too hot for any extended periods. Because you don't want to take that risk, testing is the only way to be sure. Author Mike Chin had to experiment with multiple fan arrangements in a more compact Silverstone case (LC-04) before creating a workable ventilation scheme. This also helps explain why underclocking (running a CPU slower than its rated speed) and building systems around lower-power CPUs and components is a good strategy for HTPCs.

Origen x15e HTPC Case

Our next case is one of a number of tricked-out HTPC cases currently available on the market. Although the front panel touch screen commands immediate attention, and some oohs and ahs from those who see it, the Origen x15e has a lot more going for it than just a pretty face (as shown in Figure 3-4, to the left). Figure 3-4 also includes a close-up with the right-hand side front panel door open, exposing the front panel ports (two USB, one FireWire, and three audio ports). It's got a 6-in-1 memory card reader installed where a case knockout otherwise resides as well (the card reader is available from Origen as an extra-cost option, but other cheaper options can be purchased from third parties).

The x15e is a roomy, solid, all-aluminum case that enables ample ventilation, which in turn, makes effective cooling possible. What we like best about this case is that it not only provides room for up to six full-height interface cards and a full-size ATX motherboard, but it also offers enough drive bays that those who want to install multiple hard drives in this enclosure can do so. Including the knockout where the memory card reader appears in Figure 3-4, the x15e offers four 3.5" drive bays (three internal, one external) and one external 5.5" drive bay (for an optical drive). Figure 3-5 shows a rear view of the unit, with the PSU vent at the left, next to an 80 mm rear exhaust fan aperture, and seven knockouts for expansion cards at the right. The opening at bottom center is for the motherboard's (mobo's) port block.

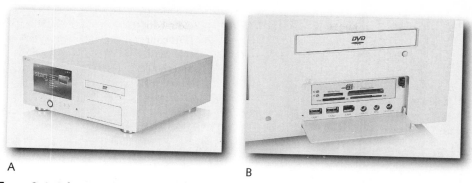

A   B

FIGURE 3-4: A front view of Origen's x15e emphasizes its touch screen at left; when closed, the open door in the right-hand close-up hides front-panel inputs.

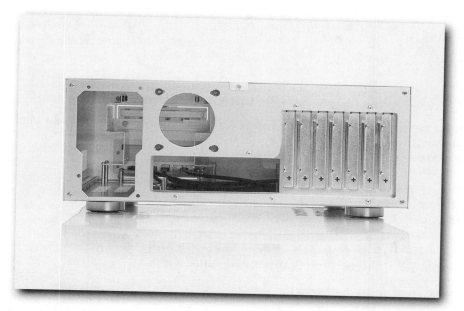

FIGURE 3-5: The rear of the empty x15e case shows openings for PSU, a fan, the mobo port block, and seven expansion slots.

Photo reproduced with permission of HTPCnews.com.

Our first impression of the case was that it lacked sufficient venting to provide adequate ventilation, but subsequent testing proved otherwise. With a quiet exhaust fan installed, case and CPU temperatures were not only acceptable, but they were on the low end of typical ranges. Communications with company engineers indicated they designed the case bottom vents (shown in Figure 3-6) deliberately to promote effective air flow and circulation when an exhaust fan is installed.

FIGURE 3-6: Strategic placement of the bottom vents and a good exhaust fan keep the x15e surprisingly cool.
Photo reproduced with permission of HTPCnews.com.

If you are interested in reading about this case in considerably more detail, check out Joshua Schipmann's excellent review from HTPCnews.com; you'll find it at `htpcnews.com/main.php?id=x15`. Table 3-2 summarizes the rest of the x15e's features and functions.

Table 3-2   Origen x15e Features and Functions

Item	Details
Type	Horizontal ATX desktop/HTPC case
Case material	Aluminum, but solid construction and good dampening produce little or no resonance
Dimensions	H 170 mm × W 435 mm × D 420 mm (6.69" × 17.125" × 16.535")
Ventilation	Vents on bottom of case, exhaust fan and PSU apertures on back
PSU	None included, but space for 12VATX PSU is available
Drive bays	Internal 3.5" (3), External 3.5" (1); External 5.5" (1)

Item	Details
Suspension	Four aluminum/rubber feet, good match to AV components
Expansion slots	Seven accessible through case rear accept full height cards
Connectors/ Indicators	Power (on/off), Power LED, front panel touch screen, front panel ports (USB, audio, FireWire), no Reset button
Roominess	Case is very roomy, but right-hand side 3.5" drive bays may be blocked by CPU cooler (experimentation advised)
Noise dampening	All drive mounts include rubber grommets, strong mechanical fit on all components, optional noise dampening kit available (but may not be needed)
Cooling	Exhaust fan not included for standard 80 mm aperture; quiet fan highly recommended especially for more powerful CPUs

The x15e does an excellent job of keeping noise pathways to the exterior long by locating all vents on the bottom of the case. Though constructed of medium-gauge aluminum, all case elements are solidly fastened, and all drive mounts include rubber grommets for noise isolation. When assembled, an HTPC built around this case using quiet components did not exhibit much noise, nor was any sound directly attributable to the case itself. In short, this case is a winner when measured for capacity, ease of installation and use, and quiet.

Cool, quiet, and roomy is about the best possible combination of adjectives one can give to an HTPC case. The catches to this case come in several forms, but only one is onerous. This case costs about $600: a huge outlay for this kind of HTPC component (other equally roomy Origen models are available for around $250 that offer everything the x15e does, except the touch screen — that's still pricey, but more reasonably so). More minor x15e quibbles include missing manuals, no grill to cover the rear fan aperture, and confusion surrounding the IR module needed for complete integration with MCE. It turns out that removing a single jumper on the IR board takes care of that issue and makes it MCE compatible.

HTPC Case Logic

Here, we elaborate on the concepts and requirements for HTPC cases that were mentioned only briefly at the outset of this chapter. As we tackle these subjects head-on, we hope to teach you how to evaluate cases for yourself (or to look in published reviews for the right kinds of information, should they be available). That's because new cases hit the market all the time, and there's a very good chance you'll be considering cases that didn't exist as we wrote this book.

Form Factor

When it comes to cases, the term *form factor* actually covers a multitude of meanings. In the most important sense, PC cases relate to those motherboard form factors they can accommodate. But the term can also be used to describe case orientation and layout, which allows us to distinguish towers by a vertical orientation, and horizontal or cube cases by a horizontal layout. Form factor can even be used as a metric of roominess, in that some cases qualify as compact or cramped, whereas others qualify as bigger and less crowded. That's why we try to be clear about which meaning applies when we invoke this term in talking about HTPC cases.

It's inarguable that a PC's motherboard must fit into its case, so that aspect of form factor is something where parts must match up perfectly. The various ATX specifications are designed so that smaller variants of the same family (such as mini-ATX or micro-ATX) can be mounted in cases that support larger variants (full-scale ATX, in this scenario). But a case that accommodates only smaller variants won't handle larger ones.

Your authors are somewhat split on the subject of form factor as it pertains to case orientation and layout. One of us believes that tower cases can be okay for HTPCs, providing they meet other criteria and don't look too out of place in the living room. The other believes that only horizontal or cube cases make sense for entertainment center furniture. But happily both of us do agree that horizontal cases are probably the best choice for most HTPCs. Of course, one of the joys of building your own HTPC is that you can choose whatever type of case (or other components) that you like best.

Finally, when it comes to roominess, the laws of physics come into play. Smaller, more crowded cases invariably run hotter than larger, roomier cases even with identical components installed. That's partly because smaller cases leave less space in which air can circulate, and partly because smaller cases build up and retain heat better than bigger ones do. It's also true that installation and upgrades are easier in a roomier case because your hands and fingers have more room to maneuver as well. Mainly because smaller cases run hotter than larger ones, we urge you to go bigger rather than smaller when picking an HTPC case (or even when buying a pre-fab HTPC system, for that matter).

Ventilation

When assessing a case's ventilation, please pay close attention to the following factors:

- The vented surface area should match the exhaust outlet surface area as closely as possible. That's because ventilation works best when intake and exhaust are matched. Vents should also be positioned to help facilitate maximum airflow through the case. The Silverstone LC-14 you toured earlier in this chapter suffered somewhat from a ratio of vents to exhausts that favored vents, resulting in less-than-optimal case ventilation.

- The internal layout of the case should be free of significant obstructions and should leave ample room for air to circulate and flow through following an effective cooling path across the heat-producing components(the CPU, video card, and hard drives. That's a primary contributor to our earlier observation that a roomier case runs cooler than a more crowded one.

■ Fan mounts should be at least 80 × 80 mm (a more or less standard PC fan size), and provide at least 25 mm of vertical clearance. Larger 120 mm fans are preferable, because bigger fans can run more slowly yet move the same amount of air as smaller fans that run faster. Rotation speed contributes to noise, so slower is better when it comes to fans. Fans should also be placed to push or pull air over the hottest components (that's why faster CPUs require dedicated fans and coolers).

The bottom line is that case ventilation is what keeps an HTPC as cool as possible. The cooler the HTPC, the less necessary it is to use fans to keep things cool. If they must run, they can run more slowly and make less noise; if they don't need to run at all, they make no noise. And of course, that leads directly into the next topic . . .

Noise Control

We begin this section by briefly reviewing why noise control is important for HTPCs. HTPCs are involved in producing sound, either by themselves for music, or in tandem with images for TV or DVD playback. Both music and multimedia use sound dynamics for effect, so that sometimes things are deliberately quiet and other times things are deliberately loud. When things get quiet, nobody wants to hear a PC grinding, buzzing, or whirring away in the background, distracting viewers or listeners from their programming material. When it comes to an HTPC, silent operation is the ideal, and as quiet as possible is a very real goal that HTPC builders should seek to attain. This makes noise control a critical factor.

There are only a limited number of things you can do about noise, so although the prescription for quiet computing involves an astonishing amount of (and attention to) detail, only a few basic principles and practices are involved:

■ Use noise (or lack of noise) as an important selection criterion when picking components for an HTPC. Much of this book is devoted to this very topic in one way or another. The basic idea is to eliminate all unnecessary noise, and to limit all necessary noise to an affordable or practical minimum.

■ Make sure that what noise is produced must travel a long way to arrive at a listener's ears. This explains why drives are at the front of most horizontal HTPC cases and exhaust fans blow out the back: sound must travel from the drives through the case, out the back, then around to the front and out the entertainment center to be heard. Hopefully, any noise will have diminished to nothing or near inaudibility by then.

■ Make sure that sources of noise are isolated from the case and the environment. The best HTPC cases (and modifications) drill out drive mount holes, so that rubber or silicon grommets may be inserted into those larger holes. This eliminates direct metal-to-metal contact between drive and case, and lowers the amount of vibration that can pass from one to the other.

Tip

Companies like Antec (which also manufactures cases and power supplies) and Mitron offer a variety of interesting sound insulation products. Antec's product line goes by the name of "Noise Killer," consists of shaped silicon gaskets and washers, and includes offerings for 80 and 120 mm fans and PSUs.

- Use sound insulation where and as it makes sense. For example, many system builders apply noise-dampening materials inside case panels for sound insulation. Although it's commonly believed that foam damping can increase temperature levels inside your case, this is generally true only if you end up blocking airflow with the material, so proceed carefully. If a case sits on a shelf in a home entertainment center, it may work better to apply sound insulation only to the front half of a panel, rather than covering the whole thing. The back half is further away, so sound must travel further to your ears, and with drives typically front mounted, insulation near the source does the most good. Some cases are built with double walls because of noise insulation between inner and outer walls.

If you recognize potential sources of noise and take steps to prevent sound from propagating (by isolation or insulation) you'll be able to reduce their impact on your listening experience as much as possible.

Materials and Construction

HTPC cases must also be built and designed to control noise. This affects the choice of building materials and the workmanship of the case. Though some experts argue that steel is preferable to aluminum for HTPC cases, aluminum's lighter weight and greater ductility make it attractive to case builders. Most commercial HTPC case designs use an aluminum shell around a steel cage or steel drive bays and card cages.

As long as a case is sturdy, and tightly enough fitted to eliminate as much vibration or resonance in its outer panels as possible, it should do the job. For example, the Origen case toured earlier in this chapter uses a heavy 8 mm aluminum front panel along with light 3 mm aluminum panels on the rest of the case (top, bottom, sides, and rear). It also incorporates two steel drive bay cages in the front of the case, and a steel expansion card and motherboard port block cage at the rear of the case. But because all mechanical connections between panels are tightly screwed together and fit extremely well, this case produces only a little vibration or resonant noise.

Some HTPC (and other) cases may come with sound-dampening materials already installed, or offer extra-cost sound-dampening kits (Origen claims to offer such a kit for the x15e, but we can't find any for sale). Other vendors such as Acousti Products offer aftermarket products like its AcoustiPack soundproofing materials that diligent HTPC users can install in their own PCs (be prepared to spend $50–$100 to do the job right). Additional sound dampening is a good idea, provided you buy dense, high-quality materials (but keep them away from sources of intense heat like CPUs, GPUs, and Northbridge or Southbridge processors — or rather, away from their coolers or heat sinks).

Appearance

This is where aesthetics come into play, and that's something that only a buyer can really appreciate in context. Make sure what you buy matches your other AV components (or at least doesn't clash with them too much). But appearance is a characteristic you'll want to consider when selecting any HTPC case for purchase. We found little or no difference between going with standard black or silver cases ourselves, probably because our AV setups already include a mix of black and silver elements. If you've been more single-minded in your color schemes, you will want to pick an HTPC case that matches.

Table 3-3 mentions numerous vendors who offer PC cases designed specifically for HTPC use. Of these, we've gotten good results with cases from Antec, Silverstone, and Origen.

Table 3-3   Case Vendors with Usable HTPC Offerings

Name	Type(s)	Price Range	URL/Remarks
AHANIX*	horizontal	$180–280	www.ahanix.com; many models worth investigating; roomier cases make best choices, be sure to check vent/exhaust ratios
Antec*	horizontal, tower, and cube	$50–220	www.antec.com; P180 specially recommended
Coolcases	tower	$100–200	www.coolcases.com; Chenbro PC-610 custom case recommended, company will also install fans and PSU for extra fee
Origen	horizontal	$250–600	www.origenae.com; touch screen models very pricey; all cases recommended
Silverstone*	horizontal	$110–220	www.silverstonetek.com; nearly all models worth investigating; roomier cases recommended
Thermaltake	horizontal	$100–up	www.thermaltake.com, numerous new offerings forthcoming, none reviewed yet

*All the companies whose names are asterisked were kind enough to furnish cases for this book.

Picking Proper Power Supplies

In most of the PCs we've owned, the number one source of noise in all of them has been (and remains) the power supply. And although you can indeed find fanless (and therefore silent) PSUs from numerous reputable vendors, only a few of them exceed 240-watt power ratings, and therefore don't really cut it for most HTPC systems. Those that do offer 300 watts or more without a fan to keep them cool run pretty hot and cost a pretty penny (see the sidebar later in this chapter entitled "Pros and Cons of Fanless PSUs" for more information). Thus, our primary coverage in this part of the chapter is on the quietest of power supplies that do include fans, simply because they're more affordable and widely available, and hence make more sense for most HTPC designs.

To begin this discussion, it's important to discuss what a power supply does for a PC. Basically, it's a sophisticated power transformer that takes alternating current (AC) from a wall socket and transforms it into various direct current (DC) outputs at voltages in the range from −12 V to +12 V, with customary stops at 1.65 V, 3.3 V, 5.0 V, and 12.0 V. PSU sophistication comes into play because they actually grab and convert no more AC into DC than the PC draws at any given moment, because they can balance electrical loads carefully across multiple devices, and keep voltage steady even as devices turn on (which draws power down) or off (which can cause power to spike momentarily).

In the introduction to this chapter, we identified the characteristics of power supplies that factor into their selection for HTPC use. Here, we explore those factors in greater detail to help you understand why they're important and how to weight them when choosing a PSU for your HTPC.

PSU Cooling Approach

Modern PSUs equipped with fans employ fan speed management to slow the fan down when loads are lower and speed the fan up as loads increase. Their distinguishing characteristics vary by how good a job of managing fan speed and regulating its temperature a PSU does, as well as whether or not the PSU permits the fan to shut off entirely at any time. More expensive PSUs generally offer more capable fan speed regulation, and a few models turn off the fan entirely when loads are low (as when a PC is running idle, servicing only occasional background tasks or the System Idle Process on Windows machines). The Seasonic S12 380W PSU (here, S12 stands for the "silent 120 cm fan" that adorns the side of the PSU case, visible through the fan grill in Figure 3-7) is an excellent case in point and is available for around $60.

FIGURE 3-7: The Seasonic S12 380W PSU makes all the right compromises between power consumption, efficiency, and cooling.

A PSU should also be designed to shed heat efficiently. This means that most modern PSUs are encased in metal with at least short heat-conducting fins on the outside, or in cases that are extensively ventilated. Such units will also include one or more heat sinks inside the PSU enclosure. They also employ a large fan (120 mm is best, 92 or 80 mm more typical) to provide cooling when and as it's needed.

PSU Noise Output

Though electromechanical noise (humming, buzzing, and so forth) is sometimes a characteristic of lower-quality power supplies, any decent unit that costs $50 or more (most HTPC-capable PSUs tend to cost $60 and up) should produce little or no such sounds. The biggest issue with any actively cooled PSU is its fan and is a function of the type of fan used as well as the characteristics of the fan controller. What's ideal is a large fan (120 mm) that ramps up in speed gradually and smoothly as PSU loads increase. The best PSUs produce little or no noise at startup (some are measured as low as 18 dBA/1m) and produce less than twice as much noise under a full load (some are measured as low as 33 dBA/1m at outputs over 400 W).

PSU Power Connections

Once upon a time, PSUs didn't extend a veritable mass of cables to their installers for installation and use. A motherboard cable bundle with an AT or ATX modular connector, and up to half a dozen Molex connectors for hard disks and floppy drives was just about it. But today's modern PCs and their constituent components demand considerably more. Here's what you're likely to see provided on most higher-end PSUs nowadays:

- 20-pin "old standard" ATX motherboard connector or 24-pin "new standard" ATX motherboard connector (the four pins added are to provide power to the PCI-E port for a graphics card). Most newer motherboards sport 24-pin connectors, so buy a compatible PSU (this standard is called ATX 2.0, and its latest version is the ATX 2.2 specification; be sure to look for 24-pin ATX connector support especially if your motherboard has a PCI-E X16 graphics slot and you plan to use it).

You can indeed buy an adapter to plug a 20-pin connector from a PSU into a 24-pin connector on the motherboard (in fact, they only cost about $4). But this puts a serious strain on your power supply and its electrical connections to the motherboard. It might do in a pinch, but it's not recommended. The absence of a 24-pin connector may mean that the PSU conforms to an earlier specification (ATX12V v1.3, for example), which has considerably different requirements than the latest specification.

- 6-pin PCI Express power cable for a PCI-E X16 graphics card. If your PSU doesn't have one, nor a 24-pin motherboard connector, you can buy an adapter that will let you draw power from two unused 4-pin Molex outputs from your PSU (assuming you've got them to spare) and then plug into the 6-pin power input on the graphics card.

Measuring Sound Levels

From the preceding paragraph, you can probably guess with some degree of confidence that 18 dBA/1m is a pretty quiet sound level, but you may not be able to put the higher sound level cited (33 dBA/1m) into context to help you understand what that means. Here, we explain the measurement and provide some common numbers that should make sense to you. The unit of measure is a decibel, which is abbreviated dB. Any kind of sound is measured in the form of a sound pressure level (SPL) in decibels (dB) using a tool called a sound pressure level meter (SLM) in combination with a very sensitive microphone. If a sound measurement is expressed as dBA/1m, that means the microphone on the sound pressure level meter is positioned precisely one meter away from the sound source. The "A" in dBA refers to the A-weighting curve electronically applied to the dB measurement as a compensation for the difference between the way human beings hear different frequencies and the way an SLM hears them. Unlike an SLM, we perceive low and high frequencies much less acutely than mid-range ones; the A weighting seeks to model non-linear human hearing.

That said, the following list gives you some common decibel values to help you put all this into context. The contents of this list are adapted from "What is Sound? And Noise?" by Mike Chin from SilentPCReview.com and reproduced by permission.

- 0 (Human hearing threshold) — Inaudible at any kind of distance
- <15 (Human body sounds: breathing, digestion, and so on) — Normally inaudible
- 15–20 (Super quiet/fanless PC) — Barely audible
- 20–25 (Quiet whisper, very quiet PC, ambient sound level in recording studio) — Very quiet
- 25–30 (Bedroom at night, very quiet PC) — Quiet
- 34–45 (Quiet office or library, typical PC) — Somewhat audible
- 50 (Conversation speech at 1m, noisy PC) — Clearly audible
- 60 (Restaurant, Department store, Noisiest gamer PC) — Noisy
- 80 (Curbside on busy street, Office with tabulating machines) — Very noisy
- 100 (Machine shop with lathes, Subway or train station, Printing press) — Extremely noisy
- 120 (Boiler room (maximum output/sound levels), Ship's engine room (full speed)) — Almost intolerable
- 140 (30 meters from military jet at take off) — Threshold of pain

From reading this table, you can conclude without much coaching that a PSU with a sound level of 18 dBA/1m is extremely quiet, and one that measures 33 dBA/1m is still pretty quiet. When informed that ordinary PSUs emit sound levels from 35 to 50 dBA/1m, you should recognize that there's a big difference between a quiet PSU and a "normal" one.

- 4-pin Auxiliary 12 V ATX power cable for square motherboard connector. This provides power to the CPU and should never be used to make up for the four "missing pins" on a 20-pin connector.

- One or more small 4-pin power connector(s) for floppy drive(s). If there's more than one, they may be daisy-chained on one or more power cables (often with 4-pin Molex connectors for hard or optical disks).

- Four or more 4-pin Molex connectors for hard or optical disks (the 500 W power supply under examination as we write this chapter has eight such connectors and can handle eight drives with ease).

Tip

Check your parts and save receipts! Making sure things fit may take a little effort, and it may even require you to return a purchase should you discover a mismatch. That's why it's always a good idea to lay out your parts and match connectors up by eye before you start putting them together. That's also why it's smart to save all receipts and to make sure you can exchange or return items that don't work out.

PSU Electrical Efficiency

Simply put, efficiency in a PSU measures how much incoming AC is converted to electricity. An 80-percent efficient PSU would require 100 W of incoming AC to produce 80 W of DC output. What happens to the other 20 percent, you wonder? Good question, because it's important for HTPC design: it turns into heat. That's why you want to purchase the most efficient PSU you can afford. It keeps the heat produced down and lowers the amount of cooling you must apply to keep a system operating within safe temperature ranges. As you already know, a cooler system is very often a quieter system so by increasing efficiency of the PSU you also automatically lower the system's overall heat output. Of course, higher PSU efficiency also results in lower overall consumption of electricity and is not just good for your HTPC, but also for the environment.

Typical commercial PC PSUs used to seldom exceed 70-percent efficiency. However, higher efficiency is increasingly emphasized, with Intel's standard-setting PSU guides now recommending 77-percent efficiency at full load and 80-percent efficiency at typical load. More efficient PSUs cost more than less efficient ones for all kinds of reasons that range from requiring more (and more expensive) circuitry, higher-quality components, and so on. Nevertheless, you should make an effort to buy a quiet and efficient PSU for your HTPC, simply because you'll be better pleased with the quality of the system you build. But not all PSU vendors publish efficiency statistics, so what's an HTPC builder to do? Read on for pointers to some helpful and informative sources of information.

Cross-Reference

The best sources for finding PSU noise and efficiency information is in PSU reviews from reputable Web sites. One of your authors, Mike Chin, has reviewed numerous PSUs for his Web site, SilentPCReview.com and invariably includes meticulous sound and efficiency measurements as a key part of what he reports. Other good sources for this kind of information include EfficientPowerSupplies.org and 80plus.org (this last source lists only PSUs that achieve electrical efficiency ratings of 80 percent or better).

Pros and Cons of Fanless PSUs

As attractive as a fanless PSU might sound, they come with numerous cons to offset their relatively silent operation (the only noise potential a fanless PSU offers is the hum often associated with the large electrical coils found in any transformer). But before you buy a fanless PSU, please consider the following cons:

- Fanless PSUs are more expensive than fan-cooled ones, often incredibly so. We know of at least one 350 W fanless PSU that goes for around $200. Ordinary 350 W PSUs cost less than $50 these days; even quiet 350 W PSUs cost less than $80.

- Fanless PSUs typically leave more heat inside the case than fan-cooled ones do because they have no fan to help move heat out of the case. Just because a PSU doesn't have a fan, doesn't mean you can build a fanless PC. If anything, a fanless PSU makes a cooling fan more necessary than it otherwise would be!

If you're seeking to investigate fanless offerings, check out PSU recommendations at Silent PC Review, which mention specific fanless models from Silverstone and Antec as worthy of consideration, but also as requiring special attention to case temperatures, ventilation, and airflow.

When it comes to buying a cool and quiet PSU for your HTPC, some research and thought will be required. Hopefully, you'll find Table 3-4 helpful in this regard, because it identifies companies that sell especially quiet and efficient PSUs.

Table 3-4 PSU Vendors with Usable HTPC Offerings

Vendor	Wattage	Price Range	URL/Remarks
Enermax	325–700	$80 and up	www.maxpoint.com; wide range of offerings at many power levels not as quiet as others but very efficient
Nexus	300–400	$60 and up	www.nexustek.nl; quiet at idle, noisier when loaded, reasonably efficient
Sea Sonic*	300–430	$60 and up	www.seasonic.com; wide range of offerings at many power levels, quiet and efficient
Zalman	300–400	$90–110	www.zalmanusa.com; quiet at idle, noisier when loaded, reasonably efficient, nice package and fan support

*All the companies whose names are asterisked were kind enough to furnish PSUs for this book.

How Much PSU Wattage Is Enough?

When you add up the wattage for a typical CPU, motherboard, PCI-E graphics card, TV card, drives, and other devices, you'll normally come up with a number somewhere between 150 and 300 watts. For most HTPC users a 350-watt PSU should be adequate. But if you buy a big case and have room for other components in the future, perhaps 400 or 500 watts may make more sense. Just be sure to pick a PSU that's as quiet and efficient as possible, and it's hard to go wrong.

The Barebones Alternatives

Numerous PC hardware vendors sell so-called "barebones systems" in addition to components on the one hand (especially motherboards) and complete systems on the other hand. Simply put, a barebones system is one that at least includes a case, a motherboard, and a power supply (though some offerings may include other components as well). The strength of the HTPC phenomenon is validated in some sense by the recent appearance of so-called multimedia or AV barebones systems, sometimes even called a Windows Media Center barebone.

Shuttle SB83G5

Well-known small-format system vendor Shuttle offers its SB83G5, also known as a Media Center Barebone, in one of its traditional cube cases, as shown in Figure 3-8. The front panel includes a Vacuum Fluorescent Display (VFD) that shows system temperatures, fan speeds, and status information. There's a drop-down door into a 5.5" bay (most likely an optical for a DVD/CD drive of some kind) at the top front, and another drop-down door at the bottom that covers two audio jacks, two USB ports, and a FireWire port. The SB38G5 is a compact case that offers room for only two expansion cards: one PCI-E X16, the other conventional PCI.

The SB83G5's innards do make a pretty convincing start to an HTPC. The proprietary Shuttle motherboard features socket 775 for current Pentium 4 or Celeron processors, Intel 915G Northbridge and ICH6-R Southbridge processors, and a pair of dual-channel DDR 400/333 memory slots. Although the motherboard offers a PCI-E X16 slot for a higher-end graphics card, it also integrates Intel's Graphics Media Accelerator 900 and Realtek's ALC658 5.1 channel high-definition audio. Some HTPC builders may be content to use these capabilities instead of adding either a separate PCI-E graphics card or a different sound card. A Marvell 88E8001 chipset also integrates Gigabit Ethernet onto the motherboard, which can run in 10/100/1000 mode.

Though compact, the case also leaves room for two 3.5" drives and a single 5.5" drive. It also supports two 150-Mbps SATA devices as well as RAID 0 and 1 should two drives be installed. The motherboard also works with ATA 100 drives as well (and surprisingly, includes a ribbon cable rather than a more modern and airflow-friendly round ATA cable). There's even a floppy connector, even though there's no room to install a floppy drive.

FIGURE **3-8:** The front panel of the SB83G5 looks pretty sleek when all the doors are closed.
Photo reproduced by permission of Shuttle, Inc.

The unit we received also included an ICE heat-pipe module that offers fanless cooling for the Socket 775 CPU. It also includes a Shuttle Silent X 250W PSU, which not only features a 120 mm temperature-controlled fan, but also gets pretty good noise ratings. The case is also engineered to help manage noise through attention to sound paths and all-steel construction. The Northbridge cooler and PSU fans are slightly audible, but nowhere near "noisy PC" levels. As an HTPC platform the SB83G5 isn't at all bad, but it also can't compare to what you can build from scratch, either (though at costs that are probably double what you'd pay for this barebone system).

Bundles for the Shuttle SB83G5 vary, so prices do as well. But the barest of barebones offerings (no TV card and no remote control or IR transfer device) is available for under $300 in today's marketplace. When you consider that this includes case, motherboard, and PSU, all of which were selected for HTPC use, this is actually a pretty good deal.

AOpen XC Cube EA65-II MCE

The AOpen machine is very much like the Shuttle, except a little less up-to-date. The motherboard supports Socket 478, and uses the Intel 865G Northbridge and ICH5 Southbridge processors. It also offers an 8X AGP graphics card slot instead of a PCI-E X16 slot. Otherwise, many of its characteristics are the same: memory type supported, 10/100/1000 Ethernet, similar number of USB and FireWire ports, and so forth.

What the AOpen has that the Shuttle lacks is a five-in-one memory card reader (it handles Secure Digital or SD and Multimedia card or MMC memory cards in one slot, Compact Flash or CF in another, SmartMedia or SM in a third, and Memory Stick or MS in the fourth). On the other hand, the AOpen EA65-II's integrated graphics are not up to HTPC standards, which means buying an 8X AGP graphics card is necessary. The AC'97 and 5.1 audio may not be enough for discriminating audiophiles, either, so it may also be necessary to buy a sound card. And then, where would your TV tuner card go?

The pros to this system as compared to the Shuttle include a lower price ($250 instead of around $300), cooler operation (older socket 478 Pentiums run cooler than do newer LGA 775 Pentiums), and a slightly more powerful PSU (the AOpen unit is rated at 275 W, whereas the Shuttle is rated at 240). But the AOpen also runs a bit noisier than the Shuttle, so you'll want to take that into account as well.

Table 3-5 provides URLs for Shuttle and AOpen and mentions other vendors that offer barebone products that target the HTPC market (but very few of these offerings have been reviewed with noise ratings or real tests of HTPC suitability so proceed with caution).

Table 3-5   Barebone HTPC Offerings

Vendor	Socket	Price	URL/Remarks
AOpen	478 775	$250 $300	www.aopen.com; MCE compatibility claimed for both MCE offerings, but we tested only the socket 478 model (and it proved acceptable, but not outstanding)
MSI	775	$300	www.msi.com.tw; Mega PC 865 Pro, some vendors are selling complete systems around this platform, 10/100 Ethernet only, reviews are mixed
NMedia	478 754 775	$229–265	www.nmediapc.com; Intel 775 and 478 and AMD 754 offerings appear to provide good value for the money, use quality motherboards and PSUs, cases are good looking, several good reviews
Shuttle	775	$300	us.shuttle.com; MCE 2005 compatibility claimed, reasonably capable, quiet system

Wrapping Up

Picking the case for an HTPC is driven by another primary consideration: the motherboard. The motherboard must fit into the case with sufficient room for CPU cooler, expansion cards, and drives. Indeed you can do preliminary matching between case and motherboard based on form factor, but you'd also be wise to look for product photos, information, and reviews to help you address how much space a case provides for other components. In this chapter, you learned about a variety of key considerations to ponder when choosing a case for your HTPC, including form factor, ventilation, noise control, appearance, and cost. All must be weighed carefully when choosing a case.

Whether it's included as part of the case or purchased separately, the PSU is also a key HTPC component. While delivering enough power for all HTPC components, it must also be as quiet as possible. This means that PSUs with temperature-controlled fans are nearly always preferable, whether or not such units can operate with the fan turned off under low loads. The factors to consider when picking a power supply include maximum power rating, cooling approach, motherboard and other power connections, and noise output. The quietest PSUs cost more, but are essential to the most positive HTPC experiences.

If price and convenience appeal more to you than absolute control over each and every system component, a barebones HTPC like those from Shuttle or AOpen reviewed in this chapter may also be appealing. If possible you'd want to get noise rating information on these systems to help you pick and choose. You also need to think carefully whether two expansion card slots will be enough to allow you to build the HTPC system you really want.

The PC Motherboard

I t's arguable that the motherboard is the single most important component in a PC. However, it's inarguable that the motherboard provides the platform into which nearly all other system components connect, and the pathways for data and instructions to make such components do their jobs. When you're buying or building any PC, the choice of the motherboard drives most of the other equipment choices you'll make for that machine.

It's not only important to understand what a motherboard does and the broad outlines of how one works, but also to understand the kinds of key components, device support, and capabilities that modern motherboards typically include. Only when armed with that knowledge can you make an informed decision about which motherboard to buy—whether you're buying a motherboard by itself as part of a system you're building yourself or as part of a pre-fab system somebody else has built to sell.

In this chapter, you get a detailed look at the features and functions a PC motherboard supplies. You also take a tour of a modern motherboard, to get a sense of what these things look like (or how they show themselves in hardware). Along the way you learn about the following items, all of which are worthy of investigation and consideration when evaluating or selecting a motherboard for your HTPC:

➤ **Form factor:** Motherboards come in various sizes, including ATX, micro-ATX, ITX, and others. One reason why a motherboard is arguably the most important component in a PC is because any given case will accommodate only certain motherboard form factors. As it happens, for Home Theater PCs (HTPCs) choosing the case is particularly important, and because that also determines compatible motherboard form factor(s), it's important to consider what cases will and won't work with specific motherboards, and vice versa.

➤ **CPU socket:** Another reason why a motherboard is only arguably the most important component in a PC is because each motherboard accommodates only one CPU socket; in turn, this dictates what kind of CPU you can install. You could argue that everything starts with the CPU, which narrows the choice of motherboards to those that can accommodate it. You could also argue that everything starts with the motherboard, which dictates what type of CPU you must purchase. Both must be considered carefully, and both are important. You can decide which you'd like to choose first.

➤ **Chipsets:** The important jobs that motherboards handle are many, including handling the PC's memory, its CPU, Accelerated Graphics Port (AGP) data transfer or PCI Express (PCI-E) graphics, and the primary PC expansion bus known as PCI (Peripheral Component Interconnect). This is the job of the *Northbridge or Memory Controller Hub*, generally considered to be a key element in the motherboard's chipset that manages system operation. The communications pathways to the elements are known as the CPU bus, the memory bus, the AGP bus, and the PCI bus, and the Northbridge not only handles those pathways, but it also plays traffic cop in managing ongoing communications over all those buses. Modern motherboards with built-in graphics capabilities (of which there are many) may also deliver onboard graphics functions to the Northbridge processor as well.

Athlon 64 systems lack a traditional Northbridge because the memory controller that's the primary function of the Northbridge now resides on the processor die itself.

Built-in motherboard graphics and related functions are covered only briefly in this chapter, but are discussed in much more detail in Chapter 9 as a possible alternative to installing a separate graphics card in your HTPC.

Also important on any PC is access to storage, networking, and other devices, which means using various communications pathways called secondary buses to interact with them. The *Southbridge or I/O controller's* job is to control numerous secondary buses including USB, IDE, PS/2, Ethernet, and so forth. This enables most storage devices, some interface cards, and other PC components to interact with the CPU and memory for processing. The speed of the pathway between the Northbridge and Southbridge processors is also important because it determines maximal performance for the PC (more on this later in this chapter).

■ **Front-side bus:** Simply put, the front-side bus (FSB) is the data bus between the PC's CPU and the Northbridge processor, which also connects to the RAM via the memory bus. The speed of this bus and the amount of data it can move also help determine maximal PC performance (more on this later in this chapter, too). Faster is better when it comes to comparing FSB speeds, because a faster FSB means a faster PC. The Athlon 64 does not use the older front-side bus approach, because the memory controller resides on the host CPU itself. But memory access speeds remain important, FSB or not.

■ **Graphics card support:** Modern motherboards not only support standard bus sockets for a graphics card, but most of them also support a special high-speed graphics connection to the Northbridge processor. An AGP (Accelerated Graphics Port) was once the fastest such socket around, but these days PCI-E (PCI Express) X16 cards appear to head the list by bus speed (more on this later in the chapter).

- **Expansion slots and bus:** In addition to special, high-speed graphics slots and data channels, motherboards need to provide pathways to other interface cards as well. The older, slower PCI technology is the expansion bus/slot standard most widely supported, though an increasing number of motherboards now offer slots for PCI-E X1 interface cards as well.

- **Peripheral (storage) support:** Standard interfaces for up to 2 E-IDE (Extended Integrated Drive Electronics) and/or ATA (Advanced Technology Attachment) devices and floppy drives appear on the vast majority of modern motherboards. Increasingly, you'll also find support for newer, faster hard disk interfaces as well. These include from two to four Serial ATA (SATA) or Parallel ATA (PATA) sockets, as well as a socket for IDE RAID (Redundant Array of Inexpensive Disks) that support up to four additional IDE drives, with onboard RAID support as well.

- **Ports:** In addition to typical keyboard, mouse, serial, and parallel ports, most modern motherboards offer two or more USB ports, along with one or more FireWire ports as well.

- **Built-ins:** Networking, sound, graphics, and sometimes other functions are more and more common on most motherboards nowadays. Most of the motherboards covered in this book offer at least two of these, and many offer all three.

- **Cables and accessories:** When you buy a motherboard, its manufacturer may or may not provide all the cables and connectors you need to hook up all devices that could be attached to the motherboard. In general, the more you pay, the more likely it is that these extras are included. Also, many motherboards include software bundles: most of the units covered in this book included some kind of DVD burning software, and many of them also included system or security tools such as Norton Ghost, antivirus software, and so forth.

By considering each of these factors when weighing motherboards, you can steer yourself in the right direction. As far as HTPCs go, it's reasonable to consider a motherboard that handles the latest chip sockets (for Pentium 4, Athlon 64, or Pentium M processors) but you may very well decide to pick a slower (and less expensive) CPU to lower the power requirements (and heat produced) to help keep your system quieter.

The section that follows looks at some motherboards so you can identify the various components discussed, and understand the impact of price on performance and functionality.

A Guided Tour of Two Motherboards

Before you look at and dig into some photos, a bit of terminology: motherboards are often called *mobos* in a truncated form of address. Because you'll see that term used so many times throughout the rest of this book, please remember that mobo is just another, shorter name for motherboard.

Chaintech VNF4 Ultra

Figure 4-1 depicts the Chaintech VNF4 Ultra motherboard. It supports socket 939 for the latest generation of Athlon 64 processors (at least, as we're writing this); this socket is supposed to work with the newer dual-core Athlon 64 processors as well, so there's some room for upgrades using this board. The large white grid at right center is the 939 socket; the fan to its right is the cooler for the Northbridge processor. Four 184-pin DIMM sockets take up the lower right-hand side of this mobo; three PCI sockets and a PCI-E X16 socket for the graphics card sit at the upper left. At the moment, this middle-of-the-road mobo costs somewhere around $90 to $100 retail.

FIGURE 4-1: The Chaintech VNF4 Ultra is a decent, usable, and affordable micro-ATX mobo for Athlon 64 socket 939 CPUs.

Table 4-1 summarizes the rest of this motherboard's features and functions.

Table 4-1   Chaintech VNF4 Ultra Features and Functions

Item	Details
CPU	AMD Socket 939 CPU: Athlon 64 FX/Athlon 64
Chipset	nVidia nForce4 Ultra
Form factor	ATX, but smaller than most
FSB	2000 MHz
Memory	4 184-pin DDR DIMMS up to 4GB, Dual-channel DDR 266/333/400
Expansion slots	PCI Express X16 slot for PCI Express graphics card 2 PCI Express X1 slots 3 PCI slots (v2.3)
Audio	nVidia 7.1 channel audio, AC'97 Rev2.3 specs, 6 audio jacks with auto-sensing, SPDIF output
SATA	4 SATA 1.5 Gbs devices 4 SATA2 3.0 Gbs devices Hot-swap capability, optimized for nVidia RAID, supports SATA ATAPI devices
UltraDMA IDE	2 UltraDMA-66/100/133 IDE ports
System monitoring	Temperature sensing for CPU and system; fan speed monitoring and control for CPU and system
Networking	nVidia 10/100/1000 Base-T Gigabit Ethernet

The external ports on the Chaintech VNF4 Ultra are depicted in Figure 4-2. What you see there from left to right is as follows (colors are mentioned where applicable, though they can't be distinguished in this monochrome photo):

- Mouse port above (green), keyboard port below (purple); both are PS/2 (DIN-9) receptacles

- Parallel port above, two serial ports below

- Two USB ports

- RJ-45 network receptacle above, two USB ports below

- Six audio jacks, three on the left: line-in or digital optical out (blue), line-out (green), microphone (pink), and three on the right: rear speaker-out (gray), side speaker-out (black), and center/subwoofer speaker-out (yellow)

FIGURE 4-2: The Chaintech VNF4 Ultra offers a nice collection of external ports for access on the back side of the case.

On the motherboard itself, buyers will also find power connectors for up to four fans, three additional USB connectors for up to six more USB ports, additional audio connectors, a front panel character display connector, and more. Accessories included in the package are as follows: one each IDE and floppy drive cables, two SATA2 cables, a driver CD, and a Value Pack CD (with antivirus, data protection, system restore, and disk imaging utilities, among others). What's missing? Onboard graphics and FireWire, but neither of these disqualifies the board for HTPC use. All in all it's a pretty reasonable mobo for a very nice price, and reviews are pretty complimentary about overall performance and capability.

ASUS P5AD2-E Deluxe

The next motherboard is the ASUS P5AD2-E Deluxe, shown in Figure 4-3. It's an Intel-oriented mobo, with socket 775 support for the current generation of Pentium 4 and Celeron processors. But because this mobo uses the Intel 925 XE Northbridge processor, it can't handle Intel's latest dual-core Pentium processors; those CPUs require the 915 or 955 Northbridge instead.

The large gray block in the right center is where the CPU plugs in; the Memory Controller Hub (MCH) is off to the left with the large heat sink attached. Four 240-pin DIMM sockets appear near the bottom right of the mobo; two are yellow, and the other two black, so those using dual memory configurations can arrange to match up pairs of DIMMS. The floppy and IDE sockets and the ATA power connector appear beneath the memory sockets. The ai proactive chip in the lower left automates network connectivity diagnostics and troubleshooting and works with both wired and wireless network links; it also manages advanced CPU, memory, and voltage controls for overclocking. In the upper-left quadrant, you can see three PCI sockets and a PCI-E X16 socket for a graphics card. At this time, this upper-tier (but by no means top of the line) mobo costs about $200 retail.

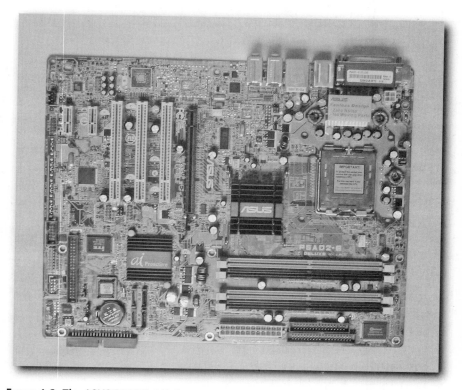

FIGURE 4-3: The ASUS P5AD2-E Deluxe is an upper-tier, feature-laden mobo for Intel Pentium and Celeron socket 775 CPUs.

Table 4-2 summarizes the rest of this motherboard's features and functions.

Table 4-2   ASUS P5AD2-E Deluxe Features and Functions

Item	Details
CPU	Intel Socket 775 CPUs: Intel Pentium 4 and Celeron
Chipset	Memory Controller Hub: Intel 925XE I/O Controller Hub (Southbridge): Intel ICH6R
Form factor	ATX
FSB	1066/800 MHz
Memory	4 240-pin DDR2 DIMMS up to 4GB, Dual-channel DDR2 600/533
Expansion slots	PCI Express X16 slot for PCI Express graphics card 2 PCI Express X1 slots 3 PCI slots (v2.3)
Audio	Intel high-definition audio, C-Media CM9880 7.1-channel audio, 6 audio jacks with autosensing, Dolby Digital, coaxial and optical SPDIF outputs
SATA	Up to 4 SATA 1.5 Gbs devices Supports RAID 0, 1, 0+1 array configurations
UltraDMA IDE	2 UltraDMA-66/100 IDE ports IDE RAID for up to 4 IDE drives, may be used as a disk array
System monitoring	Network virtual cable tester CPU and mobo temperature sensors Fan speed monitoring and Q-Fan speed control Voltage monitoring and reporting
Networking	Marvell PCI Express 10/100/1000 Base-T Gigabit Ethernet controller

The external ports on the ASUS P5AD2-E Deluxe are depicted in Figure 4-4. What you see there from left to right is as follows (where colors are mentioned it's to help those who have the real thing in front of them, we know you can't distinguish them in this monochrome photo):

- Mouse port (green), keyboard port (purple), coax (yellow) and SPDIF (black with gray cover) audio out; parallel port above

- Two USB ports below, one FireWire port above

- RJ-45 network receptacle above, two USB ports below

- Six audio jacks, three on the left: line-in or digital optical out (blue), line-out (green), microphone (pink), and three on the right: rear speaker-out (gray), side speaker-out (black), and center/subwoofer speaker-out (yellow)

In addition, the P5AD2-E also has numerous internal connectors, including an optical drive audio connector, two more USB connectors, a game/MIDI port connector, an additional serial port, plus connectors for two chassis fans, a power supply fan, and the CPU cooler fan. It also has a system panel connector for those who might wish to install front panel visual displays on their systems. The included accessories comprise all the cables you might need (though they provide flat ribbon rather than round cables for the IDE and floppy drive sockets), plus a raft of software, starting with numerous ASUS tools for flashing the BIOS, monitoring your PC, and tweaking the ai chip, along with Norton AntiVirus, a voice editor (so you can create your own audio POST messages), and Adobe Acrobat.

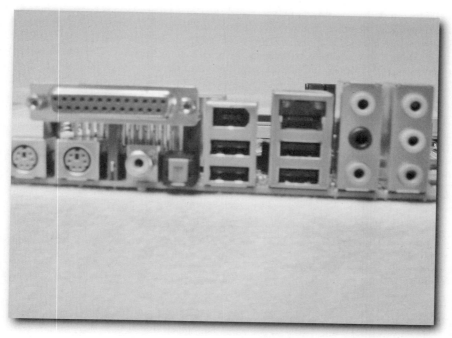

FIGURE 4-4: The ASUS P5AD2-E adds coax, SPDIF, and FireWire to the same collection of external ports for access on the back side of the case you saw on the Chaintech mobo in Figure 4-2.

The P5AD2-E Deluxe has a fair number of bells and whistles and supports more capabilities than the Chaintech board reviewed at the head of this section. Onboard graphics aren't built into this board, probably on the assumption that most system builders will want something more powerful and faster than onboard graphics typically provide. What do you get for spending twice as much as the Chaintech? You get more, and more sophisticated, ports, better system management, and more overclocking capabilities, plus faster DDR 2 memory. For HTPC applications this is already stretching the limits of what's really needed to do the job.

Mastering Motherboard Components

Having taken a look at a couple of motherboards and been exposed to major mobo elements, now take a look at the most important characteristics you should consider when deciding what kind of motherboard to buy, and which particular make and model to choose. In the sections that follow, you learn key motherboard terms, concepts, and items you can factor into your own decision making process.

Form Factors

One of the most important ways motherboards may be characterized is by their physical dimensions. This terminology didn't originate on the basis of size — it originated from the type of computer with which the motherboard was associated. Starting with the original IBM PC in 1981, there have been at least 10 different named form factors for PC motherboards. But rather than present you with all this history, we restrict the contents of Table 4-3 to those types of motherboards you can actually buy nowadays. We also indicate which ones are suitable for HTPC use.

Table 4-3   PC Motherboard Form Factors

Name	Vintage	HTPC?	Explanation
ATX	1995	Yes	Intel spec combines best of AT and LPX features and capabilities, 12" × 9.6" (smaller unofficial version called Mini-ATX, 11.2" × 8.2" also exists).
Micro-ATX	1997	Yes	Smaller version of ATX introduced for smaller, lower-cost systems; also fits into ATX cases, 9.6" × 9.6".
Mini-ITX	2002	Maybe	VIA Technologies spec, smallest form factor around uses proprietary processor, 6.7" × 6.7".
BTX	2004	Maybe	Comes in three sizes: picoBTX (7.9" × 10.4"), microBTX (10.3" × 10.4"), and BTX (12.7" × 10.4"). Rearranges faster, hotter components for better heat dissipation (also uses taller standoffs for better air circulation). Very few HTPC cases mention BTX support yet.

Advanced technology extended (ATX) and a reduced-size version of the ATX known as the micro-ATX are the best choices for most HTPC build projects. Not coincidentally, ATX and micro-ATX are also the most widely used motherboard form factors for all PCs nowadays. And indeed, though it may be possible to build a usable Media Center PC around a mini-ITX motherboard, the extremely small number of commercial products built on this platform (we can find only one such product, and it's not for sale in the United States) and its severe limitations on expansion cards (no more than two can be accommodated) make it an unlikely choice. Only an extremely experienced system builder, who's willing and able to find exotic hardware and prepared to make immature and largely untried technology work, should consider tackling a mini-ITX project. And though some cases do mention support for BTX motherboards nowadays, we found none, in the HTPC category that do so, while researching this book. That's why we recommend only ATX and micro-ATX motherboards for HTPC systems and cover mini-ITX and BTX no further in this book. This may change in future editions, however.

Tip

When it comes to picking platforms for any PC construction project—and HTPC is certainly no exception to this rule—your best bet is to pick platforms that are widely available and commonly used. For PC motherboards, this means that despite a large number of form factors introduced since the initial PC shipped in 1981, ATX and micro-ATX are the two that make best current sense for do-it-yourselfers.

CPU Sockets

Each family of CPUs fits one or more type of CPU socket, which provides the necessary connections between a motherboard and the CPU. When you buy a motherboard, you can buy one without a CPU installed for a lesser price, or you can buy one with a CPU installed for a higher price. As mentioned earlier in the chapter, the CPU you choose will narrow your choice of mobo, or the mobo you select will do likewise for the CPUs you can install.

Caution

If you are concerned about the real potential for damage to the motherboard and the CPU should you attempt to install the CPU yourself, you may want to consider buying a CPU/motherboard bundle. You'll have fewer choices, but the CPU will be pre-installed, which minimizes the risk to one of the most expensive and delicate components. It's invariably cheaper to buy the CPU and mobo separately and put them together yourself, but it can cost $200 or more to replace damaged parts (worst case is when both CPU and motherboard must be trashed) when assembly efforts go awry. If you choose to buy the CPU and motherboard separately and haven't installed a CPU and its cooler before, find a friend who has done the job to help you or pay a local PC repair shop the $50 or so they'll charge to install the CPU and its attendant cooler. That's much cheaper than having to buy a CPU and/or mobo twice!

For any given CPU socket, you'll generally find multiple options available that you could plug in for your PC. You'll generally have two kinds of choices to make when building a system:

- For the particular socket, you can choose among various processor lines to favor price over performance (cheaper processors that are slower and less powerful) or performance over price (more powerful and faster processors that cost more).

- Within any given processor line, you can choose faster or slower models, where the usual price-performance trade-off also applies (faster models cost more but get things done more quickly, slower models cost less and get things done more slowly).

On the Edge: Leading, Bleeding, and . . .

There's an interesting phenomenon at work in the computer hardware world. You'll find it almost anywhere you look—motherboards, CPUs, graphics cards, disk drives, and so forth. Those who want to buy the newest, fastest technologies typically have to pay a substantial premium. Using a motherboard example, this explains why those motherboards with the Intel 955X Memory Controller Hub cost $225 or more: the 955X is Intel's most recent Northbridge as this is being written, and one of the very few that supports dual-core Pentium processors for socket 775. If you look at a slightly older motherboard, like the ASUS P5AD2-E Deluxe you toured earlier in this chapter, its North- and Southbridge processors are a generation back, and the motherboard costs less than $200. Go back to the earlier Intel 478 socket for the Pentium 4 processor, and those motherboards top out at around $100.

Today's absolute latest and greatest Intel and AMD processors use dual-core technology. You learn what that means in Chapter 5, but for now it suffices to say this represents the most powerful CPU technology available to buyers. Such processors can cost anywhere from slightly more than $1,200 to not less than $260. By comparison, you have to buy at or near the top of the AMD Athlon 64 or Intel Pentium 4 processor lines for the preceding socket models (939 for AMD, and 775 for Intel) to spend as much money as the cheapest options in the latest line will cost you.

This helps distinguish what we like to call "edge choices" when buying computer hardware:

- **Bleeding edge** refers to the top of the latest and greatest technology offerings. You'll usually pay a hefty premium to buy in at this level (in fact, you could spend as much on such a CPU as you could spend to build an entire budget HTPC).

- **Leading edge** refers to something from the bottom or middle of the latest and greatest technology offerings. You'll pay something more than you would to buy top of the line one generation back, but it might be very little if you shop carefully.

- **Middle edge** refers to deliberately buying one generation back from the bleeding edge to realize the best possible price-performance trade-off. This approach works reasonably well, except when a new generation to replace the bleeding edge is imminent.

- **Trailing edge** refers to deliberately buying near the bottom end of the preceding generation, or more than one generation back. It represents a strategy that favors saving money over realizing computer performance.

When it comes to HTPCs, both leading-edge and middle-edge strategies work pretty well. Your budget constraints will help you decide where you fall in this spectrum and often determine the strategy based simply on how much you can afford to spend.

If you recall that in an HTPC it's often best to trade power or added capability for quieter operation, you'll understand why we recommend that although you should pick motherboards and CPUs that use the most current socket format you can afford, you needn't buy the top processor line, or the fastest model within whatever line you choose.

Socket candidates for most HTPCs will probably boil to down to one of the elements of Table 4-4 for most buyers. There are some especially interesting options worth considering for the middle edge in several cases here.

Table 4-4   Sockets and Related CPU Families

Name	Edge	Type	CPU Families
LGA 775	Bleeding/leading	Intel	Pentium Extreme Edition (Dual-Core), Pentium D (Dual-Core), Pentium 4 Extreme Edition, Pentium 4, Celeron D
Socket 478	Middle	Intel	Pentium 4 Extreme Edition, Pentium M, Pentium 4, Celeron D
Socket 370	Trailing	Intel	Celeron 766
Socket 939	Bleeding/leading	AMD	Dual-Core Athlon 64, Athlon 64 FX, Athlon 64
Socket 754	Middle	AMD	Athlon 64, Sempron
Socket A	Trailing	AMD	Athlon XP, Athlon, Duron, Sempron (Socket A, also known as Socket 462)

Some of the best deals around are in the middle-edge categories for both Intel and AMD processors, but if you go shopping for trailing-edge items, you'll observe that a great many more are available for older AMD processors (Athlon, Duron, and Sempron) than for older Intel ones (Celeron 766). Also especially noteworthy are CPUs originally designed for laptop use, such as Intel's Pentium M. By design, these CPUs consume less power and produce less heat while offering acceptable desktop performance. Because such things lend themselves well to quiet operation, they're great for HTPC use. So don't be surprised when you see one of our projects using a Pentium M CPU/motherboard combination for that very reason! Just for the record, the Pentium M uses a 479 socket that rightfully belongs on the middle edge next to its 478 sibling.

Chipsets

You already know about the roles that the Northbridge and Southbridge processors play, and the impact they can have on PC performance. Here, you learn a bit more about the various players and what kinds of options they bring to the table. Table 4-5 names the leading chipset vendors, associates newer chipsets with CPUs, and explains a bit about what the various offer to buyers.

Table 4-5   Major Chipset Vendors and Offerings

Vendor	Name	CPUs	More information
Intel	955xx	P4 Extreme, LGA 775	Dual-core support, PCI-E X16 and X1, RAID, high-definition audio, Dual-channel DDR2, up to 4 SATA 150 or 300 devices.
	925xx	P4, LGA 775	PCI-E X16 and X1, Dual-channel DDR2, RAID, high-definition audio, up to 4 SATA 150 devices, ATA 100.
	94xx	Pentium D, P4-HT, Celeron D, LGA 775	FSB up to 1066 MHz, PCI-E X16 and X1, Dual-channel DDR2, up to 4 SATA 150 or 300 devices, high-definition audio, RAID. "G" models include Intel GMA950 integrated graphics.
	915x	P4-HT, LGA 775	FSB up to 800 MHz, hyperthreading, graphics media accelerator, PCI-E X16 and X1, Dual-channel DDR or DDR2, high-definition audio, up to 4 SATA 150 devices, ATA 100. "G" models include Intel's GMA915 integrated graphics.
	910	P4-HT, Celeron D, LGA 775 or Socket 478	FSB up to 533 MHz, hyperthreading, graphics accelerator, Dual-channel DDR, high-definition audio, up to 4 SATA 150 devices, ATA 100.
	875x	P4-HT, Socket 478	FSB up to 800 MHz, Dual-channel DDR, AGP 8X, up to 4 SATA 150 devices, RAID, AC'97 digital audio.
	865x	P4-HT, Celeron D, Socket 478 (Socket 775 in a few models)	FSB up to 800 MHz, Dual-channel DDR, hyperthreading, graphics accelerator, ATA 100, up to 4 SATA 150 devices, RAID, AC'97 digital audio.
	84xx	P4, P4-HT, Celeron D, Socket 478	FSB up to 800 MHz, some models do hyperthreading, DDR memory, AGP 8X, up to 4 SATA 150 devices, some models do RAID, AC'97 digital audio.
nVidia	nForce2	Athlon XP, Sempron, Socket 462	Dual-channel DDR, single-chip architecture, AGP 8X, hypertransport, integrated Gigabit Ethernet, Firewall, audio, 2 SATA 150 devices, ATA 133.
	nForce3	Athlon 64, 64FX, Sockets 940, 939 and 754	Dual-channel DDR, single-chip architecture, AGP 8X, hypertransport, integrated Gigabit Ethernet, Firewall, audio, 2 or 4 SATA 150 devices, SATA RAID, ATA 133.

Vendor	Name	CPUs	More information
	nForce4	Intel P4 socket 775 Athlon 64, 64 FX, Sempron	Dual GPU (SLI) support, Dual-channel DDR2, up to 4 SATA 150 or 300 devices, up to 4 PATA devices, various RAID types, ATA 133, integrated Gigabit Ethernet and security, PCI-E X16 and X1.
SiS	SiS966x	Southbridge	Works with 761, 656, 649 Northbridge processors to provide Gigabit Ethernet, high-definition and AC'97 audio, SATA, ATA, and so on.
	SiS965x	Southbridge	Works with 756, 656, Northbridge processors to provide Gigabit Ethernet, AC'97 audio, SATA, ATA, RAID, and so on.
	SiS964x	Southbridge	Works with 655 Northbridge processor to provide Fast Ethernet, AC'97 digital audio, Dual ATA 133.
	SiS963x	Southbridge	Works with 755, 748, 746 Northbridge to provide Fast Ethernet, AC'97 digital audio, ATA 133.
	SiS761xx	Athlon 64 X2, 64 FX, 64, Opteron, Sempron Socket 939	Hypertransport compliant, PCI-E X16 and X1, graphics engine, Gigabit Ethernet, high-definition audio or AC'97, ATA 133.
	SiS756xx	Athlon 64 X2, FX, 64, Opteron, Sempron Socket 939	Hypertransport compliant, PCI-E X16 and X1, AC'97 audio, ATA 133.
	SiS755xx	Athlon 64, Opteron, Sempron, Socket 478	Hypertransport compliant, AGP 8X/4X, Fast Ethernet, AC'97 digital audio, ATA 133.
	SiS748	Athlon XP Socket 478	FSB up to 400 MHz, AGP 8X, AC'97 digital audio, Fast Ethernet, ATA 133.
	SiS746xx	Athlon XP Socket 478	FSB up to 333 MHz, AGP 8X/4X, Fast Ethernet, AC'97 digital audio, Dual ATA 133
	SiS741	Athlon XP Socket 478	FSB up to 400 MHz, AGP 8X/4X, integrated graphics engine, DDR 400 memory, up to 2 SATA 150 devices, Fast Ethernet, AC'97 digital audio, Dual ATA 133.
	SiS656x	P4-HT, Pentium D, LGA 775	FSB up to 1066 MHz, Dual-channel DDR2, PCI-E X16 and X1, up to 4 SATA 150 devices, AC'97 or high-definition audio, integrated Gigabit Ethernet, ATA 133.

Continued

Table 4-5 *(continued)*

Vendor	Name	CPUs	More information
	SiS655x	Intel P4-HT	FSB up to 800 MHz, Dual-channel DDR, AGP 8X, integrated USB 2.0 and FireWire, integrated 10/100 Ethernet, ATA 133.
	SiS649FX	Intel P4, Pentium D, LGA 775	FSB up to 1066 MHz, DDR and DDR2 memory, PCI X16 and X1, up to 4 SATA 150 devices, Fast Ethernet, ATA 133, AC'97 or high-definition audio.
VIA	K8 series	AMD Athlon 64, 64 FX, Sockets 754, 939, 940	DDR memory, PCI-E X16 or AGP8X/4X, integrated audio, Gigabit Ethernet, 2 or 4 SATA 150 devices, SATA RAID, ATA 133.
	K7 series	AMD Athlon XP, Duron, Socket 462	Dual- or Single-channel DDR, AGP 8X/4X, integrated audio, Gigabit Ethernet, 2 or 4 SATA 150 devices, SATA RAID, ATA 133.
	C series	VIA CPUs	DDR memory, AGP 8X/4X, integrated graphics, video, audio, Gigabit or Fast Ethernet, 2 SATA 150 devices, SATA RAID, ATA 133.
	P4 series	Intel Pentium 4, Celeron, Sockets 478 and 775	HT support, FSB up to 1066 MHz, Dual-channel DDR and DDR2, integrated audio, Gigabit Ethernet, 2 or 4 SATA 150 devices, SATA RAID, ATA 133.

Once again, what may appear to be an overwhelming array of choices slims way down as soon as you decide what kind of motherboard and CPU socket combination you want. As the galaxy of options drops to a relatively small number, you can apply the following bits of advice:

- If you're going to use an Intel processor, you'll want a compelling reason to use a non-Intel chipset (for rabid overclockers, this is easy to justify; for HTPC builders, it's somewhat less so). In that case, we suggest you look for the motherboard that has the best set of features and built-ins for the money (and $100 to $150 should be more than enough, unless you want to spend more than $1,500 on your total system).

- nVidia chipsets are fast and offer great system tweaking and tuning functions. The nForce4 Ultra chipset capabilities (as described for the Chaintech VNF 4 Ultra you toured at the beginning of the chapter) can be compelling. nVidia also often uses a single-chip implementation for both graphics hub and Southbridge functions that can be faster than two chips with a bus in between them. Note that nForce chipsets for AMD processors differ substantially from nForce chipsets for Intel processors, just as the processors themselves do. Not all nForce chipsets are alike!

- VIA gets high marks for its Athlon chipsets, both for its built-ins and for overall performance. Checking comparative rankings, ratings, and benchmarks actually turns out to be a decent way to pick a winning motherboard from a group of potential candidates. Performance does tend to trail nForce4, however.

- SiS is also known for graphics cards and some of its chipsets feature integrated graphics. These work best for undemanding desktop use and may not be entirely suitable for watching TV or DVDs through your Media Center PC. But SiS also offers chipsets that don't include graphics, and some of them get pretty good reviews, too. SiS gets more mixed reviews than any of the other chipset vendors, so proceed carefully as you make your selection.

We should also point out that graphics chipset and card maker ATI also makes motherboard chipsets as well, but is a relatively new player in this market. The Radeon Xpress 200 chipset series is available for both AMD and Intel processors, and you may occasionally come across the company's CrossFire chipsets in some motherboards. As we write this book, companies like ASUS, MSI, and ECS each offer one or two products built around this chipset, but we've had insufficient experience with them ourselves to either recommend for or against them.

Front-Side Bus

If you recall, the FSB is Northbridge territory; it's what connects a PC's CPU to other key system resources: system memory (RAM), the chipset, the graphic card, the PCI bus, and other peripheral buses (through the Southbridge processor). The speed of the FSB and the speed of RAM is every bit as important to PC performance as is the clock speed of the CPU. Historically, FSB speeds have increased more slowly and over longer intervals than CPU clock speeds. That said, it's also important to observe in Athlon 64 (and newer) AMD processors that the memory controller is integrated with the CPU so there's no separate Northbridge or memory controller at work.

As recently as 2002, many AMD processors were built for memory clocks that ran at 200 MHz. This jumped to 333 MHz in late 2002, and to 400 MHz in 2003. AMD's HyperTransport bus (which works with 64-bit Athlon processors) doubles this again to 800 MHz in both directions (from CPU to other devices, and vice versa). Over the same time frame, Intel's memory clocks (which do work through an FSB) have jumped from 533 MHz to 800 MHz to 1066 MHz in most current offerings. You will see FSB settings in the BIOSes of motherboards for Athlon 64 processors, but that just changes the speed of a clock generator that interfaces with system memory. Because the memory controller is inside the Athlon 64 (and newer) CPUs, it runs at the same speed as the CPU itself.

When you look at a motherboard, the maximum FSB or memory speed that your chosen CPU will support must match some FSB speed that the motherboard delivers. It doesn't have to be the fastest possible — and indeed, the principle of quiet HTPC operation argues that running more slowly may actually produce a better system, provided it can still deliver necessary performance.

Tip There's also more to FSB speed than may meet the eye. Total FSB speed uses a multiplier based on the actual bus clock rate (how many times per second the clock ticks, as it were) and the number of data transfers possible in any given clock cycle. Claims of 800 MHz FSB speed often turn out to involve four simultaneous data transfers during each clock cycle on a bus with a 200 MHz clock rate. To figure this out, it's necessary to read a lot of fine print.

Graphics Card Support

To some extent extremely fast graphics don't qualify as "do or die" for HTPC machines. That said, a Media Center PC can put some real demand on a graphics card when you use it to watch TV (especially if you use a dual-tuner TV card to watch one program while recording another, or run HDTV through your PC), display DVDs, or anything else that calls for smooth display of complex graphics. Top-of-the-line graphics cards usually require either AGP 8X or PCI-E X16 slots to work (but they also cost from $250 to $600 in round numbers). Top-of-the-line graphics cards also include lots of video RAM and extremely powerful graphics chips, invariably with their own fans to keep these insanely fast processors sufficiently cool.

Because HTPC deployment means stepping back from the bleeding edge to a fast and capable graphics card, but one that preferably does not require its own onboard cooling, the middle edge is where you'll find the cards that meet your needs and your budget. This means AGP 8X/4X is more than sufficient; it also means that a PCI-E X16 graphics card may be overkill. Whatever interface your motherboard supports, try to find a capable card that has no fan.

As another point of comparison consider that most commercially available Media Center PCs use AGP or PCI-E graphics cards nowadays. A fair number of them rely on graphics capabilities built into their motherboards (including low-end offerings even from high-end vendors like Hush Technologies). Only a very small number of offerings include PCI-E graphics cards among their various options. Graphics cards like the nVidia GeForce 6600 (available in AGP and PCI-E versions) and the ATI Radeon 9600 (AGP) or X300/X700 (PCI-E) appear to be among the most frequently used in commercial Media Center PCs.

Expansion Sockets and Buses

Modern motherboards usually include four or more expansion sockets, and usually offer at least three different types of buses to connect them to their Southbridge processor. Though history is littered with the washed up remains of older, no longer used PC buses, the following are the most likely to occur on any motherboard you might think about buying these days:

- **PCI (Peripheral Component Interconnect):** In Figures 4-1 and 4-3, the PCI slots appear in the upper-left quadrant of each motherboard. On each mobo you see three parallel plastic sockets with a small divider near the bottom. Today, these sockets are used for just about anything except a graphics card. The original 1992 implementation used a 33-MHz bus clock and 32-bit data transfers for maximum data transfer rates of 132MB/sec.

- **AGP (Accelerated Graphics Port):** Increasing demands for high-speed, 3-D graphics, especially for computer games, so taxed the PCI bus that Intel decided to develop a PCI variant specifically for graphics use. Introduced in 1997, AGP is a point-to-point data channel (which means only one AGP device per motherboard) that permits the graphics card to access system memory without requiring the CPU's help. Its base version is 32 bits wide and runs at 66 MHz, for a total bandwidth of 266MB/sec (this also corresponds to 1X AGP, so that 2X is 533MB/sec, 4X 1066MB/sec, and 8X 2133MB/sec).

- **PCI Express (PCI-E):** PCI Express maintains the PCI addressing model but separates physical implementations from higher-level bus communications in a layered protocol-based approach that works like the OSI Network Reference Model does for networking. Unlike PCI, which is a shared bus, PCI-E connections are point-to-point, so that each PCI-E device has the interface to itself. Each PCI-E link consists of one or more full-duplex 250MB/sec lanes along which data can travel (because data can travel in both directions, aggregate bandwidth doubles, and is thus 500MB/sec per lane). Thus, X1, X4, X8, or X16 is used as a multiplier on that base number to produce corresponding bandwidth of 0.5GB/sec, 2GB/sec, 4GB/sec, and 8GB/sec, respectively). That the top end for PCI Express more than doubles that for AGP 8X also explains why PCI-E X16 is emerging as the new standard for high-speed graphics interfaces on motherboards. Interestingly, if you look at the PCI-E X1 connectors on most motherboards, you'll see that the X16 connector supplied for a graphics card is indeed much bigger than its X1 counterparts. As with AGP, the X16 PCI-E is a single point-to-point link to the FSB bus just for the graphics card to use and also allows it to interact directly with system memory. Unlike AGP, you can have more than one PCI-E X16 graphics slot in a system.

It's no accident that both motherboards you toured at the outset of this chapter had PCI-E X16 graphics slots; it's hard to find new motherboards right now that offer AGP instead. If you do decide to install a graphics card in your HTPC rather than using capabilities on the motherboard itself, plan on buying a PCI-E X16 graphics card.

Storage Support

Modern motherboards typically include support for various types of storage as a matter of course. Though the number and types of connections do vary from one to another, nearly every motherboard for sale today includes one or more of the following types of connections (and the related device controllers are built into the motherboard as well):

- **Floppy disk drive:** Although floppies aren't used as much nowadays as they were in the 1990s, every motherboard we looked at included a single floppy drive socket and a built-in floppy controller. But really, you don't need a floppy drive anymore, unless you need to install a driver for a customized disk controller (such as IDE RAID). Windows XP, including WMCE, still requires a floppy disk for installing proprietary disk controller drivers.

Tip

Some modern motherboards make SATA drivers available to MCE in the BIOS; others don't. Read your mobo manual carefully to see if you need to supply SATA drivers during the Windows install. If so, you'll want to buy a cheap floppy drive (most cost less than $15 these days) and a floppy cable (which may come free with your motherboard) to keep around when it's needed. We just pop open the case, plug the floppy in for as long as it's needed, then remove it and button things back up when we're done. You can easily (and cheaply) do the same!

- Most PCs use drives that adhere to the **Advanced Technology Attachment (ATA)** interface standard, available on PCs since the introduction of the IBM PC-AT in 1984. The most current version of this standard is Ultra ATA and runs at either 100 or 133 Mbps. Every motherboard we looked at included two Ultra ATA sockets and built-in controllers. Because each socket supports a maximum of two drives (one the master, the other the slave), you can install up to four Ultra ATA drives. ATA is also sometimes called Parallel ATA or PATA, because it transmits data in parallel along the data path from drive to controller, and vice versa.

Tip

You can easily recognize cables for floppy and ATA (or PATA, if you prefer) drives: They're multi-line ribbon cables that can be up to 2 inches wide. When we gave you a guided tour of a generic PC in Chapter 1, we had to take the ribbon cables out of the way to make its innards more visible.

■ **Serial ATA** is a newer, faster refinement to PATA that first appeared in 2002. It currently comes in two forms: SATA1, which offers bandwidth of 150 Mbps, and SATA2, which offers bandwidth of 300 Mbps (SATA3 at 600 Mbps is due to market in 2007/ 2008). The faster type is backward compatible with the slower so you could use a 150 Mbps controller with a 300 Mbps drive, or vice versa — though you'd only get the slower speed, of course. SATA not only goes faster, but it's also been redesigned to use much smaller, narrower cables, to be easier to install and use, and to work better in disk arrays. SATA also consumes much less power, and permits longer cables to be used than PATA. It needn't be given a unique bus ID as with SCSI, nor does it need to be configured as a master or a slave as with ATA. All the motherboards we looked at for this book included at least two SATA connectors (one per drive is the rule for SATA); many of them included four.

■ **RAID** stands for Redundant Array of Inexpensive Disks. Basically, it's a way of linking up multiple drives in various ways so they behave like a single logical drive as far as the operating system is concerned. Numerous types of RAID exist identified by a trailing number. The RAID types most commonly available through motherboard controllers are as follows:

  ■ **RAID 0:** Organizes all drives in the RAID set as a single logical drive and spreads data across all drives in constant size containers called stripes. RAID 0 offers no fault-tolerance or data redundancy, so the term RAID is something of a misnomer, though commonly used.

  ■ **RAID 1:** Also known as disk mirroring, uses pairs of drives that exactly copy or mirror each other without striping. RAID 1 offers automatic fail-over from the primary to the secondary drive and 100-percent data redundancy.

  ■ **RAID 5:** Uses striping and parity data to store information about data written to any given drive across all other drives. If any single drive fails, the distributed parity data can be used to reconstruct the lost data.

  ■ **Other RAID Variants:** You may occasionally see references to RAID 3, RAID 10, RAID 0+1 and others, which all vary somewhat in their data integrity and performance capabilities, but are not embedded on many motherboards today.

Many RAID controllers also offer something called JBOD that does not logically aggregate multiple physical disks, but lets up to four drives share a single controller interface. Believe it or not JBOD stands for "Just a Bunch of Disks." Most but not all of the motherboards we looked at offered either IDE or SATA RAID support. Some offered RAID for both types of drives (but in separate arrays). Most offered support for RAID 0 and 1; some offered support for RAID 5 and JBOD as well.

Given the smaller cables, faster performance, and easier installation for SATA drives, we recommend using those types of drives in your HTPC. Because you typically may have two or four such drives, this should be plenty for most needs (and with USB or FireWire external drives as cheap as they are nowadays, it's easier to add more external storage than to install more drives inside your case anyway). Thus, we'd have to say that SATA is at least something that's nice to have on your candidate motherboards, and that you should probably buy only a motherboard with at least two SATA connectors.

Ports

Ports provide ways for data to enter and exit the motherboard and your PC, usually to communicate with various types of devices. As Figures 4-2 and 4-4 illustrate, most modern motherboards come equipped with numerous ports that are ready to use. It's also the case that most motherboards also come equipped with additional onboard connectors for various common ports as well, especially for USB and FireWire, and sometimes also audio. These are intended to hook up to cables that terminate in ports on the front of the PC case (built-in port blocks are invariably situated to project out the back of the case) or to provide support for internal devices that don't need an external port for attachment.

A quick review of what's on our two sample motherboards also shows what's typical for most modern motherboards, and where motherboards may differ. Table 4-6 lists ports by name with typical quantities and uses; it also indicates whether they're often, usually, or only sometimes present.

Table 4-6   Motherboard Ports

Name	Qty	Appear	Used for
Mouse port	1	Often	DIN-9 or PS/2 connector for mouse plug-in
Keyboard port	1	Often	DIN-9 or PS/2 connector for keyboard plug-in
Serial port	1	Often	Male 9-pin D connector (sometimes on optional cable)
Parallel port	1	Often	Female 25-pin D connector
Audio out	1 or 2	Sometimes	SPDIF optical and/or coax audio out for entertainment center link-up
FireWire	1 or 2	Sometimes	Standard IEEE 1394 connector for networking, camcorders, video and TV, storage, printers, scanners, and so on
USB	4-8	Usually	Standard USB connector for storage, flash drives, keyboard, mouse, infrared links, video and TV, printers, scanners, and so on
RJ-45	1 or 2	Usually	Ethernet 10/100 or 10/100/1000 network links (most mobos have 1, some have 2)
Audio block	1	Usually	6-jack sound card inputs and outputs
Graphics	1 or 2	Sometimes	Driving VGA and/or DVI devices, sometimes also S-Video or TV

For HTPC applications, it's likely that built-in graphics won't suffice for some time yet because of desire to display good quality TV and DVD images in real time. Onboard audio continues to improve, and it might be worth listening to high-definition audio or newer versions of AC'97 before buying an add-in replacement sound card. If the mobo offers an SPDIF optical audio out, that produces the best results when connecting to a receiver or pre-amp/processor for high-quality multichannel audio playback from your HTPC.

If you intend to use FireWire (IEEE 1394) devices as part of your HTPC setup, consider that FireWire controllers cost from $10 to $50 depending on how many ports you need and factor this into your cost analysis when selecting a motherboard. At a minimum, you wouldn't want to purchase a motherboard that didn't have networking and USB built-in. By pricing interface cards for other components that sometimes appear on motherboards, you can figure out what it's worth to get them built-in instead as you make your selection.

Built-Ins

As more and more computing functions shrink down to specialized chipsets, such functions are also finding their way onto motherboards. These chipsets provide the basis for various kinds of built-in functionality, including support for some of the ports mentioned in the preceding section, various types of storage devices, and common functions already identified earlier in this chapter. Table 4-7 provides a laundry list of common motherboard built-ins to bring all this information together in one place.

Table 4-7   Motherboard Built-Ins

Name	Type	Appears	Explanation/Remarks
IDE controller	storage	Always	At least one Ultra ATA 100 or 133 controller is typical nowadays, some mobos have two.
Floppy controller	storage	Usually	With dropoff in floppy disk use, no longer a must-have.
SATA controller	storage	Usually	Faster, more efficient disk storage features narrow cables for better case airflow (look for SATA2 for faster drives).
RAID controller	storage	Sometimes	Permits multiple ATA or SATA drives to be combined into single logical drive to improve reliability or performance.
USB controller	expansion bus	Always	Having more ports is better given demand on HTPCs.
FireWire controller	expansion bus	Sometimes	At least one FireWire port is handy on an HTPC.
Audio	audio	Usually	High-definition audio and recent AC'97 (2.3) versions make pretty good sound.

Name	Type	Appears	Explanation/Remarks
Networking	Ethernet	Usually	10/100 (Fast Ethernet) or 10/100/1000 (Gigabit Ethernet) are increasingly common on mobos, some even include wireless (802.11b or 802.11g) links.
Graphics	graphics	Sometimes	Onboard graphics remain marginal for HTPC use.

When it comes to choosing a mobo based on built-ins, USB and SATA are must-haves (but also available on most motherboards). High-definition audio or AC'97 (2.3) is worth a try for audio link-ups from your HTPC, but may not offer good enough sound quality for serious audiophiles. Because so many HTPCs do best with wireless network link-ups, wired networking is nice but not absolutely essential. FireWire may be a better characteristic to look for. Graphics support still isn't fast enough for good TV or DVD video, so built-ins are unlikely to be used in most HTPCs.

Cables and Accessories

When you buy a modern motherboard, it's always interesting to unpack the box it comes in and see what else you'll find. The closest experience we can think of is dumping out your stocking on Christmas morning, in fact. More expensive motherboards should include cables galore: one each for every storage interface is typical. You'll also find other cables as well, including power-on and reset button links for the case. The ASUS P5AD2-E Deluxe mobo also included an extra FireWire port to mobo cable, plus a two-port USB to mobo cable, and a game or MIDI port to mobo cable. In general, the more you pay for a motherboard, the less you should have to spend on cables later. One important exception to this rule is that it's almost always worth replacing standard ribbon cables (which can impede air flow inside your HTPC case) with round cable replacements (such as the very reasonably priced Thermaltake round IDE cables available from www.xoxide.com).

Other important accoutrements usually included with a typical motherboard include a CD with drivers, diagnostic and monitoring tools, and other items from the manufacturer. Many motherboards also include OEM versions of various kinds of software as well. Items such as antivirus software, antispyware programs, system utilities, and DVD-burning applications are pretty typical.

You probably shouldn't let your choice of a motherboard stand or fall by what else is in the box to be sure. Just follow our example and treat it like a Christmas stocking: if all you get is a lump of coal, then better luck on your next mobo purchase!

What About the BIOS?

As you might recall from Chapter 1, a PC's basic input/output system (BIOS) provides all kinds of controls related to recognizing devices and helping the PC to boot (or start up). Some PC gurus argue that the features and functions you get from a particular BIOS are important if not downright essential. You'll often hear the same things said about the motherboard's CMOS settings used to establish and tweak a PC's configuration and performance.

That said, if you stick to buying motherboards from reputable vendors, you should be okay. Though some BIOSes have their foibles, and hardware incompatibilities with interface cards will occasionally crop up, you should be able to build a perfectly workable HTPC if you work with the better known motherboard vendors. These include the companies listed in Table 4-8, all of which make motherboards well-suited for HTPC systems.

Table 4-8   Mobo Vendors with HTPC-Capable Offerings

Name	URL
ABIT	www.abit-usa.com
ASUSTek*	www.asus.com
ASRock	www.asrock.com
AOpen*	www.aopen.com
CHAINTECH*	www.chaintechusa.com
DFI*	www.dfiusa.com
ECS	www.ecsusa.com
GIGABYTE	www.giga-byte.com
MSI	www.msi.com.tw
QDI	www.qdigrp.com
Shuttle*	us.shuttle.com
Soltek	www.soltek.com.tw
WinFast	www.foxconn.com

All the companies whose names are asterisked were kind enough to furnish motherboards for this book. The Hush Technologies system that one of your authors purchased while researching this book uses a GIGABYTE motherboard from that company's P4 Titan series.

Wrapping Up

Picking the motherboard for an HTPC is driven by two other primary considerations: the case and the CPU. The case will determine the motherboard's form factor, and the CPU will determine what kind of socket the motherboard must provide for that CPU. In this chapter, you learned about a variety of key motherboard components, of which the chipset, front-side bus, memory sockets (as well as speed and type of RAM accommodated), and expansion buses are all key components to ponder when choosing a motherboard for your HTPC. You also learned about ports and built-ins found on modern motherboards, and which ones should count most when selecting a motherboard.

The Central Processing Unit

It is often said that the *central processing unit* or *CPU* is the brain of a computer. It is a programmable device that carries out the instruction, logic, and mathematical calculations in a computer. Great investments in time, effort, and money are made by some of the world's powerful corporations on the development of ever more capable CPUs. Mid-2005 (the time during which this book is being written) is an exciting time in the world of X86 central processing units. The industry is in transition between single-core and multi-core processors, and 64-bit computing is beginning to arrive at the consumer desktop.

As a result, there are more CPU choices for PCs than ever before, with multiple processor types from Intel, AMD, and VIA. For an end user assembling his or her own system, the choices are somewhat more limited. An open-ended discussion of all the various CPU flavors available today will take far more time and space than we have here; however, the practical aspects of processors upon which to base your purchase choice for your HTPC is more pertinent to this book's discussion anyway.

This chapter quickly reviews what the CPU does and what specifications such as clock and bus speed and cache mean. It examines the main processor options from AMD and Intel, along with a comparison of their features, their strengths, and their weaknesses. You also learn about what it takes to keep the various processors cool, about heat sinks, fans, and airflow, and how cooling ties in with aspects of case design and even the power supply. Overclocking and undervolting are also examined. During these discussions, you learn if there are any traits of processors that are of particular importance for an HTPC. Along the way you learn about the following items, all of which are worthy of investigation and consideration when evaluating or selecting a CPU for your HTPC:

➤ **CPU socket:** The CPU socket is one of the key differentiators between processor types. It is the electronic/physical pin interface between the CPU and motherboard. It determines the type of CPU you can use. The CPU and motherboard work hand-in-hand, but in our point of view, it's the CPU you should choose first. You can find motherboards with similar features for virtually every type of CPU, but the processors themselves have more distinct characteristics these days, and you may find reasons to prefer one type over another more than with motherboards.

Chapter 4 on motherboards is mandatory reading for obvious reasons. If the CPU is the engine, the motherboard comprises the chassis and drive train.

➤ **Thermal Design Power or TDP:** This is the term used to describe the power required by a processor when it is working as hard as possible. It is a critical aspect of any PC design — cooling, heat sinks, system layout, and even power supply decisions are all impacted by TDP, which also describes the amount of heat a processor generates.

Chris Hare's Processor Electrical Specifications (http://users.erols.com/chare/elec.htm) is a complete listing of basic electrical specifications of every processor made for at least the past 20 years. The data comes from manufacturers' published specifications and includes the TDP or Maximum Power Dissipation.

➤ **Heat sinks:** The processors in the first PCs only generated a couple of watts and were cooled with a tiny piece of extruded aluminum. Today's CPUs require serious heat sinks that generally weigh over a pound, often made with copper for its higher heat dissipation qualities and equipped with a high-speed fan. In an HTPC, such noise makers are unsatisfactory, and high-performance heat sinks that can run with slower, quieter fans are much preferred.

A Two-Horse Race

A casual look at the pages of any computer enthusiast magazine will give the impression of the CPU world being dominated by two brands, Intel and AMD. In fact, this is a somewhat misleading impression. The market is almost entirely dominated by Intel, which still has close to 85 percent of the processor market share, despite inroads by AMD in recent years. This says a lot about the business prowess of Intel, and it does not mean that AMD makes worse processors. As you will see, the second-place brand makes very good processors that compare well in virtually every way.

Desktop processors for the PC platform are made by other companies, such as IBM, but their products are almost entirely OEM, and you will rarely — if ever — find them on the retail market. VIA still makes the C3, but this is woefully underpowered for a good HTPC and uses an outmoded socket 370 interface. VIA's most powerful mini-ITX embedded CPU motherboards are suitable for a tiny HTPC, but poor distribution in the United States makes it a non-starter. Finally, VIA's new C7 looks powerful and highly efficient, but it has not been released yet.

That brings us back to AMD and Intel. Although the sockets and the CPU types they support were touched upon in Chapter 4, it's worth examining them again here (see Table 5-1).

Table 5-1   Sockets and Related CPU Families

Name	Edge	Type	CPU Families
LGA 775	Bleeding/leading	Intel	Pentium Extreme Edition (dual-core), Pentium D (dual-core), Pentium 4 Extreme Edition, Pentium 4, Celeron D
Socket 478	Middle	Intel	Pentium 4 Extreme Edition, Pentium 4, Celeron D
Socket 479	Leading/middle	Intel	Pentium M, Celeron M
Socket 939	Bleeding/leading	AMD	Dual-Core Athlon 64, Athlon 64 FX, Athlon 64
Socket 754	Middle	AMD	Athlon 64, Sempron, Turion 64

CPU Packages

The next sections go through the basic physical differences among the various CPU packages that fit different socket types. You may notice that we've left off the socket A (also known as socket 462), which was on the motherboard list in Chapter 4. That was deliberate. Yes, they exist, but if you want the ultimate HTPC, socket A is not a good option. The Athlon XP socket A CPUs are at the end of their product life.

LGA 775

This term refers to the 775-land Flip-Chip Land Grid Array (FC-LGA4) package with an integrated heat spreader (IHS). Intel processors in the LGA 775 package were introduced in 2004. This socket will eventually replace the older socket 478 introduced with the second generation of Pentium 4 processors. Its 775 contacts are tiny pads of gold plated copper that contact pins on the motherboard socket. This flips the traditional arrangement where the pins are on the CPU and the motherboard has a socket with tiny gripping contacts in tiny holes that the CPU pins fit into (see Figures 5-1 and 5-2).

FIGURE 5-1: Bottom of CPU has tiny pads of copper instead of pins.

FIGURE 5-2: Bottom of CPU has tiny copper pads and the 775 socket on the motherboard has matching pins.

For this design, Intel was criticized for offloading CPU bent-pin issues to the motherboard makers, because the exposed contacts in the LGA 775 socket are much more prone to damage than previous socket types. More than a dozen times of insertion and removal of the CPU was found by some researchers to be enough to damage the LGA 775 socket. Intel claims that LGA 775 allows higher current to be distributed more evenly to the CPU, which was necessary for them to reach higher clock speeds. Another point is that the value of a CPU is usually much higher than that of a motherboard if one or the other has to be replaced.

Like the socket 478 processors, the LGA 775 processor package incorporates an IHS made of thin copper that aids in heat dissipation to a properly attached fan heat sink. More importantly, the IHS protects the silicon die of the processor from physical damage when it is being handled during installation, and especially when the heat sink is installed. Processors destroyed by dies chipped and crushed during heat sink installation must have reached a peak toward the end of the Pentium III/socket 370 life cycle when massive heat sinks with high-pressure mounting clips first became popular. Among the processors listed in Table 5-1, only the mobile processors Pentium M, Celeron M, and Turion 64 have bare dies, as shown in Figure 5-3. A processor equipped with an IHS is very difficult to damage (see Figure 5-4).

FIGURE 5-3: The exposed core of Pentium M CPU is much more easily damaged.

FIGURE 5-4: AMD A64 CPU has an integrated heat spreader (IHS), which is found on all current desktop CPUs from both AMD and Intel.

The heat sink mounting mechanism for LGA 775 also differs from previous socket types. A plastic heat sink retention frame is bolted to the motherboard around the 478 socket. The heat sink is installed by using four clip holes at the corners of the retention frame. With the LGA 775, the heat sink attaches directly into the motherboard, using four holes at the corners of a square pattern around the CPU socket. Usually, the heat sink mounting bolts are equipped with springs that apply a specific amount of total pressure on the heat sink/CPU interface. Many aftermarket 775 heat sinks also provide a back support plate to be mounted on the other side of the motherboard.

The processors available in the LGA 775 package are variants of Pentium 4, mostly with higher clock speeds and larger cache.

478-Pin Package

Officially known as mPGA478, this socket/package should be familiar to anyone who has worked with an Intel-based system in the past few years. (Only one guess for the number of contacts in the 478-pin package.) This is the package where IHS was first introduced. Several varieties of Pentium 4 processors are available in this package.

The heat sink retention bracket around the socket used to be attached to the motherboard via plastic pins. They now use a more secure system of screws and threaded metal insets in the corners of the bracket, along with a back support made of plastic or metal. Standard heat sinks clip to the plastic retention bracket. Some aftermarket heat sinks dispense with the top retention bracket and bolt through the board.

479-Pin Package

The 479 ball Micro-FCBGA package is used exclusively for the Intel Pentium M and Celeron M processors. The pin pattern is just about identical to the socket 478, except for the extra pin, and the assignments for the pins are different for the two socket types.

This package does not have an IHS and care must be taken during installation not to chip or damage the exposed die. Pentium M was originally intended for use in notebooks, and two socket types are in common use: one that locks down the CPU with a lever, and another that uses a small slot screw, as shown in Figure 5-5. They have the same functionality.

FIGURE 5-5: Socket 479 with rotating screw mechanism for locking the CPU.

939-Pin Package

The 939 Micro-FCBGA package is for AMD's high-end 64-bit compatible CPUs. It is similar to the now-defunct 940 socket first used for high-end Athlon 64s, and has the familiar pins-on-CPU and holes-on-socket arrangement. This package has an IHS to help protect the die and improve cooling.

The boards come with heat sink retention bracket that attaches to the motherboard with two sturdy bolts and a back support plate. Standard heat sinks use clips that engage three hooks on two sides, and then lock with a lever.

The range of processors available in this package goes from a fairly modest Athlon 64 to the high-end Athlon 64 FX, and the bleeding-edge Dual-Core Athlon 64.

754-Pin Package

The 754 socket/package is for AMD's value processors. It also has an IHS and uses the same heat sink retention bracket as socket 939 (see Figure 5-6).

Athlon 64 and Sempron processors are available in the 754-pin package.

FIGURE 5-6: Socket 754. The same sturdy 6-lug heat sink retention bracket, which bolts through the board to a back support plate, is used on AMD sockets 754, 939, and 940.

Key CPU Parameters

Table 5-2 lists some key CPU parameters for some of the major CPU choices for your HTPC.

Table 5-2   Key CPU Parameters

Name	Type	L2 Cache	Bus/Clock	Heat	Edge
Pentium EE (dual-core)	Intel 775	2 × 1MB	800 MHz/ 3.2 GHz	Extremely high (130 W)	Bleeding
Pentium D (dual-core)	Intel 775	2 × 1MB	800 MHz/ 2.8–3.2 GHz	Very to extremely high (95–130 W)	Bleeding
Pentium EE	Intel 775, 478	2MB	800-1066 MHz/ 3.2–3.73 GHz	Very to extremely high (92–115 W)	Leading
Pentium 4	Intel 775, 478	1–2MB	800 MHz/ 2.8–3.8 GHz	Very to extremely high (90–115 W)	Middle
Celeron D	Intel 775, 478	256K	533 MHz/ 2.26–3.20 GHz	Moderate to high (73–84 W)	Middle
Pentium M	Intel 479	2MB	533 MHz/ 1.5–2.13 GHz	Extremely low (21–27 W)	Leading
Celeron M	Intel 479	1MB, 512K	400 MHz/ 1.2–1.5 GHz	Extremely low (21–24.5 W)	Middle
Dual-Core Athlon 64	AMD 939	2 × 1MB 2 × 512K	1 GHz HT/ 2.2–2.4 GHz	Very to extremely high (95–110 W)	Bleeding
Athlon 64 FX	AMD 939	1MB	1 GHz HT/ 2.2–2.6 GHz	Very high (89–104 W)	Bleeding
Athlon 64 (939)	AMD 939	1MB, 512K	800 MHz HT/ 1.8–2.4 GHz	Moderate to high (67–89 W)	Leading
Athlon 64 (754)	AMD 754	1MB, 512K	800 MHz HT/ 1.8–2.4 GHz	High (89 W)	Leading
Athlon Sempron	AMD 754	256K, 128K	800 MHz HT/ 1.5–2.0 GHz	Moderate (62 W)	Middle
Turion 64	AMD 754	1GB, 512K	1 GHz HT/ 1.6–2.0 GHz	Extremely to very low (25–35 W)	Leading

This may seem a very wide range of options to wade through, but if you approach it logically and systematically, your decision making can become simple.

Bleeding-edge processors are generally the most powerful at crunching data and processing, naturally. They are also the most expensive, reaching a current maximum of more than $1,000. So the question you have to ask is whether they will be better for an HTPC than a less capable processor.

Dual-Core Processors

The latest and greatest are the dual-core processors from AMD and Intel. In a nutshell, what they offer is the equivalent of two CPUs in one casing that fits into a single socket. True to the adage that two heads are better than one, dual-cores are much better at multitasking — doing many things at the same time, especially many CPU-intensive things. Other than that, the ultimate limits to performance are still clock speed, bus speed, cache, memory bandwidth, and latency, and all the things that apply to single-core CPUs.

The question is whether you will use an HTPC for a lot of multitasking — watching a movie while playing Doom and writing a novel? Maybe not. Okay, how about recording a TV show while watching a movie or processing a video clip from one format to another? That's the kind of thing a dual-core will be better at than a similarly clocked single-core processor from the same company.

Differences also exist between dual-cores from Intel and AMD. The consensus among the hardware community is that

- Current AMD models are faster and more capable.

- Despite high power dissipation numbers, AMD processors run substantially cooler than Intel's models, especially at idle, where power demand drops to just 60 percent of maximum. Intel models' power usage is substantially higher at maximum and drops by only 30 percent at idle. Intel's latest CPUs incorporate enhanced SpeedStep, a technology for gating processor clocks, so the latest Intel CPUs will run somewhat cooler at idle — but "somewhat" is a relative term.

- Most importantly, any 939 socket motherboard will run the AMD dual-cores. All that might be needed is a BIOS flash upgrade.

If you decide to go the dual-core route, you will need to pay close attention to ensure adequate cooling. You can also forget about a very quiet setup unless you've already scoured and understood everything at www.silentpcreview.com.

High-End Single-Core Processors

It's interesting to note that, at time of writing, both Intel and AMD have not abandoned high-end single-core processors after they launched the dual-cores. Intel's dual-cores go up only to 3.2 GHz clock speed, whereas its Pentium EE single-core model goes up to 3.73 GHz, and the 670 and 570 models reach 3.8 GHz. Excessive thermal output is the likely reason for Intel's current cap on its dual-core clock speeds, as its 3.2 GHz model already hits 130 W. AMD 2.4 GHz Athlon 64×2-4800+ dual-cores and 2.8 GHz Athlon FX 57 single-core show a similar differential in clock speed, but the absolute performance difference between the two is smaller.

Again, the question is whether or not your HTPC is better served by these powerful and hot processors. Our answer is probably not, especially when price—including the price of cooling—and noise are factored in.

Thermal Limits

This brings us to the question of whether there are thermal limits for a quiet PC of any kind, never mind an HTPC. The answer is yes, unless you are an experienced system builder and modder. As a rule of thumb, any processor that exceeds 100 W will be very difficult to run quietly in all but the most carefully configured systems using top-notch cooling gear. So a hotter processor will cost you more money to buy, then more money to cool, and it will probably prevent you from getting the lowest level of noise.

In the best mid-tower and larger cases, it is possible to assemble a bleeding-edge gaming rig that still manages to stay very quiet, say below 30 dBA SPL measured from a meter away. However, this is with the advantage of the better airflow/thermal management designs available in the larger cases, and with someone truly experienced tweaking every detail of the system. Such advanced thermal/cooling design really has not come to the horizontal AV component style PC case—at least not yet—which explains our recommendation to keep CPU power under 100 W. In fact, there are compelling reasons to go far over to the other side, the super cool processors.

Midrange CPUs

Midrange processors usually combine the best balance of value and performance. They include Pentium 4 in both 775 and 478 sockets in speeds ranging up to 3.2 GHz, and Athlon 64s in both 939 and 754 sockets, going up to 4000+ (2.4 GHz). With both Intel and AMD, the more recent higher pin-count socket platforms go higher in clock speed and offer better performance and features. This is especially true between the 939 and 754, where the former has dual memory channels and the latter has a single memory channel.

The offerings from AMD have a couple of significant advantages: They are all 64-bit ready, and despite similar power dissipation numbers, run significantly cooler than the Intel equivalents, whether at low or high load. For these reasons, the AMD A64 processors are preferred, although with some careful planning, Intel's midrange CPUs can also be made to run fairly quietly.

Powerful Computing, Low Thermals

Looking closely at the power dissipation figures, you will see that the Pentium M, Celeron M, and Turion 64 processors stand out with their extremely low wattage. The best of the lot are under 30 W. All of these are meant for use in notebook computers, which explains their low power, but at least a few socket 479 desktop motherboards are available, and the Turion 64 will run without fuss on standard 754 desktop motherboards, because in essence, it is little more than a rebadged Athlon 64 tweaked for operation at lower core voltages and clock speeds (both in the name of reduced heat and power demand). They are all bare-die processors; they do not have an IHS. The first question in your mind will probably be, "Are they powerful enough?" And the answer is yes, with the exception of the Celeron M. We will set that one aside, and look at the Pentium M, Dothan core, and the Turion 64.

Industrial desktop boards for the Pentium M have been around almost as long as the processor itself. AOpen and DFI were the first to introduce consumer-friendly P-M boards in Q4 2004. These were based on the older Intel 855 chipset, which had a few limitations, the biggest being single channel memory. The DFI board was equipped with a small proprietary heat sink whose fan still had to work pretty hard to keep even the P-M cool enough, but the AOpen board featured a socket 478 HS retention bracket that made it possible to use any of a huge range of capable aftermarket heat sinks for super quiet cooling (see Figure 5-7).

FIGURE 5-7: i855GMEm-LFS: AOpen's first Pentium M motherboard, equipped with socket 478 heat sink retention bracket.

The Pentium M is not priced low in the retail market, where the latest 2.13 GHz Dothan part (780) is fetching greater than $700. But back off to the model 760 (2.0 GHz) and you're down close to $400.

Extensive performance-oriented reviews showed that for a huge number of applications, including games, a lowly 2.0 GHz Pentium M could keep up with and even beat the fastest Pentium 4 and Athlon 64 behemoths. The 2MB L2 cache and advanced pre-fetch logic of the P-M Dothan core helped a lot. All this with *total* system power often at less than 100 W, as much as three to four times lower than the power hungry competition.

The performance results seemed slightly spotty but part of the reason was that the P-M was limited by its single-channel memory bandwidth, and its 400 MHz bus speed. It's easy to compensate for this by *overclocking* the CPU, of course — a topic we'll get into later in the chapter. The new Intel 915GM chipset brings 533 MHz bus support and dual-channel memory to the P-M; AOpen already has a new board with this chipset saddled — unfortunately — with a small proprietary heat sink that's not easily replaceable. However, another desktop Pentium M micro-ATX board is being introduced by MSI; this appears to be a 915 chipset version with socket 479 heat sink mounting. Given the increasing awareness of the Pentium M as a capable desktop processor, there will likely be many more 479/915 chipset desktop boards available by the time you read this.

An alternative approach comes from Asus, which created the CT-479 adapter that you plug a Pentium M into and then plug this adapter into one of their socket 478 boards (see Figure 5-8). The less-than-$50 adapter works transparently with five Asus boards that have BIOS support for the Pentium M. The main advantage is price: Pentium M boards carry a premium of at least $200 for a micro-ATX, whereas ATX socket 478 boards from Asus start at well below $100. One potential issue: The adapter raises the overall height of the CPU so that standard socket 478 heat sinks will fit too tightly and possibly damage the exposed CPU die. This is why the adapter comes with its own proprietary heat sink/fan. It is possible to modify some aftermarket 478 heat sinks for use with the CT-479 adapter; the trick is to compensate heat sink positioning for the absence of the heat spreader and the presence of the adapter.

FIGURE 5-8: Asus CT-479 adapter allows Pentium M processor to be used on its 478 boards.

The AMD Turion 64 is about as powerful as the Pentium M at the same clock speed — perhaps a little better for video encoding type functions — slightly higher in its power demand, and cheaper and simpler to implement. The key here is that being a standard 754 socket part, it will work on just about any 754 socket motherboard. Because these boards are positioned at the "value" end of Athlon 64 board, they start at well below $100, compared to at least $150 for the minimum P-M requirements — a 478 board plus Asus CT-479 adapter. Pricing for the Turion 64 processor is similar to the Pentium M.

Most heat sinks that fit the socket 754 and 939 sockets will work fine on the Turion 64. The only thing to watch out for is its very slightly lower profile compared to desktop CPU models due to the absence of the heat spreader, and the greater fragility of the exposed die.

Heat Sinks

These are also referred to as coolers and heat sink/fans or HSF. Modern CPUs from Intel and AMD simply cannot run without an HSF or some other serious cooling device. The concept of a heat sink is simple: Heat is conducted into a device with low thermal resistance and then dissipated into the air via a large heat radiating surface. The greater the thermal conduction, the bigger the radiating surface area, and the higher the airflow across this surface, the better the cooling. The challenge of modern CPU cooling is to wick away upwards of 130 W of heat — think of a 100 W bulb — from an integrated circuit chip with an area no bigger than a fingernail. No wonder the heat sinks are getting so big, heavy, and elaborate.

Retail processors from Intel and AMD come packaged with a stock HSF. Generally, these work well enough, if not superbly. They are almost never quiet; acoustics are low on processor makers' priorities, especially when the HSF is a freebie. They use fans that are often thermally controlled, and when conditions get hot enough, the noise from the high-speed fan can make one think of a banshee. Unless you don't mind hearing such noise routinely, you'll want to replace the stock HSF with something better, preferably much better. Figure 5-9 shows a modestly priced quiet HSF.

FIGURE 5-9: The Super Silent 4 Ultra TC is a modestly priced extruded aluminum heat sink with an integrated thermal speed-controlled fan by Arctic Cooling that cools better and works more quietly than it has any right to do.

Each socket type has specific requirements for mounting, and most of the better models include hardware that allows it to work with socket 775, 478, or any of the K8 (current generation AMD CPU) sockets — 754, 939, and 940 have identical mounting systems.

Many of the best heat sinks today employ heatpipe technology, which is a method of efficiently moving heat quickly over short distances, or of spreading it around evenly. Copper is widely used for its higher heat coefficient (ability to conduct heat), but a large all-copper HS can be dangerously heavy. The recommended HSF weight limit for all the CPU socket types is 450 grams. Any HSF that exceeds this weight substantially — say more than 20 percent — should be removed before the system is transported to avoid physical damage to the motherboard or CPU.

Some rules of thumb about low noise heat sinks:

- The basic heat sink design should incorporate fairly wide spacing between fins to allow slow, low-pressure air to flow through them.
- It should have a very secure, easy-to-use mounting system.
- The base that makes contact with the CPU should be flat and smooth.
- Good quality thermal interface material (TIM or thermal goop) should be applied sparingly between the CPU and the heat sink base.

Some heat sinks incorporate or come supplied with a fan, whereas others give you the option of using whatever fan you fancy. The former type is simpler to use, but enthusiasts often prefer the flexibility of choosing a specific fan. For best noise performance, look for fans that are 80 mm or larger in diameter, such as the Zalman model in Figure 5-10. Smaller ones have to spin too fast to create any useful airflow.

FIGURE 5-10: The Zalman CNPS7700Al-Cu is a large, innovative high-performance HSF with good fin spacing that allows excellent cooling even with the fan at low speed. The pictured sample has been modified with a super quiet 120 mm fan from Nexus.

One detail to consider is the direction of airflow in your heat sink. Conventional heat sinks generally have the fan mounted atop so that it blows down on the heat sink. Other components around the CPU benefit from the downward airflow, including the chipset and the voltage regulators around the CPU socket. These voltage regulators can get awfully hot with power-hungry processors, and motherboard makers routinely assume a certain amount of airflow from the CPU fan to help keep them cool. The downside of the downward flow fan is that the hot air from the heat sink gets spread around, which means some of it will just get recycled back through the heat sink again, thereby increasing the temperature of the CPU and the overall temperature inside the case over time.

Some heat sinks position the fan so that the air flows across the fins in a plane parallel with the motherboard, like the Scythe Ninja in Figure 5-11. The best airflow direction with such HSF is toward the back of the case, where a case fan just a couple of inches away should whisk the hot air out of the case. This is a superior airflow pattern to the conventional blow down method because it incorporates the CPU fan into the overall airflow in the case, which must include generous-sized intake vents not choked by restrictive grill covers.

FIGURE 5-11: Scythe Ninja heat sink utilizes six heatpipes and multiple well-spaced fins for passive cooling, but has clips for a 120 mm fan as shown, blowing across for airflow parallel to the motherboard. Unidirectional fins and fan positioning on any side allows air to be blown in the ideal direction.

Some heat sinks of this type have unidirectional fins that allow the air to flow through only in one direction. If it ends up that the fan blows up toward the power supply unit (PSU), this can cause problems. The power supply now sees a steady stream of hot air at its fan intake, and this adds to the heat it generates by itself. The thermally controlled PSU fan ramps up in speed to try and keep itself cool. The end result is a power supply that's getting hotter than it needs to and produces a lot more noise. So take care to examine the fan airflow directionality in such types of heat sinks. Choose one that can be set to blow toward the back panel fan.

Expect to spend up to $50 or more on a good HSF. It is an important part of the cooling system and a key source of noise.

°C/W

The technically correct way to gauge the cooling power of an HSF is by its temperature rise per watt or °C/W value. Hardware review Web sites that do a good job of HSF testing take note of the following parameters:

- Ambient temperature
- Rated thermal design power of CPU on test system

A special stress program such as CPUBurn (http://pages.sbcglobal.net/redelm/) is then run on the test system to put an extremely high computational load on the processor. The internal temperature diode in the CPU is monitored through a utility such as SpeedFan (www.almico.com/speedfan.php), which accesses the sensor outputs in the motherboard, and the stress test is run until the CPU temperature stops rising. The difference between final and ambient temperatures is the temperature rise. Divide this number by the TDP of the CPU, and you get the °C (degrees Celsius) rise per watt of heat for the tested HSF. The lower the °C/W value, the more effective the cooling of the HSF.

The best HSFs have °C/W values below 0.20, and any HSF that manages to reach 0.25 can be considered excellent. In general, the higher the TDP of your CPU, the lower the °C/W value of your HSF should be. The target is to try to keep the temperature of your CPU at maximum load below about 65 degrees C. This is designing for the worst-case scenario and should ensure perfectly safe thermals for your system over all. The good thing is that even if the CPU temperature goes higher as a result of some unforeseen circumstance or human error, most modern processors feature a built-in emergency speed/voltage throttling and shutdown that prevents them from burning the way earlier processors used to do.

There is a catch to using the °C/W specification to assess heat sinks. The fan is an integral part of the °C/W value, and a mediocre heat sink could be transformed into a much higher-performance unit by simply using a fan that blows a lot of air. The price, of course, is a lot of noise. Performance-oriented hardware review Web sites often seem indifferent to fan noise. But HSF evaluations that don't consider noise along with cooling performance make no sense for an HTPC.

For heat sink reviews that thoroughly evaluate noise as an integral part of heat sink performance, please go to the Cooling section of the Silent PC Review Web site (www.silentpc review.com/article_index.php#cooling). There is a large database of reviews on mostly quiet, high-performance heat sinks, generally tested the same way at the same noise level with the same fan. A Recommended HS page (www.silentpcreview.com/article30-page1.html) provides rankings and summary information about quiet and effective heat sinks.

Because heat sinks come and go rapidly, it is difficult to make a list that will not be outdated almost immediately. However, some brands have a reputation for high quality and good design. Some of these are noted in Table 5-3. Note that there are many dozens, if not hundreds, of heat sink brands, and at least a few of their products will be good, quiet performers.

Note Watercooling is a performance option not discussed in this chapter because it is a complex subject that calls for more time and money and dedication than direct air-cooled heat sinks. It's generally not practical for the HTPC A/V component type of case.

Table 5-3   Recommended HSF Makers

Name	Suggested Current Models	Notes
Arctic Cooling	Freezer series Super Silent Ultra TC series VGA Silencer series	Mostly inexpensive, well-engineered, low-noise heat sink with integrated fans. Not for the hottest CPUs, but excellent overall.
Alpha Novatech	8592 8150	Highest production standards, very good performance.
Scythe	NCU-2000 Ninja Shogun Katana	Innovative, performance oriented, with extensive use of heatpipes. Some meant to be fanless. New fans promise to be very quiet.
Swiftech	478-V	Highest production standards, very good performance. Brand more focused on watercooling now.
Thermalright	XP-120 XP-90 V-1 VGA cooler	High-performance heat sink usually sold without fan, catering mostly to overclockers, but still among the best with low-airflow fans.
Zalman	9500 7000 7700 VF700 VGA cooler ZM80 VGA Cooler Chipset coolers Reserator fanless watercooling	A pioneer in quiet cooling, Zalman makes a wide range of products, including fanless cases. Its heat sinks always come with a fan, sometimes integrated, and a fan speed controller. Fan noise quality is not always the best.

Overclocking

It used to be an arcane and subversive activity practiced only by wild gamers and computer geeks, but now *overclocking* is pretty mainstream. The term describes using a CPU at a higher clock speed than intended to obtain higher performance. All the adjustments needed for overclocking are in the motherboard's BIOS controls — or not. There used to be a great divide between motherboards that could be overclocked and those that couldn't, but now it's a rare board that doesn't offer BIOS settings for overclocking.

Processors achieve their rated clock speed by applying a multiplier to the frequency of the system clock in the motherboard. For example, an Intel P4-2.8 works on a system clock speed of 200 MHz and has a multiplier of 14, which gives it the operating speed of 2.8 GHz. Almost all current retail processors are multiplier locked; you can't just dial in a different multiplier to increase clock speed. Instead, you have to increase the system clock speed that the CPU sees — going back to the preceding P4-2.8 example, this means increasing the system clock from 200 MHz to 220 MHz for a 10 percent increase in clock speed. Clock speeds for other devices such as the memory, PCI, and AGP can be affected by changes in the system clock speed, and running those devices at higher than normal clock speeds is unwise. Most motherboards have options to control these clock speeds separately from the system clock, however.

So the question is whether or not it is worth doing. That depends. If you've got a bleeding-edge processor, chances are, you won't want to. The CPU will run even hotter than usual, and the amount of headroom available may make only a minor degree of speed increase possible. Why bother?

On the other hand, the middle range and mobile processors are perfect candidates for overclocking. Their heat dissipation is more modest, so if you install an effective enough HSF and ensure efficient airflow for the whole system, you could obtain a speed increase of 20 percent or more from your system just by changing the system clock. (Just how much your processor can be overclocked depends on many factors — the particulars of your CPU sample, the RAM, the motherboard, the cooling system, and even your power supply, not to mention plain, simple luck.) This can be pretty exciting, depending on what a 20 percent faster processor would cost you to buy. But you need to test the system for stability at the overclocked setting. Something like Prime95 (available at www.mersenne.org/freesoft.htm) is a good tool for system stress testing; if there is any system instability, the program will crash. Try reducing the speed and test again. Keep repeating this process until it can run 24 hours without any errors. There is no shortage of hardware enthusiast Web sites that can guide you through the overclocking process in minute detail.

One further practical point about overclocking is the simple question of whether it makes any real difference to anything you do with your computer — that is, does it provide a tangible improvement in your enjoyment of the system that you appreciate? If not, again, why bother? The system will suffer somewhat higher temperatures, and electricity consumption will be slightly higher. If there's no real gain, then it's not worth doing.

Undervolting

This also used to be an arcane activity practiced only by silent PC fanatics, but undervolting has moved more mainstream recently. It's distantly related to overclocking. At an early point in the history of PC overclocking, it was discovered that running the CPU at higher than normal voltage allowed higher stable clocks to be reached. The cost was greater heat and power consumption, considered acceptable by overclockers. Silent PC enthusiasts seek lower heat in order to run fans at slower speeds for reduced noise. They began experimenting with decreasing the CPU core voltage and found that many could run stably at reduced voltage but normal clock speed. The end result is a drop in CPU temperature, which allows the cooling fan to be run a little slower for less noise.

This assumes you have a fan speed controller. Many motherboards now come with software- or BIOS-accessible fan speed control systems, sometimes tied to thermal sensors on the board or in the CPU. You can also get simple hardware voltage controllers that let you manually dial in the speed you want, such as the Fanmate from Zalman, which actually is supplied with most of their heat sinks. Many HS makers are integrating fan controllers into their products. Multiple fan speed control add-ons are also available. Just check in the accessories section of your favorite PC stores.

Both clock speed and core voltage affect the power consumption and heat dissipation of the CPU. The relationship between clock speed and power is linear; a 10 percent increase in clock speed results in a 10 percent increase in power. But the relationship between voltage and power is essentially exponential. It has a much bigger impact on power and heat. A 0.1 V drop in core voltage from 1.5 V to 1.4 V might give you a 5 W drop in CPU heat; a 0.2 V drop could give you 15 W — the details depend on the particulars of your CPU. In any case, undervolting is worth trying if you seek the lowest power consumption, heat, and noise. As with overclocking, you have to check for system instability. Again, Prime95 or a similar program can be used in the same way as described for overclocking.

Wrapping Up

The wealth of processor options for do-it-yourself HTPC builders becomes manageable when you apply simple filters such as cost and thermal limits. In terms of computing power, if you follow our recommendations, it's difficult to make a bad choice. Even if you choose to go beyond the recommended thermal limits, it's still feasible to have a system that's not overly noisy. It will just take more money, cooling power, ingenuity, and planning. But some people love a challenge.

Whatever processor you choose, you will want to mate it with a suitable HSF. Once the system is assembled and MCE installed, run some CPU and system stress tests with the programs mentioned earlier, CPUBurn or Prime95, to ensure that your PC can run free of errors at high loads.

HTPC Memory

The old adage goes that "you can never be too rich, or too thin." Adapted for modern Windows systems in general, and HTPC systems in particular, that saying might read something like "you can never have too much memory, or too much disk space." Although we cover disk issues in the next chapter, this chapter deals with memory on HTPC systems; we address the various roles that memory plays on these PCs, as well as how much and what kind of memory they need.

To a large extent, the amount of RAM that a Media Center PC requires depends on how you plan to use that machine, and what kinds of media files or streams you expect to audition. Microsoft's minimum recommendation for Windows MCE is 256 megabytes (MB). But if you look carefully at the base configurations available from official Windows Media Center PC vendors, or from system builders who join up into the "Designed for Windows XP Media Center Partner" program, you'll quickly realize that most commercial offerings start at 512MB, and go up from there.

In an April 2005 online chat on Microsoft's Expert Zone one expert explained memory requirements for Windows MCE 2005 as follows: "The minimum recommendation is 256MB. I would go no less than 512MB. If you have dual tuners and an OTA HD card, I would even go 1GB." (Note: OTA is an acronym for "over the air" and HD refers to High Definition Television, also known as HDTV.)

No matter how you slice it, the need for RAM in Windows systems may be succinctly stated as "more is better." In this chapter, you learn about the types of memory you're likely to need for an HTPC, about memory speed and access timing settings, and how to investigate and tune your memory setup to get the best stable operation out of what RAM you've got installed. Along the way, we dive into the following topics:

> **Memory terms and operation:** A lot of specialized acronyms and terms are associated with PC memory — such as DRAM, SDRAM, DDR, and DDR2, to pick just a few moderately important examples. This section of the chapter walks you through how memory works, and what types of memory are in use in PCs today. Along the way, we explain the many terms and acronyms it helps to understand to hack your way through this otherwise impenetrable thicket of terminology.

➤ **Memory organization and structure:** Computer memory comes in banks, which can be single or dual. It is also organization into channels, which may also be single or dual. We explain the concepts and how they can be identified and put to work on your HTPC, where applicable.

➤ **Memory modules:** Here you look at the most common forms that memory takes, how it's laid out, and how it should be inserted into a PC. We also explain how to distinguish among various types of memory modules, and why some cost more than others.

➤ **Memory timing:** Modern motherboards permit their memory controllers to be manipulated at a surprising level of detail. Although default settings are almost always safe, even minor adjustments can make big differences in system performance. You get a chance to understand what memory timings mean, how they can be manipulated, and where you probably want to draw the line on tweaking for stable HTPC operation.

➤ **Memory consumption:** It's interesting to consider where memory goes on an HTPC and what it's used for. In this section, we explain the types of media that benefit most from having more memory around and show where that memory goes.

➤ **Memory tools:** A couple of excellent donation-ware utilities are available to help you inspect your (HT)PC's memory configuration and performance. We explain where to find them, how to install them, what tests to run or values to inspect, and what to do about them (if anything).

All this said, there's a simple solution when it comes to equipping an HTPC with RAM. If you plug in as many of the biggest memory modules as your motherboard can handle, you won't have to mess with memory on your system again, ever. That said, this may involve more expense and produce more heat in your system than you might like, so you'll have to temper this go-for-broke strategy with a little reality check. But because PC memory types and speeds change so frequently, and prices for older types of memory seldom go down so much over time (though newer RAM products keep getting bigger, faster, and cheaper all the time), maxing out right away is neither unwarranted nor completely stupid.

In the sections that follow, you get the chance to understand the key roles that memory plays on any PC, but also get a sense of its special significance on a Media Center PC. And as usual, you find a table of recommended memory vendors near the end.

Memory Terms and Operation

Inside a PC, memory is organized like a giant table of values, organized into rows and columns. But those rows and columns are themselves broken up into various areas, much like a large number of items stored in cubbyholes, where a single case contains a fixed number of cubbyholes. Retrieving any value from memory involves the following:

- Identifying the case where the required cubbyhole resides
- Accessing the case

- Counting off the rows and columns on the edges of the case to pinpoint the cubbyhole
- Retrieving the contents of the requested cubbyhole

In fact, the same approach also works when storing something in a particular location or cubbyhole. Most memory controllers are also smart enough to retrieve anything else in the same case that needs to be fetched, or to return anything to other cubbyholes in the same case that needs to be stored.

The reason this analogy is important is because it includes most of delays that occur when PC memory is accessed. To begin with, there's a delay involved in getting from one case of cubbyholes to the next. Then, there's a delay to count off the right number of rows from the upper left-hand corner (things always start from there by convention), followed by another delay to count of the right number of columns from the upper-left column as well (because that's where counting starts). Finally, there's a delay involved in putting something into the cubbyhole (writing a value) or grabbing something from the cubbyhole (retrieving a value). Whether the memory controller is in the Northbridge processor or in the CPU itself (as with the latest generations of AMD processors starting with the Athlon 64 and Opteron families), all these sources of delay remain the same.

If you think of the memory controller as a kind of imp whose job it is to wander around the cases where individual cubbyholes reside and to put things into or get things out of them, you're not too far away from understanding its job. About the only thing you can do to speed up memory, in fact, is to speed up the causes of delay by making the imp move faster or by speeding up the time it takes to put things into or pull them out of the individual cubbyholes. This is a rough explanation of why faster memory and speeding up memory access timing controls can combine to improve system performance.

As you know, RAM stands for random access memory. What this really means is that it is organized so that the memory controller can access any arbitrary case (which translates into a chip on a specific memory module) and get to any row and column inside the case (which translates into a specific memory address) to access its corresponding cubbyhole.

The type of RAM used in modern PCs is a special type of dynamic RAM, or DRAM. DRAM maintains the values it stores by maintaining the electrical charge in each cubbyhole and refreshing its contents periodically. This explains why turning (or losing) the power on a PC wipes away what's stored in memory. The type of DRAM that the vast majority of new PCs use nowadays is a type of synchronous DRAM, or SDRAM, because it handles one operation (read, write, lookup, find address, and so forth) each time the front-side bus clock on the PC makes a single tick.

In fact, modern memory comes in two forms on most new PCs. One is called DDR (double data rate) SDRAM, because it's been sped up to perform two operations for every clock cycle. The other is called DDR2, which reduces the core clock rate of the RAM chips by half, but increases the effective frequency to move more data per operation. DDR2 also requires less voltage (1.8 V versus 2.5 V for DDR) and therefore consumes less power and runs cooler than DDR. To make them easy to tell apart, DDR and DDR2 modules are packaged differently and use different memory sockets. You get into these details in a couple more sections as you dig more deeply into memory modules; some photos will help you distinguish between these two types of memory.

Memory Organization and Structure

The cases into which cubbyholes are organized are known more formally as *memory banks*. Each bank of memory maps more or less into a memory module (though some memory modules can actually handle two banks at a time) and is identified in terms of the number of bits it can handle in a single operation or memory transfer. DDR and DDR2 modules are both 64 bits wide, which matches the bus width of modern CPUs like the Athlon 64, Athlon, Pentium 4, and Pentium M processors. This critical match-up enables handling of one or more entire memory operations in a single clock cycle.

Memory modules are built of multiple memory chips soldered onto small pieces of circuit board. Depending on the capacity of individual chips built into the module, you can find anywhere from 4 to 16 memory chips on one or both sides of such devices. When RAM does not include hardware support for built-in error correction codes (called ECC logic, or more succinctly, just ECC), the number of bits of memory that the module can hold equals the total capacity of all the chips on the module. When ECC memory is used, the number of chips goes up by 1/8 because one error correction bit is stored for every 8 bits of data. Thus, a 64-bit data path requires 72 bits' worth of storage on ECC memory, so that you essentially need 9 chips to store 8 chips worth of data, whatever their size may be.

Tip   Most conventional desktop PC motherboards don't support ECC memory, which is used in higher-end servers and workstations. Because it requires more chips and more complex circuitry, ECC memory costs more than non-ECC memory. It also runs slightly slower because of the overhead involved in calculating or checking ECC data for each 8 bits' worth of data read or written. If you need ECC memory, your motherboard manual will tell you so in no uncertain terms.

One Bank or Two?

Some memory modules double up on the number of memory chips and may even have chips on both sides so that you can install more memory on a single device and maybe even two memory banks from a single memory module. This creates the distinction between dual-bank memory modules and single-bank memory modules.

Your motherboard manual will tell you when it's important to pay attention to the distinction between dual- and single-bank memory modules. In most cases, this applies only when the number of memory banks that a motherboard can accommodate is less than twice the total number of memory slots. In that case, not all slots can be populated with dual-bank modules, and there may even be restrictions on which slots can handle dual-bank modules and which ones cannot. In other cases, some systems with four memory sockets can support only six banks of memory. Here again, your motherboard manual and installation instructions should make these limitations crystal clear.

Channeling PC Memory

PC memory is also organized into *memory channels*, which may work either in single-channel organization or which may also (or only) support dual-channel organization. If you recall, DDR gets its name (double data rate) from its ability to perform two memory operations in a single clock cycle. Dual-channel memory organization permits two matched memory modules to work together and act like a single logical memory module that's twice as big as either one taken separately. Of course, the memory controller has to be able to operate in dual-channel mode for this kind of memory organization to work, but it's another technological trick that permits memory speeds to double up again since each operation on a matched pair of modules involves twice as much data (128 bits) as any operation on a single (64-bit) module.

This explains many aspects of dual-channel memory systems. For one thing, it makes it clear why memory manufacturers and PC experts alike all recommend that any dual-channel memory installation use the same make, model, and type of memory modules for both modules in a pair. It also explains why motherboard manufacturers routinely color-code memory sockets so that each socket in any dual-channel pair is easy to see (and use). And finally, it makes it clear why some high-performance memory vendors sell matched pairs of memory modules that have been tested to make sure they can work together as closely as technology can determine (for a higher price, naturally): that's the best way to milk maximum performance from more dual-channel memory installations.

Politics and Economics of Matched Memory Modules

If you start shopping for DDR or DDR2 memory, it won't take you long to observe that buying matched pairs of memory modules is more expensive than buying the same parts individually and unmatched. In most cases, you'll pay a premium of 50 percent or more over the cost of buying the same (or similar) parts individually. What makes this expense worthwhile to some people (most notably PC performance freaks and overclockers) is that such matched pairs can be tweaked and tuned to deliver faster performance than unmatched pairs. But unless you're incredibly flush with cash or a total perfectionist, this kind of thing may be largely wasted on a living room HTPC. Indeed, the amount and speed of the memory you use makes a modest difference in HTPC performance, but probably not enough for most people to justify the added expense.

Memory Modules

Today's memory modules are usually called DIMMs, which stands for dual inline memory modules. The dual nature of the module comes from having separate leads on each side of the package where it plugs into the RAM socket. Not all DIMMs have memory chips on both sides, but all have dual sets of connections on their socket ends.

Modern DDR and DDR2 DIMMs are laid out differently to make them easy to distinguish from one another. DDR DIMMs plug into 184-pin sockets; DDR2 DIMMs plug into 240-pin sockets. Figure 6-1 shows a DDR socket next to a matching DIMM; Figure 6-2 shows a DDR2 socket next to a matching DIMM. Right now, DDR memory has a slight price edge on DDR2 memory, but the performance advantage is all the other way.

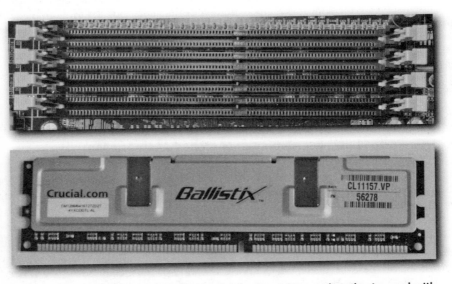

FIGURE 6-1: DDR DIMMs use a 184-pin module and matching socket; they're used with AMD and older Intel (pre–Socket 775) CPUs.

FIGURE 6-2: DDR2 DIMMs use a 240-pin module and matching socket; they work only with the newest Intel chipsets right now (AMD CPUs don't yet work with DDR2).

It's also important to understand that increases in memory speed don't scale linearly to match increases in overall PC performance. In plain English, doubling RAM speed doesn't double PC speed. That's because many other factors contribute to PC performance, including CPU speed and the nature of the workload the PC handles. In most cases, if everything else is equal and memory speed is doubled, users might notice only a slight increase in overall performance. But they might also notice more of an improvement during memory-intensive tasks, such as when loading or exiting applications, booting up or shutting down, or processing large amounts of data where memory activity is high.

When choosing DIMMs for HTPC use, a couple of words of warning may be in order. Higher-performance DIMMs often include fancy packaging with extra heat transfer shielding wrapped around the circuit board and its built-in memory chips (as shown in both Figures 6-1 and 6-2). Some even mount LEDs on the upper edge of the package (the side opposite the socket connector) to show memory activity or temperature. These fancy packages not only cost more, but they're also bigger and bulkier than their lesser counterparts.

On many smaller motherboards, space is at a premium so you'll want to make sure you can shoehorn those big packages into the memory slots before buying them — if you can. If you must buy them to try them, make sure you can return them if they don't fit. Also, be sure that you understand and adhere to the restrictions that so often apply when individuals seek to return computer components post purchase (save receipts, keep original packaging, no scuffs or marks, and so forth). This advice goes double if you're building an HTPC inside a compact or small form factor case (if so, we urge you to use the slimmest DIMMs available).

Memory Timing

Return for a moment to our earlier example of the cubbyholes in cases as an illustration of how memory is addressed and navigated. Normally, when you see memory timing specifications, they take the form CL2.0-2-2-5 or CL3.0-3-3-8. Here, we explore what's up with these numbers and what they mean.

The four numbers always appear in the same order and they correspond to timing information for the following memory activities, measured in clock cycles:

- **CAS latency:** The CL at the head of the example strings stands for CAS latency, which counts the number of clock cycles between when the memory controller receives a "read" command and when it begins to read a chip on some specific memory module. The reminder about our analogy makes sense when CAS is expanded to mean column address strobe and explained to mean the delay in locating the correct column of values on some specific memory chip. The strobe is a regular series of electrical pulses (clock ticks) used to jump from one memory location to another. Experimentation shows that adjusting this value downward (making latency shorter) by itself has little impact on memory performance in many types of applications. Applications that are memory intensive may benefit from lower CAS latency, but the difference is only about 3 to 5 percent.

- **RAS precharge:** Because of how CAS expands, you can probably guess that RAS expands to row address strobe. This value addresses how many clock cycles elapse between the precharge (which gets memory ready to read) and activation (which enacts the read action) commands. Row activation time depends on how long it takes to jump from one row to the next in a memory chip, or when jumping from one arbitrary memory location to another. It's basically the time involved in finding the right row, so it's safe to think of it as more or less equivalent to row latency. Here again, experimentation shows that adjusting this value downward (making RAS precharge shorter) by itself has little impact on memory performance.

- **RAS to CAS delay:** This measures the amount of time it takes between when any particular memory bank is activated (a module or part of a module is identified) and when a read or write command may be sent to that memory bank. This has the biggest impact when memory values are read in random order, making the next read unlikely to occur in the same bank as the previous read. Experimentation shows that lowering this value has the biggest overall impact on memory performance.

- **Cycle time:** This measures how long it takes memory to stabilize after reading or writing so that another sequence of operations can begin, or between the activation and precharge commands. This influences row activation time and the time required to jump from one arbitrary memory location to another. Experimentation shows that lowering this value also has little impact on memory performance.

Taken as a whole, lower latencies in all categories can boost performance in certain classes of memory-intensive applications by 3 to 8 percent. However, the majority of applications don't really see much gain, and the headache of trying to tweak memory settings is best left to those users who are knowledgeable about the risks.

When tweaking memory in BIOS, another value that's not part of this typical timing data (which you can obtain for nearly all memory modules by digging into the manufacturer's Web site, if it's not printed on the module itself or on a label attached to the module) is the *memory controller command rate*. This value indicates how many clock cycles the memory controller grabs and holds the command bus for memory access. Smaller values mean the controller can issue commands more quickly. Lowering this value also produces significant increases in memory performance.

When you set up your motherboard for the first time, you'll set these values (or allow the motherboard to set them for you) for the first time. It's neither smart nor safe to try to trim them immediately. It's best to start at recommended or default values, then conduct some experiments to see if you can trim values here or there and keep the system running smooth and stable. Two profound signs of overly aggressive memory timings are regular system crashes or crashes after the system warms up (and possibly overheats). HTPCs aren't good candidates for overclocking anyway because real-time signal processing for TV, DVD, and music gets flaky as clocks go faster. Better you should use this information to make sure things are set up correctly than to try to squeeze extra speed out of your system.

You'll sometimes see timing values with fractions, such as CL2.5-3-3-5 for some memory. This is because DDR actually permits values to be cut in half, and half of five in this case is 2.5. Don't let it throw you; it's just one of those things you learn to accept in the wild and wacky world of RAM timing.

Where Does Memory Go on an HTPC?

The answers to this question vary, depending on what's running on your system. But it's easy to check where memory is allocated at any given moment, so we can tell you where a lot of it is likely to be tied up or in use. If you get to know the Windows Task Manager, you can even check on memory allocation and usage any time you like (more on this later). Judicious use of this tool, however, shows that the biggest memory consumers on MCE installations include the following:

- **Windows** itself runs 20-plus processes and requires about 30MB to run XP Professional; switch to MCE 2005 and that total jumps to over 50MB (and that number goes up as more services that share common DLLs load and run, and more instances of the svchost. exe process run).

- **RemoteRecordClient.exe:** 32MB while recording TV.

- **ehshell.exe:** 28MB all the time; Windows MCE primary support file.

- **WUSB54Gv4.exe:** Driver/LAN support file for Wireless 802.11g network access (likely on most HTPCs to avoid extra wires, but not really part of Windows MCE per se).

- **ehrec.exe:** 22MB all the time; used to integrate recording from a TV tuner card with Media Center Edition.

- **rrtray.exe:** 18MB all the time; apparently this is fallout from downloading music from the MSN Remote Record Service.

- **ehRecvr.exe:** 16MB all the time, Windows MCE support file.

- **Internet Explorer (explore.exe):** 16MB to start up and slightly less than that for each browser window left open.

- **Windows Media Player (wmplayer.exe):** 16MB to start up, and about 3MB for each radio station or music source activated.

- **Windows Explorer (explorer.exe):** 18MB to start up, and about 4MB for each additional file browsing window opened; regularly observed 27MB when MCE was running.

To make a long story short, we observed typical memory commit charges (the total amount of physical RAM that Windows is using) on our Media Center PCs in a range from 415 to 507MB of RAM when engaged in typical activities such as watching TV or a DVD, recording TV, or listening to music. This also validates the notion that 512MB of RAM is the barest practical minimum for an HTPC running Windows MCE 2005.

Working with Windows Task Manager is pretty easy; it's the best way to check which processes are consuming Windows memory resources. To launch this program perform the Windows three-fingered salute: hold down the Ctrl, Alt, and Del keys at the same time, and it pops right up. Here's how to use it to check Windows memory status, and to see where the memory's going:

1. If the Performance tab isn't already selected, as shown in Figure 6-3, click that tab to bring up the Performance tab display. In the upper right-hand pane below the two right-hand graphs (CPU Usage History above, and Page File Usage History below), you'll see the legend Physical Memory (K). This displays how much memory is installed on the system (1.5GB on the machine in the figure) and how much remains available for use (989,332K or about 966MB). Also of interest is the Commit Charge pane at the lower

left: it tells you how much memory is currently in use (Total), how much can be used altogether (Limit), and the most memory used since the system last booted (Peak). Microsoft says that available memory should never fall below 4,096K, which also means that the peak value should never get closer to the limit than by the same amount.

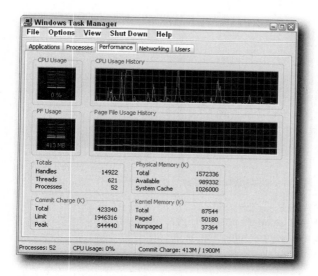

Figure 6-3: The Task Manager's Performance tab shows all kinds of useful statistics, including numerous important items about memory.

2. Next, click the Processes tab to display the list of active Windows processes. By default processes show up in alphabetical order, but you can rearrange them by clicking once on any column heading to sort values from lowest to highest, and clicking again to sort from highest to lowest. Do that with the Mem Usage column heading, and you'll see a display something like what's shown in Figure 6-4.

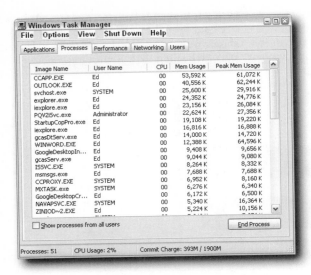

Figure 6-4: The Task Manager's Processes tab shows all active Windows processes. Click twice on the Mem Usage column heading to see the top memory consumers on your HTPC.

3. Careful examination of the listings that show up on the Image Name heading will let you know where your memory is going. If you don't recognize a name, simply copy and paste it into your favorite search engine, and it will help you figure out what's what.

4. When you're finished using Task Manager, click the X button at the upper right to close this utility (if you minimize it, it maintains a CPU utilization indicator in the system tray, but you can't see that while the Media Center interface is running).

This is a great way to keep tabs on your system and get to know what's running in your MCE environment. You can't keep Task Manager in the foreground for long while MCE is running, but you can sneak a peak at it whenever you'd like.

Memory Tools

In addition to Task Manager, some other great tools can help you investigate and check out your memory setup and configuration on a Media Center PC. These are all standard Windows programs, so you'll have to use the Alt+Tab sequence (press both keys simultaneously) to shell out to the normal Windows desktop, then go through the Start → All Programs menus to access and run them.

CPU-Z

CPU-Z is a free detection program that recognizes all the hardware on your system it can find. After you download, install, and run the program it will provide information about your PC hardware, organized by tabs into coverage of your PC's CPU, Cache, Mainboard (what we've called motherboard in this book), Memory, and SPD. The results are shown in Figure 6-5, which displays the Memory tab data, and Figure 6-6, which displays the SPD data for the memory module in slot 1 on the system it was run on.

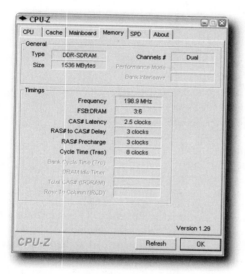

FIGURE 6-5: CPU-Z's memory tab shows memory type, total RAM installed, and the presence of dual memory channels on the test machine.

In Figure 6-5, you also get the PC's memory settings from the BIOS in the Timings panel at the center of the CPU-Z window. Though it shows 198.9 MHz as the frequency, this is actually specified as 200 in the BIOS itself. That it's really DDR memory is confirmed by the two-to-one ratio of FSB:DRAM also shown in the timings panel. Notice the various timing settings match those shown in Figure 6-6 for 200 MHz as well (as they should).

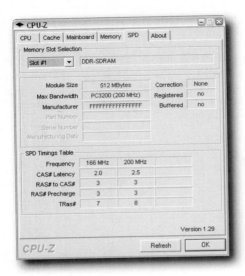

FIGURE 6-6: CPU-Z's SPD tab shows automatically detected timing information for each memory module installed on the system.

In Figure 6-6, the mysterious string SPD crowns the tab depicted there. This stands for serial presence detect and picks up data encoded on DDR and DDR2 memory modules that stores their timing information. This comes courtesy of JEDEC, a global semiconductor standards organization that created the SPD specifications that permit such data to be stored on and then retrieved from the memory modules themselves. What you see in Figure 6-6 is information about the memory module itself, but also its SPD timing table. This is what you'd check against in your PC BIOS to make sure your FSB:DRAM ratio is correct, as well as the four standard timing values.

Cross-Reference

You can download CPU-Z from www.cpuid.com/cpuz.php. It's freeware, but the makers do encourage donations to help support their work. We think it's worth at least $5!

PC Wizard 2005

PC Wizard comes from the same organization that's behind CPU-Z and offers easier access to the same kind of data that CPU-Z provides. For memory, the difference is primarily one of display because the program makes it easier than in CPU-Z to examine data from all memory modules installed (you can scroll instead of having to switch from one display to another). It also more clearly indicates what kind of memory modules are in use and labels the chipset/ memory controller information unambiguously. As one of your authors was researching this chapter, he ran this utility and noticed the memory on his test machine was running at half its

Check Out Receipt

Elbridge Free Library (EL)
315-689-7111

Wed, Aug 20, 2008 04:30:17 PM

87279

Item: 398500271270086
Title: Build the ultimate home theater PC
Material: Book
Due: 09/10/2008

Total Items: 1

Thank You!

rated speed. After a quick jump into that PC's BIOS to select SPD timings instead of Auto timings, memory speed doubled. This produced a much-appreciated 10-percent boost in system performance. Figure 6-7 shows the initial sections of PC Wizard's Physical Memory details.

FIGURE 6-7: PC Wizard 2005 provides all the same data that CPU-Z does about memory, but does so in a clearer, more accessible form.

To get to this display, launch the program from the Start menu and click the mainboard icon (second from left, top row, in the left-hand pane). Then click Physical Memory in the Mainboard pane to display the memory information in the details pane below.

Cross-Reference

You can download PC Wizard 2005 from www.cpuid.org/pcwizard.php. It's freeware, but the makers do encourage donations to help support their work. We think it's worth at least $5, too!

HWiNFO32

HWiNFO32 is a shareware program that detects and displays all the information it can elicit from every item of hardware on your PC. It delivers a bit more information than either CPU-Z or PC Wizard, but you must pay for this software if you use it longer than 14 days ($25 for home PC users, $30 for business PC users; discounts available for multiple licenses).

As Figure 6-8 illustrates, this program actually calculates timings for each memory module, and identifies the SPD version to which it conforms. It also reports on the presence or absence of numerous advanced features, and showed us that one of our memory modules was enough older than the other two that it might benefit from being replaced (it conformed to SPD 1.0 while the other two conformed to SPD 1.1, and also showed slower SPD timing settings).

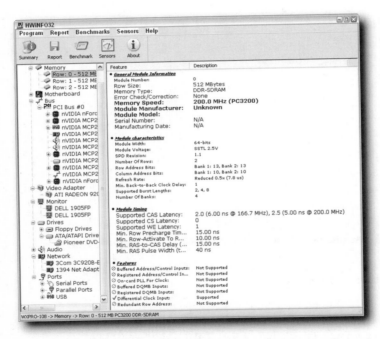

FIGURE 6-8: HWiNFO32 provides even more data about memory, but only on a per-module basis.

To launch this program from the Start menu, select All Programs ➜ HWiNFO32 ➜ HWiNFO32 Program. Once open, click the plus sign to the left of the Memory icon in the left-hand pane to open its listing of memory modules and then click any memory module in the left-hand pane to bring up its complete detail listing in the right-hand pane.

Cross-Reference Download HWiNFO32 from www.hwinfo.com. It's shareware, and costs $25 for home users to register, $30 for business users. We think it's worth the money, and worth using on your HTPC.

When Is BIOS Tweaking Safe?

It's okay to use one or more of the aforementioned utilities to help you investigate your HTPC's memory and make sure its settings agree with what the manufacturer says it can handle. Overclockers and system tweakers may be inclined to push things past their stated limits, but we're not convinced that's worthwhile on an HTPC. That said, as long as you know how to flash your BIOS or return it to its factory settings, you can play around if you must. We like to make sure we're doing as well as we should be, but usually steer clear of trying to do better than that. These utilities can help you tweak to your heart's content, should you be inclined to push your luck.

Table 6-1 mentions numerous vendors that offer high-quality DDR and DDR2 RAM suitable for HTPC use. Of these, we've gotten great results with DIMMs from Kingston, Crucial, and Corsair (all of whom were kind enough to loan us memory for testing and system builds for this book).

Table 6-1   High-Speed/-Quality RAM Vendors

Name	RAM tool?	URL/Remarks
Corsair*	Yes	www.corsair.com; high performance and value options available, noted for speed and stability
Crucial*	Yes	www.crucial.com; high performance and value options available, noted for speed and stability
Kingston*	Yes	www.kingston.com; multiple performance and value options available; one of best-known vendors, good high-performance line
OCZ Technology	Yes	www.ocztechnology.com; expensive ultra high-performance memory down to value lines available, motherboard search tool is clunky
PNY	Yes	www.pny.com; aims more at OEMs than at end users, do your homework before considering this brand
Samsung	No	www.samsung.com; aims more at OEMs than end-users, good speed and timing info, though
TwinMOS	Yes	www.twinmos.com; also aims at OEMs, but provides good motherboard lookup tool, performance memory gets good reviews

All the companies whose names are asterisked were kind enough to furnish RAM for this book. Those with a "Yes" in the RAM tool column offer motherboard lookup tools to help you match memory to your mobo.

Wrapping Up

Buying enough memory for an HTPC is important. It can make the difference between smooth and choppy video in a two-tuner TV configuration, or between faster and slower performance under many circumstances. Whenever streaming data is involved — music, video, TV, and so forth — more (and properly tuned) memory can improve your media experience. That said, it's always important to get the right kind of memory for your motherboard; you should get no less than what you need, but no more than it can handle. Though faster memory does work on slower motherboards, that extra capability (which does cost more) will go unused.

We can't recommend building an HTPC nowadays with less than 1GB of RAM. On dual-channel systems, that means two matched 512MB DIMMs for a top-of-the-line implementation, or at least two identical DIMMs from the same vendor (remember, two DIMMs on a dual-channel system will always be faster than a single DIMM of double the size). Slower 512MB DIMMs are available for as little as $80 each as this chapter is being written, whereas a pair of matched high-performance DDR2-533 DIMMs costs $400 and up. To find the best memory for any given motherboard, visit the Web sites of major RAM manufacturers (like those in Table 6-1) and look up your motherboard for their recommendations, or visit the motherboard manufacturer's Web site, look up your motherboard, and check their memory recommendations.

The best rule of thumb here is to buy as much fast memory as you can afford. If you can't spring for the best and fastest right away, get at least 1GB of budget memory, and then upgrade later as your circumstances and budget permit.

Hard Disk Drives

Hard disk drives (HDD) are the storage centers of your PC system. The hard drives represent the most critical of the many types of permanent storage that can be used your computer. The operating system, programs, and data all reside in the hard drives and load to RAM when they are needed.

The hard disk plays a significant role in many aspects of the PC:

> **System performance:** System boot speed, access to programs, saving or transferring data, and general random access to files and data — all of these tasks are closely affected by the hard drive.

> **Storage capacity:** For an HPTC, adequate storage space can quickly becomes critical as you start collecting music, video, and movie files, many of which easily reach several gigabytes.

> **Support for software:** Many program need lots of disk space and fast disk performance to work well. Windows XP alone needs upwards of 1GB.

> **Reliability:** Disable the hard drives, especially the one containing the operating system, and your computer becomes useless. Lose the drive that holds all your music and movies, and you could be losing weeks or even months and years of work. Hard drive reliability is probably more important than that of any other component in your system.

This chapter touches on basics of how hard disks work, and how data is formatted and stored. We consider performance issues and the various interfaces that connect hard disks to the PC. A discussion about external HDD options including USB, FireWire IEEE 1394, network attached storage, and external SATA is included along with data backup schemes. Finally, HDD issues and options specific to HTPC are considered.

HDD Overview

Back in the day when Bill Gates said that no one will ever need more than 640K of memory, storage space in the PC was limited to those big 5.25" truly floppy disks hardly anyone even remembers anymore. The first ones only held 100K. The first PC hard drives were just a few megabytes, then it moved to a few hundred, and finally, in the early 1980s, the gigabyte barrier was broken.

in this chapter

☑ HDD overview and options

☑ HDD performance

☑ Thermal issues

☑ Acoustics and vibration

☑ External and network attached storage

The 3.5" HDD appeared around this time; before then, they were 5.25". By the late 1990s, we had HDDs of 40GB capacity running at 7200 RPM.

Currently, the largest drive for desktop use has a capacity of 500GB or half a terabyte, and it is still in a 3.5" package and spins at 7200 RPM. The most common interfaces for HDDs are Parallel ATA with 80-conductor ribbon cables and the newer, more convenient Serial ATA. Although SATA offers higher maximum bandwidth capacity for faster data transfers, the practical reality is that no single ATA/IDE hard drive processes the data fast enough to make the interface a bottleneck.

HDD Options

Many different ways exist to handle data storage in a PC these days. To keep things manageable, we'll make the assumption that you want at least one hard drive to boot from, and to run your operating system and program. The best way to get a handle on hard drive options is to do a simple survey of suitable types and the key features of each (see Table 7-1).

Table 7-1   Hard Drive Families for Desktop PCs

Form Factor	Interface	Speed (RPM)	Capacity	Notes
3.5"	Parallel ATA	5400, 7200	40–500GB	Still widely used, cost effective, easy to use. Most models are much quieter than they used to be even a year ago.
	Serial ATA	7200, 10K		Higher bandwidth than PATA, but no real-world gain. Much easier to manage cabling.
	SCSI	7200, 10K, 15K	20–400GB	Still the fastest overall, due to an embedded processor that manages the data flow more efficiently. Expensive.
2.5"	Parallel ATA	4200, 5400, 7200	20–100GB	A different connector, but it's desktop compatible. Speed is very good with large cache in the 5.4K and 7.2K drives. Several dBA better than the best 3.5" drives, with much less vibration.
	Serial ATA	5400, 7200		Much like PATA, but much better cable management. Just starting to appear on the retail market.

The inclusion of 2.5" notebook drives may have you raising your eyebrows. You should be aware that Seagate, the 800-pound gorilla among HDD makers, introduced Savvio, the first 2.5" enterprise drive, in early 2004. This is a 10K RPM Serial Attached SCSI (SAS) interface drive designed to take on the fastest 3.5" enterprise drives in the world, including Seagate's own. The research firm Gartner predicted then that 2.5" enterprise-class drives would be the predominant HDD form factor in multi-user environments in 2007. Figure 7-1 shows clearly the size difference between the two form factors, a difference that's similarly reflected in the amount of heat they produce.

The shift from 3.5" to 2.5" form factor is occurring for much the same reasons 5.25" drives were displaced by 3.5" ones: the drive for higher data capacity in smaller, cooler, more power-efficient packages. At least three 2.5" drives will in fit the space of one 3.5" drive, and performance, thermals, and storage capacity will be better — so the argument goes. If these benefits of 2.5" drives are good enough for serious IT applications, there may be good reasons for us to consider them for HTPC as well. More on that later in the chapter.

FIGURE 7-1: The very quiet Samsung P120 SP2004C 200 GB 3.5" SATA drive dwarfs the Western Digital Scorpio WD800VE 80G 2.5" drive. Note the adapter for IDE cable and 4-pin power connector needed for the notebook drive to be used with a desktop motherboard.

HDD Performance

There's no question that a high-performance hard drive will make a system feel quicker and more responsive. The time that it takes for the PC to load the operating system or a program is most affected by hard drive speed. Hard drive access usually measures 4–15 milliseconds (thousandths of a second), whereas RAM speeds typically run 60–70 nanoseconds (billionths of a second). The mechanical limitations of the hard drive are clearly a major bottleneck compared to the other pure electronic devices such as the processor and RAM. The simple fact is that when the HDD is being accessed, the rest of the system is simply waiting.

The performance of hard drives is not at all a simple matter to determine. Much depends on the type of work being done, and there are innumerable testing methods, along with a host of technical specifications that can be measured. As with every other component in a PC, the performance of hard drives is examined and dissected with gusto by numerous hardware review Web sites. Many words are produced in long and detailed discussions on the significance of these various technical parameters and the merits they bestow on the drives. But in comparative assessments of several hard drives, you'll find that many specifications vary less than 10 percent between the best and the worst. Unless you are much more perceptive than us, you won't be able to notice this difference even if it can be isolated for an A/B comparison, and certainly it will be "lost" in the mix of other components that determine the overall PC experience.

So what level of performance is needed from a hard drive in an HTPC, specifically? The general answer is that it merely needs to be adequate. That is, almost any modern drive will do. The most common application for an HTPC is playback of music and video. The performance requirement of an HDD for this task is extremely low. Much more is demanded of the sound and video cards than of the hard drive. The same can be said about recording or copying music and video files as well. The only HTPC-specific activity that would benefit significantly from better than pedestrian performance is media editing with repeated saves of large files or snippets. But even here, it is RAM and the CPU that do much of the high-stress work. We've already covered the reasons for going with gobs of RAM. So in a nutshell, almost any hard drive will perform fine for HTPC.

Having said that, we suggest getting a drive that's been on the market for a relatively short time, say one year or less. This is because hard drive technology moves quickly enough that an older drive will always be outperformed by a newer one. This difference is bigger than the differences between current drives of similar price and format.

The main benefit of a really high-performance drive (think: expensive, large-capacity SCSI drive with SCSI interface card) for an HTPC is quickness — how quickly the system boots up, how quickly programs and files load up. Compared to a normal drive, it's kind of like a Porsche compared to a Honda. The Porsche is quicker to get up to speed and navigate through traffic to get on the freeway, but once you are there, you're just cruising at the speed limit like you would be with the Honda.

SATA versus PATA

This is a common choice hard drive buyers are faced with: the Serial ATA interface or the Parallel ATA. There is no perceivable performance or reliability advantage in the SATA, despite the fact that it has higher maximum data handling capacity. We're far from saturating the PATA bus with a single hard drive. SATA is the logical choice for future upgradeability and for improved cable management. The SATA data cable is much thinner than the ribbon cable needed for PATA, which can hinder airflow in a case if not managed well (see Figure 7-2).

FIGURE 7-2: Much smaller cables represent a big benefit of SATA drives over the large IDE cables for Parallel ATA.

On the other hand, there are two gotchas with SATA:

- Some cables don't fit well and can be easily knocked off. SATA2 connectors are better. Certainly you should replace cables that don't feel secure.

- If your motherboard does not have a "native" SATA controller that is recognized by Windows (or the OS of your choice), you will need to load the driver provided by the HDD maker, often with a floppy drive, in a somewhat convoluted procedure that really should have been left back in the DOS and 640K RAM age. Examine the motherboard documentation in detail to avoid this potential headache.

Thermal Issues

Elsewhere in this book, the virtues of high energy efficiency and low thermal output have been emphasized repeatedly. It's no different with hard drives.

The average power draw of typical IDE hard drives in 3.5" and 2.5" form factor are shown in Table 7-2.

Table 7-2   Comparing 3.5" and 2.5" HDD Power

HDD	Activity	Power
3.5", 80GB, 7200 RPM, 8MB cache	idle	7–9 W
	start	14–20 W
	seek/write	12–15 W
2.5", 80GB, 5400 RPM, 8MB cache	idle	<1 W
	start	2.5 W
	seek/write	2.5 W

It's abundantly clear that the amount of heat generated by a notebook drive is many times lower than that of a 3.5" drive. A SCSI drive tends to draw the most power, by a small margin. The actual amount of heat may seem small when compared to the CPU or video card, but it all adds up in the case and has an impact on overall temperatures and required forced airflow — that is, fans and their noise.

The maximum operating temperature for 3.5" drives cited by most manufacturers is 55–60 degrees C, but for thermal insurance, it's best to shoot for under 50 degrees C at maximum load, and 40 degrees C or lower at idle. In general, without some exposure to airflow or tight mounting to the chassis for heat conduction, most 3.5" drives will overheat.

Acoustics and Vibration

Acoustically speaking, the tight mechanical coupling of the hard drive and chassis necessary for adequate HDD cooling is the source of a lot of problems. Drive manufacturers have known for some time that vibrations are a primary source of noise for an HDD in actual use.

Seagate's excellent Technology Paper entitled *Disk Drive Acoustics* (www.seagate.com/support/kb/disc/tp/acoustics.html) is well worth quoting:

"The acoustic noise of a disc drive mounted in a chassis comes from two sources. The first source, airborne acoustics, is what all drive manufacturers currently specify as the sound power value. It is the sound that comes from the drive through the air to the observer. This value is measured with the drive suspended in space by wires. The second noise source is generated from the drive's vibration during idle and seek. This vibration energy is transmitted directly to the PC chassis structure and causes the chassis to act as a speaker. This form of noise is structure-borne acoustics.

"When drives are mounted in a chassis (frame for a PC or other product) and enclosed in a box (plastic body of PC or other product), the vibrations that cause acoustic noise can be attenuated (reduced, muffled) or amplified. For example, the plastic enclosure tends to attenuate noise emanating from the box because it muffles airborne acoustics.

"The chassis, on the other hand, may pick up, redirect, or even amplify the vibrations caused by the drive, which may result in more structure-borne noise emanating from the box, or through a specific portion of the box. Seagate has considered the total effect of drives on a PC system and can show that structure-borne noise is the dominating source of disc drive-induced PC acoustics. In fact, testing has shown that changes in stand-alone drive acoustics had little effect on the overall system acoustics when drives were hard mounted in the chassis."

Structure-borne acoustics is the cause of the often-loud humming noise that emanates from most computers. A spectrum analysis will show that a predominant portion of this noise is centered on the spin frequency of the HDD in the PC. For a 7200 RPM drive, this is 120 Hz (7200 times per minute = 120 times per second, which cycles per second or Hertz). For a 5400 RPM drive, the main low-frequency noise is centered at 108 Hz. There will also be harmonics (multiples) of this frequency that appear at higher frequencies. A well-damped, inert case will have fewer harmonics whereas a less sturdy, more resonant case will have more harmonics.

For a low-noise computer, a quiet drive should be chosen but not hard mounted to the chassis. Effective hard drive decouple mounting requires very soft mounting. Elastic suspension, such as that pioneered in the NoVibesIII accessory from Germany (see Figure 7-3), eliminates not only the audible hum at idle, but also most of the chatter of seek and write noise. The end result is an eerie silence (assuming the rest of the PC is quiet) that you will soon find yourself luxuriating in.

Most rubber grommet + screw mounting options supplied in HTPC cases are not effective at eliminating the noise from hard drive vibrations. A shortcoming of 3.5" HDD silencing accessories is that they invariably adopt the optical drive form factor to accommodate the mechanical additions required. The main problem is cooling. Most cases have very poor airflow around the optical drive bays, and a standard 3.5" hard drive soft mounted there will usually run quite hot. Too hot, in our opinion.

FIGURE 7-3: The NoVibesIII floats a Hitachi 7K400 HDD in an elastic suspension made from high-strength industrial rubber O-rings, rigged up in a special tray designed to fit into an optical drive bay.

Given these facts, you can make several choices in order to avoid the woeful reality of an HTPC humming loudly amongst your audio/video gear:

- Choose a quiet, low-vibration hard drive. There's no substitute to starting with less noise; then it's so much easier to suppress what little noise is there. At present, there is only one source of reliable, thorough acoustics-focused reviews of hard drives: www. silentpcreview.com.

- Use something like the NoVibesIII HDD vibration reduction device, and custom-mount it in a position where there is some airflow, ideally near an intake vent or in the path of an intake fan's airflow. (Velcro is a good way to affix the device.) It takes only a very small amount of airflow to keep a hard drive cool.

- You can also invent your own DIY HDD suspension or try one of the many methods, discussed at Silent PC Review, both on the main Web site as well as in its forums: www. silentpcreview.com/section14.html and http://forums.silentpc review.com/viewtopic.php?t=8240.

- Use a quiet 2.5" notebook hard drive and a rig up an HDD suspension or decoupled mounting in a 3.5" drive bay. There is enough space.

- Don't install any hard drive in the HTPC case. Instead, use an External SATA interface to locate your hard drive up to two meters away in a noise-insulated closet or drawer. More on this radical option later in the chapter.

Tip

One recent development among notebook drives is the introduction of SATA. They've been around since some time in 2004, but not been released to the retail market because the laptop makers have been slow to adopt them. Fujitsu appears to be the first one out of the gate with a SATA notebook drive for the general market (see Figure 7-4). The big advantage for desktop use is that the connections and cabling are identical to desktop SATA, which obviates the adapters needed for conventional notebook connections.

FIGURE 7-4: The Fujitsu MHT2080BH 2.5" 80G notebook drive sports SATA interface, making adapters and bulky ribbon cables like those on the WD Scorpio drive unnecessary. The Fujitsu MAV2073RC on the right is an enterprise class 10K RPM Serial Attached SCSI drive designed for industrial storage and servers.

Notes on 2.5" Drives

Specifications of 2.5" drives don't usually match 3.5" drives in most ways. But anecdotal evidence suggests there is little or no perceived slide in performance for most users of 2.5" drives in desktop systems. Still, to obtain the best from a 2.5" drive, consider these suggestions:

- Opt for a 5400 RPM drive with at least 8MB of cache RAM. The additional cache helps performance. 4200 RPM drives are noticeably slower, and the louder noise of 7200 RPM drives tends to eliminate the acoustic advantages of a notebook drive. Quieter 7200 RPM notebook drives may be coming, however.

- The quietest drive will be a single platter (or disc) drive. These are now at 40G capacity, which may seem low, but remember, you can easily store data on an external high-capacity drive.

- SATA connections are much easier to deal with, so if the acoustics and performance are similar, then opt for the SATA drive.

- There are virtually no thorough reliable sources of notebook HDD noise performance. The exception is www.silentpcreview.com and its storage section, which has a growing number of notebook HDD reviews.

External Drive Options

External storage boxes are so common these days that they hardly need any introduction. They can be found in almost any computer shop, whether brick and mortar or online. There are two basic types: enclosure only and complete with hard drive. The first type has all the connectivity and its own power supply, ready for your choice of drive. Usually, these enclosure-only storage boxes accept only standard IDE/ATA drives. It's simple to install the drive, and this can be a good way to use older or noisier drives that you don't mind running some of the time. The second type is an integrated package complete with the hard drive. All you have to do is power it up and plug it in for Windows to recognize it.

USB 2.0 and IEEE 1394

The typical external HDD consists of an ATA (usually Parallel ATA) hard drive installed in a metal/plastic box slightly larger than the drive itself, powered by a small wall-wart type DC power supply and connected to the PC by USB 2.0 or IEEE 1394 (FireWire) connections. Often, both connections are provided. A bridge chip in the external box translates from the ATA protocol to USB/1394 protocol used for the connection.

In theory, both USB 2.0 and 1394 protocols are very fast. But in practice, the 480 Mbps maximum speed of USB 2.0 is shared among all the USB devices on a hub and subject to numerous overhead issues that makes it only almost as fast as 1394 (450 Mbps) under ideal conditions. Neither achieves much better than 30MB/sec transfer rate under ideal conditions, which is certainly much poorer than PATA drives connected directly to the motherboard. However, both are plenty fast enough for playing back movies and music, although video editing would be a stretch.

One obvious way to minimize the amount of HDD noise and heat in the HTPC is to use an external large-capacity drive for media storage, using USB or 1394 connectivity. This strategy allows the external drive to be located up to 4.5 meters away with standard 28-gauge conductor cables. It allows a small inexpensive notebook drive to be located inside the PC for the operating system and programs, and the most cost-effective large storage HDD to be located far away in a closet or drawer where its noise and heat become non-issues.

Network Attached Storage

The term network attached storage (NAS) refers to any device that is attached to a network and dedicated to nothing but storage. In commercial networks, this is often a relatively low-power PC with many hard drives. Recently, NAS devices have come into the personal arena, with the simplest devices being a single drive in an external box much like USB and 1394 boxes. In fact some of these small NAS devices offer USB or 1394 as well as network connection via 100 Mbps Ethernet.

Small devices containing multiple drives for storage capacity approaching a terabyte or more are also becoming available. These are not much bigger that the 2 to 4 drives they hold and are equipped with their own power supply (see Figure 7-5).

FIGURE 7-5: One of many similar 4-HDD network attached storage servers for small office, home office, or home users is ideal for centralized music and video storage in a home.

Here, access and transfer speeds are essentially limited by the network, but again, it is plenty fast enough for serving up movies and music. The huge advantage is the ability to access the media storage from multiple computers in the house, although not always simultaneously. As with the USB/1394 devices, remote location to keep the extra heat, vibration, and noise of additional drives out of the HTPC is a big plus.

Tip

Look for clever combinations of hard drive storage, combined with a network router, and even a USB hub that are beginning to make their way onto the market. They can help reduce the clutter of gear around the HTPC by consolidating several necessary ancillaries into one box.

External SATA

This concept was first explored by do-it-yourself enthusiasts who took long SATA and power extension cables to locate standard SATA drives outside the PC. Recently, the SATA International Organization established new protocols for an official eSATA specification (www.sata-io.org/esata.asp). Seagate teamed with NetCell in the spring of 2005 to demonstrate an external Serial ATA (eSATA) storage solution, as shown in Figures 7-6 and 7-7. The eSATA specs include more robust connectors, a back panel interface for PCs, and up to 2-meter standard gauge cables.

Benefits for eSATA include:

- Up to three times the bandwidth of USB and FireWire. Essentially no different from internal SATA.

- Interface transfer rate of 150 Mbps to increase system performance, with eSATA solutions providing 1.5Gbps or 3Gbps interface speeds.

- Cost-effective and higher performance alternative to tape backup.

- Can be deployed in RAID configurations to deliver high levels of performance and data protection.

- The biggest benefit of all: You can boot from an eSATA drive. What this means is that you could leave the HTPC completely free of any HDDs to add either noise or heat, locate an eSATA drive up to two meters away in a sound isolated position, and use that drive as your primary OS and programs drive. The rest of your data could be stored on NAS or other external drives or drive arrays. The only noise sources in the system would then be fans(in the power supply, on the CPU heat sink, and for case exhaust. If you plan wisely, these fans could all be running at very low speed, producing very little noise.

Adding eSATA is as simple as installing an eSATA host bus controller for desktop systems, to which a number of eSATA drives can be connected. Motherboard makers are talking of integrating eSATA as another one of the many built-in connectivity devices.

At the time of writing, there does not appear to be any eSATA drives available for retail purchase. Market supply can change very quickly, however; we see no reason why eSATA products would not be in the marketplace by the fall or winter.

FIGURE 7-6: Two external SATA storage devices shown by Seagate and NetCell at the Spring Intel Developers Forum, 2005.

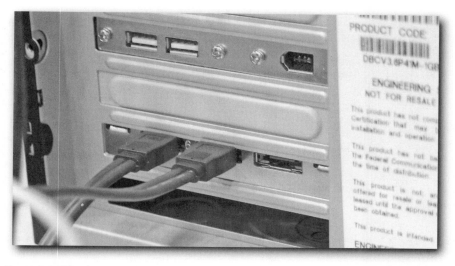

FIGURE 7-7: The demonstrated eSATA PCI card could handle up to three eSATA storage connections.

Table 7-3 lists major HDD makers.

Table 7-3	HDD Makers	
Name	**URL**	
Fujitsu	www.fujitsu.com	
Hitachi	www.hitachigst.com	
Maxtor	www.maxtor.com	
Samsung	www.samsung.com	
Seagate	www.seagate.com	
Toshiba	www.toshiba.com	
Western Digital	www.wdc.com	

Wrapping Up

Many more storage options are available now compared to even the recent past. Quiet SATA drives in 3.5" and 2.5" form factors are both viable options for the primary drive, and external storage options with USB and 1394 abound. NAS makes offloading the storage tasks out of the computer to a remote location very viable. External SATA will make a PC without any local hard drive possible, for absolutely no HDD contribution to noise, heat, and vibration. All of these options require thinking through your own situation, likely use patterns, and budget.

Optical Storage and HTPCs

The optical drive has become a basic ingredient in personal computers. Without at least a CD-ROM drive, it's almost impossible to install basic items like the operating software and any programs you want to use. The vast majority of computers come not just with a CD-ROM drive, but a CD-RW (read and write) drive, often one that can also access DVDs. For the more advanced users reading this book, DVD/CD-RW devices are not unfamiliar, either.

In an HTPC, a DVD drive of some kind is an absolute necessity. You must be able to play DVD movies at the very least. You may also want to make DVD copies of home movies, programs recorded from TV, or backups of material that is already on DVD. Use in an HTPC also requires some attention to optical drive noise (where we seek to recommend the quietest possible drives in keeping with our design philosophy). Although there is often little to differentiate DVD burners from one another on the basis of features and functions, attention to size (slimline designs are essential or desirable in smaller cases) and noise output can have a big impact when selecting an HTPC optical drive.

Bundling issues can also sometimes come into play: many of the more expensive DVD burners include DVD recording and editing software, whereas some of the cheapest such offerings omit everything except basic software — including the decoder software so necessary to enable DVD players to play back DVD video inside the Windows MCE 2005 environment.

This chapter walks you through the various and sundry functions of CD and DVD optical drives, the media choices, and some of the software that's available for use with optical drives. It also explores what kinds of items are bundled with various drives, to help you understand related value adds.

Optical Storage Basics

Because the optical drive has been a part of the PC for nearly two decades, there's much about this technology that you already know. A quick review of basics is worthwhile because despite their similarities, the functionalities and capabilities of CDs and DVDs in read-only, writable, and re-writable forms have significant differences and compatibility issues.

Compact Disc

Compact Disc was originally invented by Philips and Sony primarily as a music storage medium. Several essential characteristics that led to wide adoption over the vinyl LP record and cassette tape include instant random access to any track, absence of background noise, convenience, and portability. It quickly gained favor as a fast and convenient storage medium for all kinds of digital data and was broadly adapted by the PC industry in the late 1980s.

The first CD drives were read-only memory (ROM), which allowed you to access CDs with music or data but not record anything on them. CD-R (recordable) and CD-RW (re-writable) devices soon followed. These drives allow you to record to blank CD discs, including reusable blanks that can be treated like tape or a hard drive, removing old data and storing new.

Basic CD technology is well known. A digital stream of data is converted into a long spiraling line of microscopic physical pits on a clear polycarbonate plastic disc with a thin reflective layer of aluminum. A thin acrylic layer protects the aluminum. These pits are one of two sizes, to represent the zeros and ones in a digital data stream. To convert a sequence of pits on the CD back into digital form, the disc is spun while a laser beam on a tracking mechanism reads them in linear order. To maintain a constant linear velocity, the speed of rotation varies from 200 RPM when the laser is on the outside edge of the disc, to 500 RPM on the inner edge. When you consider that the spiral is just half a micron wide and that lines are separated by just 1.6 microns, it's a minor miracle that CD technology works at all, especially given the casual abuse they receive from most users, and at the very high speeds at which the latest drives access the media — 52 times the original CD speed. Note that there is space dedicated on every CD to encode error-correcting codes, including on the CDs you burn.

In general, we buy only two types of data-encoded CDs: Audio CD and CD-ROM ISO. The former contains music, and the latter software or data. However, there are numerous subcategories, especially for discs burned with a CD-RW, including Mixed-Mode CD (audio and data), CD Extra, Video CD, Super Video CD, mini-DVD, Bootable CD-ROM, CD-ROM UDF, CD-ROM Hybrid, and CD-ROM UDF/ISO. The original CD spec allowed up to 74 minutes of dual-channel audio at 16 bit/44 KHz sampling or 783 megabytes.

A CD-R recordable blank is quite different from a manufactured audio or data disc that you buy. There's the same plastic substrate and aluminum layer, but between them is a layer of dye. When you write to a CD, the writing laser heats the dye to make microscopic portions non-reflective. The end result is functionally the same as burning pits. Just remember that the dye is light sensitive, so avoid exposing CD-R discs to bright light.

CD-RW works by changing the laser exposed area from crystalline to amorphous form. A CD-RW disc is much less reflective than CD and CD-R, and not all optical drives can read this medium well. But CD-RW discs can be rerecorded 1,000 times or more, assuming they don't get too scratched up. Commonly available CD-R/RW discs can hold 650MB or 700MB of data, or 74 or 80 minutes of music.

DVD

DVD is an acronym that stands for nothing. The DVD forum started out calling it Digital Video Disc. Some members lobbied for Digital Versatile Disc. In the end, they agreed that the official term is just three letters. A DVD looks almost identical to a CD and works similarly but has some key differences, the single most significant one is its capacity to store more than 4GB of data. That's seven times more than a CD can store. It's this capacity that allows high-resolution 720p movies of up to 133 minutes long with 5.1 channel Dolby surround sound soundtracks in up to eight languages and subtitles in up to 32 languages to be encoded on a standard DVD disc.

CD drives cannot read DVDs, although DVD drives can read CDs. This relates to the way that data is encoded on the disc. Smaller sizes for pits/bumps and tracks delivers most of a DVD's increased capacity, where the rest comes from improved efficiency in error correction, which requires less data overhead. An ability to encode two layers of data on one side naturally doubles capacity, and using both sides of a disc quadruples it.

As Table 8-1 shows, the smaller size of the data track is one of the big differences between DVD and CD drives. A DVD laser uses a wavelength of 640 nm, compared to the 780 nm for a CD laser. This explains why a CD drive cannot read a DVD; its laser beam is too big.

Table 8-1   DVD and CD Compared

Parameter	DVD	CD
Storage capacity	4.38GB on standard single side, one layer 7.95GB on single side, double layer 8.75GB on double side, single layer 15.9GB on double side, double layer	650 or 700MB
Track details	Pitch: 1600 nanometers Minimum pit length: 830 nm Minimum pit length: 400 nm	Pitch: 740 nanometers

Movies in DVD are formatted for either the NTSC or the PAL systems, using MPEG-2 40:1 compression. Depending on the track format, a DVD can hold movies up to about 2 hours long (single side/single layer), 4 hours (single side, double layer), 4.5 hours (double side, single layer), or over 8 hours (double side, double layer). Given the running time for most Hollywood movies and the amount of extra features included, two layers are the norm for most commercial video DVDs. Normal resolution for a DVD movie is 480 horizontal lines, progressively scanned.

 Cross-Reference Differences between NTSC and PAL are briefly explained in Chapter 9; for additional information on these differences please consult the informative article entitled "NTSC vs PAL" at Microcinema International (www.microcinema.com/index/ntsc).

The preceding discussion refers specifically to DVD-Video, but there are several other DVD formats:

- **DVD-ROM** uses the same technology but with computer file formats for data storage.

- **DVD-RAM** has 4.7GB per side and can be re-written more than 100,000 times so is treated almost like a hard drive. However, this format is almost out of the picture on consumer desktop PCs. It's dominant in U.S. consumer electronics devices, owing mainly to the efforts of Panasonic, but most DVD-RAM recorders also support DVD-RW.

- **DVD-R** and **DVD-RW** is similar to DVD-RAM, but uses sequential read-write access more like a vinyl record. It can be re-written up to 1,000 times. It's one of two competing formats. Discs burned in DVD-R or DVD-RW formats can be viewed on most DVD-ROM players.

- **DVD+R** and **DVD+RW** is the other competing format. (More on this format race later.) Discs burned in DVD+R or DVD+RW formats can be viewed on most DVD-ROM players.

- Finally, there is **CD Audio**, which is different enough to warrant a separate discussion of its own (more on that later).

DVD-Audio and Super Audio CD

DVD-Audio Disc has been discussed for years, but it is since 2003 that either music or drives that support it have become available. DVD-Audio (DVD-A) lets recording producers choose from various sampling rates and word sizes: 44.1, 48, 88.2, 96, 176.4, or 192 KHz, with 16-, 20- or 24-bit words. With Meridian Lossless Packing (MLP), a lossless compression algorithm that does not discard data, this results in an upper frequency limit of 48 KHz, and a dynamic range of 144 dB for recordings made using maximum 192 KHz/24-bit resolution.

This compares favorably to CD Audio, which operates at 44.1 KHz sampling and 16 bits. The end result is much higher resolution potential, with greatly improved accuracy in waveform playback. The maximum theoretical number of output level gradations on a CD is 65,536; that number skyrockets to 16,777,216 using the highest-resolution DVD-A format. Of course, you will need a sound card capable of handling 192 KHz/24-bit D/A conversion to access DVD-A. Most (if not all) DVD-A discs have a standard DVD audio track in Dolby 5.1 for playback on standard DVD hardware/software. Standard audio on DVD is capable of being encoded at 96 KHz/24-bit in Dolby 5.1.

In reality, weaknesses elsewhere in the recording and reproduction chain (such as lower-resolution original masters) may obscure DVD-A advantages, but if you're looking for the best sound quality, this is probably the future. DVD-Audio is encrypted with CPPM (Content Protection for Prerecorded Media), an advanced and aggressive copy-protection scheme. DVD-Audio playback software for PC has only just begun to appear. These include software that comes with Creative's SoundBlaster Audigy 2 and WinDVD's DVD-Audio add-on. However, these tools do not allow copying of DVD-A in digital format. The record companies appear even more paranoid about digital piracy of DVD-A than other formats.

Cross-Reference As noted in Chapter 10, you can't even use SPDIF outputs to pump DVD-A audio from a PC into an optical or wired link to a home entertainment center. For the time being, the only way to listen to DVD-A audio is to buy equipment that can decode it in a home entertainment center environment, or to attach speakers to a PC that's equipped to decode this high-end audio format. We're hopeful that this missing connection will find its way into the next release of Windows Media Center Edition, however.

The audio standards are similar to Super Audio CD (SACD), introduced by Sony and Philips as an answer for those who lament low CD audio resolution, some 20 years after the original. SACD utilizes technology similar to DVD, including dual layers, six discrete channels, 24-bit word length, and up to an amazing 2.8 MHz sampling rate. It does sound better than CD on an appropriately high-resolution playback system. Again, this assumes an original recording that employs high-resolution data capture is available for remastering, which is often not the case.

Support for SACD is fairly strong. There appear to be at least a couple thousand such titles available for purchase. Unfortunately, because SACD uses a digital processing scheme called Direct Stream Digital instead of the PCM technology used for ordinary CDs, SACD doesn't work on ordinary CD players or drives. It certainly cannot be saved in digital format. That explains why almost all SACD discs are hybrids that contain two layers: one for native SACD data, the other normal two-channel CD audio tracks.

DVD Format Race

On the PC DVD scene, DVD-RW and DVD+RW are competing non-compatible formats, much like Beta and VHS. (However, unlike Beta and VHS, the two recording formats do hew to the same physical form factor, and are the same size.) DVD-RW was developed and is backed by Pioneer, whereas DVD+RW has Philips behind it. There is really little point in getting into all the details of the differences between the two, because for the most part they are functionally insignificant. The bottom line is that the optical drive makers have succeeded in making drives that operate in either mode for single-layer recording. As this chapter is being written, however, only DVD+RW format offers dual-layer recording. Give DVD-RW a bit more time, and surely drive makers, too, will follow suit, along with drives that record dual layers in both formats.

The total available storage space on a recordable DVD is the same as on a manufactured DVD. The basic writing technology for DVD is the same as for CD. The primary differences relate to the wavelength of the laser beam used, which is narrower than CD.

Dual-layer burning is also more complex and requires a dual-layer blank with two thermally sensitive dye layers, each with its own semi-reflective metallic layer. The two layers do not have the same reflectivity, because the laser must be able to read through the first layer to access the second. A single-layer DVD has a wobbled pre-groove in the polycarbonate base to control rotational speed and provide addressing information. A dual-layer recordable DVD has a wobbled pre-groove for each layer. The laser optics try to focus on one of the two layers and to detect an Address in Pre-groove (ADIP). Once the DVD burner determines the media type, the laser can focus up and down between the two recordable layers. This is the same way the disc is read. The two layers have a contiguous address stream for recording. Recording is started on the first layer outward from the inside hub area. Once that layer is filled, the laser continues from the outside edge going inward, ensuring no pause for continuous recording or access.

Optical Drive Types

You have basically four different types of optical drives to choose from: CD-ROM drives, CD-RW drives, DVD-ROM drives, and DVD recordable drives. To get right to the point, there's really only one choice for an HTPC, and that's a DVD recordable drive with CD-RW compatibility. This device lets you play and record CD-R, CD-RW, DVD+R, DVD+RW, DVD-R, and DVD-RW. The most advanced of these drives can also record dual-layer DVD+R. Prices are so incredibly modest given the truly amazing capabilities of these multi-function optical drives that there's no good reason not to buy one. The reasons for owning a recorder with portable media haven't really changed since the days of the audiocassette. The uses are limited only by your imagination. But that explains why we focus exclusively on this single type of drive in this book.

A BenQ DW1640 DVD, shown in Figure 8-1 with all capabilities mentioned previously and up to 16X DVD burn speed complete with Nero CD/DVD burning software, is currently available for as little as $50 from a reputable online shop. BenQ is a retail brand created a year or two ago by Taiwanese PC component giant Acer, and offers surprisingly quiet, efficient operation at a pretty low price.

A similarly featured PX-716A/SW from Plextor, traditionally the most respected brand in the optical drive market, costs around $100. Unlike the BenQ drive, which users an E-IDE/ATAPI interface, the S in the Plextor 716's product name indicates it supports a Serial ATA (SATA) interface. SATA drives use narrower cables that promote better airflow in HTPC cases (this effect is easy to mitigate for IDE-based optical drives, however, simply by purchasing a round IDE cable to replace the flat ribbon cables included with most drives and motherboards).

Another good DVD burner for HTPC use is the NEC ND-3520A DVD-R±W IDE. It's available for as little as $40 from Newegg, and from many other reputable vendors for between $40 and $50. Some HTPC aficionados rate this drive as the quietest around, though we were able to detect little or no difference among the various models mentioned here during DVD or CD playback.

Tip   All DVD burners are pretty noisy when burning DVDs or CDs. That's why we recommend that you avoid burning any kind of optical media while you're trying to watch a movie or listen to music. Better to expect to make noise and plan accordingly, than to be bothered by inevitable noise involved in the media burning process!

On the low end, the Sony DW-D26A, NEC ND3540A, Asus DRW-1608P, and Toshiba SD-R5372 all feature similar capabilities for $40–45. We'd recommend any of these drives for HTPC use, with an emphasis on the BenQ, Plextor, and NEC models mentioned in this section of the chapter and elsewhere in this book (particularly in the HTPC build chapters, which are Chapters 18 through 20).

FIGURE 8-1: The BenQ DW1640 DVD offers maximum optical disc record and read compatibility and can be found online for as little as $60.

The only reason you may want any other optical drive is that some DVD drives have trouble reading some CD-RW discs. If you think you'll be wanting to use CD-RW often, go ahead and get a CD-RW drive. Models 52X write, 32X rewrite, and 52X read speed CD-RW drives from AOpen start as low as $23. It's not exactly a purchase you'll have to consult your spouse about.

Optical Drive Software

The amount of software designed for use with optical drives is simply staggering. Although you do indeed get some software that can burn DVDs with Windows MCE 2005, it's not really suitable for general-purpose use with movies and music. That's because this software — known as Movie Maker 2 with DVD Burning — can only create DVDs that use a proprietary Microsoft format that's not suitable for playback on standalone DVD players. Options for burning CDs are likewise limited in Windows MCE 2005, which makes some kind of general-purpose recording and archiving tools for movies and music a must. As a rule, commercial Media Center PCs include such software as part and parcel of their built-in capabilities: you can purchase similar software for your home-made Media Center PC at relatively low cost.

Here is a very short list of items we have used and feel confident to describe:

- **Nero,** the current version of which is called Nero 6 Ultra Edition, has evolved into arguably the best suite of optical disc burning tools available for Windows. We've personally been Windows and Nero users for years and have trouble finding reasons other than sheer curiosity to try other offerings. This Ahead Software product includes tools for both DVD and CD burners, supports just about every disc format available, and is probably bundled with more optical burners than any other software. Expect to pay about $90 for this software should you decide to buy a full retail edition.

Tip When searching for CD/DVD burning software packages, don't forget to look for deals on OEM versions. As long as you use a drive from a supported manufacturer, this software should work with your drive. Prices can be as low as 10 to 20 percent of retail for such offerings. Better yet, be sure to look for one of these packages in the bundle that accompanies your DVD player, and pay even less!

- **Easy Media Creator** is Nero's closest competitor, and it, too, is highly regarded. Like Nero, it features many tools for optical burning, plus others such as creating movies and photo slide shows and so on. As with Nero, there are both simple and more advanced tools so that both amateurs and pros can be well served. The latest version is Easy Media Creator 7.5. Expect to pay around $70 for a full retail edition.

- **AnyDVD** is a useful tool for removing encryption, copy protection, region codes, and other potential impedimenta to recording from DVDs. It can decrypt on the fly without saving data to a hard drive. It supposedly works on any DVD and any DVD drive. It is not a simple tool, nor is it totally bug free, but may be worth a look if you're interested in burning or copying DVDs. Expect to pay $26 for a full retail edition.

- **1Click DVD Copy** lets you easily copy DVD movies. It supports dual-layer media, and uses LG1X encoding technology for perfect video quality. It supports both NTSC and PAL DVD formats. It's more expensive than AnyDVD but also friendlier and easier to use; expect to pay $59 for a full retail edition.

- **PowerDVD** and **WinDVD** are the main movie playback programs for Windows. They appear to be equal in their functionality, although some users claim lower CPU load with one and better compatibility with certain DVD drives. Most DVD drives come bundled with one or the other of this software. For full retail editions, expect to pay $40 for PowerDVD from CyberLink, and $50 for WinDVD from InterVideo.

Tip Both InterVideo and CyberLink offer enhanced products (such as CyberLink's PowerCinema 4 or InterVideo's Home Theater 2) that can also provide time-shifted recording capabilities, improved TV handling capability, and enhanced DVD playback as well. These are not always entirely compatible with Windows MCE 2005, but work outside that environment just fine.

Ideal HTPC Optical Drive Qualities

In keeping with our general design philosophy for HTPCs and in selecting drives for HTPC use, several characteristics loom large when considering an optical drive for inclusion in a build.

Though we don't know of any single optical drive that leads the pack across all these characteristics, the following qualities are worth considering as you ponder your own optical drive options:

- **Low noise** is a nice feature to look for, but it's difficult to find in any drive once drive speed exceeds about 16X. This is because the main item that's spinning, the polycarbonate plastic disc, is not necessarily balanced. It's not like the platter in a hard drive or a platter in a high-end analog turntable, which must be balanced to very tight tolerances for them to work well. The natural imbalance works against good acoustics when the optical disc is spun fast. At 52X read or write speed, you simply cannot get away from the high wind-turbulence noise or the high-pitch whining noise.

  Having said all that, some drives still do manage to sound better, if not always clearly quieter, than others. The draw mechanism, the bearing noise, in short, all the mechanical functions, are better damped and more silky smooth on some drives than on others. Recent BenQ and AOpen drives have these qualities, as do the Asus QuietTrack, Samsung, and LG drives. There may be more brands that offer quiet performance, but we don't have hands-on experience to say for sure.

  Even with one of these quieter optical drives, the best way to ensure that the noise is kept low is to limit the read speed with software. The Nero burning software that comes with virtually all optical burners these days has a tool called DriveSpeed that allows you to limit read speed with a software switch. Find your level of acoustic comfort, and use the tool.

- **Serial ATA** is not that common on optical drives yet, but it's coming, and it is preferred. The primary advantage is not increased bandwidth. ATA/IDE has no problem handling the data stream from any optical drive. The main advantage is its narrow cable, so easy to route and manage inside an HTPC case as compared to the wide bulky ribbon cables used with most IDE optical drives. Look at the photo of the back of a standard optical drive in Figure 8-2. A SATA connection makes a tidy case interior much easier to achieve. The gain is not just visual. Low airflow impedance is a key part of cooling a PC effectively and quietly, and thinner cables help in a big way, especially in a slim, low-slung case where everything is a tight fit.

- **Depth** varies with optical drives, sometimes by as much as 2 cm. This may not seem like much, but in a small case, any size reduction can be beneficial. Newer drives are often shorter than older ones (as shown in Figure 8-3). Just look at the dimensions as a final check if you need to choose between two very close drives.

- **Height** is the same for most optical drives, and is designed to fit standard 5.25" drive bays (which are 1.75" tall). But some optical drives — particularly those designed for laptops — advertise themselves as "slimline drives." These offerings are more expensive (anywhere from $110 to $175 is typical) but they can be essential when looking for optical drives to use in smaller HTPC cases. Vendors like IBM, Panasonic, and Toshiba all offer good products of this type for HTPC use. Slimline drives tend to lag behind full-height optical drives in terms of drive speeds, which actually makes for quieter operation.

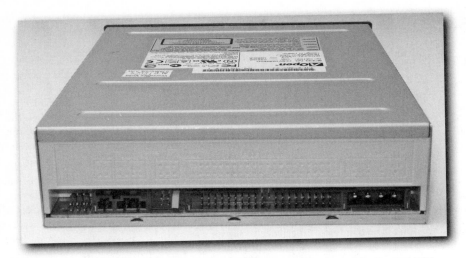

FIGURE 8-2: The back end of the traditional optical drive is dominated by the IDE/ATA connector. A Serial ATA connection reduces this by half.

FIGURE 8-3: A recent BenQ/AOpen DW1620 DVD writer on the right is a bit shorter than an older Toshiba DVD-ROM drive on the left.

What About Performance?

This may seem like heresy to some readers, but we don't think optical drive performance matters very much. Invariably, high performance in computing is related to speed: The machine that does things faster with fewer errors is considered better. But what if the differences are 10 minutes to burn two hours of movie instead of 12 minutes? Does that two minutes really matter to you? You're not going to sit there waiting for it to finish; you will be doing something else anyway.

To us, the more interesting characteristics for HTPC optical drives include dependability and good media latitude. Does the drive always make a clean, low-error copy? Does it accept a variety of different blanks without complaint? (A rule of thumb: To make the best low-error copy on most blank media on most optical burners, turn burn speed down.)

This kind of information is best found on Web sites that specialize in optical storage reviews. Optical drive models come and go so quickly that it's difficult to keep up to date in any other kind of publication. Some of these Web sites are listed in Table 8-2, along with a couple of other relevant sites.

Table 8-2   Optical Drive Information Web Sites

Web Site	URL/Remarks
Burning Bits	www.burningbits.com
CD Freaks	www.cdfreaks.com; established in 1997; very authoritative
CDR Labs	www.cdrlabs.com; established in 2000
cd-rw.org	www.cd-rw.org
CD Media World	www.cdmediaworld.com; established in 1998
CDR Info	www.cdrinfo.com
DVD Forum	www.dvdforum.org; the main industry group that promotes and develops DVD technology.
Extreme Tech	www.extremetech.com; look for articles on DVD burners

Finally, Table 8-3 lists some of the better known optical drive brands and their Web sites.

Table 8-3   Selected Optical Drive Brands

Vendor	URL
AOpen/BenQ/Acer	www.aopen.com; www.benq.com; www.acer.com
Asus	www.asustek.com

Continued

Table 8-3 *(continued)*

Vendor	URL
Hitachi	www.hitachi.com
IBM	www.ibm.com
LG Electronics	www.lge.com
LiteOn	www.liteon.com
NEC	www.nec.com
Panasonic	www.panasonic.com
Pioneer	www.pioneerelectronics.com
Plextor	www.plextor.com
Samsung	www.samsung.com
Sony	www.sony.com
TDK	www.tdk.com
Toshiba	www.toshiba.com

Wrapping Up

An optical drive, particularly a DVD drive, is a mandatory component for HTPCs (in fact, this is a requirement that Microsoft imposes on all would-be vendors of Media Center PCs). Because so much music and video are on CD or DVD without an optical drive, there's no way to access these from a PC. Although it's perfectly feasible to build an HTPC that incorporates only a single multiformat DVD drive, to ensure the best overall ability to read every type of optical media, installing a second CD-specific burner may be wise. The ability to not only read from but also to record onto a variety of media is important, but sticking with a brand of CD or DVD blanks that you know works well with your particular drive may be the best way to avoid hassles. Low noise is an important quality, especially during straightforward playback. Price is really not much of an issue these days with prices seldom breaking $100, and the difference between the most and least costly multi-format drives is small.

HTPC Graphics and Video

To a large extent, HTPC hardware choices sometimes suffer from what math wizards like to call *overdetermination*. In plain English, this means they are subject to enough constraints to make simple, no-brainer solutions hard, and sometimes impossible. This is particularly true for graphics and TV tuner cards, where MCE compatibility requirements limit choices and options, and where HTPC use adds additional requirements to that mix.

In slightly different terms, MCE compatibility imposes technical requirements on the width of a graphics card's memory bus, the size of its onboard memory, and also requires support for certain specific capabilities. The details require some explanation — and make up a significant chunk of this chapter — but it's appropriate to note that even official minimum requirements more or less dictate reasonably modern, fast, capable graphics cards. HTPC use dictates quiet operation and also makes the in-case footprint (vertical and horizontal clearances) a potential issue, especially in smaller horizontal cases like the Ahanix D5 or Silverstone LC02.

When it comes to integrating TV with a Media Center PC, Microsoft likewise imposes certain compatibility requirements. Earlier versions allowed only one tuner card, but 2005 doubles that limit. Nevertheless, it's wise to pick a TV card from the company's compatible products list (and we explain where to find it, and provide input as to which items included therein are worth buying).

You'll find another topic covered in this chapter as well. It introduces the subject of DVD decoders, explains how they work and why one is required to enable MCE to play back DVD movies and other recorded content, and lists available choices, before recommending certain specific selections.

This chapter thus falls into three major sections; each is described in its order of appearance, along with more information about topics covered therein:

- **Graphics cards for MCE HTPCs:** Starting with a discussion of Microsoft requirements for compatibility with MCE 2005, this section addresses what kinds of features and capabilities that suitable graphics cards must possess before moving on to suggest what kinds they should possess. It also addresses needs specific to HTPC use, and then lists a handful of suitable candidates that you might want to consider for your build.

- **TV (and HDTV) cards for MCE HTPCs:** Following the model established in the preceding section, we begin with a discussion of Microsoft requirements for TV and HDTV compatibility with MCE 2005. Then we describe suitable candidates for your build in each of these niches, and ponder limitations specific to HDTV in North America.

- **DVD decoders:** Additional software is required on a Media Center PC to decode and render DVD digital images into forms suitable for display on a monitor or TV set. In this section, we describe what this software does, list compatible choices, and then recommend leading options as we've done in the preceding sections.

Note Near the end of the three main sections in this chapter, there's a table containing vendors and products mentioned, with URLs to follow for more information on capability and where or how to buy things.

Although there's a fair amount to chew on in each of the three primary sections, there really aren't a huge number of options for any of the three Media Center PC components to which they relate. When all is said and done in each section, you should know enough to evaluate upcoming products for yourself and find pointers to a handful of worthwhile options in each of the various product categories.

In the sections that follow, you'll develop a decent understanding of the special roles that graphics and (HD)TV cards play on a Media Center PC and get a sense of where DVD decoders fit into a Media Center PC.

Graphics Cards and Media Center PCs

Among the many items devoted to Windows XP Media Center Edition, Microsoft maintains a set of pages that it calls "Designed for Windows Media Center Logo Program." There, you'll find compatibility requirements for the following types of components, along with lists of products that have been tested for compliance:

- DVD decoders
- Media Center remote controls
- TV tuner cards

- Video cards
- Wireless network access points and bridges

The three topics from this list that we tackle in this chapter fall under a single heading called the graphics subsystem, under which they include a graphics accelerator, graphics memory, video connectors, an NTSC video output encoder, and associated software drivers. The next section looks at and explores base graphics subsystem requirements.

Microsoft Graphics Subsystem Requirements

Table 9-1 lists Microsoft's requirements more or less verbatim. In the text that follows this table, we explore these topics and explain their importance to Media Center PCs.

Table 9-1   MCE Graphics Subsystem Requirements

Item	Requirements	Comments
Graphics frame buffer memory	128MB minimum DDR or equivalent	256MB offers better performance and viewing
Graphics interface support	AGP 4X, PCI Express, or equivalent	AGP is becoming more outmoded, PCI-e more common on newer motherboards
DirectX 9 hardware acceleration	DirectX 9 device driver support DXVA hardware decode YUV single pass mixing and deinterlacing	Hardware decode is demanding stuff! Video decode of MPEG2, including progressive and interlaced 1920 × 1080 and 1280 × 720 content Using DXVA deinterlaceBLITEx interface, expose YUV2RGB and YUV2RBG extend caps
Graphics modes	DVI, VGA format	Provides output to display devices, must support standard interfaces if proprietary ones are supported
TV	Graphics adapter must be TV-out capable	Enables output to TV from graphics card
TV-out interface	Video parameters supported 720 × 480, 60 Hz display mode 720 × 540, 50 Hz display Standard VGA support Standard TV support	Permits software to help produce best viewing quality Matches conventional NTSC TV signaling Helps optimize Media Center for TV display Devices identify themselves as such Devices identify themselves as such

Without some explanation and discussion, much of what's in Table 9-1 makes sense only to those who already know a lot about how graphics are handled in Windows, and how TV signals are captured, manipulated, and displayed on various devices. We dig into these topics next, matching entries from the table to subsection headings to drive our coverage of what's really going on inside Table 9-1 and what it means to you and your HTPC.

Graphics Frame Buffer Memory

Memory on a graphics card provides high-speed storage for the graphics processor to use when manipulating or formatting image data. A frame is basically a unit of graphical data that represents one screen's worth of information in an ongoing stream of images for display. Normal television is sometimes called SDTV (Standard Definition Television) or NTSC (National Television System Committee); either way it uses 540 scan lines per screenful of data (of which only 480 scan lines are visible on the screen, which is why it's often identified as a 480-line standard), each line of which is 720 pixels wide. Each frame of television data consists of 540 lines times 720 pixels, plus additional data for one or more sound channels and subtitles (think of second audio program, or SAP, for access to foreign language soundtracks and subtitles for the hearing impaired).

DVD movies and HDTV use larger frames that may be interlaced (every other line is scanned on each frame) or progressive (every line is scanned for every frame). A DVD video frame is typically 704 × 480, 720 × 480, 704 × 576, or 720 × 576. An HDTV video frame is typically 1080 lines by 1920 pixels (likewise either interlaced or progressive mode). Frame rates for HDTV and DVD-Video run between 24 and 60 per second, which produces pretty hefty data streams given the size of individual frames. Progressive scan produces much better-looking output, but also requires twice as much data to represent.

The long and short of this discussion is that handling TV and DVD movies requires buffer space, so the graphics card can capture incoming data, decode or otherwise manipulate it, and then send it to a display device for rendering. HDTV only increases the need for buffer space because it uses even more data per frame. That's why a graphics card for MCE requires at least 128MB of frame buffer memory, and why we recommend nothing with less than 256MB, especially for those considering running HDTV through their Media Center PCs. Although this isn't enough to handle the extreme frame rates that games like *Half-Life*, *Doom 3*, and *EverQuest II* (which can easily top 100 fps on a high-end graphics card), it's enough for the multimedia that an HTPC will typically handle.

Graphics Interface Support

Basically, Windows XP MCE 2005 adds a variety of data format decoding (MPEG2, in particular) requirements to Windows' existing graphics handling needs. Moving image data for television and DVD movies requires frame rates of anywhere from 24 to 60 frames per second (fps). For now, let's just say this involves moving so much data that a bus like ISA or PCI isn't really up to the job (ISA tops out at 33 MHz, and PCI tops out somewhere between 66 and 133 MHz). That's why Microsoft states that AGP 4X, PCI-E, or some equivalent is required for a Media Center PC graphics card — simply because those buses are the only ones that can transfer all the necessary data fast enough.

That said, faster is clearly better when it comes to graphics interfaces. More bus speed makes a graphics card better able to move large volumes of data over time. With frame resolutions increasing dramatically (HDTV requires moving over eight times as much data per second as conventional TV, and DVD movies three or more times as much data per second as conventional TV), faster buses are clearly better able to handle such loads.

Thus, although Microsoft recommends only AGP 4X and PCI Express, we hasten to point out that PCI Express X16 is significantly faster than even AGP 8X. That's why we recommend buying only motherboards for HTPC machines that support PCI-E X16 graphics cards. Because these are likely to support 8-channel audio and Gigabit Ethernet as well, they make more sense for HTPC use for many reasons. Table 9-2 compares speed and bandwidth of numerous typical PC buses and shows the cumulative differences in the bandwidth column for the items mentioned. As you examine these numbers, remember that PC buses are invariably shared (and any CPU involvement likewise) so that total bandwidth represents the aggregate that all processes must share and which no single process can monopolize (or at least, not for very long).

Table 9-2   Typical PC Bus Speeds and Bandwidths

Bus Type	Width (bits)	Speed (MHz)	Cycles (/clock)	Bandwidth (MBps)
ISA	32	8.33	1	33
PCI	32	33	1	133
PCI-X 66	64	66	1	266
PCI-X 133	64	133	1	1066
PCI-E X1	1	2500	0.8	250
PCI-E X16	16	2500	0.8	4000
AGP 4X	32	66	4	1066
AGP 8x	32	66	8	2133

DirectX 9 Hardware Acceleration

MCE's media playback capabilities are rooted in Windows Media Player, which in turn depends on DirectX for handling video and sound. DirectX is a multimedia application programming interface (API) that Microsoft has been working on since 1995, designed to provide a standard interface to permit software to interact with graphics and sound cards, input devices, and so forth. It was originally known as the GameSDK (SDK means software developer's kit) but DirectX has come a long way since then (and no longer applies specifically to games, either). DirectX 9 represents the ninth generation of this API and includes support for 2-D and 3-D graphics, drawing, sound, music, input, networking, and video display. Windows MCE 2005 is the only Microsoft OS that ships with DirectX 9 support built in, although you can upgrade versions of Windows as far back as Windows 98 to support this latest version of the API.

The key requirements under this heading in Table 9-1 all relate to DirectX 9 hardware acceleration. In the simplest of terms, this means any graphics card you consider for use in a Media

Center PC must support DirectX 9 in hardware (and probably states this explicitly in its specifications). The reason for these requirements is to make sure the graphics card can handle the kind of graphics information that MCE sends to it and can operate on it quickly and efficiently (that's why device driver and hardware decode support each include DirectX 9 support as requirements).

The tie-in may become clearer when we expand the DXVA acronym to read DirectX Video Acceleration. DXVA was introduced in DirectX 8.0 and allows MCE to depend on and access a set of MPEG2 decoding routines built into a graphics processor's video engine. This means that the graphics card actually handles the most processor-intensive parts of MPEG2 decoding, and lowers overall demand for CPU processing time. This is even more important when dealing with HDTV: laboratory tests show that pure software decodes of HDTV streams require a 3 GHz CPU or faster, whereas a system that includes a DVXA-capable graphics card can get by with a CPU that runs between 1.8 and 2.0 GHz. The resolution requirements specified help to ensure proper support for HDTV (1080i or 1080p) and DVD-Video (720i and 720p).

YUV is a way to model video color in terms of three components, where Y represents a luminance (brightness) component, and U and V represent chrominance (color) components. As with the RGB (red-green-blue) color model, any color can be represented in terms of three values, one for each of Y, U, and V. YUV is used in the PAL system of television broadcasting, the standard for much of the world outside North America (which uses RGB). This capability gives MCE the ability to work with TV signals from all over the world, and to convert readily between RGB and YUV (and vice versa).

This collection of requirements basically ensures that graphics cards can handle and provide a hardware assist in dealing with incoming encoded video streams, and turn them into formats they can display on an analog television set or a digital counterpart, or an analog computer display or its digital counterpart.

Graphics Modes

Modern graphics cards must be able to drive all kinds of devices, some of which use different cabling and connectors. The digital video interface (DVI) requirement is intended to make sure an MCE-compatible graphics card can interface with and manage output on consumer digital television displays. The VGA (video graphics array) interface and its many successors (EVGA, XVGA, and so forth) have long been used to attach graphics cards to computer displays, which an MCE-compatible graphics card must also be able to interface with and manage as well. Even when a manufacturer chooses to include and use any kind of proprietary interface, MCE-compatible graphics cards must include both of these standard interfaces as well.

Tip

Most modern graphics cards can drive two monitors, because they typically include two device connectors. Many cards include one VGA and one DVI connector; some cards offer two DVI connectors instead (but conversion adapters to go from DVI to VGA are both cheap and readily available, if not included with monitors or graphics cards). Driving two monitors is a great way to extend your desktop on a normal PC; on an HTPC, it's a great way to drive a computer monitor and a TV set from the same graphics card. That said, if you want to move the cursor from one screen to another using this kind of setup, you must switch MCE from full-screen mode to windowed mode to regain full cursor mobility. Do this by clicking View in Window in the upper-right corner of the title bar, or by double-clicking the Media Center window title bar. This happens because Microsoft uses DirectX to create the full-screen display that MCE uses so often and so well.

TV Capabilities and TV-Out Interface

Driving a TV set means being able to produce the right signals and formats, but it also means supporting the right kinds of physical connections to cable a graphics card up to a television set. That's why so many modern video cards include S-Video ports nowadays and why some video card manufacturers include other devices (sometimes called dongles) to provide attachments for component video, coaxial cable (CATV), and so forth. So many modern digital televisions support DVI inputs nowadays that finding a way to interconnect a graphics card and a television set is seldom a problem. But given TV's important place in MCE's capabilities, this requirement makes sure that all MCE-compatible graphics cards are able to attach to a conventional or a digital TV with minimum effort and absolute assurance. This also explains why support for all of the common conventional TV frame formats is required and why MCE-compatible graphics cards must be able to drive conventional analog TV sets and computer monitors with equal ease and facility.

Graphics Chipsets, HTPC Needs, and Recommendations

Just as a handful of companies (Intel, VIA, SiS, and nVidia) dominate the motherboard chipset markets, so do a pair of powerful competitors dominate the graphics chipset or GPU (graphics processing unit) markets. In this case, the two multinational big dogs are:

- **ATI**, an Ontario, Canada, headquartered company that offers a broad range of graphical chipsets, plus TV/video processors that many vendors package and use in their designs.

- **nVidia**, a California headquartered company that offers an equally broad range of graphical chipsets, as well as TV/video processors that many vendors also package and use in their designs (many of the same vendors that use ATI chipsets in some products use nVidia chipsets in other products).

Both chipsets have their adherents and aficionados, and both offer newer products that are fully MCE 2005 compliant. In fact, Microsoft doesn't bother to list the actual products that are compatible with MCE 2005; it lists only the nVidia and ATI chipsets that such cards must include to be compatible. For ATI, this includes Radeon chipsets 9800, plus X600 and up; for nVidia, this includes GeForce FX5*xxx* and GeForce 6*xxx* chipsets and up.

HTPC Considerations for Graphics Cards

A modern GPU is an impressive piece of silicon nowadays, exceeding the capabilities of any equally modern Northbridge or Southbridge processor. Memory speeds for graphics cards typically exceed 400 MHz and can go much higher; processing rates for these cards can be outrageous. All this capability adds up to a lot of heat output, which is why so many graphics cards from the middle ($150 to $300) and the high end of the market (over $300) include onboard cooling fans nowadays.

But fans are anathema to quiet HTPC operation, and many of the fans that graphics card vendors choose to install on their products make sufficient noise to be noticeable. For the purposes of this book, we concentrated on fanless graphics cards with enough onboard RAM and GPU power to handle HDTV. This kept us from considering the kinds of ultra-premium graphics cards ($500 and up) that gamers tend to favor. We chose to favor mid-range cards with 256MB of RAM (but do mention some exceptional 128MB cards), recognizing that graphics cards with 128MB can handle MCE reasonably well provided they meet other Microsoft criteria already discussed (DirectX 9.0 support in hardware, TV-out, and so forth).

Although the graphics card market is pretty darn huge (thousands of products), our focus in the middle of the market and our requirement for fanless operation reduced the population we judged suitable to a manageable group. You'll find these products listed in Table 9-3, but you can pick your own such products by asking the following questions during your own selection process:

- Does the card provide at least 256MB of RAM onboard (DDR or faster)?
- Is the chipset on Microsoft's compatible products list?
- Is the card fanless?
- How much vertical clearance does my case allow? How much horizontal clearance? Will the card fit?

The first three questions are easy to answer by inspecting product information, spec sheets, and so on. Answering the fourth question may come down to "try it, and keep it only if it fits," if you can't find satisfactory answers from other buyers (but in most cases you can find this kind of information in online forums that cater to HTPC users, such as `HTPCnews.com`, `SilentPCReview.com`, `theGreenButton.com`, and so forth).

Recommended Graphics Cards

Jumping back a couple of sections for a moment, we want to repeat the Microsoft list of MCE-compatible chipsets — namely ATI Radeon chipsets 9800, plus X600 and up, plus nVidia GeForce FX5*xxx* and GeForce 6*xxx* chipsets and up. Based on reports from MCE users, Web sites and publications, and our own experience, we'd whittle that list down a bit further for HTPC use to read: for ATI Radeon (and related Mobility) chipsets X700 and up; for nVidia, GeForce 62*xx* chipsets and up. The other chipsets MS mentions will work, but are older and slower. By the time you limit selections to fanless models, the total number of options drops pretty dramatically, as Table 9-3 illustrates. As you look at build advice and parts lists for our own builds elsewhere in this book, notice that we follow our own advice closely, especially when it comes to graphics cards.

Table 9-3   Recommended Graphics Cards

Vendor	Chipset	Bus	Name or Part Number	Description
BFG Tech.com	GeForce 6600	PCI-E X16	BFG GeForce 6600 GT	128MB card offers single-side, narrow profile heat sink (costs about $215)
eVGA*	GeForce 6600	PCI-E X16	256-P2-N379	256MB card offers narrow profile with heat sink on front, no clearance issues (costs about $168)

Vendor	Chipset	Bus	Name or Part Number	Description
Gigabyte	Radeon X800XL	PCI-E X16	GV-RX80L256V	Wide profile card with heat sinks front and back, heat pipes, definite clearance issues (costs about $285)
Gigabyte	Radeon X700	PCI-E X16	GV-RX70P128D	Wide profile card with heat sinks front and back, heat pipes, definite clearance issues (costs about $152)
Gigabyte*	GeForce 6600GT	PCI-E X16	GV-NX66T128VP	Wide profile card with heat sinks front and back, heat pipes, definite clearance issues (costs about $200)
Gigabyte	GeForce 6800	AGP 8X	GV-N68128DH	Wide profile card with heat sinks front and back, heat pipes, definite clearance issues (costs about $197)
Gigabyte*	GeForce 6600GT	AGP 8X	GV-N66128VP	Wide profile card with heat sinks front and back; heat pipes, definite clearance issues (costs about $200)
GeCube	Radeon X800XL	PCI-E X16	GC-HP800XL-D3	256 and 512MB models available, very large heat sink on front, definite clearance issues (256 MB costs about $400 ; 512 MB costs about $500)
GeCube	Radeon X700	PCI-E X16	GC-HP700G-E3	512MB model has large front-side heat sink, but no vertical clearance issues appear likely (costs about $600, only available in the United Kingdom)
Leadtek	GeForce 6600	PCI-E X16	WinFast PX6600 TD Heatsink	256 and 128MB models available (256MB model costs about $200; 128MB costs about $155)
Leadtek	GeForce 6200	PCI-E X16	WinFast PX6200 TC TDH	256 and 128MB models available (costs about $70: a real bargain)
Powercolor*	Radeon X700	PCI-E X16	R41AB-ND3D	256MB model has heat sinks front and back, definite horizontal clearance issues, vertical clearance looks okay (costs about $145)

All the companies whose names are asterisked were kind enough to lend us graphics cards for testing; ATI also lent us numerous cards, but all proved too noisy for HTPC use. Our closing remarks may help you choose from the set of products mentioned in Table 9-3:

- In a lot of performance tests we read, nVidia showed moderate performance advantages over ATI Radeon chipsets, sometimes even when price differences went strongly the other way. ATI and nVidia both make good products, but we find nVidia's current price/performance ratios to be more compelling than ATI's. Over the years, these companies have flip-flopped in this relationship, so don't assume what's true as we write this will remain true forever.

- You can buy an adequate graphics card for your HTPC for under $100, and a good one for between $150 and $200. You can spend more than that, but unless you game on that system, you really won't need the extra performance that added costs convey.

- Your authors use nVidia GeForce 6600–based cards in their own HTPC systems finding in them a sweet spot between cost and capability. See Figure 9-1.

FIGURE 9-1: Three nVidia 6600 graphics cards. From top to bottom: the eVGA with slim heat sink, the Gigabyte AGP showing the back side of the card, the Gigabyte PCI-E X16 showing the front side of the card. Note the heat pipe that wraps from front to back (it's what causes clearance problems in smaller cases).

TV and HDTV Cards for MCE

For most people, building an HTPC means you want to record television and enable all the fancy bells and whistles like pausing live TV and recording multiple shows at once. This requires a peripheral called a *TV capture card*. In this section, we explain the Microsoft requirements for TV cards, how TV signals differ from those your PC uses, and what hardware you need to record TV. Finally, we discuss the state of HDTV recording support in Windows XP Media Center Edition today.

Microsoft TV Card Requirements for MCE 2005

As in the preceding section, this is one of the areas where Microsoft states specific requirements against which hardware is judged for compatibility with MCE 2005. Though we must simplify these requirements just a bit to avoid diving too deeply into television technology details, the basics appear in Table 9-4.

Table 9-4   MCE TV Tuner/Capture/Compressor Subsystem Requirements

Item	Requirements	Comments
Analog signals	Single or dual analog tuner compatible with NTSC-M/J, PAL, or SECAM broadcasts	Varies by location: NTSC in North America, PAL and SECAM outside (PAL in Europe). Dual tuners must handle two complete video capture and compression paths independently at the same time.
Digital signals	Single digital tuner compatible with DVB-T or ATSC broadcasts	DVB-T is the European digital standard, ATSC in North America.
Tuners	Low signal attenuation and quality	Various requirements for lock signals, adjacent channels, signal-to-noise ratios, and so forth (all designed to provide decent reception and handling for broadcast TV).
Analog tuners	Connector outs for switchable S-Video/Composite and audio	One set per tuner, able to use S-Video or Composite for video, plus 1-1/8" phono plug or dual RCA plugs for audio.
Copy Protection	Various forms must be supported (VBI line 21 and Macrovision)	Provides Digital Rights Management protection for video materials.
Vertical Blank Interval	Raw VBI with support for SAP, MTS, NICAM, AM/FM, plus PAL, SECAM	Provides access to data for second audio program (SAP), multichannel TV sound (MTS) and so on.
FM Tuner	If present, integrated into capture card with separate antenna input	Provides access to over-the-air radio broadcasts through MCE.
A/V Capture	Audio video capture occurs on single device, uses WDM drivers and meets related standards	Makes sure all devices will work with MCE and can identify themselves to the software for proper handling.
Tuner Driver	Works with MCE drivers, supports proper formats and compression services	Governs how video data is represented, captured, sampled, what form compressed video streams take, and handling of variable bit rate compression, all to ensure compatibility with MCE.

The driving principle here, as with other subsystems for Windows XP Media Center Edition 2005, is to make sure that compatible hardware works easily and well with existing equipment, especially conventional, digital, and high-definition TV sets. By imposing stringent standards on vendors, Microsoft makes things easier for users (and for Media Center PC builders as well).

You'll find this information online under the heading "TV Tuners" at www.microsoft.com/ windowsxp/mediacenter/partners/dfw/partnerlisting.mspx. Of the 46 items listed there as this chapter was being written, we worked with over half of them to provide recommendations listed later in this chapter.

TV Signals Versus PC Signals

A standard television signal differs quite a bit from the display signals PCs use. Television signals generally come as a package of sound and video. The video is generally combined into one signal; by that we mean the red, green, and blue elements are smashed together into one signal. This is called a composite signal. To add to this complexity, standard television is interlaced. This means that at any one time only half the screen actually shows something, by tracing every other scan line on screen. In one cycle, even-numbered lines on your TV set light up; in the next cycle odd-numbered ones do likewise, and your brain fills in the rest.

A PC displays screens of data differently. It uses a high-quality signal where red, green, and blue elements are separate signals to provide maximum clarity and resolution. A modern PC typically can display resolutions well past 1600 × 1200, if your monitor can handle it. These signals are non-interlaced (in home theater jargon this is "progressive scan") so that all portions of a PC monitor actively display data for each screenful. This produces greater detail, which in turn makes your PC easy to read and lets you view fine details with clarity and ease.

Regular TV Tuner Cards and Signals

A TV capture card — also called a *TV tuner card* — is a device that receives TV signals and converts them to a digital format your PC can understand.

A typical inexpensive standard TV capture card enables your PC's central processor to bear the brunt of recording TV signals in standard PC format. Media Center requires a more advanced TV card that records to MPEG2 (the same digital video standard that DVDs use) using onboard hardware, leaving your processor free to do other things. Thanks to onboard MPEG encoding your HTPC can support two TV tuners and can record two programs at once. This way you can record one program while watching another, or record two programs at the same time while you're off on vacation.

Table 9-5 lists leading TV tuner card vendors for MCE.

Table 9-5   Leading TV Tuner Card Vendors for MCE

Name	Price Range	URL/Remarks
Hauppauge PVR-150MCE/500MCE	$65–$150	www.hauppauge.com; the leader in hardware encoding offers single (150MCE) and dual tuner (500 MCE) cards.
ATI TV Wonder Elite	$150	www.ati.com; ATI's Theater 550 Pro–based capture card; includes Remote Wonder II (not suited for MCE use).
AVerMedia UltraTV 1500MCE and AverTV PVR 150 Plus	$65–$75	www.avermedia.com; AVerMedia has made capture cards for years, and has two MCE compatible offerings.
PowerColor Theater 550 PROTheater	$80	www.powercolor.com; less expensive version of 550 Pro with basic remote (not fully functional in MCE).
Sapphire Theatrix Theater 550 Pro	$80	www.sapphiretech.com; less expensive version of the Theater 550 Pro includes basic remote (not fully functional in MCE).

All companies listed in the preceding table were kind enough to lend us their cards while we were writing this book.

Top Choices

Hauppauge is a capture card vendor that has made quality TV cards for quite some time. It was also one of the first vendors to offer hardware encoding cards; as such, they've become a de facto standard for home-built HTPCs. Its current models are the PVR-150MCE and PVR-500MCE. The PVR-150MCE is a single tuner card and is reasonably priced. The Hauppauge PVR-500MCE is a dual tuner card; it delivers two PVR-150s on a single PCI card. Thus, the PVR-500MCE can handle and record two programs at once, but consumes only one PCI slot in an HTPC.

The second choice falls to a group of capture cards based on the same TV chipset. ATI recently introduced a TV capture chip designed specifically for Media Center 2005 called the ATI Theater 550 Pro. It offers advanced features that help with noisy signals, and more. Cards that incorporate the ATI Theater 550 Pro are available from numerous ATI vendors, such as PowerColor and Sapphire. And, of course, ATI uses the Theater 550 Pro in its own TV Wonder Elite product.

The State of HDTV and Media Center PCs

As we write this book, Media Center offers support only for OTA HDTV broadcasts in North America. OTA, or over-the-air, means HDTV broadcasts from local TV stations. To receive HDTV broadcasts, you must use an antenna much like that for standard broadcast TV. In most major metropolitan areas, local network affiliates (NBC, CBS, ABC, and so on) broadcast digital TV as well as standard analog TV. In major metropolitan areas, it's normal for more than a dozen stations to offer OTA HDTV programming.

Tip

To identify which local stations broadcast HDTV, how far away they are, and for suggestions on what type of antenna you need to receive such signals, check out `www.antennaweb.org`.

Recording HDTV is different from standard TV; there is no conversion process involved because HDTV is digital. An HDTV tuner card simply tunes into the frequency for a digital broadcast and starts recording to an HTPC's hard drive. There's no processing burden to convert that data into digital, because HDTV is already encoded in MPEG2 format (called Transport Stream). More taxing activity occurs when viewing or playing back high-resolution HDTV signals. Media Center requires a 2.4 GHz P4 processor (or equivalent) and a more powerful video card than is necessary for standard TV (that said, we found 1.8 GHz Pentium M and 2.0 GHz Athlon 64 processors also equal to this task).

Tip

Sample HTPC configurations described in Chapter 15 are ready for HDTV recording and display: simply add an HDTV tuner card and you are ready to enjoy! Of course, you'll also need an HD-capable TV set or other equivalent display to see the hi-def picture in its full glory.

Table 9-6 lists leading HDTV tuner card vendors for MCE.

Table 9-6   Leading HDTV Tuner Card Vendors for MCE

Name	Price Range	URL/Remarks
AVerMedia A180*	$100	`www.avermedia.com`; a well-known name in TV cards, this inexpensive no-frills card works well.
ATI HDTV Wonder*	$150	`www.ati.com`; ATI's HDTV offering includes an HDTV antenna. Remote Edition includes a remote control that isn't ideal for MCE, and adds to the cost.
DVICO Fusion 5	$100–$150	`www.dvico.com`; lesser known company has a great product: its Fusion 5 series is a fourth generation offering.
Vbox DTA-150/151	$150	`www.vboxcomm.com`; this small Israeli company was first to design MCE-compatible HDTV tuners in early 2004. Spotty availability in the United States, but Vbox is working on distribution deals.

Top HDTV Choices

The Fusion 5 series is the latest in a line of well-made HDTV tuner cards from Korean manufacturer DVICO. DVICO's cards are a cult classic in the HTPC community, though they don't enjoy ATI's name recognition. The Fusion 5 line is a solid family of cards that utilize the newest HDTV reception hardware (helpful in regions where HDTV can be hard to receive).

AVerMedia recently released an HDTV tuner card made specifically for Media Center 2005 called the AVerTVHD MCE A180. It is available only in a white box version made for system integrators, but is available for under $100.

ATI's HDTV Wonder is our third choice. Thanks to ATI's brand strength, the HDTV Wonder is for sale in most retail stores. The retail bundle includes a small directional HDTV antenna. This antenna may or may not be useful, depending on where you live (check www. antennaweb.org to determine whether or not it is likely to work).

All companies whose names are asterisked in Table 9-6 were kind enough to furnish HDTV cards for this book. You'll find a group shot of the Hauppauge PVR-150MCE and the AVerMedia AVerTVHD-MCE-A180 cards in Figure 9-2.

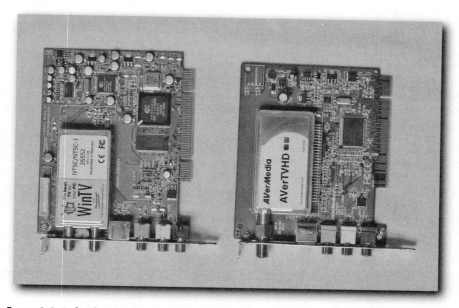

FIGURE 9-2: Left: The Hauppauge PVR-150MCE TV capture card; right: The AVerMedia AVerTVHD-MCE-A180. Both use metal shields around tuner circuitry for added shielding.

DVD Decoders

Simply put, a *DVD decoder* is a piece of software that permits a Windows PC to understand, interpret, and render both audio and video content from DVD MPEG2 files so that users can play back and watch DVDs. Microsoft recommends that users install an MCE-compatible DVD decoder on Media Center PCs, to enable MCE to work directly and seamlessly with DVD entertainment media.

There's a small number of compatible DVD decoders listed on the MCE compatibility list. It includes decoders from three vendors:

- **CyberLink PowerDVD:** Versions 5.0.2027C, 6.0, and 6.0.1.1102
- **Intervideo WinDVD:** Versions 5.0 and 5.0 Build 11.670
- **nVidia DVD Decoder:** No versions specified

None of this software lists for more than $69; most is available at substantial discounts (you can buy usable versions of any of these for under $20, if you shop carefully).

But do you really need to buy and install one of these programs? Maybe yes, maybe no. If you download and run the utility described in the next section, you'll find out for sure!

Check DVD Decoder Status

Microsoft offers a free diagnostic tool called the Windows XP Video Decoder Checkup Utility. It loads onto any Windows XP system, including MCE 2005, and reports on DVD decoders it finds installed. Because all DVD decoders must register in the Windows Registry, this is actually pretty easy to check.

Where this utility's value comes into play, however, is that it reports back if decoders it finds are compatible with Windows Media Player 10 and Windows XP Media Center Edition. Because so many vendors include DVD decoders as part of software they ship with DVD players (many of these bundled offerings are compatible with MCE), it's worthwhile checking to see if you need to install a DVD decoder or not. Figure 9-3 shows the output that this program produces (it found a compatible decoder installed with software for a graphics card on a test machine, to our surprise and delight).

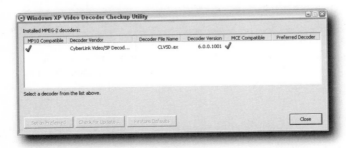

FIGURE 9-3: The Decoder Checkup Utility grants a green checkmark to compatible decoders, like the Cyberlink entry shown.

To download this utility, search for Video Decoder Checkup Utility, or visit `www.microsoft.com/windowsmobile/portablemediacenter/decoder.mspx` instead. It's a 163K download and takes less than a minute to install. The default install makes this program accessible through the Start menu (Start⇨All Programs⇨Windows Media). Simply click the program name to run it: it's easy! Select a compatible entry as your preferred decoder for best results with MCE.

Two other tools that can come in handy when dealing with video files are:

- **GSpot:** A tool that identifies which video codec and audio compression method is used on .avi files, and indicates whether or not a matching codec is installed, plus all kinds of other helpful information.

- **AVIcodec:** A multimedia file analyzer that reports on individual files, including codecs needed and where to find them.

Grab either or both of these tools from this good general codec resource online: Free Codecs.com at `www.free-codecs.com`. You'll also want to visit this site if you decide to investigate free codec software, like that mentioned in the next section.

If You Need a Decoder, Get One!

If the checkup utility shows no decoder installed, you can visit any online shopping service to look for a compatible decoder from one of the three vendors mentioned earlier. On the other hand, numerous free decoders are available that many experts have found to be entirely workable on a Media Center PC (but not all of them show up should you re-run the Decoder Checkup Utility following their installation, so don't be surprised if that happens to you). Even if you have to pay for a DVD decoder, however, you can find them for $15 or less, if you shop carefully.

Wrapping Up

It's hard to overstate the importance of the display side of MCE. Without the right components in place — which for this chapter means a graphics card, a TV capture card, a DVD decoder, and possibly also an HDTV card — you can't count on MCE to handle and display TV programming nor play DVD movies properly. That's why it's important to stick with components that Microsoft identifies as MCE compatible whenever possible. Even within those option sets, some are better than others, which is why we try to steer you toward certain choices in each of the three component areas covered in this chapter.

Sound Cards and HTPC Audio

I n the age of iPods and MP3s, it may seem perfectly natural for your computer to play music, but this was not always the case. Even today, audio is hardly a necessary feature of a basic computer, but it is a crucial part of an HTPC. Without some way of playing back audio files, your HTPC is only as good as the silent cinema of the early twentieth century — and even this was accompanied by live music. A twenty-first century home theater is not complete without some way of producing high-quality digital audio, preferably in 5.1, 6.1, or even 7.1 surround sound. The cheap speakers that came with your office computer aren't going to cut it. This chapter explores digital audio: what it is, where it comes from, and what you (and your HTPC) need to produce it.

Your investment in audio equipment for your home theater may be substantial, and it may extend beyond parts for your Media Center PC. What you need depends on your playback needs, your budget, and what equipment is already available to you. If you already own a receiver and a surround speaker system, you may simply want to connect your Media Center PC up to your existing equipment. On the other hand, if you're completely new to the home theater market, you may not want yet another box cluttered around your television. After all, the idea of a Media Center PC is to centralize and simplify your entertainment center, not just pile another component on the stack. If this is the case, you'll want to treat your HTPC as a virtual receiver with the ability to handle every aspect of audio playback. The only external components you should need in this configuration are speakers (covered in Chapter 11).

To decide which of these configurations is right for you, you must have a good idea of exactly what happens in the process of transforming a digital file into a perfectly balanced movie soundtrack. If you plan to use your Media Center PC to play back music as well as movie audio, you may also want to explore buying and downloading music over the Internet. Finally, you'll also need to decide which audio card is right for you — or even whether you need to buy one at all. All this, and much more, is covered in this chapter, including:

in this chapter

☑ Digital audio

☑ Playback

☑ Receivers and amplifiers

☑ Sound cards

☑ Best HTPC sound card options

- **Introduction to digital audio:** For something as simple as music or dialogue, digital audio sure can be complicated! Here we discuss how audio is stored in digital form to how it is transformed into audible sound waves and everything in between. You'll also find a little about what is needed to achieve this transformation.

- **What you need to play digital audio:** A basic rundown of everything you need to play back digital audio, including a source medium, hardware, and software for your Media Center PC, and external equipment like speakers or an audio-video receiver.

- **Sources of digital audio:** Digital audio is not just restricted to the realm of computers. CDs, DVDs, and satellite radio are all examples of digital audio that doesn't require a computer for playback. With a little knowledge and the right tools, however, your computer can play back audio from all of these sources, as well as the audio embedded in digital video files.

- **Playback:** A quick-and-dirty outline of the process of playing digital audio on your Media Center PC, no matter what the format. Media Center can play back many common formats automatically and can play back unsupported formats using additional software. You will also find what you *can't* play; rampant piracy has made record companies wary, causing them to restrict playback for certain formats.

- **Receivers and amplifiers:** If you plan to grant your existing receiver or amplifier a role in your home theater system, you need to know how to hook it up to your HTPC and how this changes the components involved.

- **What a sound card does:** A sound card (or equivalent circuitry on some motherboards) provides the link between the software inside your Media Center PC and the rest of your audio equipment outside it. Find out exactly how digital files end up as audible sound waves.

- **What you need in a sound card:** Many motherboards come with sound processing capabilities onboard, but a number of manufacturers also produce add-on sound cards. Which is right for you depends on the level of fidelity you seek and on the rest of your system's capabilities.

- **Installing your sound card:** Even if you don't buy an add-on sound board, you still need to set up Windows MCE to recognize your hardware and take advantage of its particular capabilities. You also want to test several different types of media to make sure everything is working properly and at full resolution.

- **Best HTPC sound card options:** If you're feeling slightly overwhelmed by possibilities presented in this chapter, we help you out by recommending a few of our favorites.

After reading this chapter, you should have a good idea of what's involved in playing back digital audio, and what you need to do to configure your system to play it back. Keep in mind that, like many other aspects of the computer industry, countless obscure and incompatible formats exist that aren't covered in this chapter. Topics such as lossless compression, open-source codecs, and the legality of copying music for personal purposes are also relevant to playing digital audio but are beyond the scope of this book.

Hydrogen Audio (www.hydrogenaudio.org) is a good place to start learning about the ins and outs of the various audio compression formats. Another useful site is Doom9 (www.doom9.org), which has plenty of information about playing and converting between the numerous file and audio formats, although it focuses primarily on digital video and DVD compression. Many free tools and more unasked-for information about copyright issues around the world can be had there as well.

On the hardware side of things, you can find plenty of discussion and in-depth articles about the latest sound cards and what they support on the ExtremeTech Web site at www.extremetech.com/category2/0,1695,838538,00.asp. If you're interested in the nitty-gritty technical details of what goes on inside your sound card (or any other piece of computer hardware for that matter), this is a great place to start.

Introduction to Digital Audio

In its most basic form, digital audio is a numerical representation of an analog waveform. Analog audio can be thought of in terms of *amplitude* (volume) and *frequency* (pitch) and is usually represented visually as a two-dimensional graph with amplitude plotted on the vertical axis against time on the horizontal axis. This visual graph is called an *audio waveform*.

Digital audio stores only one of the two aspects of analog audio: amplitude. The oldest and most basic format for storing digital audio, *PCM* (pulse code modulation), is a sequence of numbers, each of which represents a specific amplitude. The frequency information is reconstructed based on the specific order of the sequence. How is this done? Just as motion can be captured in a sequence of still frames to make up a movie image, sound can be reduced to a sequence of very short sequential data points, called *samples*. When played back in a continuous sequence, these samples reproduce the original sound fairly well. To do this accurately, however, the frequency at which samples are played back must be very short: at least twice as fast as the highest audible frequency. For most humans, the upper range for hearing is somewhere around 22 KHz. Digital audio is typically sampled at 44.1 KHz or above.

The key to reconstructing frequency information that is not stored in digital audio is this *sampling frequency*, which states how often individual samples are played back. The sampling frequency remains the same throughout a single piece of digital audio, and must be known beforehand to play it back at the correct pitch. Most common audio formats specify sampling frequency before playing back any samples. Once the sampling frequency is known, the sequence of individual samples begins to make sense. Take a simple example assuming a sampling frequency of 44.1 KHz. The information in a single sample represents the amplitude of the analog waveform exactly 1/44,100th of a second after the previous sample. Using the information in the digital samples, a reconstruction of the original analog waveform is produced.

Even if you didn't completely follow the technical explanation just given, the most important things you need to know about digital audio are its *sampling rate* and its *bit depth*. Bit depth is a measure of how much information about each individual sample is stored. Bit depth is measured in bits (strange but true!), the basic unit of computer storage. Most digital audio is stored in 16-bit form, which holds slightly more information than most humans can actually hear.

Each additional bit doubles the number of possible values a sample can have, so a digital audio clip with an 18-bit sample depth contains four times as much information as one with a 16-bit depth. On the other hand, it requires only about 10 percent more space on your hard drive.

Although the sampling rate and bit depth alone are enough to reproduce any individual sound, there's another aspect of digital audio that has been left out. Most musical recordings are made in stereo, which means that two separate audio channels must be played back simultaneously. If more than two channels are used, these must also be stored.

You can find a more complete discussion of multichannel audio in Chapter 11.

Digital Audio Formats

Although sampling rate and bit depth make up the underlying form of digital audio, there are many ways to store the digital bits that make up this information. What this means in practical terms is that even though digital audio can always be thought of in terms of sampling rate and bit depth, the way it is actually stored on your hard drive can vary a lot, and not all formats can be played by all software players. Two basic types of format exist: the file format and the data format. These two are often confused, and that problem is made worse because the same name is sometimes used for an instance of both formats, especially when they are often found together, as is the case with MP3 or WMA files.

The *file format* can be thought of as a container for the data format. Basically, your computer needs something to tell it what it is looking at when it sees an audio file, and the file format acts as a computer-readable label with information about sampling rate, bit depth, what kind of software should be used to play it back, and additional information about the file, such as the artist or the name of the song.

The *data format* is the specific way in which the audio data is stored. Because uncompressed audio takes up a lot of storage space, compression is often used to reduce file size to a manageable level. Data formats may be uncompressed, or utilize either lossless or lossy compression. Data formats that involve compression are commonly called *codecs*, short for coder/decoders. The simplest format is uncompressed PCM audio (used on CDs), which simply stores the individual samples in sequence. This format requires the least amount of computer resources to play back, but takes up the most disk space. Lossless codecs can reduce the file size of uncompressed audio by almost half, but any further reduction in file size generally requires a lossy codec of some kind, which means that some audio information is lost when the file is compressed, or *encoded*. The amount of information lost depends on the quality of the encoding algorithm, the limitations of the codec itself, and the target file size. Generally, a compression ratio of between 5:1 and 10:1 can be achieved without a noticeable decrease in audio quality, although the exact ratio varies depending on the quality of your hearing, your playback system, and what you are listening to. Common lossy codecs include MPEG layer-III (MP3), Windows Media Audio (WMA), and Advanced Audio Coding (AAC).

Lossy codecs are often compared on the basis of how much audible information is lost at a given bit rate, the number of bits used to store a single second of digital audio. Bit rates are typically given in kbps (kilobits per second). Better codecs sound closer to the original uncompressed file, or are more *transparent*, than a lesser codec when encoded at the same bit rate. Lossless codecs are always transparent and are best judged by comparing the bit rate necessary to compress the same audio file. Uncompressed audio also has a bit rate, which is directly derived from its sampling frequency, bit depth, and the number of channels it has.

Tip   You can find a much more in-depth discussion of digital audio on the ExtremeTech Web site: `www.extremetech.com/article2/0,1697,1460716,00.asp`.

What You Need to Play Digital Audio

Once your Media Center PC is all set up, you should be able to play most audio files at the click of a mouse, but first you need to make sure you have everything you need to play it. The basic components necessary for PC audio are as follows:

- **Source media:** You can't listen to digital audio without something to listen to, so that's the first step. If all you're doing is listening to CDs, your setup should be quite simple, but if you want to play back DVDs or the songs on your iPod, you might have a little bit of work ahead of you. Above all, try and figure out ahead of time what you're going to be listening to, so you will know what your needs are.

- **Software:** Many different kinds of software are needed in the playback process, but, if you're lucky, it's all included in Windows and you don't have to worry about it. Just in case, it might be wise to read up a bit on media players (especially Windows Media Center, which is what you'll be using in Windows MCE), as well as audio drivers for your sound card, codecs for the various types of files you'll be playing, and DirectSound filters for the formats that Windows Media Center doesn't support natively.

- **Hardware and interconnects:** You need a sound card to convert your audio files to a form your speakers (or amplifier) can recognize, and cables (interconnects) to hook them up. Sound cards are discussed at the end of this chapter and cables are discussed in Chapter 11.

- **External hardware (optional):** Depending on the equipment you already own and the level of fidelity you seek, you may also want to use an external receiver or amplifier to power your speaker system properly. This topic is covered more thoroughly in Chapter 11.

- **Speakers:** You can't watch a DVD without a television, and you can't listen to music without speakers. Get the scoop on home theater speakers in Chapter 11.

Sources of Digital Audio

Digital audio comes from many different sources. CDs and DVDs are probably the most common sources, but there are many other places you can find digital audio. Every source has its own unique sampling rate and bit depth, which affects the hardware that it is compatible with just as much as the physical media itself. Although the precise details of how the various media store audio data are beyond the scope of this book, almost all sources of digital audio are converted to PCM format audio (that is, they use a specific sampling rate and bit depth to represent audio waveforms) before they are played back. The one exception to this is high-fidelity SACD discs, which cannot be played easily on a computer-based system. The most common sources of digital audio include:

- **CD:** The oldest medium for digital audio. The official specifications are for 44.1 KHz, 16-bit audio, but enhanced 20- and 24-bit CDs may sometimes be found. Most standalone players cannot take advantage of the additional bit depth, but it's possible to play them back on a PC with the right software. Windows MCE supports CD audio natively. So long as the CD-ROM drive and sound card are properly hooked up, no additional software or hardware is necessary.

- **DVD-Video:** Movie soundtracks are also digital audio, and can be stored in a variety of formats, including the basic PCM format used for CD audio. The audio on DVD-Video discs is almost always 48 KHz/16 bits, although high-resolution 96 KHz/24-bit audio is also supported. The 44.1 KHz sampling rate used for CDs is not supported, however. Most commercial DVDs ship with Dolby Digital (AC3) encoded audio in up to 5.1 channel configurations. Other supported formats are DTS and MPEG layer-II. Playing back DVDs on any version of Windows — including Windows MCE — requires a third-party software decoder. Usually, this is bundled with your DVD-ROM drive, but if you've bought a low-cost OEM drive, you may have to purchase it separately.

- **DVD-Audio:** Although a DVD-Video can be used to store audio only, a second DVD-based format designed specifically for audio is available. This format is extremely high resolution and aims at audiophiles. Whereas the PCM audio on DVD-Video discs is limited to two channels, DVD-Audio supports up to 5.1 channels at 96 KHz/24 bit, and even supports stereo audio at a sampling frequency of 192 KHz. The 44.1 KHz sampling rate of ordinary CDs is also supported. Very few PCs are capable of playing back DVD-Audio discs at their full resolution, although most DVD-Audio discs are shipped with a DVD-Video audio stream for maximum compatibility.

- **Internet sources:** Many sources of digital audio are available on the Internet, legal and otherwise. The most common format is the MP3, which will play back on almost any computer. However, most MP3s are illegal copies of CDs. Most legal audio that can be downloaded is protected by DRM — Digital Rights Management — that limits how the file can be used in an attempt to prevent piracy. Generally, these files are in WMA, AAC, or (in the case of Sony) Atrac format, of which only WMA is supported out of the box by Windows MCE. Regardless of the source, downloadable audio is almost always in the 44.1 KHz/16-bit format of audio CDs and is typically of worse quality because some audio information is lost when it is converted to a download-friendly format.

- **Radio:** Radio comes in many forms, both digital and analog. It is possible to listen to conventional AM or FM radio signals on a computer, although an additional hardware tuner must be purchased. It is also possible (for now) to receive digital satellite radio on a computer. A monthly subscription and a digital tuner are required to decode the signal, and a separate adapter box must be purchased to route the signal into your PC. At the time of publishing, industry concerns about piracy have prevented any computer card–based tuners from being sold. TimeTrax (www.timetraxtech.com) sells tuners and subscriptions bundled with its PC adapter. By far the easiest way to listen to radio on a computer is via Internet radio, streaming audio. Most major radio stations also broadcast an Internet radio stream available through their Web sites. There are also many stations that broadcast only on the Internet. These can be found using a software tuner service, such as the one in Apple's popular iTunes. Windows Media Center also includes an Internet radio tuner, but unlike most other options, you must pay for each station you listen to.

- **Digital video:** Most digital video files also contain digital audio in some form or another. Most of the time, this audio tends to be in the same formats as digital audio: MP3, WMA, or AAC. AC3 (Dolby Digital) audio is also fairly common. The difficulty with digital video files is that the format of the audio is often hard to discover, which makes it hard to troubleshoot when audio problems surface.

Playback

You should now have a fairly good idea about what digital audio is and where you can find it. Now it's time to translate this theory into practice and actually find out what it takes to play it back. The first thing you need to know is what format your audio uses. This includes the physical medium (if there is one) as well as various file and data formats. If you want to play back a digital file (as opposed to a CD or DVD), the GSpot Codec Information Appliance (www.headbands.com/gspot/) is a useful tool for identifying the audio (and video) format in use.

Once you know what format you want to play back, you must identify what kind of hardware you need. If you just want to play a digital file, all you will need is a sound card to output an audio signal to your speakers. Playing a CD or DVD requires a CD-ROM or DVD-ROM drive, details about which are covered in Chapter 8. Radio — analog and satellite — requires an appropriate tuner and possibly an adapter to play it on a computer. Internet radio requires an Internet connection and whatever hardware is required to connect. Details about network connections are covered in Chapter 13.

The next step is to make sure your format will play back properly in Windows Media Center or, failing that, at least in some Windows-compatible media player. Windows Media Center supports many formats right out of the box. However, the politics of the computer world dictate that there be few formats that Media Center cannot play back easily, among them the popular AAC format that Apple uses with its iPod. Support for open-source formats such as OGG (Ogg Vorbis) or Matroska is also fairly spotty. Fortunately, Media Center can play back most of these formats if an appropriate DirectSound or DirectShow filter is installed. Table 10-1 shows which formats Media Center can play back.

So long as you have the correct hardware and software installed, you should be able to play almost any source of digital audio in Windows Media Center. However, if you do end up with a source that is incompatible with Windows Media Center, you can often find third-party software that does work correctly. The downside of using third-party software is that the Media Center interface won't run them, which means you can no longer use a remote control to operate your Media Center PC.

Unfortunately, neither of the two main high-end audio formats, DVD-Audio and SACD, is compatible with Media Center. In both cases, this is a hardware limitation: SACDs require a special drive that is available only as a standalone device, and DVD-Audio exceeds the playback capabilities for most sound cards. However, many DVD-Audio discs include a lower-resolution version playable as a DVD-Video soundtrack. True DVD-Audio playback is supported by only a few high-end sound cards, which typically come with proprietary software that does not allow playback in Media Center.

Cross-Reference
You can find more information about Media Center and how to use it to play digital audio in Chapter 17.

Table 10-1   Media Center–Compatible Audio Sources

Source	Playable in Media Center	How to Play
CD Audio	Yes	Media Center.
DVD-Video	Yes*	Third-party DVD decoder software required; usually included with DVD-ROM drive.
DVD-Audio	No	Creative MediaSource DVD-Audio Player (bundled with high-end Creative Sound Cards that are DVD-Audio capable).
SACD	No	Not playable on any computer systems; requires special hardware.
FM Radio	Yes	Media Center. FM tuner required (built into some TV tuner cards).
Satellite Radio	No	TimeTrax (www.timetraxtech.com).
Internet Radio	Some	Media Center. Incompatible stations may be playable with Quicktime (www.apple.com/quicktime/).
MP3	Yes	Media Center.
WMA/WMV	Yes	Media Center.
AAC/M4A	Yes*	Used by iTunes and iPod. Can be made playable by installing Quicktime Alternative (www.free-codecs.com).
WAV/AIFF	Yes	Media Center. Both are file formats that contain basic PCM audio.
Ogg Vorbis	Yes*	Install OggDS DirectShow filter (www.vorbis.com) to make Ogg files playable in Media Center.

* Playback requires installation of additional software.

Digital Rights Management

As if compatibility didn't cause enough issues with Media Center, some files are *designed* to be incompatible with Media Center. For the most part, these are music files that you've down-loaded from an online music store such as iTunes or Sony Connect and have been modified to be playable using a specific program or computer. This is designed to reduce music piracy by preventing DRM-protected files from being played in programs that do not support the DRM. Media Center does support the DRM in protected WMA files, but users of iTunes or Sony Connect must use that software to play back purchased music — and no other.

Two workarounds exist to make DRM-protected music playable in Media Center. If the DRM allows it, it may be possible to convert the file into a format that Media Center does play. For example, iTunes allows CDs to be made from files downloaded from the iTunes store. Because there is no DRM on CDs, you could then re-import that CD into a Media Center–friendly format. The downsides of this approach are that it is labor-intensive, it may not be permitted by the DRM in the file, and it can affect the audio quality of the file. The other workaround is to strip the DRM from the file illegally. Software to do this can be found on the Internet, but, because it is illegal, it often works poorly and can lead to various legal and compatibility problems.

Receivers and Amplifiers

As mentioned earlier, the only essential pieces of hardware you will need to play digital audio in your Media Center PC are a sound card and speakers. Before you choose a sound card, how-ever, it is worth thinking a little about how you want to transfer audio to your speakers and what kind of speaker setup you want. For a low-end system, you will probably just want to let the sound card handle everything and buy a decent PC speaker set that plugs directly into the card. However, this approach can limit the selection of speakers, especially if you're interested in hi-fi.

Another possibility is to send the output signal from the sound card to an external amplifier or A/V receiver, which then amplifies the signal and passes it on to the speakers. If you already own a set of home theater speakers, this is probably your best option.

How you hook your speakers up to your Media Center PC will determine what you need from your sound card. If you connect to an external receiver, you may not need to spend as much on a sound card because the receiver will be able to do many things that the sound card would otherwise need to do. If you use a PC speaker system, you need a more powerful sound card that supports multichannel audio. Most important, connect up to any external receiver using a digital SPDIF interface (a PC speaker system will be fine using the analog 1/8" mini-jacks on the back of your sound card). More information about choosing a speaker system is available in the following chapter. However, before you choose a sound card, it is a good idea to decide what kind of speaker system you will use.

What a Sound Card Does

The sound card in your computer is primarily an output device. It provides a means of converting the digital bits of data in a digital audio file into analog audio suitable for delivery to a set of speakers. Alternatively, in the case of SPDIF, it may just pass along a steam of digital information to another device that knows what to do with it. However, a sound card can do much more than just convert digital audio to analog; it's also responsible for combining two or more digital sources, applying digital filters (such as an equalizer) to tweak how the audio sounds, and decoding the Dolby Digital surround sound found on DVDs. Exactly which of these tasks your sound card can do varies from model to model, but the best can do all of these and more. Tasks that your sound card cannot perform can almost always be done by the main processor with the proper software, but this adds to the load on the CPU and can affect its performance on other tasks, such as decoding a video file. An external receiver can also handle some tasks independently, such as decoding Dolby Digital or THX.

At its most basic level, a sound card works with the basic format of digital audio: PCM. A sound card works in one or more native sampling rates and bit depths, and if the source audio is not in a supported format, it must first be converted into a format that the sound card recognizes. In addition, a sound can output only a single sampling rate and bit depth at a time, so if the input format does not match the output format, the sound card must convert it before it is played. Sample rate and bit depth conversions are usually done in the sound card itself. However, decoding the file format and data format is the responsibility of the playback software and the codec (discussed previously), respectively, and is not handled by the sound card.

In addition to manipulating the sound format, the sound card is also responsible for mixing multiple sources together into a single output. This aspect of the sound card is most heavily used by computer games, which often combine multiple sound effects with the game's soundtrack. However, even a system that is intended to play back only a single source at a time may also utilize the mixing capabilities of a sound card. For example, an error message in Windows can be heard even when there is music playing in the background. The reason the error message can be heard is because the sound card has mixed the sound that Windows makes with the music that is playing so that both are heard simultaneously.

Another important responsibility of the sound card is DSP: Digital Sound Processing. Once again, this is most heavily used by computer games, which often apply audio filters dynamically to vary how certain effects sound with where they appear on screen. However, DSP is also used for equalizer effects and for simulating extra channels of sound when there are more speakers than source channels. DSP also has specialized uses, such a removing the vocal track from music for karaoke or artificially slowing the tempo of a sound file. Decoding Dolby Digital and other multichannel encoding schemes also falls under the DSP category.

What You Need in a Sound Card

Three factors combine to limit your choice of a suitable sound card—namely, the source media to which you wish to listen, how you intend to connect to your speakers, and the level of sound quality you need. At the very least, most sound cards are capable of playing back CD or DVD audio in stereo, and most can handle multichannel audio in up to 5.1 channels. If this is all you want, you may not need much more than the basic sound capabilities built into your motherboard. Conventional CDs are stored in 44.1 KHz/16-bit stereo format, which should be playable on almost any PC sound system, although some low-end sound cards may automatically up-sample the sampling rate to 48 KHz, which can diminish audio quality. Most audio from Internet sources also uses this format, including Internet radio and songs purchased from iTunes. DVDs are mastered in 48 KHz/16 bits, and may include a Dolby Digital soundtrack in up to 5.1 channels or even DTS sound in 6.1 channels.

However, if you're planning on exploring the world of high-resolution DVD-Audio, your audio requirements are more demanding. DVD-Audio supports up to 192 KHz/24-bit audio in stereo, and 96 KHz/24-bit audio in 5.1 channels. You must make sure your sound card can support these formats to get the most out of DVD-Audio. If you want to use DVD-Audio, you must also use the analog outputs on your sound card — unfortunately, DVD-Audio does not permit digital output via SPDIF because its sampling rate is too high. This limitation may make it tricky to connect your Media Center PC to an external receiver, because the most convenient and obvious connection, SPDIF, can't deliver everything you need. Furthermore, most sound cards do not use the same RCA interconnects that most receivers do, further complicating the procedure for using an external receiver with DVD-Audio.

Whether or not you plan to use an external receiver also influences what is required of the sound card. If you are using an external receiver and you don't plan to play DVD-Audio discs, all your sound card really needs is an SPDIF output to transfer the source audio to the receiver. So long as your receiver can decode Dolby Digital, the sound card need not even have more than two channels, because only the output function of the sound card will be used. If you will be using a PC speaker system, you will need to make sure that your sound card can decode Dolby Digital and (optionally) DTS audio or you better be willing to shell out money for software or hardware that can do so.

One word of caution about the SPDIF interface: The sampling rates and number of channels that can be sent across an SPDIF connection is limited, especially in the uncompressed PCM format. The official SPDIF specification allows a maximum 48 KHz/24-bit source with two channels. Alternatively, a compressed Dolby Digital or DTS bitstream can also be transported, in which case the number of channels and sampling frequency is dictated by the format of the bitstream. However, although many sound cards can decode Dolby Digital into PCM audio, very few can do the reverse. What this means is that, unless your source is in Dolby or DTS format to begin with, playback is effectively limited to stereo audio at a maximum of 48 KHz via SPDIF. This means that any multichannel source that uses the DSP on your sound card cannot be transported over an SPDIF connection without being down-converted to two channels. This includes a Dolby Digital stream that your sound card has decoded as well as the surround audio found in most computer games. A small number of sound cards can convert multichannel audio to Dolby Digital on the fly. These sound cards are capable of sending *any* multichannel signal over SPDIF, not just the ones that are already encoded in Dolby Digital. The downside of this solution is a small loss of quality that occurs in the conversion to Dolby Digital, making it unsuitable for playing high-resolution DVD-Audio.

Tip

An external receiver can still be used to play back DVD-Audio if the analog output on the sound card is used. However, additional mini-jack to RCA adapters may be required to make the proper connection. You can even continue to use SPDIF to transfer regular audio to your receiver. Just remember to select the right source on the receiver if you connect the analog and digital connectors to different inputs!

The last and probably the most important consideration is the quality of the sound card. If you're using SPDIF to transfer the audio to a receiver, the analog quality of the sound card is irrelevant, which makes it possible to use a lower-quality sound card. However, be aware that lower-quality sound cards often have less reliable timing clocks, which can degrade audio quality even over a digital connection. Plenty of reviews on the Internet claim to measure the quality of sound cards, but the best way to determine what kind of sound card you need is simply to listen to it. Once you've chosen your speakers (see Chapter 11), try hooking them up to the built-in sound on your motherboard. If you're satisfied, you may not need to buy a separate sound card at all. On the other hand, if you consider yourself an audiophile type, why not try auditioning several cards to see which one sounds best? For the most part, sound cards are cheap (~$100), and rejects can be resold on eBay if you can't return them to the seller for a refund or exchange them for something else.

Types of Sound Cards

The term *sound card* can sometimes be a bit of a misnomer. A large number of motherboards are already capable of producing good-quality sound without an additional sound card. In these cases, the tasks of the sound card are handled by special circuitry on the motherboard itself, although some features may be emulated by the software driver. Whether or not the integrated sound on the motherboard is good enough for your home theater depends on how you use it.

For a while now, almost all motherboards with audio capabilities have conformed to Intel's AC '97 specification. This specification dictates a certain minimum level of functionality and can also include a number of optional features. Because AC '97 is just a specification, the exact features and quality delivered depend on how well the manufacturer implements it in hardware and how many of its optional features are included. At the barest minimum, AC '97 supports 48 KHz, 16-bit audio in stereo—inadequate for a Home Theater PC. Fortunately, the specification also allows for multichannel audio and the 44.1 KHz CD sample rate, and most modern motherboards do support these capabilities. SPDIF is another optional feature of AC '97, although support for this feature is less common (but increasingly so, on the latest motherboards from most manufacturers).

If you don't plan to record or listen to high-resolution sources (mainly, DVD-Audio), most AC '97–compliant motherboards should be able to handle home theater audio just fine. However, motherboard audio quality varies quite significantly depending on the specific implementation, and it's not always easy to tell which ones are good enough for your needs. To a certain extent, the quality can be determined by the audio chip used, but even this is not a reliable way of judging how it sounds. One of the more common motherboard audio codec chip lines comes from Analog Devices, including the newer AD1981HD and AD1986A HD audio codecs. Another high-quality manufacturer of audio codecs is SigmaTel, whose latest offering is the eight-channel high-definition STAC9220/21 codec. Fortunately, its sound quality tends to be better than its competitors, although exactly how good it is still depends on the specific motherboard.

Recently, Intel has replaced the dated AC '97 specification with a much more robust specification: HD Audio. This increases the maximum sampling rate and bit depth to 192 KHz/32 bits, and provides support for up to 16 discrete channels. It can also drive two or more separate outputs simultaneously, although at the moment this feature is not yet supported in Windows. This allows a single computer to play a different audio track on two different sets of speakers — a movie soundtrack in one room and music in another, for example. SPDIF also seems to be more prevalent in HD Audio solutions. One final feature is of great interest to those using SPDIF: A Dolby Digital encoder can optionally be included, which allows any multichannel source to be sent over SPDIF by encoding it as a Dolby Digital bitstream. At the moment, HD Audio has appeared mainly on Intel-based motherboards, although, like AC '97 before it, it is likely to become standard on AMD and VIA systems as well.

Because it is so new, there is not a lot of information available about the quality of HD Audio, but the few tests run have shown a significant improvement in the signal-to-noise ratio that can be achieved relative to AC '97. However, like AC '97, sound quality varies depending on how well the standard is implemented. Any HD Audio–compliant motherboard should be able to handle the requirements of a home theater system with ease. The essentials, 48 KHz/16-bit audio in 5.1 Dolby Digital, are easily met by the HD Audio specification.

If you are really serious about audio and don't want to trust the unknown quality of a motherboard-based solution, you are left with two choices: a traditional PCI-based audio card or an external audio box that hooks up via USB or FireWire. Assuming your purpose for building a Media Center PC is to consolidate your home theater, it doesn't make a lot of sense to add another box to your computer, so the most convenient solution is probably an internal card. Be careful if you decide to use an internal card for this reason. Some internal audio cards use an external breakout box to house the large number of input and output connectors. External cards do have one theoretical benefit: They are isolated from the heavy electronic noise inside the computer case. Audiophiles have long recognized the importance of a clean electrical signal and power source to good-quality audio, and having an external sound card can help in both these respects. Apart from this one difference, external sound cards are essentially the same as internal cards and generally contain the same electrical components.

The sound card market is much like the motherboard and video card markets in that there are many brands out there, but their basic components are all pretty much the same. Motherboard chipsets come from either Intel, VIA, or nVidia, CPUs come from Intel or AMD, and video cards are all based on technology from either nVidia or ATI. The situation is similar for sound cards. Sound processors come from either E-MU or VIA. Creative Labs sells the lion's share of sound cards on the market. The sound processor in all of Creative Labs' recent offerings, the EMU10K series, was developed by a subsidiary of Creative Labs called E-MU. The remainder of the sound card market sells cards based on VIA's Envy24 sound processor.

The most ubiquitous sound card is the Creative Labs Sound Blaster Audigy, which comes in half a dozen versions that differ mostly in the software package that is offered. In addition to providing high-quality audio, it also includes a hardware DSP, which reduces the processing load on the CPU. Because Creative Labs designed the EAX standard that is used by many computer games, it can also conform to a more recent version of EAX than most of its competitors, who must pay licensing fees to Creative to use it. However, as mentioned earlier, DSP (and EAX in particular) is a minor consideration for home theater audio. Far more important is the quality of the audio, which, fortunately, Creative can also deliver. In its latest incarnation, the Audigy 2 series can deliver up to 192 KHz/24-bit audio with up to 7.1 channels. It also provides a digital SPDIF connection. Most importantly, the sound quality it offers is a step above motherboard audio — even HD Audio.

Unlike the EMU24K processor in the Audigy, VIA's Envy24 sound processor does not have a hardware DSP, which means it relies on software to achieve these effects. This has little practical effect, especially if the primary use of the card is not gaming. Like the EMU24K, the Envy24 supports up to 192 KHz/24-bit audio and 7.1 channels. Most Envy24-based sound cards are similar in quality to the Audigy, although some tests have given the Audigy a slight advantage. It is notable that Envy24-based cards dominate the Pro and Audiophile markets, however, so this advantage may be mainly theoretical.

Tip

An excellent resource for sound card reviews is the audio section of the ExtremeTech Web site (`www.extremetech.com/category2/0,1695,838538,00.asp`). Here you can find in-depth tests of audio hardware, including signal-to-noise ratios, CPU usage, and more.

Going Pro: Audio Interface Cards

At the top end of the audio card market are professional "audio interface" cards that retail for hundreds of dollars. If you're sparing no expense on your Media Center PC, you may want to know what additional benefits this kind of card provides. The short answer to this question is, "Not much." Professional-caliber audio interface cards are typically used for mixing and recording audio — not playing it back. Unless you plan on setting up a recording studio in your living room, you don't need the multiple inputs, low-latency mixing, or additional MIDI support that these cards provide. Audio interface cards are built around the same audio processors and chipsets that are used in the consumer market, and there is little difference in the playback quality between professional audio interface cards and consumer-level sound cards.

Perhaps the only reason to use an audio interface card is to connect your Media Center PC to an external receiver via an analog connection, as is required by DVD-Audio. The additional connectors that professional cards typically offer may make it easier to make this connection without running the signal through several quality-degrading plug converters. In fact, such a card may be necessary to take full advantage of the quality offered by DVD-Audio.

Installing Your Sound Card

The process of installing a sound card has two parts: hardware and software. If you're using your motherboard's onboard sound, there is no hardware installation required: It's already built into the motherboard. However, no matter what kind of sound card you are using, you will always need to do some software configuration before you can use all the features of the card.

Hardware Installation

Installing a sound card is quite simple. If you're using an internal sound card, you simply need to slide it into an open PCI slot on your motherboard and connect any internal plugs. Some cards may require an external power source and should be plugged in using the appropriate plug from the power supply. There may also be internal input cables, typically from the optical drives in your system. The plugs for these connections are typically located along the top edge of the card, where they can be easily accessed even when the card is installed in a case (see Figure 10-1). These internal connections are rarely essential. Even if the optical drives are not connected directly to the sound card, it is still possible to play back CD or DVD audio by routing the signal through the computer itself.

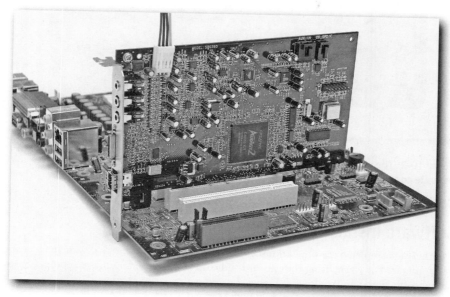

FIGURE 10-1: Sound cards plug into a PCI slot (the white box on the motherboard). Our sound card also needed to be plugged into an external power source, which can be seen at the top of the card.

In addition to plugging in the sound card internally, some sound cards have external breakout boxes that need to be plugged in. All of these cards have slightly different connectors, but the connection on the Sound Blaster Audigy 2 Platinum ZS Pro is fairly typical (see Figure 10-2). It consists of a main data cable and a FireWire-style connector, both of which must be plugged in for the breakout box to function.

External sound cards are even simpler. Because they're self-contained, there's just one USB or FireWire plug that plugs into the back of your motherboard. Make sure you check that your motherboard supports whichever connection your sound card requires. Keep in mind that there are two versions of USB: 1.1 and 2.0. New motherboards should all support USB 2.0, which is faster and backward compatible with USB 1.1 devices. However, if you're using an older motherboard, make sure it either supports USB 2.0 or that your sound card supports USB 1.1. About half of the motherboards currently on the market support FireWire (sometimes called IEEE 1394). If your sound card requires a FireWire connection, make sure your motherboard supports it. Some external sound cards may also require a separate power source.

FIGURE 10-2: The external breakout box for our Audigy 2 Platinum ZS Pro required two separate connections to the main sound card.

Software Installation

After you've completed the physical installation of your sound card, its software must be installed and configured. If you're using the onboard audio on your motherboard, the appropriate software can probably found on the driver CD that shipped with your motherboard. Most likely, it can be found in the setup utility on that CD under the name of Intel HD Audio or SoundMAX, although many other names are possible. A separate sound card has its own driver CD and may come with a software bundle in addition to the basic driver software. No matter how much software your sound card comes with, the only essential software is the driver for your sound card; the other applications should be installed only if you think you have a use for them.

The installation of the software driver is different for every card, but generally speaking most cards come with good instructions for this portion of the setup. Most of the time, the software installation should be as simple as putting the CD in your computer, finding the appropriate menu option, and following the instructions in the installation wizard.

Configuring the software is a little more complicated. Although the documentation for your sound card can tell you *how to do things* (and hopefully does a good job of it), it cannot tell you *what you need to do*, because this depends on your intended use. The specific details of configuring a sound card vary depending on the manufacturer and capabilities of the model, but because all are capable of roughly the same things, they should have similar options. Unless you have exactly the same model as our demo (a Creative Labs Audigy 2 Platinum ZS Pro), the precise process you follow to set up your sound card for home theater audio will be different from ours, but the basic idea should be the same.

The exact configuration required depends a lot on how you have connected your speakers. If you are using SPDIF, you need to make sure that the sample rate of the SPDIF connection is correct, that you have disabled the Dolby Digital decoder on your sound card, and that your sound card does not attempt to play audio that cannot be carried over SPDIF.

Depending on the model of your sound card, you may need to enable the SPDIF output. This option may also be called digital output, because some PC speakers use SPDIF. For best audio quality, the sample rate of your SPDIF connection should match the sample rate of your source: 48 KHz for DVDs, and 44.1 KHz for most other sources. Dolby Digital and DTS sources do not require the sample rate to be set. Not all sound cards allow the user to change the SPDIF sample rate, so don't worry if you can't find this option. Rest assured that your sound card will take care of things for you.

Because the main reason for using SPDIF is to allow an external receiver to handle multichannel audio, it is important that you don't let your sound card try to decode a multichannel Dolby Digital or DTS signal before it gets to the receiver. Make sure you find the option to disable on-card decoding; otherwise, you won't get true multichannel audio from your receiver (see Figure 10-3). At best, your receiver may try to simulate multiple channels by applying Dolby Pro-Logic II to the stereo signal it receives from the sound card. The last thing you should do in an SPDIF configuration should be to set the number of speakers to 2/2.1, even if you actually have more. This is because SPDIF audio is limited to stereo unless Dolby Digital or DTS encoding is used. As long as you disable the Dolby decoder on your sound card, setting the speaker configuration to 2/2.1 ensures that stereo sources remain in stereo, while 5.1 or 6.1 sources in Dolby Digital or DTS format pass through untouched.

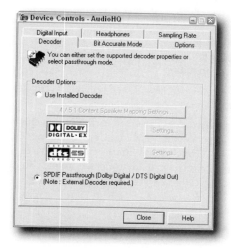

FIGURE 10-3: Dolby Digital and DTS decoding should be disabled when using an external receiver and enabled when using a PC speaker system.

Configuring your system for use with a PC speaker system is more straightforward. PC speaker systems can be connected in two ways: Older systems use analog 1/8" mini-jacks to receive their signals, but some newer systems receive the signal via a special SPDIF connection (for 2.1 systems) or a special 1/8" jack that carries a digital signal (for multichannel systems). Some sound cards require the proper output format to be selected. Look for an analog-only or digital-only output option to select the proper output format. You should also make sure that Dolby

Digital decoding is enabled on your sound card. This will ensure that multichannel DVDs play back properly. If your sound card doesn't support Dolby Digital, you can purchase a software decoder. The last — and most crucial — configuration item is to set the number of speakers correctly (see Figure 10-4). Most likely this will be either 5.1 or 7.1, but a number of other settings can be used. The number you choose should match the number of physical speakers you plug in, but don't forget that the subwoofer counts as .1, and isn't included in the first number.

FIGURE 10-4: The speaker setting should match the number of physical speakers you have unless you are using SPDIF. If you have digitally connected speakers, you need to make sure that the output signal is also digital.

The last aspect of software installation concerns the codecs discussed earlier in this chapter. Should you wish to use any file or data formats that Windows Media Center does not support natively, you must install the proper programs and DirectSound filters before you try to play them. Codecs can be installed at any time, but installing too many codecs at a time can cause conflicts and make certain formats unplayable.

Best HTPC Sound Card Options

The best technique for choosing an HTPC sound card is probably to audition the onboard audio that comes with your motherboard first and then explore add-in sound card options if you're not satisfied. Motherboard audio chips come from a variety of manufacturers, including Analog Devices, AKM, Sigmatel, Crystal, Creative, Yamaha, Avance Logic, Realtek, and VIA, but reliable information about them is hard to find. So, the best way to judge sound quality is simply to listen to it. Most major manufacturers use Analog Devices for AC '97 sound (SoundMAX), and the most common HD Audio chips come from Realtek. It's probably best to find a motherboard that supports HD Audio if you're seriously considering using onboard audio, because that specification offers better features and sound quality.

If you decide that motherboard audio just isn't for you, Table 10-2 offers an overview of what's available. In terms of quality, the sound card market picks up where motherboard audio leaves off, but some onboard audio chips may sound better than a cheap external card. The cleanest and best sounding cards, however, offer better sound than any motherboard audio. As befits its position in the market, we list several products from Creative Labs. This reflects the large number of Creative products more than an outright recommendation (although they are very good). Unless otherwise noted, all products support up to 192 KHz/24-bit audio in stereo and 48 KHz/24-bit audio for up to 7.1 channels. They also all support SPDIF output, although not all will take SPDIF input.

Table 10-2   Quality Sound Card Vendors

Vendor	Model	Remarks/URL
Creative Labs	Sound Blaster Audigy 4 Pro	The top offering from Creative Labs. Differs from the Audigy 2 ZS Platinum Pro only in a slightly higher-rated signal-to-noise ratio. Costs about $270 (www.creativelabs.com).
Creative Labs	Sound Blaster Audigy 2 ZS Platinum Pro	Top of the Audigy 2 line. Comes with an external breakout box. Costs about $210.
Creative Labs	Sound Blaster Live! 24-bit	Low-end card with 96 KHz/24-bit capability in 7.1 channels; quality on par with top-end motherboard audio. Costs about $30.
Creative Labs	Sound Blaster Extigy	External USB sound card based on original Audigy internal card. 96 KHz/24 bit in 5.1 channels. Costs about $130.
Chaintech	AV-710	Budget product with audio quality on par with or above Audigy 2; based on VIA Envy24 sound processor. Costs about $25 (www.chaintech.com.tw).
M-Audio	Revolution 7.1	Bottom-tier card from well-known pro audio company; based on VIA Envy24 chip. Popular in audiophile market. Costs about $90 (www.m-audio.com).
E-MU	1212M	Professional-caliber card from company that designed the EMU10K sound processor that powers the Audigy line; uses higher-quality DAC components. Costs about $200 (www.emu.com).

Continued

Table 10-2 *(continued)*

Vendor	Model	Remarks/URL
AudioTrak	Prodigy 7.1	Another Envy24-based card that competes with the M-Audio Revolution 7.1 in audiophile market. Costs about $90 (www.audiotrak.de/eng/).
HiTec Digital Audio	X-Mystique 7.1 Gold	New high-end card featuring Dolby Digital encoding on the fly, also known as Dolby Digital Live; based on a audio processor from C-Media. Maximum sample rate 96 KHz. Costs about $100 (www.ihda.co.kr or www.bluegears.com [U.S. Distributor]).

All these are well-known vendors and offer good value for HTPC use. Creative Labs was kind enough to lend us a Sound Blaster Audigy 2 ZS Platinum Pro for this book.

Wrapping Up

Digital audio (and audio in general) is an immensely complex topic, with many ins and outs we could skim past in this chapter. At the moment, there's no one product that does absolutely everything. Although the best-quality audio comes from using an SPDIF connection and an external receiver, this option is incompatible with DVD-Audio and won't play back EAX-compatible sound in games properly. On the other hand, a PC speaker system can bypass these problems, but may not be as good a choice for hi-fi sound.

Much depends on what you expect in terms of audio capability. If you can't afford a high-end speaker system, the onboard audio on your motherboard may provide sufficient sound quality. In that case, you probably don't need a sound card to experience surround sound in 5.1 or 7.1 channels. On the other hand, if you want to mortgage your house to build a Media Center PC, audio is an excellent place to sink more than a few dollars.

HTPC Audio Setups

S ound is an increasingly important form of output on many PCs, but it's arguably more important on HTPCs, where sound includes a wealth of options. Of course, sound is pretty much all there is to music and radio, but it's also important to multimedia playback, especially television programs and movies.

When you set up a Media Center PC, producing sound means taking one of two possible paths. Together these define the basis for this chapter. In general, you must decide if you want to integrate your Media Center PC with existing audiovisual equipment to make use of its speakers and playback controls, or if you'd prefer to drive speakers from your HTPC instead.

As we lead you through various options involved in making either approach work, you have a chance to dig into some interesting issues related to making the most of PC audio. In this chapter, we cover those issues in this order:

➤ **Loudspeaker primer:** There are many kinds of speakers and also many kinds of speaker configurations. Here you get a chance to tell the woofers from the tweeters and understand what speakers (and speaker components) do to deliver sound to your ears.

➤ **PC sound outputs:** Whether built into your motherboard or installed in an adapter card slot, PC sound cards offer a cornucopia of outputs. Here you examine them, what they're for, and why they're there.

➤ **Connecting to output gear:** Whether you are dealing with a receiver, a pre-amplifier, or a speaker controller setup, you can take various routes to ferry sound from your HTPC to your loudspeakers. We distinguish among types of connections available and explain how they compare and contrast. We also cover the pros and cons of attaching speakers directly to your Media Center PC versus linking your Media Center PC's audio outputs to inputs on audiovisual equipment (at least some of which you probably own already).

➤ **Decoding multichannel sound:** In a time when sound cards (and motherboards with built-in audio) can produce or decode all kinds of multichannel formats, making use of that capability raises interesting considerations (if not outright challenges). Here, we explain those options and tell you how to decide if you can (or can't) use them.

➤ **Speaker placement:** Various types of multichannel sound assume certain speaker configurations. Here we describe the number and types of speakers associated with multichannel sound schemes and describe prevailing ideas on optimal placement.

➤ **Best HTPC speaker options:** This is where we recommend potential gear for your Media Center PC, plus a few tried and true online resources to help you dig more deeply into high-end PC audio should you feel so inclined.

The quality of sound in any environment depends on many characteristics. Some, like the shape and size of the room in which the equipment lives, go beyond the scope of what a book about building Home Theater PCs can cover. Others, like discussing the vices and virtues of high-end loudspeakers and components, likewise go way beyond what we can explore or explain in any depth. Thus, this chapter maintains three primary foci as it tackles the topics just listed:

■ **Making the most of your PC audio outputs:** We explain what kinds of connections and cables you can use to hook things up, but also indicate which of them are most likely to produce the best-sounding results.

■ **Doing the decode thing:** We describe various multichannel sound schemes, such as Dolby Digital, THX, and DTS, and what's needed to use them to their fullest effect.

■ **Making the best sounds:** We describe the kinds of equipment you can use and rules for speaker placement intended to create the most listenable sounds possible.

In the sections that follow, you'll get the chance to understand the special significance of audio for a Media Center PC. And as usual in these chapters, you'll also find a table of recommended PC audio vendors near the end, with a special emphasis on loudspeakers.

A Loudspeaker Primer

Simply put, a *loudspeaker* is an electromechanical device that uses some mechanical means to turn electrical signals into audible sound. At the most fundamental level, this usually means somehow forcing a flexible surface to vibrate so that it emits sounds in the audible spectrum. For most humans, this runs from about 30 cycles per second, or hertz (Hz), up to about 21,000 cycles per second, or 21 KHz. Some loudspeakers use powerful magnets that cause conical paper elements to vibrate (and most conventional speakers use this kind of technology); others use pieces of aluminized mylar, metal ribbons, or crystal films instead (as in electrostatic, planar-magnetic, or piezo-electric speakers, respectively).

Because the audible sound spectrum covers a moderately broad range, you'll also find speakers that incorporate separate elements intended to produce sounds in specific sub-ranges of the overall spectrum. These include the following:

■ **Bass elements (woofer or subwoofer):** Because low-frequency sounds are essentially omni-directional (and often sound like they come from everywhere), most speaker systems include only one subwoofer. These large, heavy enclosures often include an integrated amplifier as well as a sizable 8" to 20" loudspeaker. The typical frequency range for such a device is from 0 to 200 Hz, or the very bottom of the sound spectrum.

- **Midrange elements (driver or midrange):** This is the part of the sound spectrum that humans hear best and falls in a relatively narrow range between 200 Hz and 2,000 Hz. Another set of medium-sized speakers that may be somewhere between 2" and 8" usually delivers sounds in this range.

- **High-frequency elements (tweeter):** This part of the sound spectrum runs from 2,000 Hz to the limits of human hearing. Most audio equipment is tested only to 20,000 Hz, though hearing tests indicate that some exceptional individuals can hear as high as 23,000 to 24,000 Hz. Small speaker elements appropriately called tweeters handle this chore. Most such elements are 2" in diameter or smaller; many such elements use special materials to deliver clean, crisp sound at these frequencies.

There's another element in the picture that coordinates the activities of all the elements in a modern loudspeaker system. It's called a *cross-over*, or an *electronic cross-over*, and it basically divides up sound streams on the basis of frequency range, so that low sounds go to the woofer or subwoofer, midrange sounds go to midrange speakers, and high-frequency sounds to the tweeters. The cross-over points described in the preceding list items (200 Hz to divide bass from midrange, and 2,000 Hz to divide midrange from high-frequency) are more illustrative than prescriptive. Actual audio components vary these numbers, but these divisions exist to reflect the physics of sound: low, slow sound waves are big, and require larger mechanical elements and surfaces to generate them whereas fast, high waves are small and require smaller, faster mechanical elements and surfaces to create them. This electronic division of labor allows speaker components to concentrate on those parts of the sound spectrum they handle best and helps to produce realistic, fully dimensional sound.

Most home and PC audio systems handle multichannel sound. This term covers a multitude of formats from stereo (two channels) up to various forms of eight-channel sound (which usually consists of right and left channels for front (2), side-middle (2), and back speakers (2), plus one center channel at the front, and one subwoofer channel for low-frequency sounds). In general, the more you spend on a speaker system, the better the sound (and also, the larger the volume of space that you can fill with the sound produced).

PC Sound Outputs

Audio is an interesting collection of technologies and playback devices, as much for PCs as it is for home entertainment and audiovisual equipment. This world is rife with proprietary sound encoding schemes as well as more generic multichannel schemes. Most high-end PC sound cards (or their built-in motherboard equivalents) support at least half the items in the following list, as do many home receivers or pre-amplifiers:

- **Stereo:** Basic two-channel sound divided into right and left channel. Most commercial music and radio broadcasts are in stereo, including music CDs. Other common digital music formats easily decode into stereo.

- **2.1:** This is a simple extension to stereo that sends low-frequency sounds to a subwoofer along with right and left channels for midrange and high-frequency sound. It's a minimal form of surround sound technology where the idea is to create three-dimensional sound by mixing the sounds for each speaker to enhance spatial effects.

Note Surround sound specifications tend to take the form *n*.1 to indicate the presence of a single subwoofer, along with *n* channels; 2.1 thus indicates only right and left front channels.

- **5.1:** This is a more sophisticated approach that adds a center channel in the front to the left and right speakers, with two rear (surround) speakers to provide enhanced spatial effects and sound. The sixth channel is the bass channel, also known as the low-frequency effects or LFE channel.

- **6.1:** This adds a single center rear to those defined for the 5.1 scheme.

- **7.1:** This adds left and right channels on the left and right side positions relative to where listeners are sitting. Thus, they have three or four speakers in front of them (right and left front channels, center channel, and bass channel, though the latter can go almost anywhere in a room), two more speakers to their right and left (center-side channels), and two more speakers behind them (left and right rear channels).

- **Dolby Digital:** A trademarked name for Dolby Laboratories proprietary sound encoding schemes. These come in various formats, the most common of which gives its name to this list item. It uses a 5.1 format but also supports stereo and mono playback as well. Other Dolby offerings include Dolby Digital EX, which can simulate either 6.1 (single rear surround channel) or 7.1 (dual rear surround channels) formats; Dolby Digital Surround EX, which creates true 6.1 or 7.1 formats; and Dolby Digital Plus, which increases encoding bit rates for higher fidelity and supports up to 13.1 format.

- **DTS:** Digital theatre system, a proprietary multichannel surround sound format used for commercial- and consumer-grade sound systems, especially for movie soundtracks on film and DVD. The basic DTS format is a 5.1 surround sound scheme, but other formats are also supported. The most common of these is DTS-ES, which adds information for one or two rear channel speakers, for playback in 6.1 or 7.1.

- **THX:** A proprietary sound playback system for home and movie theaters from the company of the same name. THX home theater is a certification system that requires consumer devices and equipment to meet certain criteria to qualify; covered devices include DVD players, audio equalizers, receivers and pre-amplifiers, amplifiers, speakers, and cables. THX is compatible with both Dolby Digital and DTS.

Why do these various schemes matter? They matter mostly because home theater users want to reproduce the sound encoding schemes on their DVDs or for TV shows, generally with the hope that a home theater can be made to sound as much like a real movie theater as possible. But the real reason for seeking support for any multichannel sound format is to reproduce a sound track with the same fidelity as the original was recorded.

The fundamental principle that applies to playing back multichannel sound is this: every element in the playback chain must support the format, or at least be able to pass it on unaltered. Thus, if your sound card can produce some or all of these formats, they must then be handed over to a receiver, a pre-amplifier, or a speaker controller. Otherwise, the sound card might simply take a digital data stream and send it out the SPDIF output port without doing anything more to it. But only if the device that handles the digital input understands and can reproduce these formats will the right sounds be directed to the proper speakers. And of course, the playback setup has to match the same number of channels and speakers as used to record the original. Otherwise, the best you'll probably be able to do is either good quality stereo output or some form of synthesized multichannel sound — which never sounds as good as "the real thing."

Tip

Let's call this fundamental principle end-to-end multichannel playback. It's something we'll return to throughout this chapter, and something that's very important to getting the right results from any audio setup, with or without an HTPC.

Connecting to Output Gear

If you'll recall the information presented at the beginning of this chapter, it posed two choices for where to take output from your Media Center PC. Option number one is to some piece of AV gear — probably an AV receiver or pre-amplifier — so you can use your existing gear to play back content that originates from your PC, as well as your other signal sources. Option number two is to cable up your Media Center PC to some kind of multichannel speaker setup, possibly skipping other typical AV equipment completely.

The Entertainment Center Still Rules

Although it's obvious to anybody who appreciates MCE's ability to handle radio, TV, music, and DVDs that Microsoft is aiming at a home entertainment center takeover, there are still plenty of reasons why connecting a Media Center PC to AV gear makes sense, including the following:

- **Existing investments in speakers and gear.** Unless you really need to buy new, why not use what you've already got? Besides, anybody who's serious about audio still wants more inputs, speakers, and signal processing equipment than all-PC rigs enable.

- **Legacy audio inputs still appeal to many families, especially those with members who have large collections of vinyl disks, audiotapes, and what have you.** For those with large laser disc or videotape holdings, the same thing also applies. To some extent the Media Center PC appeals to this crowd as a means to digitizing and archiving existing collections of older media and music, but it can by no means simply step in and sweep all that history away. Many long hours and lots of pleasant effort are likely to be involved first!

- **What best fits many large living and family rooms is still an entertainment center and a whopping big set of speakers set around some kind of big display** (mostly rear-projection TV because of its high value-to-cost ratio, but also an increasing number of LCD and plasma displays). A Media Center PC is welcome to make a place for itself there, but it lacks the infrastructure and support to supplant that kind of setup as yet.

- **Because of fallout from legal and regulatory controls planned for HDTV in North America (the story's different in Europe), Media Center PC can't yet do for HDTV what it does for standard television.** Until Media Center PC can handle satellite and cable-based HDTV as well as it currently handles conventional TV, TV buffs will continue to buy and use other gear in their home entertainment centers to do the job. This probably won't change until 2006 or perhaps even 2007, in some future version of MCE. Today, MCE's HDTV support is best described as "half-hearted."

- **Output capabilities on high-end AV gear still outstrips PC equivalents.** Serious home theater buffs won't accept the kind of DVD playback you get from most PC DVD players. Lack of progressive scan is just one of the most glaring nits that real home theater aficionados are happy to pick with PC-based DVD offerings. Other buffs are happy to pick nits with other types of gear (CD players, amplifiers, signal processing) as well until the cows come home.

So why bother with a PC-only home entertainment setup? Good question. Though the family or living room may not be the place for this, it's still worth considering for other circumstances. These include office setups, dorm rooms, or other small spaces where the large footprint of a typical home entertainment center chock-full of AV gear is too much for its surroundings. That's when a Media Center PC with a good set of self-amplified 5.1 or 7.1 speakers does a nice job indeed of playing back the various kinds of inputs that MCE handles. Some of this gear even provides its own crafty ways to integrate other devices as well, including high-end CD or DVD players, and MP3 or other mobile music players likewise.

Making the Sound Connection

When you cable up from your PC to some kind of sound output, you've got your choice of two kinds of connections: SPDIF and speaker channel ports. As described in more detail in Chapter 12, SPDIF stands for Sony/Philips Digital Interface. It defines an all-digital transmission mechanism to move audio information from one device to another. Speaker channel ports usually map directly to specific speaker channels such as front right and left, center and LFE, and surround right and left.

SPDIF connections come in two formats. Although one is universally called digital coax (short for digital coaxial), it uses the same kind of RCA jack common for many types of audio cables. The other is an optical jack format called TOSLINK, a way of using fiber optic cables to interconnect audio devices. Toshiba originally developed TOSLINK as a way to link high-end audio CD players to receivers (the generic name for this standard link-up is EIAJ optical); today most receivers and pre-amps offer four or more optical input jacks for CD and DVD players, as well as other devices — such as a Media Center PC. Optical digital cables cost nearly twice as much as coax digital, THX certified or not.

So-called digital coaxial cables are indistinguishable by eye from ordinary RCA cables. That said, they're built to carry much greater frequency ranges than conventional audio cables (to accommodate all eight channels in a 7.1 scheme, you need at least three times the bandwidth of a conventional uncompressed audio cable to convey all the data). If you plan to play back THX-encoded movies, the company claims you must use THX-certified cables for best results. These cables cost two to three times the price of ordinary digital audio RCA cables, but may still be worth the added price.

Conventional wisdom says that because of its vastly higher bandwidth and immunity to electromagnetic interference (EMI) and radio frequency interference (RFI), optical cables are preferable to coaxial. Either does the job, yet some audiophiles express strong preferences for one or the other (but unfortunately, some favor optical with the same rabid passion that others favor coaxial). One of your authors opted for optical because a large (42") CRT-based television set loomed immediately above the AV receiver, but both have used optical and coaxial cables with acceptable results.

Either way, digital outputs are preferable to speaker channel outputs from your PC (these are sometimes called direct attachments, or direct speaker attachments). These appear in Chapter 4 in Figures 4-2 and 4-4, and use various colors (such as lime green, black, and orange) to label speaker channels to which they correspond. RCA mini-jacks are the most common type of connectors for such outputs, which link up to similar inputs on speaker rigs (but not to the various receivers and pre-amplifiers we surveyed for this book). Better PC speaker rigs — including those we reviewed for this book — support both optical and coaxial digital audio inputs as well (and that's what we used for our auditioning, mostly because it was much easier to hook up one cable instead of three or more).

Decoding Multichannel Sound

The principle of end-to-end multichannel playback means that your receiver, pre-amp, or speaker rig must be able to recognize any multichannel format you want it to play back. This is a case where careful reading of product specifications or features lists is critical, because that information is normally buried somewhere inside the documentation.

At the risk of oversimplification, here are some suggestions you should put to work, to figure out if the link-up you're considering (or trying to make work) does what you want:

- If your sound card or the sound circuitry built into your motherboard supports your chosen format (be it more generic 5.1, 6.1, or 7.1 formats, or proprietary formats like Dolby Digital and DTS), you're off to a good start.

- If your receiver, pre-amp, or speaker rig documentation specifically mentions support for your chosen format, keep going.

- If you hook your Media Center PC to your receiver, pre-amp, or speaker rig and it recognizes your chosen format as you try to play some material recorded in that format, you're in good shape.

- If playback occurs and you can hear output from all the speakers in your setup, you're home free — things are working like they should.

The worst case occurs when your receiver, pre-amp, or speaker rig doesn't recognize your chosen format. In that case, you must either replace that gear, or see how well or poorly it handles things. Considering that a 7.1-capable AV receiver or pre-amp costs at least $250 (all the way up to stratospheric five-figure prices for high-end audiophile pre-amps), you may decide to live with the status quo for a while before buying anything new.

If the product documentation claims it recognizes the format but doesn't in practice, you must poke around in your device setup — user support forums for audio equipment online are many, and all are chock-full of the nitty-gritty details so often essential to make things work. If a device recognizes input but there's no output on all channels, check your speaker cables to make sure everything's properly connected. If the wires are right, re-read the previous bit of advice and double-check your device configuration. If all else fails, go online or try a phone call for some tech support. Good luck!

Speaker Placement

Speaker placement is an interesting mix of art and science because the shape of the listening room and the acoustic characteristics of its surfaces (walls, ceiling, and floor, along with any objects in the space) have much bearing on what you hear, as well as where you put the speakers you use. The key is to identify that part of the room where you want things to sound best, and to combine careful listening inside that area with whatever tinkering or experimenting you undertake to arrive at what sounds best.

That said, the experts do have some recommendations for speaker placement worth pondering, if not following. Before we convey this advice, with the help of a diagram, we introduce some terminology related to 5.1 and 7.1 speaker layouts:

- The front speaker array consists of the front right and left channel speakers (the only two channels for conventional stereo, in other words) plus the center channel speaker.
- The subwoofer handles the really low sounds, to provide low-frequency effects (LFE).
- The speakers to the side on left and right are called the left surround and right surround, respectively (they are part of a 7.1 configuration, but omitted from its 5.1 counterpart).
- The speakers to the rear are sometimes called the left surround back (or rear) and right surround back (or rear). In 6.1 schemes, there's only one "center rear."

With this terminology not only in mind, but also with a look at the diagram in Figure 11-1, here's what most audio experts recommend for speaker placement guidelines:

- The front speaker array should be placed at or near listener ear level. Let's assume everybody's sitting on the sofa shown in Figure 11-1 and facing the front array. Achieving proper placement often means raising speakers for right and left channels off the floor on stands, and making sure the center channel's traditional spot on top of the TV isn't too high above ear level.

  If you've got big speakers, you may not have precise control over speaker height. But if you examine such speakers closely, you'll see that the midrange and tweeter elements tend to be between 30 and 40 inches off the floor, which corresponds to normal ear height for most seated humans over 15 years old.

  Arguments about right and left channel speaker placement can get boisterous among experts, but many take the approach shown in Figure 11-1 — namely angling the speakers so that their center axis lines up on a 45-degree angle splitting the corners of the listening room. This can improve sound if you have that luxury, but it's not worth stressing over if you don't. What's more important is that right and left front speakers are positioned on the edges of the prime listening zone (the right- and left-hand ends of the sofa in the figure as shown).

Tip One point on which the majority of audio experts and audiophiles do agree is that placing speakers some distance from the back wall (at least two feet, if not more) results in better sound than placing them right up against the wall. Basically, this lets you use the wall as a natural sounding board that improves sound quality at least a little.

- Subwoofer placement is the least critical of that for any speaker, but it's smart to experiment with multiple positions and let your ears help you make a final choice. That said, big, heavy subwoofer enclosures often end up underneath coffee or end tables simply to get them out of the way, so be practical when choosing your options.

- Surround speakers should be roughly three feet (about a meter) above listener ear level and placed directly on either side of the prime listening area (as shown in Figure 11-1, they are centered on either side of the couch).

- The rear surround speakers should also be about three feet (or a meter) above listener ear level and roughly parallel with the front channel speakers.

As nice as these ideal rules of placement might be, you must live with the realities of room dimensions, available furniture, and issues involved in running wires to speakers. That means making compromises here and there, but this tells you where to aim.

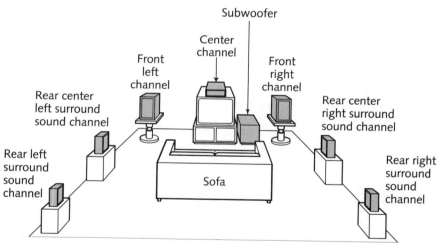

FIGURE 11-1: Speaker placement works best when you identify and then work around a "prime listening area" (shown as a sofa here).

Wiring Is Key

If you're serious about a living room 5.1 or 7.1 sound system, you must spend some money on wiring. The best options for surround speakers (whether to the side or to the rear) usually involve one of two options: first, running wires through the space above the room and then fishing down into the walls for final positioning; or second, purchasing special flat-format under-carpet wiring to bring wires up from the baseboard near the proper position.

Audio cables come in many sizes and grades and vary from wires that look like phone cords to massive wire bundles. Generally, it's smart to spend extra money and buy the best audio-grade wiring you can afford, so as to deliver the cleanest signal to your speakers. This is a case where heavier gauge wiring is better than narrower gauge — paradoxically this means a smaller numbered wire gauge, so that 12-gauge wire is bigger than 24 gauge. Well-known audio vendors such as Monster Cable, Acoustic Research, and PureAV (a subsidiary of Belkin), among many others, all offer top-notch audio wiring.

For home installation, it may be cheaper to buy entire spools rather than purchasing only prefab cables in fixed lengths. If you hire a cable installer or home theater specialist to run your cables, make sure they purchase digital audio-quality cable.

Matching Speakers to Your Needs

When it comes to selecting typical speakers for 5.1 or 7.1 sound schemes, interesting options are available from speaker vendors. Many of those that sell 5.1 or 7.1 speaker sets use identical elements for all speakers except the subwoofer. Although this may seem counterintuitive, it's actually not a bad strategy. It keeps things simple and easy to install, and also creates a consistent look in your family room. Numerous products of this kind — often marketed as surround speakers, or surround speaker systems — are available from lots of vendors, including PC-oriented companies like Logitech and Creative Labs, as well as audio outfits like Bose, JBL, Klipsch, and many others.

Comparing and contrasting speakers is beyond this book's scope. Let's just leave this subject by observing that for as little as $100 to $200 or for as much as you'd care to spend, you can find listenable 5.1 or 7.1 speaker systems for a home entertainment system. For under $1,000 you can buy some highly regarded products, if you'd care to spend a bit more. Figure 11-2 shows a very acceptable Logitech speaker system.

FIGURE 11-2: For about $400 the Logitech Z-5500 speaker system not only offers great sound, but also includes a snazzy, powerful control unit.

Best HTPC Speaker Options

Table 11-1 mentions numerous vendors that offer high-quality 5.1 or 7.1 speaker systems suitable for home theater (and HTPC) use. Of these, we've gotten great results with products from Logitech, Creative Labs, Bose, and JBL. But many vendors make good to great speaker systems, so you needn't restrict your options to outfits we explicitly mention. Appendix H provides numerous pointers to Web sites and publications that cater to home theater aficionados or to outright audiophiles; please consult them to help your own selection process along.

Table 11-1   Quality Speaker System Vendors

Vendor	Types Available	URL/Remarks
Bose	6.1, 5.1	www.bose.com; compact, attractive satellite speakers usually offset by powerful subwoofers (with built-in amplifiers for all channels); look for home theater speaker systems; prices from $700 to $1,300; individual speaker pairs/ elements also available.
Creative Labs	7.1, 6.1, 5.1, 4.1, 2.1	us.creative.com; compact, attractive satellite speakers with self-amplified subwoofers; look for speaker systems; prices from under $100 to $500.
JBL	7.1, 6.1, 5.1	www.jbl.com; conventional speaker components widely used in movie theaters and recording studios; prices in the company's HT (home theater) series range from $450 to $2,000 each (typical 5.1 configuration costs $4,200).
Klipsch	7.1, 6.1, 5.1	www.klipsch.com; conventional and folding horn speaker components revered by many audiophiles; prices in the company's THX Ultra2 series range from $1,250 to $1,400 (typical 5.1 configuration costs $5,350).
Logitech*	6.1, 5.1, 2.1, 2.0	www.logitech.com; compact, interesting satellites with self-amplified subwoofers and capable control heads available, prices range from $79 to $400; sound is fine for smaller spaces.

All these are reputable vendors and offer good values for their products. Logitech was kind enough to lend us speakers for this book, and we already owned or were able to audition systems from the other vendors mentioned here.

Wrapping Up

Though it may not yet be time for a Media Center PC, a TV set or equivalent display, and a set of speakers to be all the equipment in your family or living room, there's a case to be made for this kind of setup for smaller rooms like dorms or offices. That's okay, though, because a Media Center PC can make itself a part of a typical home entertainment setup by hooking up to an AV receiver or pre-amplifier. As long as outputs from the PC match up with inputs on the gear (which shouldn't be a problem for those who own equipment no more than four or five years old), the connection should work. Things get interesting when multichannel sound comes into play, so we also describe how to make sure that what the Media Center PC produces, the other equipment can consume.

It does make for a pretty satisfying experience to hear high-quality Dolby Digital sound while watching a favorite TV show, or to let THX or DTS bring surround sound to a DVD. It's also great to let your Media Center PC take on the role of digital jukebox, because it arranges and makes it easy to listen through your entire music collection.

Monitors and Displays

The video screen is the final interface between an HTPC and you, the user, or the audience. You could also call it the whole point of an HTPC system. In whatever way you like to think of it, on-screen visuals are the means by which you control the computer side of HTPC *and* watch movies, videos, or TV — the theater side of the machine. It's the centerpiece for any home theater system, PC-based or otherwise. Naturally, the display comprises a major component in any HTPC system, whether it is meant for a one-person audience in a cramped studio apartment or dorm room, or a custom-built screening theater.

We're pretty sure that most people reading this book fall somewhere between those extremes. You want something bigger than a normal PC monitor, but you may not have the space or extravagant budget for a dedicated theater setup.

The assumption we make is that HTPCs are used most for video and music entertainment and occasional video editing, not for general computing. A large display some distance away from the keyboard and mouse may be okay for occasional conventional computing, but you may want a smaller conventional monitor for such use. With most video cards, it's easy to hook up a TV display as well as a PC monitor to your PC (or HTPC).

In this chapter, we consider larger display choices for HTPC. It is a bewildering array, indeed, with conventional CRT, rear projection, LCD, and plasma monitors of all shapes and sizes, along with widely varying specifications and connectivity. Although it's feasible to use a standard 17"–21" PC monitor with an HTPC, our focus is on larger displays more suitable for a theater entertainment experience with Digital HDTV and DVD. It is here that the choices are also most interesting.

The relationships between displays, graphic cards, Media Center Edition (MCE), and TV video parameters are complex. Keep in mind that it's the most restrictive specification that limits your choices, so focus on those parameters to take the most practical approach.

Video and TV capture cards work hand-in-hand with displays. Do read and refer back to Chapter 9 as necessary. The sources discussed in Appendix F are also relevant to understanding more about the role of TV digital feeds and standards whatever display you might choose.

The Input to the Display

The first thing to discuss is HDTV. You've read elsewhere in this book that MCE only supports High Definition TV that is "broadcast," not propagated via cable or satellite, even though these delivery systems are the primary sources of HDTV. Never mind. It's a rapidly evolving arena with technology, government regulations, and commercial interests all vying for market share, and interacting in a confusing mish-mash. MCE is evolving, too, and the next big MS update may provide broader HDTV support (but don't hold your breath). The main observation that applies to HDTV is that to get the best from it, you need a compatible display. We'll go into a bit of alphabet soup in this discussion, because there's simply no way to avoid it.

HDTV is a subset of Digital TV (DTV) as defined by the Advanced Television Systems Committee (ATSC) in 1995. Digital TV means that the signal is delivered in digital form, but many programs on digital cable and satellite feeds began in analog and were converted to digital fairly late in the transmission process. Often there are many conversion artifacts, as well as signal losses that may have occurred in analog prior to conversion. This means far from everything you see on DTV is high resolution or digital in origin. The best DTV begins in digital form and stays that way for maximum signal fidelity. At its best, it is better than most DVD content.

Two classes of DTV exist(standard and high definition. A standard-definition DTV screen shows 480 active scanning lines, which can be interlaced or progressive. Standard-definition pictures may be 16:9 or 4:3 (standard NTSC analog TV). An in-between standard, known as Enhanced Definition (EDTV), uses a screen frame with 480 lines progressively scanned in a 16:9 format.

When it comes to TV display signals, *progressive* refers to the lines being scanned continuously. 480p means 480 lines are scanned or painted on the screen 30 times every second. (Thirty times because TV motion is 30 frames per second.) With progressive scan, each video frame is a discrete unit. *Interlacing* refers to the odd lines being scanned or painted first on the screen, followed by the even lines. 480i, or standard analog TV, means that every other line on the screen is displayed 30 times a second. Interlacing began with conventional analog TV to save transmission bandwidth (it's a long story you don't really need to know about) and works fine today on smaller screens. But blown up to 50" and larger screens, interlacing at 480 causes jaggies (smearing on vertically moving images) and other artifacts that are easily visible. This is especially true for fast moving images found in sports coverage or action movies. PC monitors are non-interlaced or progressive, by the way. This is particularly an issue with CRTs, which use a scanning electron beam to paint images on the screen. It takes one pass of the electron gun to paint a single frame of video on the screen, whereas it takes two passes to paint a single video frame—one pass paints the even-numbered scan lines, and the other pass paints the odd-numbered scan lines.

HDTV is always widescreen format, 16:9. The frames can be 1080 or 720 scanning lines. Each line in a 1080-line picture has 1920 horizontal pixels. Each line in a 720-line has 1280 horizontal pixels. It can be interlaced or progressive — in other words, 1080i or 1080p, and 720i or 720p. However, 1080i and 720p appear to be the most common. NBC, CBS, and PBS use 1080i for their HDTV broadcasts, but PBS stations can produce 720p programs. ABC and Fox use 720p.

Most CRT-based HD displays support only 1080i in HDTV mode. This means whether the input is 1080i or 720p, it's shown at 1080i. Digital displays(LCD, Plasma, and micro-display Rear Projection(convert the signal to their native progressive display, usually 1280×720 (720p) to 1366×768 pixels, with the newest models offering 1920×1280.

Almost all modern TV sets support input connections for S-Video, the primary output on video cards for TV monitors. Remember that S-Video is an analog connection, and cannot transfer progressive scan images from a video card to a display. You need a DVI, HDMI, or Progressive Scan Component Video Output to preserve progressive scan signals.

Figure 12-1 shows an HDTV and a conventional TV side by side.

FIGURE 12-1: The difference in aspect ratio between HDTV and conventional TVs is easy to see by comparing units side by side (HDTV is longer and offers a more movie-like picture, conventional TV is more square).

Sony products pictured with permission of Sony Electronics, Inc. Syntax photo reproduced by permission of Syntax Corporation.

How Big?

How big a space do you have and how many people do you want to accommodate at any one time? The best view is within a 30-degree arc; the field of view can be expanded by getting closer to the screen or by getting a bigger screen. The trouble with getting closer and with bigger screens is that the scan lines and picture grunge are more easily seen, especially with standard NTSC TV's low 480-line resolution. The solution for viewing regular analog TV on an HDTV is to sit farther back so the grunge is less visible. It's much better with HDTV or DVD, so you can sit closer or use a larger display in a smaller room.

Table 12-1 summarizes the relationship between viewing distance, screen size, and the resolution of the input signal. Four feet have been added to the minimum distance for regular TV watching to obtain the minimum room length. This is to allow for the depth of the display and the seating. Naturally, your own 60" widescreen may look wonderful in the showroom, but could make watching standard cable TV in your 14-by-12-foot den less pleasant than with a regular TV. (Figure 12-2 shows both a 32" LCD HDTV and a 60" rear-projection HDTV.)

Table 12-1   Size Matters

Diagonal Screen Size	Best Distance, HDTV/DVD	Best Distance, NTSC TV	Minimum Room Length
26" widescreen	3–5 feet	5–8 feet	9 feet
34" widescreen	4–7 feet	7–11 feet	11 feet
42" widescreen	5–8.5 feet	9–14 feet	13 feet
50" widescreen	6–10 feet	10–16 feet	14 feet
60" widescreen	7–12 feet	12–20 feet	16 feet
32" standard (4:3)	3.5–6 feet	8–13 feet	12 feet

Tip

The term *widescreen* refers to a display with an aspect ratio of 16:9. It is the most common screen shape for HD displays, which is a good thing, allowing widescreen DVD and HDTV programs to be viewed without much letterboxing or cropping.

Figure 12-2: The difference in size between a 32" LCD HDTV (left) and a 60" rear-projection HDTV (right) is hard to see in side-by-side photos, but notice the stand on the 32" model and the hefty base on the 60" model. The former weighs 45 pounds with stand, the latter 112 pounds.
Sony products pictured with permission of Sony Electronics, Inc.

How Much?

It's a basic matter you may feel we're overstating, but price is a good way to narrow your range of choices. Table 12-2 summarizes prices for various types and sizes of HD displays in the U.S. market at the time of writing. Prices vary tremendously based on brand, model, features, and so on; the ones noted here are low starting prices based on various Web shopping search engines (expect to pay more than this, when taxes, shipping, and handling come into play, or when best deals may not be available).

Table 12-2   Pricing

Diagonal Screen Size	CRT	RP, CRT	RP, Micro-display	LCD	Plasma
26–27" widescreen	$600	N/A	N/A	$1100	N/A
34–36" widescreen	$1000	N/A	N/A	$1400	$2200
42–44" widescreen	N/A	$1100 (46–47")	$1800	$4300 (45–46")	$2500
50–52" widescreen	N/A	$1300	$2500	$6000 (50")	$5000
60–62" widescreen	N/A	$1600	$3500	N/A	$9000
32" standard (4:3)	$400	N/A	N/A	N/A	N/A

What's interesting is that some display technologies have an ideal value range. For example, the current cost of producing large LCD screens with the required low defect rates is reflected in the huge jump in cost from 34–36" to the 45–46" size.

The good old CRT is very good value, but they simply can't be made as big as the other types; you won't find one much bigger than 36". Rear-projection TVs represent excellent value, especially the newer micro-display types, which we'll be discussing a little later on. They start at around 42" diagonal screen size, where they are less than half the price of similar sized plasma displays.

Thin, flat panel displays are the cat's meow today, and plasma is the only choice once screen size exceeds 50". LCD displays are relatively affordable under 40", at only 40–50 percent more costly than similar size CRTs. Still they tend to be the most costly per square inch of screen. As mentioned earlier, prices rocket up as screen sizes increase.

Plasma displays are more costly than LCDs in the under-40" size category, so you won't find many models under 40", but surprisingly, cost does not appear to go up much in the 40–42" size range, a sweet spot for plasma right now.

Display Technology

The sections that follow dig a bit deeper into the display technologies used to make common display types work, including multiple flavors of standard CRT, LCD, and plasma displays. Along the way, we point out features of special interest or significance for HTPC use, and try to recommend various options within each category.

Standard CRT

The cathode-ray tube TV remains popular. It is less expensive than ever before, extremely reliable, and the best models set high standards for performance, especially new, large HDTV models, with their excellent brightness and contrast. A CRT's ability to display blacks and dark colors is unmatched by newer technologies. Around $1,000 will get you a decent 34–36" HD-ready TV, although you can certainly pay more. The downside is that they are limited to about this size, consume a fair bit of electricity, and get decidedly warm with extended use. CRTs are also bulky and very heavy. A picture tube does get dimmer over time. A typical estimate is 10,000 to 20,000 hours before it fades enough to need replacement. That's 7–14 years based on an average of four viewing hours per day.

Rear Projection, CRT

These sets start at 46" and are now down to just over $2,000, although we found one model for a mere $899. Even a 60" model will set you back only a little over $1,500. The CRT RP (RPTV) represents the value category for large screen TVs. They work best in a darkened room. If properly tweaked for viewing, they also work really well for movies and prime time programming. Even under ideal conditions, though, RPTVs simply cannot match the brightness and contrast of standard CRT TVs, which makes standard CRTs preferable for viewing fast action sports. RPTVs also require occasional adjustment for convergence calibration. As is common for all CRTs, RPTVs don't have a problem with fixed pixel sizes, because they're able to scan images in variable resolutions.

RPTVs use three 7" CRTs to project red, green, and blue onto the screen through lenses and mirrors. Alignment of the three beams is critical and should be performed by pros if it goes out of whack. CRT-based RPTVs are *really* big and heavy, invariably floor-standing. Liquid gels are used to cool the three tubes. Some rare leakage of these gel packs has caused problems in the past, so keep on the lookout for leaks.

The actual screen on which the image is projected is susceptible to image burn-in from things like continuously displayed station logos or window box lines from long-term display of 4:3 aspect ratio programming. This is also a problem with the other RPTV displays as well, due mostly to their bright, powerful projection light bulbs. Estimated life of a projection bulb is somewhat shorter than for standard TVs, but the three picture tubes should last almost as long. Almost every big brand offers CRT RPTVs, but some are actually discontinuing them in favor of micro-display types.

Rear Projection, Micro-Display

This is a general category of rear-projection displays that uses small solid-state chips instead of CRTs. There are three different types:

- **Liquid crystal display (LCD) rear projectors (RP)** shoot a bright light through small LCD panels that display a moving image and project it through lenses and mirrors onto the screen. The compact size and weight of the LCD chips, as well as their cool operation are big benefits that allow an LCD RPTV to be much smaller than a CRT RPTV display of the same screen size. They even come in table-top models. They are brighter and offer better contrast than CRT equivalents, and require no maintenance. The useful life expectancy of the projection bulb is 8,000 hours, somewhat less than a CRT. The LCD itself should easily last 20,000 to 30,000 hours.

  The downsides are somewhat higher cost and the same kind of dead pixel issue you find with LCD monitors or digital cameras. If a pixel burns out, it shows up as a constant black or white dot on the screen. The only way to fix it is to replace the entire LCD. They also exhibit something of a grainy look, often dubbed the "screen door effect," because of the difficulty of manufacturing panels with small gaps between pixels.

  One other characteristic common to all LCD monitors is that they have fixed native resolution, based on a finite number of pixels. LCD RPTV displays scale input signals to match the LCD's pixel count. For example, a 1080i input calls for a display of 1920 × 1080 pixels for a 1:1 display. If the LCD chip is 1024 × 768, the original signal must be scaled to match this pixel count, and the image must be letterboxed to show a correct 16:9 aspect ratio. Sony, Hitachi, Panasonic, Epson, and LG are among the big brands in this category.

  A consortium of LCD RPTV makers, dubbed 3LCD, is working to improve both actual quality and the perception of quality in LCD RPTVs. You can expect true 1080p LCD RPTVs to ship by the end of 2005.

- **Digital Light Processing (DLP) RPTV** displays are similar to LCD RPs. The image is displayed on a chip. Color is added as light passes through a high-speed color wheel, then reflected, amplified, and projected to the screen. The Digital Micromirror Device (DMD) chip is unique in that every pixel is a reflective mirror.

  This is a technology that has been used successfully in commercial theaters, with digital movies stored on hard drives feeding a DLP projector shooting the image to the screen. However, these high-end projectors use three DLP chips, and don't need a rotating wheel. The color wheel in DLP RPTVs is a source of visual anomalies for some users (as indicated later in this section).

  Most DLP RPTVs use a 1280 × 720 native resolution chip that can show every pixel of 720p HDTV, which gives a very sharp high-definition picture. The newest 2005 models offer 1920 × 1080 resolution for 1:1 display of 1080 HDTV, but are substantially more expensive. Aside from sharpness and high definition, DLP also has very good black rendition. LCD is getting better, but DLP still leads. Like LCD RPTVs, DLP models are much thinner, smaller, and more energy efficient than CRT counterparts.

A peculiar artifact of DLP RPTV is called the rainbow effect, a brief flash of colors becomes visible quickly across the screen during viewing that some people notice. Faster color wheels, now in excess of 10,000 RPM in the latest Samsung models, have reduced this effect quite a bit, and many people never notice them. No maintenance is required, and life expectancy of the projection bulb is about the same as with LCD RPTV. Pricing is similar to LCD RPTV. Samsung, Toshiba, Mitsubishi, Panasonic, RCA, and LG are among the big brands in this category.

- **Liquid Crystal on Silicon (LCoS) RPTV** is offered by only a few manufacturers. It had a strong start with many big players who produced one generation and then backed away in favor of other RPTV technologies. Neither prices nor performance are as compelling as for either LCD or DLP RPTV models. JVC and Philips are the main players in this category, which appears to be shrinking over time.

LCD Flat Panel

Sexy, widescreen, ultra-thin flat panel displays have become symbols of the rich modern lifestyle in movies, ads, and other imagery that pervades pop culture. It's no wonder they provoke consumer envy and lust.

There is actually some substance in the hype. LCD flat panels have pretty much taken over the PC monitor world. Their space- and energy-saving qualities are as compelling as the generally excellent performance they provide for all-around computer use.

For entertainment, LCD displays don't suffer geometry problems such as pin cushioning of the CRT and RPTV displays and offer extremely bright, sharp, high-contrast images that are great for bright environments. The slower response time that was the biggest weakness of earlier LCD technology has been engineered out of the latest LCD displays, so streaking and blurring are less problematic. The low heat, power consumption, and thin size are great benefits. All this comes at a price, and a basic size limit. As you venture much beyond 30" diagonal size, the price of LCD displays increases dramatically. Very few LCD displays are bigger than 40".

LCD panels consist of two bonded panels of polarized transparent sheets, one with a polymer coating that holds liquid crystals. Electric current passing through individual crystals passes or blocks light as required, forming an image on the screen. Fluorescent tubes behind the transparent material provide the illumination. The crystals don't produce light and thus do not emit radiation like a CRT.

One last weakness of LCD displays is their ability to show black. In earlier models, blacks were rendered as grays, and this often lent a flat look to scenes. Again, this is much improved to the point where it's difficult to notice in current models. Newer technologies that use LEDs to backlight LCD displays hold the promise of substantial improvement in black levels over more traditional fluorescent backlights.

LCD flat panels do not suffer from screen burn. They also last longer than any other type of display, about 50,000 hours on average.

Virtually every major TV brand offers LCD displays. One big benefit is that they are often very much cross-platform devices, with connectivity for PC hookups such as DVI and FireWire as well as HDMI and Component Video. This makes them ideal for use with an HTPC in rooms where their size limitations don't restrict the number of viewers too much.

Plasma Flat Panel

Our first glimpse of a large widescreen flat panel TV a few years ago was a plasma mounted on a wall at Sound Plus, Vancouver's premier high-end audio-video store. This CA$17,000 device showed an HDTV feed from a news program. The display might have been 40 inches, with a small black colored bezel. We can't recall what brand it was or what the news was about, but we do remember thinking how the combination of HDTV and plasma screen managed to make it look beautiful, like cinematic art, even though it was just routine news with a few on-the-scene clips. We watched only for a few minutes, in the middle of a busy day, and wonder whether our first impressions would have held up under closer, longer scrutiny. Still, it was a compelling experience, one that many other casual viewers also report.

Plasma flat panel displays have come down in price since those days, and they are the only choice for flat panels over 40". Although neither can be considered cheap (compared to CRT), plasma is cheaper per square inch than LCD.

The core of a plasma screen is a flat, light surface covered by millions of microscopic phosphor-coated glass bubbles, each containing a gas-like substance, the plasma. Each of these bubbles has the ability to emit light in red, green, or blue. An electric current is passed through the flat screen, causing the plasma in specific bubbles to emit UV rays that cause the phosphor coating to glow in the appropriate color. It requires a fair amount of electricity to operate, and produces a lot of heat as well as light. Most large plasma displays are fan cooled, and can sometimes be noisy.

The performance of plasma doesn't hold up to the dreamy first impression described previously, but the overall performance is excellent, and shows blacks better than LCD displays. Plasma displays can portray scenes with richness and lots of detail, though perhaps with a bit less brightness and contrast than an LCD can.

The resolution of the smallest plasmas (42") is usually 852×480, and rises to a more appropriate HDTV resolution of 1280×720 at around 50".

Almost all major TV brands offer plasma displays.

Who Sells What?

Convergence is an overused word, but it's truly relevant when it comes to displays. Television and computer screens have converged to such a degree that most PC monitor brands offer products that either double as TV displays or actually make TVs, and most TV brands offer many products that can double as monitors or be easily connected to a PC. As long as the tuner is in your PC, if it can accept the output from your video card, any of these display devices will work with an HTPC. Finding one with precisely the balance of features you seek at the price you want is getting easier, but it's still a bewildering maze as available options continue to expand and evolve. Table 12-3 shows a short list of vendors that offer HDTV displays. Check any TV or PC monitor brand, however, and you'll find more options than you might believe possible.

Table 12-3   **HDTV Display Vendors**

Name	Type(s)	URL
Daewoo	CRT, Plasma, LCD RP	www.daewoo.com
Dell	LCD, Plasma	www.dell.com
Hitachi	CRT, CRT RP, LCD RP, DLP LP, LCD, Plasma	www.hitachi.com
HP	LCD, Plasma	www.hp.com
JVC	CRT, CRT RP, LCoS RP, LCD, Plasma	www.jvc.com
Panasonic	CRT, CRT RP, LCD RP, DLP RP, LCD, Plasma	www.panasonic.com
Philips	CRT, CRT RP, LCoS, LCD, Plasma	www.consumer.philips.com
RCA	CRT, LCD, CRT, DLP RP	tv.rca.com
Samsung	CRT, CRT RP, LCD RP, DLP RP, LCD, Plasma	www.samsung.com
Sharp	CRT, DLP RP, LCD, Plasma	www.sharpusa.com
Sony	CRT, CRT RP, LCD RP, LCD, Plasma	www.sony.com
Syntax	LCD, LCoS	www.syntaxgroups.com
Toshiba	CRT, CRT and DLP RP, LCD, Plasma	www.toshiba.com
Zenith	CRT, CRT RP, LCD RP, DLP RP, LCD, Plasma	www.zenith.com

Recommendations

- **Standard CRT:** It's hard to recommend a standard CRT set because of two primary issues: first, CRT sets are susceptible to burn-in, and second, CRT sets are limited to 480p and 1080i resolutions. Interlaced resolution is never ideal for PC use, either.

- **Rear projection, CRT:** This technology has aged badly and isn't recommended for a modern home theater. RPTV CRT sets are highly susceptible to burn-in and like their standard CRT cousins are able to resolve only 480p or 1080i, thus making them less than ideal. Because the CRT electron guns need convergence on a regular basis, owning one can be a real hassle.

- **Rear projection, micro-display:** This new generation of rear projection encompasses three display technologies: LCD, DLP, and LCoS. If you have room for a rear-projection HDTV set, these new technologies represent the best value for the money. All three technologies are better suited to HTPC use than RPTV CRT. All support native resolution of 720p or 1080p, perfectly suited to a PC that assumes a progressive display. None of these technologies suffer from burn-in, nor do they need convergence. Which one you choose is mostly subjective. Well-liked vendors in this category include Samsung, Mitsubishi, and Sony.

■ **LCD flat panel:** If you are tight on space and need a TV in the 26"–37" range, an LCD is what you want. LCD displays generally have a native resolution of 720p or higher. Sharp makes excellent LCD TVs, and the Syntax Ölevia series is a great budget buy.

■ **Plasma flat panel:** If you want the largest flat display you can buy, plasma is about your only choice. Modern plasma sets combined with proper screen calibration and turning off your TV when not in use combat burn-in. Inexpensive plasmas support 854×480 (EDTV), the bare minimum for high-definition HTPC use, whereas larger units support 720p or higher. Panasonic, Sony, and Pioneer are well-respected brands in this category.

Wrapping Up

A direct view CRT display retains its position as the most popular choice among all technologies. It has many strengths, including dependability, low price, and excellent performance in the best models. But they only come in sizes under 40", however.

Rear-projection TVs offer the best value in large-screen displays, with LCD- and DLP-based models competing for top position. Substantial improvements have improved the handling of motion and blacks, while reducing visible glitches and screen artifacts.

LCD flat panel displays boast impressive lists of benefits and panache, but with price tags to match, and are really practical only up to <40" size. Plasma displays perform much like LCD displays, but cost less per square inch, and get much bigger. Heat and short lifetimes are issues with plasma, however, that don't apply to LCDs.

Whichever display type you choose, make sure to get the best connectivity for your HTPC. Especially if you want to maintain the highest-resolution HDTV your system can deliver, DVI, HDMI, or Component Video connections are desirable, if not downright necessary.

For a more in-depth comparison of display technologies, check out Ray Soneira's four-part series on ExtremeTech.com (www.extremetech.com/article2/0,1558,1734380,00.asp). Dr. Soneira covers all four primary technologies in sufficient technical detail to satisfy most video engineers, but in a highly readable style that should be equally compelling for interested laypeople and HTPC aficionados.

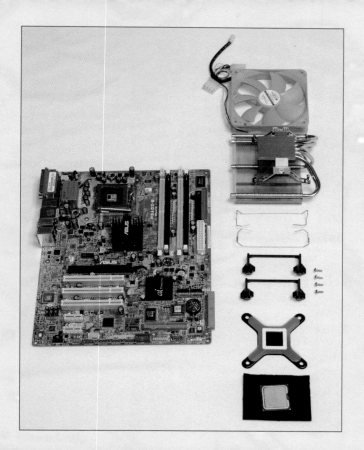

The Pentium 4 motherboard, with CPU (lower right), backplate and mounting brackets (with screws), fan clips, CPU cooler (CPU side up), and cooler fan (listed from lower right to upper right).

The Pentium 4 has no pins on its back, which makes it easy to drop and lock it into position with a locking lever (front view left). The cooler backplate attaches to the motherboard with four small screws that tap into the mounting brackets on the front side (back view right).

The **Thermalright XP-120** cooler rocks into the bracket on the memory slot side and then clamps down to the bracket on the port block side of the CPU socket. Don't forget to apply thermal paste to the CPU before installing the cooler.

A profile view of the **Antec P-180** with expansion cards installed shows how roomy and well built this case really is.

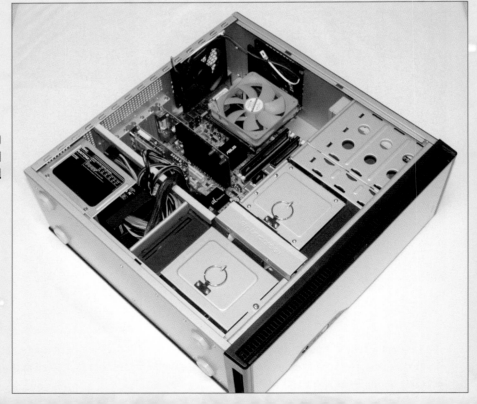

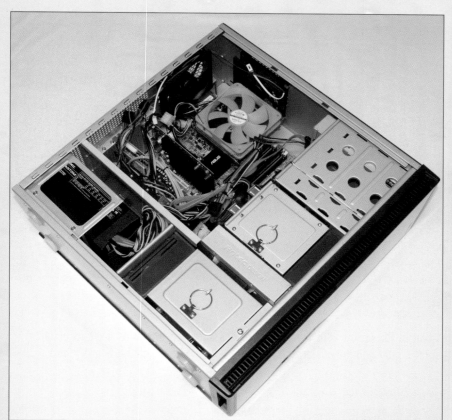

Even with all cables in place, there's plenty of room for air to circulate in the Antec P-180 case, shot in profile view (note how cables route from the PSU in the lower chamber), through a porthole into the upper chamber to reach the motherboard, drives, fans, and so forth. This build produced one of the coolest-running P4 systems we've ever encountered.

The AOpen i915GMm-HFS motherboard (above) with cooling fan and mounting screws (leftmost), cooler, CPU, and backplate (rightmost). AOpen supplied all these parts with the motherboard (except the CPU, of course).

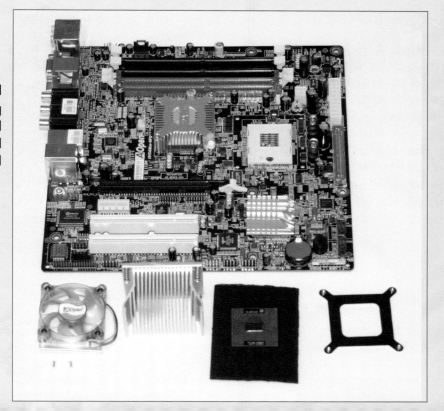

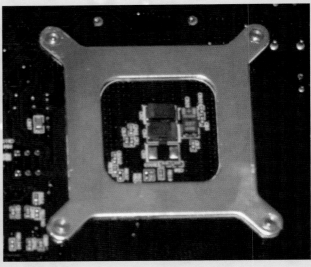

The Pentium M locks into position in its socket with the half-turn of a small screw (left); the backplate matches up to spring-loaded screws built into the cooler that AOpen provides with the motherboard (right).

The AOpen cooler is a snap to mount, thanks to its spring-loaded screws that are easy to turn with your fingers (once you get one screw started, the job goes quickly thereafter). The fan slides into place on top of the cooler (it's shown halfway on in the photo) and fastens into place with two tiny screws.

An isometric view of the Ahanix D5 case with expansion cards installed doesn't really show how tricky it is to work with the drive cage or to cable the drives up.

An isometric view of the Ahanix D5 case with everything cabled up only hints at how cramped power and interface cables proved to be for both the hard disk and the optical drive in this build.

The Chaintech VNF4 Ultra motherboard (below), with the cooler (top left) and Athlon 64 3500+ CPU (top right).

The Chaintech motherboard ships with the cooler mounting bracket (left) and the backplate (right) already installed. All you need to do is drop the CPU in place and clamp it into position, and you're ready to mount the cooler.

The AVC cooler that AMD furnished with the Athlon 64 3500+ for our use snaps into position on the Northbridge side of the board and then locks on with a lever clamp on the port block side of the board (shown in the up position in this photo). This proved to be very easy to install.

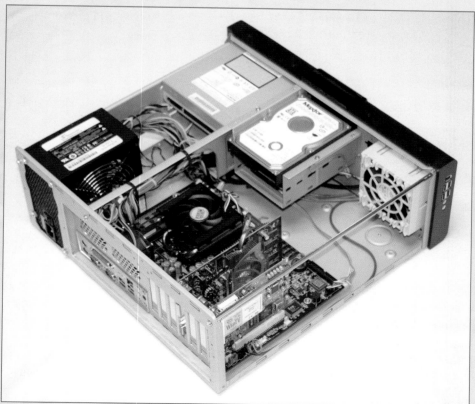

An isometric view from the rear of the Silverstone LC04 case shows how the open side (front right) makes it easy to slide the motherboard into position during the build. We like the ease of access, roominess, and ventilation in this case.

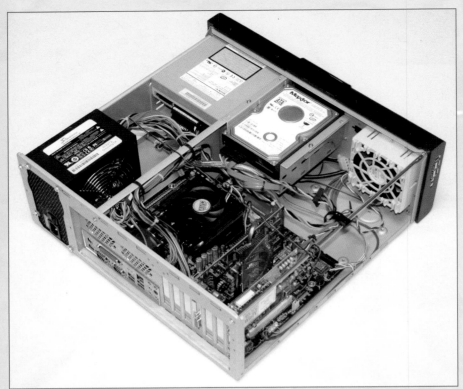

An isometric view from the rear of the Silverstone case also shows how nice the case made routing cables and tying them down. Note how we used the center rail for motherboard and fan cables, and the right-hand rail for fan and control cables.

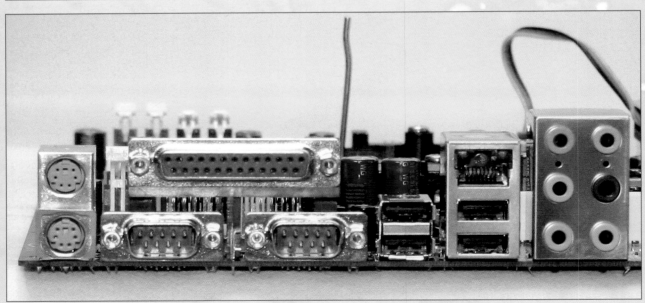

Color coding helps determine where to plug in various connectors. The green port on the left is for the mouse, the purple port beneath it for the keyboard. To the far right, the blue port functions as line-in for an RCA connector, and with an optical adapter, as the digital optical output (SPDIF out). The green port underneath it is an RCA line out port for speaker or headphone connections. The pink port at the bottom of that column is an RCA microphone port. The gray port at the top right is for rear surround speakers in 4-, 6-, or 8-channel configurations. The black port at middle right is for rear side surround speakers in 8-channel configurations. The yellow port is for connecting to center and subwoofer speakers in 6- or 8-channel configurations.

Networking Your HTPC

O ne of the ingredients that has both a subtle and profound influence on HTPC technology in general, and Windows Media Center Edition in particular, is the Internet. Nobody can keep a computer up-to-date nowadays without Internet access (at least, not without jumping through lots of unnecessary hoops), nor would anybody want to set up a home media/entertainment center without Internet access, either. And in fact, MCE requires Internet access to support many of its built-in media handling and managing functions, including its program guide data for television, plus access to online databases for movie and music information.

When you set up a Media Center PC, your biggest networking question will be "wired or wireless?" rather than "networked or not?" In this chapter, you explore the role of the network interface in a PC, both in terms of local network access and in terms of Internet access. You also examine the pros, cons, and costs of using wired or wireless technologies to make your connection. You also look at what happens to network bandwidth and Internet access requirements when media access comes into play.

An important part of the MCE installation process comes when establishing and verifying an Internet link for the operating system to use. All the necessary installation details are covered in Chapter 17, but we cover all the preliminary networking bases in this chapter, including the following:

➤ **PC network interfaces:** Here you learn about how a network and your PC are able to communicate, and how this can bring the Internet into reach. You will have a chance to refresh yourself about the basics of networking links, protocols, and services, especially as they pertain to Media Center PCs.

➤ **MCE and the Internet:** The various ways in which MCE accesses and uses information from the Internet are explored and explained, as well as some of the perhaps surprising sources of media and entertainment available via an Internet link.

➤ **Network speeds and feeds:** Not all Internet links are the same, particularly when it comes to speed. We describe bandwidth requirements that various MCE setup and usage scenarios impose on a network link and explain links that do and don't make the grade.

➤ **Wired or wireless:** Bringing the Internet to a Media Center PC can present interesting wiring challenges. This makes such PCs excellent candidates for wireless link-ups, but it's important to understand the advantages and disadvantages of each approach, including issues related to cost, security, access, and more.

➤ **Your Internet link:** Depending on what you want to do with your Media Center PC, your Internet access needs may vary. You explore what various types of common Internet connections will — and won't — let you do.

➤ **Best HTPC networking options:** This is where we recommend potential links and solutions for your Media Center PC, plus a few tried and true techniques to bring security up to a safe level.

Best case, you'll simply be able to hook up to a wired network, or plug in a wireless adapter, and be off and running on the Internet with your Media Center PC. In this chapter, we do everything we can to increase the odds that this will happen, and to help you anticipate and overcome common potential pitfalls that might obstruct this oh-so-desirable outcome, however temporary they may be. And as usual in these chapters, you'll also find a table of recommended network interface and equipment vendors near the end.

The Network Interface

Today, the vast majority of PC motherboards include at least one, if not two, network interfaces that can handle up to and including Gigabit Ethernet. That means you can attach most PCs built around such motherboards up to twisted-pair networks running 10, 100, or 1000 Mbit Ethernet without installing any additional hardware.

Drivers for onboard network interfaces normally reside on the software CD bundled with a motherboard. Please don't let that stop you from visiting the vendor's Web site and checking for a newer version, if Windows Update doesn't provide one for you automatically. You can also check out various driver update sites on the Internet to help you find and install the latest and greatest version for your motherboard, such as:

■ **DriverGuide.com:** Membership is free, but it costs $19.95 to register the site's automatic driver scanning and update check tool (the DriverGuide Toolkit).

■ **Drivers HQ (**drivershq.com**):** It costs $19.95 for life membership to this site for an unlimited number of machines and the site's Driver Detective scan tool.

■ **Winfiles (**www.winfiles.com/drivers/**):** A CNET site that offers free manual search and lookup for drives, but no scanning facilities.

■ **SoftLookup.com (**www.softlookup.com/drivers.asp**):** Search drivers by category or device make/model (no scanning facilities here, either).

The real choice here is whether you want a scanning tool to check your driver status for you or whether you prefer to do that legwork yourself. You must typically pay for the convenience of the former, whereas you can visit a manufacturer's Web site or any number of driver clearinghouses (like all the sites just mentioned) and search for drivers on your own for free.

For most HTPC systems, the biggest choice system builders must make is whether they should use the built-in wired network interface(s) on the motherboard or switch to wireless access instead. The pros and cons, and technical implications, of making this decision are covered later in this chapter. But first, we dig into how and why Windows Media Center Edition needs Internet access to do its job properly.

MCE and the Internet

MCE needs access to the Internet for multiple purposes, but chief among these are the following:

- **Initial setup and configuration information during the installation process.** This applies to recognizing locations to earmark proper versions of the Electronic Program Guide (EPG) for television, radio schedules, and so forth. Language preferences and other basic data acquisition and display choices come into play during installation as well. Without Internet access, MCE can't install completely or correctly.

- **Access to Windows Update for necessary security, system, and driver updates for the systems and hardware upon which MCE operates.** This ideally occurs immediately after initial setup and configuration, and Microsoft recommends using Automatic Updates to make sure important updates, patches, and changes download and install onto MCE systems automatically. Without some kind of Internet access, MCE can't be kept current and secure.

- **Ongoing access to various online databases that MCE uses to continuously update the EPG and to look up movie, music, and other entertainment media information as and when its users request such data.** Without some kind of Internet access, MCE can't obtain and manage its programming schedules, nor can it download and use descriptive data to identify music, movies, television shows, and more.

In addition to the preceding, MCE also provides access to Windows Messenger so users can chat online while watching movies, TV, or listening to music. You can also shell out to the Windows XP desktop any time you like by pressing the Alt and Tab keys together, then picking a program icon to activate. This makes normal Web, e-mail, and other Internet services and applications readily available on Media Center PCs as well.

Network Speeds and Feeds

When it comes to working with MCE, network speeds matter in two ways. First (and for those users who don't have a local area network, or LAN, with other PCs or devices at home, foremost) is the speed of your Internet connection. Second (or not, as the case may be) is the speed at which local networks carry data. In an era when numbers for household networks are exploding, and where nearly all households with PCs also have Internet access, we feel obliged to cover both sides in this book. The section that follows covers the Internet side; the section after that covers the LAN side.

We've already established why MCE needs Internet access during and after installation. Access to the right kind of local network also offers profound benefits to Media Center PC owners, including the following:

- **Access to storage space elsewhere on the network lifts the lid on storage.** Whereas most HTPCs can accommodate only a limited number of hard disks, and it may not make sense to add external drives in an entertainment center, network access opens all kinds of possibilities to extend storage space for music, movies, TV recordings, photos, and more. Many Internet access devices include one or two USB ports where external drives can be attached; other Windows PCs on a home network can also play host to additional storage for a Media Center PC to use (though users on those machines might not appreciate the performance hit involved in reading or writing large media files on their machines). You can even buy low-cost storage devices that attach directly to your network, instead of to a PC or other network hardware.

  As this chapter is being written, external storage devices cost from $1.16/GB and up for network-attached versions, and $0.72 and up for external USB- or FireWire-based versions. All provide excellent solutions for extending Media Center PC storage outside an HTPC's case, thereby displacing additional noise and heat output, and making it easy to add more room for media collections in 100GB to 400GB increments.

- **Network connections enable use of Media Center Extenders, plus other streaming media capabilities.** Linksys offers a network-based device that grabs music, movies, radio, TV recordings, or photos from a Media Center PC for display on another television elsewhere in the house, or for listening to on another stereo. This device supports wireless as well as wired home networks.

But these capabilities impose their own bandwidth requirements on local area networks as well, as you learn in the section that follows our coverage of Internet link speeds.

Internet Link Speeds

Because so much of what MCE does involves forms of streaming media — for example, DVD movies, TV programs, and music all qualify as such, because all involve ongoing playback over time, also known as *streaming* — the speed of your Internet connection matters, as well or as much as basic Internet access. In fact, for best results Microsoft recommends that MCE users obtain broadband Internet connections like cable modem or DSL (or reasonable alternatives, such as T1/E1 links). And although it's possible to set up MCE using a conventional modem link to the Internet, Microsoft recommends against using a telephone link for streaming media.

Simply put, this is because of bandwidth requirements. *Bandwidth* is a measure of data transfer over time, usually measured in kilobits or megabits per second, if not in kilobytes or megabytes per second (there are eight bits to a byte, so it's pretty easy to convert between these units). Although music imposes less need for bandwidth than other richer, media (sound by itself requires less bandwidth than sound plus images), the primary determinant for bandwidth need comes from dividing the total number of bits in a streaming media, music, TV program, or movie file by the amount of time it runs, to calculate bit rate per second.

For example, a 2MB music file consists of roughly 128 million bits. If that file takes 8 minutes to play, that indicates a bit rate of 16 megabits per minute (128 divided by 8). Divide by 60 to get the bit rate per second, which calculates to 279,620 bits per second. Divide again by 1,024 to translate that into kilobits, for a result of 273 kilobits per second, or Kbps. That doesn't translate into much of a data requirement as media files go, but it's nearly five times faster than a 56 Kbps telephone link (ignoring for the moment that very few 56-kilobit links actually attain maximum bandwidth anyway; in our experience, breaking 48 Kbps is something of a novelty). In general, music requires somewhere between 32 and 384 Kbps to encode in compressed form (raw, uncompressed data rates run from 512 to 748 Kbps for a single [non-stereo], CD-quality audio stream).

This begins to explain why something faster than a phone link is needed if you want to do anything with media playback over an Internet connection. It also explains why file sizes for media files virtually demand faster links, simply to avoid giant download times. Normal television and DVD encodings require bandwidth from 2 to 10 Mbps, and high-definition television encodings run from 19 to 38 Mbps (raw data rates are as high as 249 Mbps for the former, and 1.6 Gbps for the latter). With various Internet video services (especially video-on-demand) increasingly available, it's not unthinkable that users are going to demand faster Internet links from service providers in the near future!

Table 13-1 illustrates typical bandwidths for various Internet connections available today. It's terribly clear to anybody who understands what's available and what's needed, that major infrastructure and service changes must be in the offing, simply because of the gap between what's possible and what's available.

Table 13-1   Typical Internet Connection Speeds

Link Type	Maximum Bandwidth (typical)	Monthly Costs (Remarks)
Telephone modem	56 Kbps	$5–$25 (telephone connections seldom exceed 42–44 Kbps)
DSL	384 Kbps–1.544 Mbps	$20–$45 (most DSL services are metered, with typical 1.544 Kbps maximum downstream and typical 384 Kbps maximum upstream bit rates)
Cable modem	384 Kbps–6 Mbps	$30–$60 (cable rates tend not to be metered, but higher-priced, higher-speed links available in many markets)
T1/DS1	1.544 Mbps	$300 and up (T1 fractions available, but maximum T1 bandwidth fixed); various T1 multiples (for example T1C at 3.152 Mbps) increasingly available
T2/DS2	6.312 Mbps	$1,000 and up (not widely available)
DS3	32.064 Mbps	$10,000 and up (outside North America only)
T3	44.736 Mbps	$7,500 and up (North America only, too much for home users)

Because most consumers can't afford service beyond DSL or cable modem, this represents the current "sweet spot" for Internet access price and performance. But given increasing appetites for higher-bandwidth digital entertainment, we can't help but see both sides creeping upward (more money for more bandwidth, in other words) in years ahead.

Local Area Network Speeds

Though there have been (and probably still are) other alternatives to Ethernet for local area networking in use somewhere, Ethernet is the predominant choice for home and office networking. Older Ethernet implementations worked exclusively on wires, including two varieties of coaxial cable and twisted-pair wiring. Modern implementations come in both wireless and wired forms. Table 13-2 describes common forms of Ethernet in use today in both varieties and lists speed and distance limitations.

Table 13-2   Common Ethernet Varieties

Name	Speed	Distance Limitations	Remarks
10 Base-T	10 Mbps	100 m	Oldest form of wired Ethernet covered, not suitable for streaming media (too slow)
802.11b	11 Mbps	30 m*	Oldest form of widely available wireless Ethernet covered, not suitable for streaming media (too slow)
802.11a	6–54 Mbps	30 m*	More complex signaling technologies make for more expensive hardware, not widely used in home networks
802.11g	54 Mbps	30 m*	Most popular form of wireless Ethernet currently available, proprietary speed doubling implementations to 108 Mbps also available
100 Base-TX	100 Mbps	100 m	Newer form of Ethernet, also known as Fast Ethernet, reasonable for most streaming media
Gigabit Ethernet	1 Gbps	25 m (100 m CAT-5e)+	Fastest form of widely available wired Ethernet, works for all streaming media

* Distances vary for wireless technologies depending on local conditions and interference, distance-boosting technologies are also available to extend these technologies; YMMV.

+ CAT-5e stands for Category-5 extended wiring and is the most widely used form of twisted-pair used for prefab cables and premises wiring. It supports standard 100 m cable runs even for Gigabit Ethernet; thus, we can't recommend anything else.

Given that HDTV signals consume bandwidth from 19 to 38 Mbps, it doesn't take a big stretch to understand that even 100 Base-TX Ethernet will be strained when such signals transit a network. Although Gigabit Ethernet is by no means necessary for Media Center PCs, it may be beneficial to set up a Gigabit Ethernet network at home anyway, to anticipate increased use and more bandwidth-hungry applications in the future. Certainly, we recommend setting up nothing less than 100 Base-TX home networks nowadays.

On the wireless front, 802.11g appears to offer the best combination of cost and bandwidth: 802.11b is simply too slow (and technically outmoded in several important ways), and 802.11a equipment is less widely available and more expensive. 802.11g even offers vendor-specific double-speed implementations up to 108 Mbps. That puts it in the same league as 100 Base-TX, as subject to typical wireless networking limits (more on that in the next section).

Wired and Wireless Networking: Pros and Cons

Both wired and wireless networks have strengths and weaknesses. Here, we cover those topics so you can weigh your choices carefully and make an informed decision—unless your choices are already made (in that case, feel free to skip this section, although you may find some interesting information here anyway).

Wireless Considerations

Wireless offers convenience and relatively easy installation and use. Doing without wires can be liberating. But when you go wireless, you must recognize that liberty comes with certain security risks. Thus, it's essential to educate yourself on what to do to prevent eavesdropping and interlopers. It's also important to understand that speed ratings for wireless networks are like those for telephone modems: they represent theoretical maxima seldom attained in actual use. For example, 802.11g PC interfaces aren't required to handle data rates faster than 24 Mbps; this number may therefore establish a more realistic upper bound on wireless network performance.

Multiple environmental factors can influence wireless network performance. The further your Media Center PC is from its wireless access point, the slower that connection runs. Also, interference can impact wireless networking, so experiment with wireless links to maximize bandwidth. For example, the transformer in a tube-based TV set can cause serious interference. An external antenna placed well away from the set may be necessary to get best results. Likewise, multiple active wireless users must share total bandwidth, so more users means less bandwidth for a Media Center PC.

Dual-channel 802.11g implementations can indeed improve performance, but such products are vendor-specific. If you use somebody's 802.11g dual-channel stuff, ensure best possible performance by purchasing all wireless gear from the same source. Otherwise, compatibility issues could lower performance (worst case means working like single-channel 802.11g at 54 Mbps, with no speed gain for the extra expense). Note that each connection to a wireless router or access point consumes a portion of the total bandwidth for that device. Thus, if multiple computers and devices share a wireless connection, you may run into bandwidth issues.

Wireless networking standards continue to evolve. For example, 802.11n promises higher bandwidth while 802.11e adds QoS (quality of service), and potentially improves throughput for streaming media files. The alphabet soup of wireless standards can be confusing, but trends are toward ever-higher bandwidth and better quality of service.

Wired Considerations

On the wired side of things other factors come into play. Even if you're using wireless networking, you'll need one wired connection to attach your Internet access device (cable or DSL modem); fortunately, most wireless access points include at least one RJ-45 for a wired Ethernet hookup. Unless you deploy an Ethernet switch, multiple wired Ethernet users must also compete for access to the network medium — a situation known as *contention*. A switch eliminates contention by setting up temporary point-to-point links between a sender and a receiver, allowing 100 percent of the available bandwidth to be used (up to the aggregate bandwidth the switch can handle). Small, inexpensive Gigabit Ethernet switches that support up to eight different link-ups and aggregate bandwidth of 2–4 Gpbs are available from numerous vendors for under $200. Please note that these devices also handle links that run at 10 and 100 Mbps.

But for all forms of Ethernet, the possibility of contention drops maximum available bandwidth to somewhere between 60 and 70 percent of the theoretical maximum. Thus, as soon as two or more users become active on a shared Ethernet segment, total bandwidth drops to around 6 Mbps for 10 Base-T, around 60 Mbps for 100 Base-TX, and around 600 Mbps for Gigabit Ethernet. Depending on what users do and how much aggregate bandwidth is available, this may or may not be a problem. But even for 100 Base-TX, multiple Media Center Extenders active at the same time, along with a Media Center PC at home base could strain even a 100 Mbps Ethernet network playing only conventional TV, prerecorded movies, or music.

Ethernet cables are also subject to distance limitations, and higher-speed versions require more expensive (and sometimes shorter) cables. In most homes, this shouldn't be much of a problem. Even so, it's still a good idea to build a wiring diagram of your network with measurements for lengths of all cables wherever possible. If you use pre-fab cables throughout, this is a trivial matter; but if your network is installed in the walls of your home, ask your builder or contractor to provide a diagram with accurate measurements as part of what you're paying for. Otherwise, you'll need to rent the necessary test equipment to determine cable lengths for yourself, or pay a cable contractor to come do it for you (either way, expect to spend at least $200 to get the job done). If you get a network installed or buy any new Ethernet cables, make sure to purchase CAT-5e cable, because it can handle everything up to and including Gigabit Ethernet.

Best Home Networking Practices

In general, we strongly urge you to use a wired network connection for your Media Center PC, preferably Gigabit Ethernet (though 100 Base-TX is acceptable). Use a wireless link only if you must.

If you decide to use a wireless network, ponder these points as you plan your implementation:

- Use the fastest technology you can afford. 108 Mbps 802.11g products are only about 25 percent more expensive than 54 Mbps alternatives, so pick 108 Mbps if you can find suitable offerings.

- If your Media Center PC is near a CRT-based TV set, get an external antenna for your wireless interface, and place it as far away from the set as possible. Or pick a USB interface with a cable between your PC and the device. Check network performance to ensure optimal antenna placement.

- Try to limit the number of users on same wireless network as your Media Center PC. If necessary, put a separate network in place for everybody else to use and give the Media Center PC its own exclusive network connection to your Internet access device.

- Consider using a MIMO (multiple input, multiple output) access point or router, which often improves throughput in locations with lots of walls and obstructions (such as a house).

If you decide to use a wired network, consider these items as you put it in place:

- Buy a Gigabit Ethernet switch and build your network around it. It will accommodate 10 and 100 Mbps links, so you can upgrade slowly over time if that's your choice. Some switches use noisy fans to keep them cool, but if they're located well away from the audio playback areas or offices, then that shouldn't be an issue.

- Build your Media Center PC around a motherboard with built-in Gigabit Ethernet and use that connection to access your home network from that PC.

- If you set up any network storage, make sure it's directly accessible over a Gigabit Ethernet link (whether attached to the network itself, to your Internet access device, or to another PC on the network).

- If your home network includes multiple PCs and you don't use Gigabit Ethernet throughout, put the Media Center PC (and any attached extenders) on a separate network if at all possible (especially if all other links are 100 Mbps or slower).

By providing as much network bandwidth to your Media Center PC as you can, you will help to ensure the best possible viewing and download capabilities.

Your Internet Link

Remember to use the fastest link you can afford for Internet access with a Media Center PC. For most users, this means broadband. Make sure you understand any limits your service provider may put on downstream (from the Internet to your location) and upstream (from your location to the Internet) traffic. Most DSL companies limit both upstream and downstream traffic; some cable companies do likewise (others limit only upstream, usually to 384 Kbps). Whatever your circumstances, make sure you understand how much Internet bandwidth you've got. Anything over 512 Kbps downstream is usually okay for home theater applications, but Internet bandwidth is one case where more is better!

You can check your Internet bandwidth using any number of Web sites (try a search on "Internet bandwidth test" with your favorite search engine to see what we mean). Table 13-3 lists some of our favorites.

Table 13-3   Internet Bandwidth Tests

Name	URL	Remarks
Bandwidth Meter	`reviews.cnet.com/bandwidth_meter/7004-7254_7-0.html`	Downstream only
PC Pitstop	`www.pcpitstop.com/internet/bandwidth.asp`	Upstream and downstream
Testmy.net	`www.testmy.net`	Upstream and downstream
Toast.net	`www.toast.net/performance`	Downstream only
Broadband Reports	`www.broadbandreports.com`	Various throughput and latency tests available

Tip

When measuring bandwidth for cable modem connections, it's important to understand that your local cable segment works like a shared Ethernet segment. That means that when more users are active, the lower your bandwidth reading will be. This explains how you can get different readings at different times of day and why upstream readings are more likely to reflect metered limits than downstream readings.

Networking Tools

Beyond checking the speed of your Internet connection, it's also a good idea to check on the health of the network to which your HTPC is attached. You can (and probably should) use the networking tab in Windows Task Manager to check network utilization. This output is shown in Figure 13-1, which displays network utilization with a large file transfer underway (much like you'd see when copying a file across your network, or saving a recording on another drive elsewhere on the network).

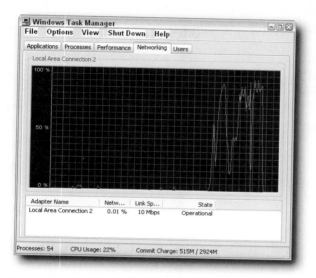

FIGURE 13-1: The Networking tab in Windows Task Manager shows that nearly 100-percent utilization is possible when only a single machine uses the network.

At the command line, lots of commands offer insight into what's up on networks to which a Windows machine is attached. The netstat command provides information about traffic into and out of specific network interfaces. Among its capabilities, you can request Ethernet statistics using the -e switch, and per protocol statistics using the -s switch. Figure 13-2 shows the output from running netstat -se. Information about errors, packets discarded, and TCP segments retransmitted are all good if crude measures of network health. Type netstat /? in a command Window to read the online help file for this command, or look up "netstat overview" at www.microsoft.com for additional documentation and usage instructions.

Cross-Reference To go beyond these rough metrics for network activity and health, you'd have to dig in and learn some things. A good place to start is in the TCP/IP Troubleshooting section in the Windows 2000 Resource Kit online. Visit www.microsoft.com and search on "Windows 2000 Overview of TCP/IP Troubleshooting." You'll find a wealth of information here, most of it directly applicable to Windows Server 2003 and Windows XP as well as Windows 2000.

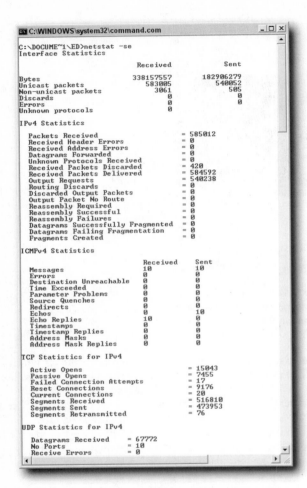

FIGURE 13-2: Run the netstat command inside a command window to get useful information about Ethernet statistics and network errors.

Best HTPC Networking Options

Table 13-4 mentions numerous vendors that offer high-quality networking gear suitable for HTPC use. Of these, we've gotten great results with products from D-Link, Linksys, 3Com, and Belkin. For brevity we use the following codes in the second column of the table to itemize what each vendor offers, product-wise:

- **GI** — Gigabit Ethernet internal interface (PCI, PCI-E X1, . . .)
- **GS** — Gigabit Ethernet switch
- **IAB** — Internet Access device, dual cable modem/DSL support
- **IAC** — Internet Access device, cable modem only
- **IAS** — Internet Access device, DSL only
- **WI** — Wireless Ethernet interface (PCI, PCI-E X1, . . .)
- **WU** — Wireless Ethernet USB interface, same indicators for 802.11x as for WI item

Table 13-4   Quality Networking Vendors

Name	Item Codes	URL/Remarks
3Com	GI, IAB, WI, WU	www.3com.com; switches available, but no low-price Gigabit versions
Belkin	GI, GS, IAB, WI, WU	www.belkin.com; also wired USB adapters for 10/100 Ethernet
D-Link	GI, GS, IAB, WI, WU	www.d-link.com; also wired USB adapters for 10/100 Ethernet
Linksys	GI, GS, IAB, WI, WU	www.linksys.com; also wired USB adapters for 10/100 Ethernet
NETGEAR	GI, GS, IAB, WI, WU	www.netgear.com; also wired USB adapters for 10/100 Ethernet

All are well-known networking technology providers and offer good values in nearly all categories covered.

Wrapping Up

Making sure network and Internet links are fast enough for your HTPC is important. Sometimes these links can have as powerful an impact on viewing or listening experiences for streaming or on-demand media as the PCs where materials are stored and auditioned. We must recommend 100 Mbps Ethernet or faster for your local network and a broadband Internet link (or faster) as networking basics for a Media Center PC.

We can't recommend slow networking technologies, such as 10 Mbps wired 802.3, 10 Base-T, or 11 Mbps 802.11b for Media Center PC use. Likewise, telephone Internet links don't cut it for HTPC use either, because their bandwidth tops out at a maximum of 56 Kbps (but usually run slower than that).

The HTPC Remote and Controlling Your Set-Top Box

Most would agree that life without a remote control for our TV set is almost inconceivable. When you come home tired, getting up to change the channel seems too much like work. Fortunately, a remote device controls nearly everything the TV can do, including changing settings, switching inputs, and more. Why should this be any different for an HTPC?

In this chapter, you are presented with criteria to help you evaluate your remote control needs. Don't worry: you also get a chance to see three of the top candidates for your HTPC, with a rundown of the pros and cons for each remote. Before you get there, however, we make a quick stop to explain some technical jargon that you encounter in this chapter. You'll find the same lingo when you go to look for a remote on your own as well. In the final portion of the chapter, you are introduced to two related topics: controlling a cable box or satellite box from your HTPC, and using a wireless mouse and keyboard with your HTPC. All of these topics share a remote connection!

The Remote: A Couch Potato's Best Friend

Most people like using remote controls with their TV sets. Given that hundreds of different kinds are available, what makes for a good remote?

- **Functionality:** Above all, you want your remote to do what you need it to do. For HTPC users much of this is the same as driving a VCR or DVD player. You need play, stop, pause, fast-forward, and rewind controls. The remote should also be able to skip chapters when playing DVDs and provide numerical keys so you can skip directly to a chapter by number, and enter any channels or codes you might need when configuring TV settings. When you are using program menus, the remote should provide arrows to navigate left, right, up, and down, an Enter or OK button to select options, and a back or previous button so you can quickly jump back to where you were before entering your most recent command. Channel up and channel down controls are important when watching TV. Also very convenient but not necessarily crucial is a "home button" that takes you back to the main menu with a single touch.

- **Layout:** The remote you choose should be logically laid out. For example, play, stop, pause, fast-forward, and rewind buttons should all be grouped together. Another layout criterion relates to size: do the most commonly used buttons align with how the remote sits in your palm? If buttons such as play, pause, and OK don't line up well then you must ask yourself "How much bother will this be to use?" "Do layout issues outweigh other advantages of this remote?" and so on.

- **Size and weight:** If a remote is too large to fit comfortably in your hand, you won't have a pleasant experience. Likewise, if the remote is shaped awkwardly or places the battery compartment in an odd spot, this can make the balance clumsy and the remote hard to hang onto.

- **Appearance:** Last but not least, if you do find the remote aesthetically displeasing you won't be inclined to use it and you sure won't want to show it off to friends. And we wouldn't want that now would we? An HTPC is supposed to be a cool tech gadget that makes you the envy of all your friends!

IR and RF Signals Explained

To help you better understand which remote is best for you, it's important to understand the signaling technology each potential candidate uses. Remotes generally use one of two types of signals: infrared (IR) or radio frequencies (RF). IR is probably what makes almost any TV remote you have seen do its job. It signals devices using light waves below the spectrum of light you perceive as red. To be more specific, a special infrared LED on the remote control uses pulses of light to send a signal to your TV to tell it to turn up the volume or change the channel.

IR generally works well but is subject to some limitations:

- **Distance:** For a signal to pass successfully from a sending to a receiving device, you must use any IR device within the same room as the receiver (for example, your TV set) for the signal to reach its destination.

- **Line of sight:** You must point an IR-based remote at the device you want to control and have an unobstructed view of that device.

- **Ambient lighting:** Because IR is itself a form of light, intense bright lights or white surfaces can disrupt or bounce IR signals. One interesting side effect is that you can often bounce an IR signal off a white wall to extend your remote's reach or to send a signal around a corner.

The second form of remote signaling uses radio frequencies (RF). RF remotes work much like cordless phones. The remote includes a low-power radio transmitter that communicates with a radio receiver on the other end. RF has advantages and disadvantages as compared to IR:

- **Distance:** RF works over fairly long distances.

- **Line of sight:** Unlike IR, radio signals travel into and around our homes or cars. When we listen to the radio, no line of site to the transmitter tower is needed. This explains why you can go into the next room and change the channel on your HTPC in the living room using an RF-based remote.

- **Compatibility:** RF's biggest downside is that most remotes and remote signal receivers are IR based. This means that RF-only remotes don't work as universal remote controls, because they can't transmit commands to devices that don't have built-in RF receivers.

Media Center Remote Control Features and Functions

As mentioned earlier, a remote should provide the common features that individual remotes for TV sets, DVD players, and VCRs deliver. These include the following:

- Record, play, stop, pause, fast-forward, and rewind.

- Channel up and down.

- Volume up, down, and mute.

- Numerical keys — Crucial for entering channel numbers directly, skipping directly to a specific DVD chapter, or entering information such as time or date.

- Chapter skip keys — Useful when playing DVDs. Many so-called universal remotes don't offer a dedicated button for chapter skips; they assign a button or button combination for this job using software called into service when you're playing a DVD.

- Arrow keys — Crucial for navigating MCE and DVD menus.

- OK or Enter button — Used to accept menu items once highlighted or selected.

- Home button — A useful function that works best when assigned a dedicated button. The home button lets you jump back to the main menu at any time; it's a great way to transition from one activity to another.

Any worthy remote not only includes these basics but also offers buttons tied to specific functions; such buttons act as shortcuts to common tasks. On an HTPC these usually include Live TV, DVD Menu, Guide, and Music buttons. Many universal remotes include generic buttons you can program to perform these tasks. For a closer look at how the Microsoft and SnapStream remotes each handle shortcut buttons take a look at Figure 14-1.

FIGURE **14-1: Close-up of the function buttons on the Microsoft remote versus the universal buttons on the Firefly.**

A nice extra is mouse emulation. The SnapStream Firefly offers a mouse mode wherein the remote behaves like a mouse (see Figure 14-2). This isn't absolutely essential, but it is handy when troubleshooting, or if you open a program that isn't remote friendly.

FIGURE 14-2: Close-up of the Firefly's mouse emulation buttons.

Finding and Buying a Remote

In Table 14-1 you'll find some of the vendors that make MCE-compatible remotes, along with information about their transmission technology and pricing, plus related comments.

Table 14-1   Remote Vendors with HTPC Offerings

Name	Technology	Price Range	URL/Remarks
Logitech Harmony*	Universal IR	$199.95–$249.95	www.logitech.com; easy-to-program universal remotes; 680 and 880 models are MCE ready.
Microsoft Media Remote	IR	Approx. $35	OEM-only kit made specifically 2005 Center for MCE 2005; also includes compatible IR blasters.
SnapStream Firefly*	RF	$49.99	www.snapstream.com; feature-packed RF remote is compatible with many programs.
StreamZap PC Remote	IR	$39.95	www.streamzap.com; basic IR remote; software is compatible with variety of media software, including MCE.

*All the companies whose names are asterisked were kind enough to furnish remotes for this book.

Top Choices

The Microsoft remote stands out as the one that's easiest to implement. That's probably because this device is built specifically for use with Windows XP MCE 2005. The remote's receiver also houses the IR blaster (emitter) controller. This is the only IR blaster hardware that is compatible with MCE. If you have a cable box or satellite receiver you will need to use the MCE remote kit. You don't have to use the remote, but you do need the remote receiver because the IR blaster(s) plugs into the back of the receiver module.

The MS remote also has a handy button found at the top center called "The Green Button." This special element triggers the MCE interface to load if it is closed. Or, if you are already running MCE, it takes you to the main menu from wherever you are.

Another excellent but expensive choice is the Logitech Harmony 680. If you can afford it, this remote is incredibly easy to program. It's a universal remote, which means it can control the rest of your home theater equipment (up to 15 devices in all) in addition to MCE 2005. The Harmony family of remotes is activity-based by design. When you press a button such as "Watch a Movie" the remote issues a series of commands that handles everything on your home theater. For example: it could turn on your HDTV set and change the input to DVI, turn on your surround receiver and set the correct input, and then select the DVD option in MCE 2005 — all with the press of a single button!

Programming the Harmony to work with your home theater devices is incredibly simple: log in to Logitech's site and choose those devices you own. Connect the USB cable from the remote to your PC. It programs all the correct codes for you. No need to test multiple 4-digit codes! The Logitech has direct shortcut buttons such as "Watch My TV" that will take you to a specified section in MCE. Take note, however, that the Harmony package includes only a remote control (unlike the MCE remote, which also includes an IR receiver and blaster cables). If you buy a Harmony remote, you must also buy an MCE-compatible remote receiver. Therefore the Harmony is more a supplement to the Microsoft MCE remote kit rather than a complete replacement for that kit.

A distant third place goes to SnapStream's Firefly. This remote enjoys the distinction of being the only RF-based remote we recommend. Its setup software is easy to use, and most of the software configuration works from your couch. The Firefly works with a broad range of

How to Buy the Microsoft Remote

Just like the Windows XP MCE 2005 software, the MCE remote is sold only bundled with system hardware. It's targeted at system builders who don't need much, if any, instruction or support. When you buy your system hardware most places will sell you an OEM copy of Windows; in this case you want Windows XP MCE 2005. Similarly, most places that sell Windows XP MCE 2005 also stock the MCE remote kit. You can buy a bundle that includes Windows MCE 2005 software and the MCE remote for around $155. PC Alchemy is one reputable online store that specializes in HTPC parts; it can sell you this bundle, as well as lots of other HTPC components you might need, such as a capture card or a case designed specifically to house an HTPC system.

applications beyond MCE 2005. Like the reference MCE remote from Microsoft, the Firefly also has a home button to take you back to the main menu. Sadly, there are two bugs with the Firefly's software and MCE that keep it from getting a stronger recommendation. You can read more about those issues in the next section.

A Tale of Three Remotes

Figure 14-3 shows all three remotes that we discuss in this section.

FIGURE 14-3: Group shot of all three remotes.

Microsoft Media Center Remote

Using the MCE remote is a plug-and-play affair — simply plug in the USB cable from the receiver module, and it is recognized automatically within a few seconds. There is no software to load or configure: everything needed is built into Windows XP MCE 2005.

The MCE remote is average sized and seems made to fit most any hand. There are no drastic curves, just a simple slope on the underside to help the remote rest in your palm. The MCE remote is labeled with functions that correlate exactly to functions within Media Center. The largest button on the remote is the Play button. The arrows and OK button are clustered right about where your thumb comes to rest. Just above this is the Play button and just below the "Green Button" flanked by the Channel Up/Down and Volume Up/Down buttons. The "back" and "more information" buttons are right next to the arrow buttons for quick access to playback options, or to a way out.

The issues with this remote are few. We found the skip forward and skip backwards buttons to be useful: they skip in 5-second increments that are just perfect for jumping past commercials. However, their small size and position (they're very close to the "back" and "more information" buttons) caused us to bump these other buttons sometimes, without meaning to do so.

Logitech Harmony 680

The Logitech Harmony family of remotes consists of many models; all are designed as high-end universal remotes. To use one of these fascinating devices, you must install a compatible IR receiver in your HTPC (Microsoft's remote receiver is the recommended device for use with MCE). The Harmony 680 can control an MCE 2005–based PC right out of the box. If you want to use it to control other home theater devices, you must program it from Logitech's Web site. Once the Harmony is programmed, its special task buttons work just like they should. Pressing the button with the TV icon turns on your TV with the right input, wakes up your MCE PC, and jumps to the My TV section in MCE. If you set up a home theater receiver, it turns that on and sets it to the correct input as well. The Harmony can also be set up so that its Volume Up and Down buttons always drive a specific device. For example, you may want to control the volume from your home theater receiver and not from your TV or HTPC.

Despite its inclusion of an LCD screen, the Harmony 680 isn't much larger than the Microsoft MCE remote. The additional batteries needed to power the LCD screen add slightly to the remote's weight, and makes the remote feel more substantial. To make the Harmony a natural replacement for the standard Microsoft MCE remote, the back and more buttons are in roughly the same spot relative to the OK button and directional arrows, and use the same icons. Better yet, the Harmony also includes a green "Media" button that functions like the special Windows "Green Button" on the Microsoft remote. It also has dedicated buttons to jump to live TV, recorded TV, and the program guide.

When you want to change which device the Harmony is controlling, simply choose its name from the list on the LCD screen. The remote has a slope in the middle where your hand can rest, and two indentations for your index and middle fingers when gripping the remote. The buttons are all within easy reach for your thumb. Sliding the remote up in the hand is necessary only when you want to use one of the task buttons, or to select a new device for the Harmony to control.

SnapStream Firefly

SnapStream's Firefly is RF based, so there are no remote codes to learn or need for an IR receiver. All you need is included in the box. After loading the Firefly software it detects that you are using Windows Media Center Edition and asks you if you prefer to use MCE or SnapStream's own basic HTPC front end called Beyond Media Basic (it's included with the Firefly). In most cases you can't tell you're using the Firefly instead of the genuine MCE remote, which is a good thing. SnapStream's Firefly software actually adds value here: if you forget which keys to use, you need only press its Help key and an overlay of buttons and their functions appears on screen. You can press the Close button or the Exit button to dismiss this screen and return to MCE.

The layout is different from the Microsoft remote; many of the button groups are inverted. The number pad is up top, and the transport controls are near the bottom. As you might imagine, the central Firefly button behaves like Microsoft's Green Button. (The functions of the Green Button are described earlier in the section called "Top Choices.")

The Firefly has a pleasing slope to help it rest in the hand. Unfortunately where it rests isn't always an ideal spot for your thumb. This means making some awkward thumb motions to play, fast-forward, or rewind media. Although these issues may simply reflect individual preferences and experiences, in testing the remote we had to slide the remote up and down in our hands to get at the areas that contained the necessary buttons. We didn't need to go through these motions when using the Microsoft remote.

Sadly, we also encountered two serious issues and one niggling issue when using the Firefly remote software with MCE 2005. Most serious is that the pause key triggers the same function as the play button. Thus, it can't pause playback properly. The second issue is also fairly serious: when listening to music, sometimes the Firefly software loses its focus on the MCE interface. To return to that interface, you must use mouse mode on the remote, or pull out your keyboard or mouse, then click your way back inside MCE. This bug appears under specific circumstances: it occurs only the first time that you select My Music inside MCE (but not thereafter). That said, closing and reopening the MCE interface causes this bug to recur.

Thankfully, SnapStream is aware of these issues, so some future update to the Firefly software should produce a truly great remote for any MCE system. (We tested the Firefly using software version 1.2.) The final issue is small and a limitation of how Firefly software supports the numeric keypad. Despite printing the standard alphabet near each number key on the remote (much like the alphabet appears on a telephone keypad) you can't use the Firefly to enter text. (Note: the Microsoft and Harmony remotes do support text entry.)

IR Blasters: Controlling a Set-Top Box

You may wonder how you can use your Media Center PC to take control of a set-top box like a cable box or satellite receiver. After all, the tuner on the TV card goes up only to channel 125, and digital cable or satellite channels go much higher. With a set-top box (a generic name we use for both cable boxes and satellite receivers) you let it tune in channels just as you would with your TV set. Does Microsoft expect you to run home and change the channel on your cable box when you need to record something? No way!

That's where a device called an IR blaster comes into play (an IR blaster is also often called an IR emitter). An *IR blaster* is an IR transmitter that's very much like a remote control. The difference is that rather than being connected to a remote control for a human to use, it's wired up to a computer for MCE software to use. When it's time to record a show, MCE sends a sequence of codes to your set-top box just as a remote control would, and changes channels automatically.

During setup, if MCE detects a set-top box it asks a few questions to see if it knows the sequence of codes your set-top box uses. As mentioned earlier in this chapter, the only IR blasters MCE 2005 supports are the two that are bundled with the Microsoft remote kit.

At the back of the remote receiver module you can see two holes labeled 1 and 2 (see Figure 14-4). These are ports where IR blaster cables plug in. The IR blasters themselves look very much like small earbud-style headphones, and they plug into the back of the MCE remote module using 1/8" mini-jacks. At the other end is a nub that houses an IR emitter. When you find the IR receiver on your set-top box, peel the backing off the IR nub and stick it to the face of your set-top box (see Figure 14-5). Don't worry: it won't block the signal from your normal remote. The plastic casing of the nub is tinted red and lights up when the IR blaster sends its codes to show that it's working.

FIGURE 14-4: Back of MCE remote module with IR blaster ports.

FIGURE 14-5: IR blaster stuck on a cable box.

Wireless Keyboards and Mice

Because this chapter is about controlling an HTPC, it's also appropriate to talk briefly about using a wireless keyboard and mouse to supplement a remote control. Because you will have full-fledged PC in your living room, you may want to perform standard PC tasks now and again, perhaps to surf the Web or start an online chat. MCE lets you use MSN Messenger while watching TV or playing a DVD, but a remote doesn't cut it for text entry.

As with remotes there are wireless keyboards and mice that use IR, RF, or a fairly new signaling method called "Bluetooth."

All keyboard and mouse combinations covered in Table 14-2 and this section of the chapter are either RF- or Bluetooth-based. IR keyboards tend to make transmission errors too apparent; sometimes it's possible to type faster than IR can handle. Or if transmission errors do occur, they show up as missed letters or incorrect characters.

Table 14-2   Wireless Keyboard and Mouse Vendors

Name	Technology	Price Range	URL/Remarks
Gyration	RF	$129.95–$179.95	www.gyration.com; unique gyroscopic mouse technology, compact keyboard for easy stowing.
Logitech*	RF and Bluetooth	$99.95–$249.95	www.logitech.com; wide range of combinations available, DiNovo series HTPC friendly, Bluetooth-enabled components available.
Microsoft*	RF and Bluetooth	$84.95–$159	www.microsoft.com; the standard for mice, Bluetooth-enabled components available.

*All the companies whose names are asterisked were kind enough to furnish keyboard and mouse kits for this book.

Bluetooth Explained

Bluetooth is a fairly new way to send data back and forth between devices. It's a standardized wireless network protocol much like Wi-Fi (802.11) that's designed for lower-power transmission inside a room rather than around the whole house. Bluetooth is most commonly associated with newer cell phones and personal digital assistants (PDAs). Rather than sending contact lists and e-mail between a PC and a portable device, a Bluetooth-enabled keyboard or mouse uses it to send keyboard codes or mouse movement data to the PC.

Top Choices

Gyration started as the manufacturer of deluxe presentation keyboards and mice with a unique mouse technology. A Gyration mouse has a small built-in gyroscope. In addition to working just like any normal optical mouse, you can pick it up and use it in the air, no desk required! As you can imagine, this capability fits HTPCs well. Gyration now produces two affordable kits that are a good match for an HTPC. Both include a compact keyboard that is well suited for use on your lap while sitting on a couch; when you're done, it's also easy to tuck away.

The first of these two bundles is the Gyration GO Mouse and Compact Keyboard Suite; this is the more traditional combination used for HTPCs. It includes the compact keyboard and a fairly typical optical mouse with a scroll wheel. The mouse includes a docking station for its rechargeable battery. The second combination, called the Gyration Media Center Suite, offers some interesting features. This desktop set includes the same keyboard as the other bundle. But instead of a typical wireless mouse, it includes a mouse with a group of buttons at its front end intended to provide basic remote controls. It also functions as a gyroscopic mouse and includes two normal mouse buttons for such use. Both of these are a bit more expensive than some other desktop sets you might consider, but both also offer conveniences that other sets don't.

Logitech offers a variety of affordable wireless keyboard and mouse combinations. Most include a full-sized keyboard. The budget choice here is the Cordless Desktop LX700. This kit uses Logitech's proprietary "Fast RF" signaling that makes mouse feedback work as if it were wired, good for those who want to game casually on a big screen. This mouse is rechargeable and comes with a recharging cradle. The next step up is the Cordless Desktop MX3100, which features a wireless version of Logitech's acclaimed laser mouse.

For a more HTPC-like feel to your keyboard and mouse Logitech offers a deluxe set called the diNovo Cordless Desktop. The diNovo features a split keyboard setup with a compact keyboard and a special media module that can act as a numeric keypad or as a media controller. The media controller has its own LCD screen. A small form-factor two-button mouse with a scroll wheel is also included. It's available in Logitech's "Fast RF" or in a Bluetooth version.

The Bluetooth version is called the diNovo Media Desktop (see Figure 14-6). It includes Logitech's deluxe MX900 optical mouse and brings the added benefit of acting as a universal Bluetooth hub. For example, if you have a wireless phone with Bluetooth capabilities, the Logitech receiver module can download your camera phone pictures to your HTPC. You can see a list of tested Bluetooth devices at Logitech's Web site. The keyboard is light, thin, and sleek: it rests easily on your lap without dominating the space around you. But the Media Pad is not incredibly useful and only adds unnecessary cost. On the other hand, the compact keyboard is great for casual use from the couch. Also, the included Bluetooth optical mouse is top of the line and handles gaming from your couch with ease.

If you're looking for a good-quality standard keyboard and mouse to use with your HTPC, don't forget the name Microsoft is synonymous with the word *mouse*. It, too, offers a Bluetooth keyboard and mouse combination that works well; it's called the Optical Desktop Elite for Bluetooth (see Figure 14-7). The keyboard is large and includes an undetachable wrist rest; although it's not an ideal HTPC keyboard, it does feel nice and sturdy. The mouse included in this bundle is the wireless version of Microsoft's excellent Intellimouse 4.0. This mouse is great for gaming on the big screen.

FIGURE 14-6: diNovo Media Desktop.

FIGURE 14-7: Optical Desktop Elite.

Tip

As this book is being written, a new keyboard is on the way from Microsoft (it's mentioned on their Web site, but we couldn't secure an advance copy for review in this book). It should be available by the time you read this. It's called the Microsoft Remote Keyboard for Windows XP Media Center Edition. This special keyboard is designed specifically by Microsoft to work with the existing MCE remote receiver hardware. The keyboard has all the functionality of the Microsoft MCE remote as well as a compact keyboard.

Wrapping Up

Choosing a remote control is intensely personal. That said, the main questions you must answer when making your choice are: "Does the remote have all the buttons I need to use my HTPC the way I want?" "Does the button layout make sense?" "Is it comfortable to use?" Buy only that remote for which you like all three of your answers to those questions.

IR Blasters enable your HTPC to communicate channel changes to a cable box or satellite receiver when it's time to record a program. If you need IR blasters, please remember that the MCE remote includes them at no extra charge.

A dedicated wireless keyboard and mouse is a boon to HTPC users and allows you to perform typical desktop PC tasks from the comfort of your sofa. Choosing a keyboard that isn't too large or awkward for lap use often persuades buyers to go for a reduced form factor, such as those included in select Gyration and Logitech desktop sets. These units to tend to be more expensive, but make up for added cost with increased convenience and more attractive features.

All the products discussed in this chapter could make fine additions for some HTPCs. But ultimately, your aesthetics and personal needs will determine which ones you actually purchase.

Planning and Building Your Media Center PC

part

III

Planning Your HTPC

Building a PC has become a task of medium complexity these days. It's neither as easy as building a sandwich, nor anywhere as difficult as building a house. But a certain amount of planning is required to pull off this task, especially given specific hardware requirements for Windows Media Center Edition 2005.

We try to make it easy for you to plan your build by including a checklist of basic pieces and parts, then walking you through the process for the Media Center PCs we build in Chapters 18, 19, and 20. Along the way, we take an occasional pause to discuss reasons for making certain selections and to indicate what kinds of cost-saving alternatives might apply, depending on your needs and budget.

Though there are many important decisions to make when planning a PC build, none is arguably more important than setting a spending limit because that inevitably puts limits on the range of choices for various constituent elements. Because ready-made Media Center PCs are available for prices as low as $900 to as high as $5,000 as this book is being written, we decided to set $1,700 as the budget for the PCs we'll build, allowing also a plus or minus swing of 10 percent (this puts our target between $1,500 and $1,900 in round numbers).

This chapter covers the following topics while walking through the planning process for building an HTPC:

- **Establishing budget guidelines:** Here you learn how to let key component choices drive overall budget projections, and how to ballpark various component costs in terms of a total figure. We also explain how we arrived at a target budget, and what we expect to get in return for our money.

- **Picking core components:** CPU, case, and motherboard all depend heavily on each other. We explain how to approach selection from each of these three angles, and cover power supply and RAM selection here, too. Along the way, we make selections for our three target systems.

- **Selecting hard drive type and size:** Depending on your noise requirements and other factors, drive selection involves making some surprisingly interesting choices. We walk through them as we select drives for our target systems.

- **Selecting optical drive and capabilities:** MCE requires a DVD player (and all modern offerings also play CDs); common sense dictates write capability as well as playback. We walk through some options and trade-offs and then make our choices.

- **Making a network connection:** We look at networking options on our chosen motherboards, and then make appropriate add-in choices. We discuss possible trade-offs here, especially speed versus capability and storage requirements.

- **Selecting sound sources:** We look at sound outputs from our chosen motherboards, and make appropriate choices about add-in sound cards. Again, we discuss possible trade-offs, especially in terms of audio quality and output requirements. We also briefly discuss speakers (two of our three targets make an entertainment center their connections for final sound processing and delivery).

- **Handling graphics and visuals:** We look at onboard graphics capabilities and outputs from our chosen motherboards and make appropriate graphics card selections. We also address display choices and decide among various options.

- **Choosing a remote control and IR receiver:** We examine our options for remote control of our HTPC and then choose among available offerings. We mention other alternatives and justify our selections.

- **Making the TV connection:** We describe available options and ponder the SDTV/ HDTV dilemma. We then select various TV tuner cards, justify our selections, and explain potential added-cost upgrades for your consideration.

- **Potential (or missing) miscellany:** Here we recount the items we had to go out and buy to complete our systems, and explain what kinds of additional elements you may need (or want) to include in your budget, along with their cost impact.

- **Adding up the bill:** Here we present tables for each machine that details choices and related costs, and then calculate various totals.

Most of our product selections during the planning phase panned out in practice during our builds. But we overlooked a few items, and some didn't make the grade for reasons ranging from insufficient clearance inside our case to apparent hardware problems with some of the items we obtained for our builds. Only one of three builds went all the way through the hardware phase without a single hitch; the others did likewise once we replaced malfunctioning components.

Cross-Reference All details about hardware and software issues are covered in Chapters 18, 19, and 20, each of which details the build-out processes and our experiences for the three machines planned in this chapter. Chapter 17 also describes the general process of installing Windows MCE 2005 to help you prepare for this activity on your own machine.

In the sections that follow, you'll get familiar with the planning process for building an HTPC and be exposed to different selection rationales as well as specific choices that resulted from them. We conclude this chapter with a recommended checklist to help you through your own budgeting, planning, and component selection processes.

Building a Budget

Before you can get started selecting PC components, you need an idea of how much money you can spend on your HTPC as a point of departure. Like many planning tools, the number you start with may not be the exact number you end up with—but it should provide a helpful target at which to aim and may prevent you from overshooting your limits (in our experience, coming in under budget is rare enough that it's seldom worth worrying about).

As this chapter is being written low-budget Media Center PCs are available for prices as low as $900 (throw in shipping, handling, and sales tax, and you're probably at or over $1,000). High-end platforms like the Hush Technologies E3 MCE or the Niveus Media Denali cost $4,000 or $5,000 and up, in round numbers. We chose a target budget of $1,700 for our systems for the following reasons:

- Numerous Media Center PCs or laptops that get good reviews from companies like HP, Dell, Ricavision, and Toshiba are available in that price range. To us, this indicates a good target price for affordable and highly functional capability.

- Hardly any systems in component-type horizontal cases are available for under $1,500 (most such systems cost $2,000 and up). Base offerings are usually a little under-configured (and might benefit from more RAM, bigger disk drives, and so on) so $1,700 seems a reasonable level to set for affordable functionality.

- The $1,700 price represents a threshold of pain for many individuals and families: spend much more than that, and it really hurts. Spend that much or less, and it can be absorbed without leaving too many scars.

- Working through numerous potential configurations with components we wanted to use, this number appeared at the middle of the price estimates we built.

If you can't afford to spend $1,700, you can cut corners at several points along the way. We'll point them out as we go through this chapter, and describe potential savings that could result. Spending more is indeed possible at all steps along the way; when it's potentially justifiable, we'll mention those things, ballpark added costs involved.

With a target budget of $1,700 in place, and a decision not to let those numbers swing by more than 10 percent (maxing out at $1,900, in other words) we can now get down to work and start picking pieces and parts.

Picking Core Components

Whether you pick the case, the motherboard, or the CPU first, these three items usually come first during the selection process. That's because the CPU/motherboard combination must fit the case, and what the motherboard can do dictates the kinds of expansion cards you must purchase to assemble a complete, working Media Center PC. The power consumption and attendant heat output of the CPU also has an impact on case selection (hotter-running CPUs generally do better in bigger cases with more room for active ventilation components and air-flow for cooling). Or, if you prefer, you can stand this logic on its head and decide you want a small compact case, and pick a micro-ATX motherboard with a Pentium M or Athlon CPU that doesn't require extreme cooling.

Because we wanted to hit all bases for potential Media Center PC platforms, we decided to pick three distinct configurations, each based around a specific CPU. At the same time, we also tried hard to pick components that would be as quiet as possible to keep noise output down. To establish a level playing field for memory, we decided to outfit all systems with 1GB of RAM (which maxes out two-slot micro-ATX motherboards when using 512MB DIMMs, and a modest amount for those mobos with three or four DIMM slots; this is also sufficient RAM for Media Center PCs to work within).

Core Components: Cost-Cutting and Higher-Dollar Measures

To cut costs further, well-ventilated tower cases generally cost only half as much as horizontal HTPC cases. You could also select lower-powered CPUs (or move down from P4 to Celeron, or Athlon 64 to Sempron processors); this also shaves related costs in half. Finally, half as much RAM (512MB instead of 1GB) also costs no more than half as much. Total savings could be as much as $300.

When it comes to spending more, you could insist on a $600 Origen case, and buy a faster, more expensive motherboard and CPU, then max out the RAM. But all these things require more cooling, which we think plays against a fundamental design goal when building any HTPC. But hey, it's your decision and your money—do what you like! You could easily spend an additional $1,000 or more this way, $2,000 or more if you go for top-of-the-line Pentium or Athlon 64 dual-core CPUs.

- **Pentium 4:** Despite at least one author's belief that Pentium 4s consume too much power and therefore require too much cooling to be suitable for HTPC use, we think some builders are going to want multi-use machines. That is, in tight quarters — such as dorm rooms, offices, or small apartments — people typically have only one PC. Thus, they must work on the same machine they also use for entertainment. If you accept that premise, a P4 machine with somewhat beefier components than a normal HTPC might require starts to make sense. To accommodate this situation and a 630 3.0 GHz P4's cooling needs, we selected an Antec P-180 tower case and an Antec Phantom 500 power supply. We also chose a midrange motherboard with moderate capabilities for this build, the ASUS P5AD2E-Deluxe.

- **Pentium M:** This chip was originally designed for laptops, where low power consumption is essential to extend battery life, and where space for active cooling is typically non-existent. These factors play nicely into building a cool and quiet HTPC; one of our builds puts these features to good use. We chose an Ahanix D5 HTPC case to house our system; it included a built-in 300 W power supply, so we didn't have to buy a PSU for this build. We also chose the AOpen i915GMm-HFS motherboard, which offers minimal graphics, but eight-channel sound capability.

- **Athlon 64:** This chip compares favorably to the P4 in terms of capability but draws only half the power of the faster, hotter Intel CPU. Cooling remains a concern, but quiet operation is easier to attain as cooling requirements abate. We chose the Silverstone LC14B case and used a Seasonic S12 380W Silent Power supply to provide the juice for this box. We also selected an Athlon 64 from the middle of that processor range — namely the 2.2 GHz Athlon 64 3500+.

Picking (a) Hard Disk(s)

The quietest HTPCs may actually choose to house their drives outside the case, either on a network-attached device somewhere else, or at the end of an external SATA connection. But because we're on a budget that precludes such choices here (they would either involve more expensive motherboards and external drives, or more expensive network storage devices), we opt for a single hard disk of moderate size (300GB) and assume additional storage is available elsewhere on your home network when and as it's needed.

Here's what we chose for the three different builds by way of hard disks:

- **P4:** The initial build includes a 300GB Maxtor DiamondMax Plus SATA 150 device. It's not the quietest drive around, but offers decent performance without excessive noise or heat output. The Antec case we chose makes adding more drives later a snap, should we decide to do so.

- **Pentium M:** The initial build includes the same drive used for the P4 build. The Ahanix case provides only one 3.5" drive bay, so that's it for this box.

- **Athlon 64:** The initial build includes a slightly faster and quieter 300GB Seagate Barracuda SATA drive.

Hard Drives: Cost-Cutting and Higher-Dollar Measures

To cut costs further, smaller drives might be the ticket. In Chapter 7, we explain how using 2.5" laptop drives cuts down on noise and heat output (but also cuts drive capacity). This could be a quieter alternative, but trying to save money at the same time probably means buying a 40GB or 60GB drive — that makes more storage somewhere else on the network for music, TV recordings, and other multimedia files that Media Center PCs work with regularly an absolute must. For 3.5" drives, cut SATA capacity to 200GB or less and save about half the cost; go smaller and save even more. Savings of $100 or more are possible for this category.

Bigger drives cost more, but often make more noise. Adding more storage elsewhere on your network is probably the best way to boost storage available to your Media Center PC. Expect to pay $600 and up for each terabyte of storage you add this way.

Choosing an Optical Drive

Case dimensions and space can sometimes dictate the purchase of a slim-profile DVD player/burner. Because they can be more expensive than their bulkier standard counterparts, we were fortunate that all three of our chosen cases could accommodate standard-sized DVD drives. Because of its quiet, competent operation and nice price of $60, we chose the same DVD player/burner for all three builds — namely, the NEC ND-3520A 16X Double Layer DVD+-RW drive.

Other factors that may come into play involve optical drive dimensions. Slim-profile drives cost more, but may be the only options suitable for slim HTPC cases. Smaller cases may also benefit if buyers consider drive length (which typically varies between under 5" to as long as 8", depending on make and model) when they choose optical drives to match their cases. Certainly, a shorter optical drive would have made our build in the Ahanix D5 case easier, where space between the backs of the drives and the front edge of the motherboard was non-existent. Check device specifications on vendor Web sites for this data; they always include outside dimensions for planning purposes.

Optical Drive: Cost-Cutting and Higher-Dollar Measures

Cheaper, noisier DVD drives can be had for as little as $25, but to our way of thinking dollars saved don't compensate adequately for noise gained. Higher priced slimline models from Panasonic and Teac are available with prices from $125–$165, for those who need them. Those looking for a SATA DVD drive might want to try the $120 Plextor PX-716SA.

Making the Network Connection

This part of the planning is absurdly easy: because all the motherboards we chose support at least one Gigabit Ethernet connection (which also work on 100 and 10 Mbps networks as well), this part's done for us. Also, there's no way to save money on something built into the motherboard, so we can't deal with cost savings for this category, either. If you decide you need a wireless link for your HTPC you will have to spend at least $30 for an 802.11g 54 Mbps USB or internal interface, but total expense could go as high as $200 if you also need to add a wireless router or access point for 108 Mbps 802.11g as well.

Note You can purchase wireless bridges that attach to the Ethernet port and permit a PC to access a wireless network. These are easier to install than a PCI card and require less CPU resources than a typical USB wireless device. Be sure to investigate these offerings, too!

Selecting Sound Sources

We're going to follow our own advice elsewhere in the book and lean on the motherboard to handle sound when 7.1 multichannel audio or eight-channel high-definition audio are supported. That means we don't need to install a sound card in any of our target builds. If you listen to the results and don't like what you hear you can add a decent sound card for as little as $25 for a Chaintech AV-710, an entirely adequate and capable sound card. Or you can spend $60 and up for a Creative Labs Audigy 2 ZS or one of its more powerful and better sounding siblings (the 2 ZS Platinum, Platinum Pro, and 4 ZS all offer more options and improved signal-to-noise ratios; see Chapter 10 for details).

Sound: Cost-Cutting and Higher-Dollar Measures

Given the near ubiquity of built-in 7.1 and eight-channel audio on modern motherboards, it's hard to save any more money than exercising onboard sound-handling affords. That's why we jump right to added-cost options: Those audiophiles or individuals seeking access to analog inputs or digital sound-editing capabilities could install higher-end Audigy 2 ZS Platinum or Platinum Pro models on any of these machines, or even spring for Creative Labs' top-of-the-line Audigy 4 Pro series for still more digital recording, editing, and decoding options. This could add as much as $350 to overall system costs, depending on which target platform and which sound card you choose. For the P4 system, you could check out other higher-end, self-powered 5.1 or 7.1 sets from other vendors such as Bose, JBL, Klipsch, and others, starting at $75 more than the Logitech array we chose and climbing into the stratosphere from there. Or you could use cheaper speaker arrays that lack integrated hardware decoders and install a Creative Labs Audigy 2 ZS card to do that job instead. Our suggestion, if you feel like spending much more than $400 on PC audio, is to invest in an AV receiver and a set of good loudspeakers as well as whatever kind of sound card add-in you think you might need.

And because we designed the P4 system as a do-it-all, standalone home theater/desktop/ moderate gaming rig, we included speakers with built-in digital decode capabilities: For this build, we chose Logitech's Z-5500 5.1 digital speaker array. These can pump out plenty of sound for a small office, dorm room, or apartment for under $300.

Handling Graphics

Here, we took the approach of wanting to install a graphics card with better graphics and video handling capability than built-in offerings could deliver. The ASUS and Chaintech mother-boards lacked graphics outputs altogether (not uncommon for higher-end models where designers assume buyers will use high-end graphics cards in any case), so graphics cards were must-haves for both of those machines. The AOpen motherboard's built-in graphics weren't really up to HTPC standards, either, so we picked one for the Pentium M system also. Here are more particulars:

- **P4:** Because this machine is intended to perform multiple computing roles (desktop, home theater, and light gaming), we decided to install a higher-end graphics card than is typical in some HTPCs. Here, we went with the Gigabyte GeForce 6600 PCI-e 256MB Silentpipe model (whose heat pipes keep the GPU cool, but require lots of space in the case for an oversize card — no problem in the Antec P-180 that houses this build).

Graphics: Cost-Cutting and Higher-Dollar Measures

If you're seeking to save money, a good 128MB graphics card works nicely on an HTPC machine. Most such models cost under $100 whether they're built on the ATI, nVidia, or some other GPU (fanless models will cost more, though). This delivers savings from $100 to $150 depending on how you downgrade, but also makes such systems useless for high-end gaming.

At the middle of the range, buyers should be aware that Gigabyte offers a Silentpipe model of the 6600GT graphics card for about twice the price of the 256MB plain 6600 with half the graphics memory (we don't think the performance boost repays the added cost). Likewise, fanless versions of the ATI X800 and X800 XL cards are also available for prices starting at about $285 and up. HTPC users with modest gaming ambitions might consider these a worthwhile buy-up.

On the high side of the graphics world, the most you can spend these days requires buying an SLI rig (SLI stands for "scalable link interface," and requires buying a special motherboard and two or more high-end PCI-E graphics cards). The most common SLI configuration doubles up the PCI-E X16 slots and makes room for two graphics cards. Figure $500–$700 each for the graphics cards, and anywhere from no added cost to an additional $150 for the motherboard, and costs could go up by as much as $1,550 (don't do this unless you go for a top-of-the-line Pentium or Athlon 64 CPU as well, preferably a dual-core model).

- **Athlon 64:** We chose the same fanless Gigabyte card for this build that we chose for the P4 build because both cases have room for this affordable monster of a card. If more space is needed to make room for other PCI cards, the eVGA fanless 6600 make a good, but more expensive, alternative.

- **Pentium M:** Our motherboard provides a PCI-E X16 slot, but less clearance above or to the sides in the Ahanix D5 than in the other cases. That's why we chose the more expensive but slimmer eVGA fanless 6600 graphics card for this build.

Remote Control and Other Inputs

Based on our survey of and experience with available remote controls, although there are many potential candidates to choose from, only two stand out. One is the Microsoft MCE Remote, the other is the Logitech Harmony 860 remote; both include an IR receiver along with the remote itself as part of the product package — but only the MCE remote's IR receiver works with MCE! The Logitech Harmony costs more than the Microsoft remote and offers more functionality. The Microsoft model shines as the intended remote control for Media Center PCs; the Harmony's USB-connector and Internet-based download of device information make it a contender for that over-used designation: "universal remote" (this appellation is too often claimed for devices that don't deserve it, in our humble opinion).

We decided to endow the P4 system with a Microsoft remote because it won't need to drive too many other devices (perhaps a set-top cable box and TV set at most). But because the Athlon 64 and Pentium M systems will sit in an entertainment center chock-full of other equipment, we endowed them with the Harmony remote. That said, remember that if you buy the Harmony remote you must still also buy the MCE remote, to get a workable IR receiver to plug into your HTPC.

Remotes and Inputs: Cost-Cutting and Higher-Dollar Measures

The remote is the hub of any Media Center PC's universe. This is not something on which you should try to save money. That said, if you don't need or want universal remote capability, the Microsoft remote is $85 cheaper than its Logitech counterpart, so you can save some money buying only the cheaper selection instead of also springing for the more expensive option.

But when it comes to a wireless (or wired) keyboard and mouse, there's a lot of room for savings and for extra expense, if you like. The cheapest keyboard and mouse available won't cost you much more than $25; the most expensive ones we could find cost $250. Compared to our picks, that represents savings of up to $50 and potential extra expense of about $200, depending on which way you go (up or down in price, that is).

See if you can find somebody who has one or both of them, and take them for a spin. Buy the Harmony if you need it to control other IR devices is the only advice we can give here. Because the same chapter that covered remote controls also covered wireless keyboards and mice, we recommend a decent Bluetooth or radio-frequency (RF) keyboard and mouse combination. For our budget we stuck to desktop sets (mouse and keyboard sold together), and picked the Logitech Cordless Desktop LX 700 (about $100 retail, discounts down to $55 available), and the Microsoft Optical Desktop Elite (about $100 retail, discounts down to $75 available). Both are comfortable, middle-of-the-pack offerings that do the job nicely.

Making the TV Connection

Here's one place where the sky is potentially the limit, depending on what you want to do with your TV and your Media Center PC. To try to keep chaos under control, we elected not to include HDTV options in these builds. Though many other options are available, we stuck with the tried and true Hauppauge WinTV PVR-150 MCE. At $65 it does its job well and affordably and works well with Windows MCE.

Tip

All HDTV interfaces that work in a Media Center PC in North America today handle only over-the-air (OTA) HDTV transmissions and cost $100 and up. If your build leaves room to occupy another slot with an HDTV card, add this into your budget and your system as you choose. Leading HDTV cards available today include the MyHD MDP-130, the DVICO FusionHDTV5, and the VBox DTA-151; other models from ATI, AVerMedia, and others are also available (the vast majority of these cost between $100 and $150; the MyHD card costs $250).

TV Connection: Cost-Cutting and Higher-Dollar Measures

The TV connection is one where saving money often means accepting a lower-quality image on your display as well, so when trying to save money on a TV card, get ready for fuzzy images especially for characters generated for onscreen display (box scores in televised sports are a great source for this kind of image data). How low can you go? You might be able to save $30 off the price of the Hauppage single-tuner card.

On the high end, lots of HTPC builders install two TV tuners in their machines. This means a dual-tuner card like the Hauppauge PVR 500 (probably the most popular offering of its kind), or sometimes, two ATI TV Wonder Elites. Figure on spending $300 for two ATI TV Wonder Elites, or $140 for the Hauppauge WinTV PVR-500MCE.

Missing Miscellany

Whenever you build a PC, you will come to some point in your build process where you need to go out and buy additional parts to complete the process. This normally involves cables and fans, on both of which we had to spend between $10 and $30 for our systems. For the Intel P4 CPU we snagged from Intel, we also had to purchase a CPU cooler (boxed retail versions include these in the purchase price, but they can be too noisy for those seeking to build quiet systems) — but we chose to regard that as a good thing because it let us choose the best and quietest coolers for the job (we spent $60 on the P4 Thermalright cooler we chose). AMD furnished us with a reasonably quiet cooler for the Athlon 64, and AOpen included a cooler for the Pentium M with its motherboard.

Expect to spend at least $25–$50 on stuff otherwise unaccounted for during the HTPC build process. If you do need to buy a cooler, it's hard to spend more than $100 on anything that doesn't involve the use of water or some kind of refrigerant for cooling. We included $35 for a miscellaneous category in our budgets as a kind of middle-of-the-road estimate, except for the P4 system, where we added another $60 for the cooler cost. Your mileage will definitely vary, as far as this category goes!

There is one more very necessary expense when building a Media Center PC that appears nowhere else in our budget, so we cover it here. It's the $120 that Windows XP Media Center 2005 costs if you purchase it from a vendor who'll sell it standalone. Look for deals on "MCE bundles" (especially the MCE Remote plus Windows XP MCE 2005), and you may be able to save $15–$20 on the combined costs we use in our budgets!

Adding Up the Bill

Based on all the items we picked for each of the builds, it's remarkable how closely we tracked our budget of $1,700 and how close in price all three systems were. The Athlon system was the cheapest, at $1,463, and the Pentium 4 and Pentium M systems nearly tied at $1,788 and $1,705, respectively. If you leave out the loudspeakers that we chose only for the "do-it-all" P4 system, it comes in at $1,518.

But as is so often the case, these numbers don't tell the entire story. If you leave the case (and where necessary, the power supply and speakers) costs out of the three equations, the results are: the Athlon 64 system is tied with the P4 system at $1,248, and the Pentium M system comes out on top at $1,480. This is probably the best way to compare prices, because the same kind of HTPC case and power supply could be used for all three systems and would therefore add a pretty typical, but constant $215 to each of those prices (ignoring the speakers yet again).

Tables 15-1 through 15-3 show the items chosen for each component category, along with their costs.

Costing HTPC Components

Whenever you buy anything that's widely available—as is true for nearly all of the components we itemize for our three HTPCs in Tables 15-1, 15-2, and 15-3—prices can vary tremendously. We picked the lowest prices we could find from reputable online vendors using tools like Computer Shopper (www.shopper.com), PriceWatch (www.pricewatch.com), Froogle (froogle.google.com), and so forth and then rounded them up to the nearest whole dollar for presentation.

What's missing from this approach? Shipping and handling costs! To keep those as low as possible buy as much as you can from a single vendor and ship it all at once, by the slowest way you can stand. Waiting takes patience, but it also saves money!

Table 15-1   Pentium 4 Build List

Component	Item Chosen	Cost
Case	Antec P180	$120
Motherboard	ASUS P5AD-2E	$207
CPU	P4 630	$220
Hard disk	Maxtor DiamondMax Plus SATA 300 GG	$150
Optical	NEC ND-3520A 16X Double Layer DVD+-RW	$60
Graphics card	Gigabyte GeForce 6600 PCI-E 256MB Silentpipe	$121
TV card	Hauppauge WinTV PVR-150 MCE	$65
Memory	1GB Corsair DDR2 PC4200 512MB	$120
Remote	Microsoft MCE and IR receiver bundle	$35
Sound card	onboard	$0
Speakers	Logitech Z-5500 Digital speakers	$270
CPU cooler	Thermalright XP-120 heat sink w/adapter	$60
Misc	Various cables and fans	$35
MCE SW	Microsoft Windows XP MCE 2005	$120
PSU	Antec Phantom 500	$150
Keyboard and Mouse	Logitech Cordless Desktop LX 700	$55
	TOTAL	$1,788

Table 15-2 Pentium M Build List

Component	Item Chosen	Cost
Case	Ahanix D5	$225
Motherboard	AOpen i915GMm-HFS	$265
CPU	Pentium M 745	$250
Hard disk	Maxtor DiamondMax Plus SATA 300 GG	$150
Optical	NEC ND-3520A 16X Double Layer DVD+-RW	$60
Graphics card	eVGA fanless 6600 256 MB	$168
TV card	Hauppauge PVR 150 MCE	$62
Memory	Crucial 2 x 512MB DDR 333	$132
Remote	Logitech Harmony & MCE	$153
CPU cooler	Included with mobo	$0
Misc	Various cables and fans	$35
MCE SW	Microsoft Windows XP MCE 2005	$120
PSU	Included with case purchase	$0
Keyboard and Mouse	Microsoft Optical Desktop Elite	$75
	TOTAL	$1,705

Table 15-3 Athlon 64 Build List

Component	Item Chosen	Cost
Case	Silverstone LC14B	$150
Motherboard	Chaintech VNF4 Ultra	$87
CPU	Athlon 65 3500+	$240
Hard disk	Seagate Barracuda SATA 300 GB	$178
Optical	NEC ND-3520A 16X Double Layer DVD+-RW	$60
Graphics card	Gigabyte Silentpipe 6600 256MB	$121
TV card	Hauppauge WinTV PVR-150 MCE	$65
Memory	Kingston HyperX DDR 400 512MB x 2	$134
Remote	Logitech Harmony, MCE Remote	$153
Sound card	Onboard	$0

Continued

Table 15-3 (continued)

Component	Item Chosen	Cost
CPU cooler	Included with CPU purchase	$0
Misc	Various cables and fans	$35
MCE SW	Microsoft Windows XP MCE 2005	$120
PSU	Seasonic S12 380W	$65
Keyboard and Mouse	Logitech Cordless Desktop LX 700	$55
	TOTAL	$1,463

The cost of the Pentium M versus the Pentium 4 may surprise some readers: but indeed, at today's prices, a 2.0 GHz Pentium M costs more than twice as much as a 3.2 GHz Pentium 4. But then, a Pentium M system like the one in our build consumes only about 80 W of power running at idle, whereas a P4 system like the one in our build consumes more like 220 W. All that extra power consumption means more heat production, which means more cooling is needed to keep the P4 system going. We report on average case and CPU temperatures at the end of Chapters 18, 19, and 20, and also provide our impressions of noise levels as well.

You may be thinking that, with prices ranging from a low of $1,463 for the Athlon 64 system and a high of $1,788 for the Athlon 64 system, we've come in on or under budget. Not so! By the time sales tax (where applicable, but often less so on items ordered online) and shipping and handling costs are added into these numbers, all of these budgets will be closer to our $1,900 high swing value, rather than our actual budget of $1,700. If you put any of these systems together, you'll find yourself agreeing with this assessment when you add up everything you've spent when the job is done!

HTPC Build Checklist and Budget Counter

The components listed in Tables 15-1, 15-2, and 15-3 provide our template for elements in a checklist you can use, except that here we list them in their most likely order of consideration (but remember, the first three items in the list are all tied for first place and should be considered together):

- **Case:** The box inside which you'll build your HTPC must fit the motherboard and be appropriate for the CPU's ventilation needs.
- **Motherboard:** The foundation on which you build any (HT)PC. Many modern motherboards offer features that make some expansion cards unnecessary, especially for networking, sound, and graphics (in that order).

- **CPU:** The central processing unit is the brains for any (HT)PC. Its selection will strongly influence motherboard and case selection.

- **Hard disk:** Storage for operating system, data, and media files. On an HTPC, 200GB is the minimum acceptable drive size, and bigger is better (as long as bigger isn't too much louder).

- **Optical:** Playback or install for software, music, and digital video.

- **Graphics card:** Drives the HTPC display, be it a monitor, a conventional TV, a digital TV, or even an HDTV.

- **TV card:** Permits the HTPC to manage TV station selection, viewing, recording, and playback.

- **Memory:** Provides room for the HTPC to get down to work while it's running. More is better for HTPCs, but we capped our configurations at 2GB in our budgets and build plans.

- **Remote:** Primary input device for HTPCs in general, and Media Center PCs in particular.

- **Networking:** Because all the motherboards in our selections had onboard network interfaces (1 Gigabit Ethernet, no less) we didn't include this capability in our budgets. If your chosen motherboard doesn't do the kind of networking you need it to, you'll have to add this item in and find a suitable network interface to do the job.

- **Sound card:** Handles audio (music, plus TV, DVD, or other multimedia sound tracks) for playback or delivery to a home entertainment center for playback.

- **CPU cooler:** Keeps the (HT)PC's brain cool enough to stay on the job.

- **Misc:** Covers a multitude of little thises and thats, mostly cables and fans, but might even include the occasional cooler or other widgets needed to complete a build.

- **PSU:** The power supply unit provides the juice (electricity) that lets all the other (HT)PC components do their thing.

- **Keyboard and Mouse:** Less necessary on an HTPC than on other PCs, we picked wireless desktop sets (which include both keyboard and mouse) for our budgets.

Vendor Information

For convenience, Table 15-4 lists all the vendors whose products appear in the first three tables in this chapter. Although you can visit these sites for product information (and probably, news about newer products as well), you should use the price comparison tools we mentioned earlier in this chapter to look for the best deals (and don't forget to check on eBay or to consult the appendixes at the end of the book, many of which also provide pointers to comparison and shopping information as well).

Table 15-4   Vendors Listed in Build Tables

Vendor	Components Mentioned	URL
Ahanix	HTPC case	www.ahanix.com
AMD	CPU	www.amd.com
Antec	Case, PSU, fans	www.antec.com
AOpen	Motherboard	www.aopen.com
ASUS	Motherboard	www.asustek.com
ATI	Graphics, TV cards	www.ati.com
Chaintech	Motherboard	www.chaintechusa.com
Corsair	Memory	www.corsair.com
Creative Labs	Sound cards, speakers, desktop sets	www.creativelabs.com
Crucial	Memory	www.crucial.com
eVGA	Graphics cards	www.evga.com
Gigabyte	Graphics cards	www.giga-byte.com
Hauppauge	TV cards	www.hauppauge.com
Intel	CPUs	www.intel.com
Kingston	Memory	www.kingston.com
Maxtor	Hard disks	www.maxtor.com
Microsoft	MCE remote, desktop sets, software	www.microsoft.com
NEC	Optical drives	www.nec.com
Panasonic	Slimline optical drives	www.panasonic.com
Plextor	Optical drives	www.plextor.com
Seagate	Hard drive	www.seagate.com
Seasonic	PSUs	www.seasonic.com
TEAC	Slimline optical drives	www.teac.com
Thermalright	CPU cooler	www.thermalright.com

Wrapping Up

Planning any PC build gets easier the more you do it. That's why we hope our discussions, plus our build- and checklists for a Media Center PC will do you some good. Use our checklist as a point of departure for your own plans, and you won't forget anything important, and shouldn't forget anything else, either.

Assembling an HTPC

After you've selected and purchased your HTPC components, it's time to unpack them and put them all together. Because Chapters 18, 19, and 20 take you through building three distinct HTPCs step-by-step, this chapter tries to explain the build process in a general kind of way, to help you prepare to do the same thing yourself. But if you're an old hand at this game, you can probably skim or skip this chapter as you see fit — the truly interesting and gory details are more likely to appear in one or more of the build chapters. What you'll find here is a litany of things to watch out for, plus lots of tips and tricks to help you understand what needs doing and how best to do it.

We try to make it easy for you to build an HTPC by covering the normal sequence of activities involved in putting one together. Along the way, we also recount potential pitfalls that ensnared us in the past (or that we encountered while building the systems for this book), as well as best practices we've learned in the 20 or so years of combined experience in building PCs, too much of it from the "school of hard knocks."

The more compact a PC case, or the more crowded its quarters and corners, the more likely it is that you'll notice that building PCs has lots in common with building ships in a bottle. But although the calm demeanor, extreme patience, steady hand, and firmness of purpose that bottled ship builders often possess in abundance will also benefit a typical PC builder, it's really not that hard — or at least, it's only that hard on rare occasions. These pose some of the most interesting potential pitfalls past which we try to steer your course, although we may have crashed onto those rocks a time or two ourselves.

This chapter covers the following topics while walking through the HTPC build process:

- **Pre-build preparation:** With a small mountain of PC parts at hand, it can be tempting to jump in and start putting things together. But before you limber up your screwdriver, or start tearing into any packages, we suggest some preparatory activities.

- **On-site inspection:** Once you unpack your case and motherboard, some visual inspection and playing around can be beneficial before you begin putting one into the other. This is also when you'll want to look for potential clearance or access problems.

- **Installing the motherboard:** This is when you start a process of attaching fasteners that will continue for some time. Pay attention to how you will access connectors or sockets later on during the installation. Note that with some compact cases, or some CPU coolers with bottom brackets, it may be necessary to install the CPU *before* fastening the motherboard into the case. Likewise, clearance issues may also dictate installing memory prior to battening down the mobo as well.

- **Installing the CPU:** This is when you mount the holder for your CPU cooler, insert your CPU into its socket, add just a smidgeon of thermal paste to conduct heat away from the chip to the cooler, and install the cooler (and possibly a fan, if your chosen cooler doesn't integrate one itself).

- **Installing memory:** You need to research and decide which memory slots you'll populate with memory modules. This goes double if you don't plan on filling all modules, because of special requirements that dual-channel memory configurations can impose.

- **Installing drives:** This is when you'll decide where to put your hard disk(s) and optical drive, and when you must decide how best to perform this sometimes tricky task. This is also where cable routing and placement can really start to look interesting, too.

- **Installing expansion cards:** This is when you'll typically stick a graphics card into an AGP or PCI-E slot, and then decide how to fit your remaining expansion cards into other remaining (and unblocked) PCI slots.

- **Working with cables and connectors:** Start by hooking up your case controls and other connectors. This may only require attaching modular connectors for switches and front panel connectors if you've got them, or it may also include cabling up any of a variety of front panel displays or touch screens). Then, you'll take a second look at what's running where inside your case and eyeball it for potential airflow problems. You may end up repeating steps to route and organize cables better, sometimes more than once. Don't start applying cable ties or other semi-permanent connectors yet.

- **Addressing ventilation:** This is where you may decide to install one or more extra fans to make sure enough air is moving inside your case to keep things cool. It's also when you'll want to hook fans to the motherboard and make sure they've got power, whether you installed them yourself or they came installed with the case.

- **Testing and burn-in:** This is where you turn the machine on and make sure it survives the POST process all the way to a boot attempt. Your goals are both modest and challenging: all you want at this point is for initial boot to complete successfully and the system to tell you it can't find an operating system or boot image to run. After that, you let things run for a while, just to make sure your mostly inert and useless PC can keep the juice flowing for at least a few hours, if not all night.

- **Clean-up and close-up:** We suggest some good ideas for establishing good cable management inside your case. We also provide you with some tips about documenting your build, and making sure you'll have ready access to manuals and software you might need later on.

The most interesting situations that are more specific to building HTPCs occur when working inside smaller, more crowded, and compact cases. Where these considerations come into play, we'll be sure to provide as much warning to help you prepare for potential gotchas as possible.

All details about hardware and software issues are covered in Chapters 18, 19, and 20, each of which details the build-out processes and our experiences for the three machines planned in Chapter 15. Chapter 17 also describes the general process of installing Windows MCE 2005, to help you prepare for this activity on your own machine.

In the sections that follow, you'll get familiar with the HTPC build process, as we talk you through the general sequence of activities, carefully leavened with cautionary tales from our own experience.

Prepare to Build

As pieces and parts start piling up, you'll be able to put your checklist to the first of its many uses. Tick off each item as you pick it up or as it shows up at your door (we got to know our local UPS and FedEx staff pretty darn well while working on this book, and you may share this experience when orders start arriving). It's not absolutely necessary to wait for every last bit and piece to arrive before you start unpacking some key ingredients, but it's probably smart to wait until the following items are on hand before going too crazy:

- **Case:** You've got to have something to build in, so it's vital to have your case on hand. In fact, fooling around with your case and motherboard is normally a key preamble before building can begin in earnest, as you'll learn in the next section of this chapter.

- **Motherboard:** The motherboard is the item to which everything else in a PC typically attaches. Don't even think about starting anything without your motherboard handy.

- **Drives:** Installing one or more hard disks and an optical drive in an HTPC often present interesting challenges, so it's a good idea to wait for them to show up before starting anything serious. That's because it's often necessary to remove drive cages, in whole or in part, to install them in a PC, and because fitting an optical drive inside an HTPC case sometimes requires interesting contortions to complete.

- **Power supply:** If your case includes a power supply, skip this item. If it doesn't, please recognize that because its cables provide power for everything inside your PC (and connect directly to the majority of devices inside your PC) it should be on hand before you start installing anything as well.

Once you've got this minimal collection of items you'll be able to start fooling around with them to see how things are going to fit in just about any kind of PC case, HTPC or otherwise. If you're building inside an HTPC case, however, we also urge you to wait for any expansion cards you plan to install so that you can assess any issues in positioning or placement that may arise, and to establish an install sequence that works for your situation. That's exactly what you'll be reading about in the next section of this chapter, in fact.

Eyeballing Pieces and Parts

There's a definite order to how you should approach a PC build. Although some of the steps may vary because of what you discover during the eyeballing process, most systems we've built use the sequence followed in this chapter. Hopefully, you won't have to diverge from it too much yourself.

Start with the Case

The first thing you should unpack is your case. As you open the box, look for an instruction manual somewhere — often, you must actually crack the case to find a smaller box with additional parts and documents inside. If your case incorporates a VFD (Vacuum Fluorescent Display), a touch screen, or some other kind of visual readout device, you should also find a CD or a diskette with drivers and instructions on how to cable this device to your motherboard, and how to integrate it with Windows. If you're really lucky, the vendor will provide install software that knows how to integrate with Windows XP MCE 2005 and does most of that work for you automatically.

Skim through the instruction manual and look for advice on how to build your system — sometimes, you'll find great information and advice between its covers. But a distressing number of components ship sans documentation; if that happens to you, visit the vendor's Web site and look for information about your case. You can often find PDF versions of manuals, how-tos, and sometimes even videos that help steer you through parts of the build process. Print what you think you might need and make sure to bookmark that page or add it to your favorites so you can return to it again.

Tip

As we build systems, we grab two big Ziploc bags, and stash all manuals and CDs for each component in one bag, and all extra parts, cables, fasteners, and so forth in the other bag. If you're building more than one system at any given moment, you'll probably also want to label those bags (a permanent Sharpie marker works well for this job) so you can associate them with the system to which they belong. We actually devoted a whole shelf in our parts closet as we were building to make it easy to lay hands on important materials at various stages during the build.

Unpack the Motherboard

Your next step is to liberate the motherboard from its packaging. Here again, you'll want to find and set aside any manuals and software you find, as well as cables, fasteners, and other ancillary parts. That said, if your mobo includes a CPU cooler amidst its treasures, put the cooler somewhere safe because it's probably too big to fit inside your hardware Ziploc (unless you're building a Pentium M system).

A Builder's Notebook or Diary

Although some people can remember everything they need to know while assembling a PC from a dozen major components and hundreds of smaller items (cables, fasteners, and so forth), not everyone is blessed with that kind of recall—including at least one of your authors. We've learned that a good way to stay organized and to save yourself from wasted time rooting around for missing parts (the smaller they are, the more likely this is to happen, in our experience) is to take notes while you are building your system. We buy a cheap, small, narrow-ruled notebook at our local grocery store and use it to record the following kind of information as we go:

- Start a fresh page each time you sit down at the system to work, and begin with the date and quick notes about what you work on. For example:

  7/18: resume Athlon 64 build
  Insert and affix TV card (Hauppauge PVR-150MCE)
  Cable up PSU to mobo
  IDE cable from optical drive to mobo
  Fan power cable to PSU, fan sensor cable to mobo

- Keep track of anything interesting that occurs, especially where access is tight or restricted and how you manage to get things installed, connected, and so forth. The same goes double for any outright problems you encounter and solve. For example:

  PSU mobo connector tight fit under 5.25" drive cage; decided to insert connector before sliding mobo into position and fastening to standoffs

  describes a situation we encountered during one test build. Later on, one of our notes for this same build observed that:

  The only suitable fanless AGP graphics card we can find (Gigabyte GeForce 6600 GT Silentpipe) has clearance issues: Heat pipes run over the top of the pcb from front to back; insufficient clearance to close case because of 1 cm of added device height.

  Combined with the other note also cited, this helped us decide to abandon that particular case selection and to try a different HTPC case. The real problem in this case (Ahanix D5) was that the combination of an older AGP mobo and available silent graphics cards for that bus proved unworkable because of the clearance problem noted.

- If you have parts left over when you're finished installing something (most often this means extra fasteners, cables, or adapter plugs) make a quick note and also indicate where you plan to store them (for us, that means noting an associated Ziploc bag on a shelf in a closet). For example:

  Finished installing PSU: cable organizers, cable ties, and misc. screws left over. Placed in Athlon 64/Chaintech VNF4 hardware Ziploc.

You don't necessarily need to go into excruciating detail in your build journal, but it's a good idea to keep track of anything that requires special effort or attention, and to note where to find parts, documentation, and software later on. If and when it's needed, you'll be grateful you can run these things down quickly and easily!

Your next step is to carry the mobo over to your case and eyeball how best to fit the mobo inside the case. Most modern motherboards use six or more plastic or metal spacers that screw into holes predrilled into the case that match up with other holes predrilled into the motherboard to create a solid connection between these two components that won't conduct electricity between them. Many cases come with such spacers, also called standoffs, already installed. Other cases are predrilled for standoffs, but you must install them yourself. Every motherboard we unpacked included some standoffs and screws to match them, and many cases also include this kind of hardware as well. Put all this stuff together, and label it if necessary, then put it in your hardware Ziploc, too.

As you look at the motherboard and case, visualize how those two parts match up. Look for parts inside the case (such as drive cages or rails) that might occlude your view or block easy access to key sockets or connectors. Try to develop a sense of how you'll maneuver the mobo into the case to put it into position, where you must mount standoffs (if necessary), and where you'll insert the screws that fasten the motherboard to them.

Tip Don't be afraid to remove drive cages or rails as part of the installation procedure. If you read the case manuals thoroughly, you'll often see that they recommend or require this activity in order to make room for the motherboard. In horizontal HTPC cases, in fact, it's pretty normal to have to remove drive cages to install the drives because there's not enough room between the outside surface of the cage and the side or back of the case to insert and fasten the necessary screws that hold those drives in position. Sometimes, you can't even get the motherboard into its proper place without removing these parts, either. Be ready for this possibility!

Go ahead and put the motherboard down in or near its intended location. At this point, it's probably a good idea to check your CPU cooler to make sure you don't have clearance issues. That means unpacking that device and simply placing it on top of the CPU socket. If this raises concerns about possible damage to the socket, cut a small piece of cardboard to cushion the cooler while protecting both cooler and socket from each other. Next, eyeball the top of the cooler (or fan, since many have fans installed on top) vis-à-vis the top or side panel of your case. Your goal is to determine if the case can accommodate the cooler once it's installed. For example, despite a great big case for our P4 build, we still had to switch from one enormous (but incredibly quiet and efficient) CPU cooler to a smaller model when we realized our initial choice was tall enough to prevent us from replacing the side panel had it been installed.

Tip Eyeballing before installing has another redeeming value: if you make a mistake and buy something that won't fit where it needs to, you can probably return it for a refund or exchange it for something else. Once you start screwing things together, you may no longer be able to make a switch or get a refund. That's why you also want to keep all of the original packaging around until you're sure you can use what you've bought. Most outfits that sell PC parts will take them back only if they're returned intact, in their original packaging. In the same vein, keep all receipts, too!

Your next job is to figure out how to route cables from the PSU to the motherboard and the CPU. You don't necessarily need to plug anything in at this point, but if your case doesn't include a PSU, you may want to go ahead and install it at this point. This normally requires inserting three or four screws through the back of the case into matching holes in the PSU (and those screws should be included in the materials provided along with that unit). Fool around with the 20- or 24-pin motherboard power connector and the 4-pin CPU power connector to make sure you can insert them easily after the motherboard is fastened to its standoffs. If so, you can start eyeballing other system components; if not, make some notes in your builder's journal to describe what you think is necessary to make things work (like the note about inserting the mobo power connector before sliding it into place described in the preceding builder's journal discussion).

Plan Your RAM Deployment

Look at the RAM slots on the motherboard next. If you have more than two of them, pairs of color-coded slots are a strong indicator that your motherboard supports dual memory banks. This has interesting implications (see Chapter 6 for the gory details) but usually means you can eke a little more performance out of your HTPC by installing pairs of DIMMs (same make, model, and manufacturer is good, matched pairs of DIMMs is best) into slots of the same color.

If you fill all memory slots, make sure they're all occupied with identical DIMMs, if not matched pairs. If you fill only two slots, make sure you pick slots of the same color to take advantage of a mobo's dual memory bank abilities. Check the motherboard manual to find out where a single bank may be installed or to see if it belongs in a particular pair of slots. Visual inspection of the mobo sometimes also provides clues: On the Chaintech Athlon 64 mobo, for example, all four DIMM slots are clearly marked DDR1, DDR2, DDR3, and DDR4. The first two slots are blue, the second two black. And indeed the manual confirms our guess that DDR1 and DDR2 are preferred when installing only two DIMMs.

Make a note about what you plan to do, which slots you plan to occupy, and double-check clearances while you're at it — we've been inside several compact HTPC cases where things went better when we socketed one or more DIMMs before sliding the mobo into position and fastening it to its standoffs. If you decide this is necessary in your case, make a note of that, too, for later reference.

Visualize Drive Placement and Position

Your next challenge is to observe the placement of drive bays or cages. It's not at all unusual to have to remove cage elements or entire drive bays to make room for the motherboard, and then to have to replace them once the motherboard is in place, along with any cables they might also obstruct. If you're lucky, you'll find clear instructions and diagrams on how to perform these tasks in the installation manual that comes with your case. If you're not that lucky, try to figure things out on your own.

Tip

If you get stuck trying to figure out how to perform a build inside some particular case, jump onto the Web and use your favorite search engine to look for reviews of that case. Most of the time, if your case has been reviewed, that review provides a blow-by-blow recitation of the build process. Even if it doesn't go to extreme levels of detail, such reviews invariably warn about potential problems or pitfalls. We had no trouble finding reviews for all the cases we tried out for this book; you should experience similar results. Sites like HTPCnews.com, SilentPCReview.com, and ExtremeTech.com all provided reviews of at least two of the cases mentioned in this book, if not more.

As you observe the drive bays or cages, you must also decide how you'll install your hard disk(s) and optical drive. In most of the cases we built systems in, we had to either remove or partially disassemble drive cages or bays to affix drives to their mounts, then put things back together after drives were mounted. It's important to pay attention to power and interface cable access at the same time. It may be easier to attach cables to the drives or the motherboard before you replace the cages or bays within which they reside. Make notes on this as you work through the eyeballing process and figure out how to get things done. Here again, you may find all the guidance you need in the installation manual for the case, or in some review — or you may not.

When it comes to the optical drive, another important issue on HTPC cases that feature DVD drawer openings rather than standard 5.25" drive bays is drawer front panel clearance. On some Sony optical drives we tried out, for example, we had to use smaller black plastic front panels and drawer fronts to enable the media drawer to slide in and out freely and clearly. In such cases, the drive's own eject button must be properly aligned with a matching button on the case front, too. This makes front-to-back drive alignment important when mounting the drive. Thus, it's smart not to tighten down drive mount screws all the way until you've made sure the two buttons are properly aligned and in close enough proximity front-to-back to work together.

Check Expansion Card Requirements

Aside from potential clearance issues — and don't forget to check side-to-side clearances as well as top-to-bottom — expansion and graphics cards seldom pose serious installation concerns, or command much attention beyond cursory checks. There are occasional exceptions, however, that make this exercise entirely necessary. In particular, the following interfaces can command your complete attention:

- For two of our builds (the P4 and Athlon 64), selecting a heat pipe–cooled graphics adapter not only meant paying attention to vertical clearance for that card, it also meant we couldn't use the PCI slot next to the graphics slot either. That's because both sides of this card are partially bedecked with heat sinks making it significantly wider than most expansion cards (even wider than some higher-end graphics cards with large fans, in fact). This also explains why the graphics card is typically the first expansion card to be installed during the build process.

- In one of our early experimental builds (on the Pentium M mobo we initially selected), we also had to install a sound card to replace the motherboard's less-than-stellar audio chipset. Because they integrate external connections with the DVD player (to bring digital audio in) and also with the case front (microphone, headphone, and audio in/out connections to the front panel are typical on most HTPC cases), examine sound cards carefully from a cabling perspective. This goes double if they include 5.25" drive bay front panel devices, or external devices, all of which involve still more cables.

Inspect the Ventilation

Most cases include one or more fan ports; some ship with fans pre-installed. Look these things over carefully to determine where power and sensor cables may (or must) run. If you need to install one or more fans, you'll need them on hand in time to complete your build. We recommend using 120 mm fans wherever they'll fit, and buying quiet, controllable fans like those from Nexus, Pabst, or Zalman if at all possible. If you turn your HTPC on and don't like the sound from any fans that may have been included with the case, you can always swap them out for something quieter. Although this may stretch the $35 allowance in our budgets for fans and miscellany, it's worth the extra money.

Also, make sure you've got enough power and sensor connections available for your fans. If you're short on power plug-ins, you may need to purchase some splitter cables for that purpose (we found some at our nearby Fry's for under $5). If you're short on sensors, you may want to consider adding a fan controller to your component list, such as the Silverstone Eudemon SST-FP52-B, which handles up to three fans—but which also requires a 5.25" drive bay (or an external drive enclosure) in which to reside.

Caution A fan controller probably isn't an option in most HTPC cases, where 5.25" drive bays are often at a premium. Unless your chosen case has two or more such bays, and one of them is unused, this approach will be unworkable for you, unless you go to the trouble of purchasing an appropriate external drive case and mount a fan controller in that enclosure. Even then, cabling issues may be tricky!

Ponder Case Cabling

HTPC cases normally offer numerous front panel connections to their users; these often include two or more USB ports, a FireWire port, and two or more audio ports. You'll also have to deal with typical on/off and reset switch connections to the front panel as well. All these items trail cables inside the case that must link up with the motherboard (and sometimes to a sound card, when one is installed). Cases that incorporate VFDs or touch screens trail even more cables, and sometimes require you to dedicate a USB pin block on the motherboard (true for many VFDs) or to route cables from inside the case to the motherboard's port block or the graphics card at the back of the case.

Cut the Static!

Before you start handling sensitive, expensive circuitry like CPUs or memory modules, or more mundane stuff like motherboards and expansion cards, consider this: in dry conditions (low humidity), static electricity can build up to the point where it can damage or destroy these things. This phenomenon is more formally called an electrostatic discharge, or ESD.

If the heat is on while you're working on a PC or you live in a dry climate (and there's no humidification in your workspace), you must take proper steps to prevent a static discharge from wreaking havoc on expensive PC parts. You can (and should) buy an anti-static wrist strap and ground yourself before picking up such components. You can (and may decide to) buy and work on anti-static mats, or to purchase anti-static spray for carpet in your work area. At a bare minimum, always touch something metal and ground yourself (we like to grab for radiators, metal filing cabinets, or the PC case ourselves) before picking up or handling electronic components.

For a different take on static, see the excellent ESD (electrostatic discharge) guidelines entitled "Your Safety First!" in the "Build Your Own Music PC" tutorial online at www.computermusic. co.uk/tutorial/build1.pdf.

All cables must travel from their points of origination to their proper connections, and you must often route them carefully around heat sinks, fans, and other impediments inside the case. This can require an exercise of imagination (you're still eyeballing things, remember?) but is worth the time and effort involved to help you get ready to build. And hopefully, you've been taking notes and hatching plans all along the way.

Congratulations! You've now made it through the preliminaries. In the sections that follow, your notes will come in really handy as the build gets underway for real.

Step 1: Motherboard (and PSU)

If your case requires a power supply, or you've decided to replace the power supply the vendor chose with something more to your liking, you'll want to start by installing that PSU. If you're replacing an existing PSU, be sure to check what kind of power supply you must replace. If it's a standard ATX or Mini-ATX power supply, it will be easy to swap out, but if it's a proprietary PSU design, you may want to reconsider your case choice if you're not sure about the built-in power supply.

Some case vendors do sell cases with proprietary power supplies whose replacement can pose serious challenges. We believe you're better off choosing a case with a standard PSU component, or a case without a PSU that accepts standard components!

Installing the power supply is usually pretty simple. Check out the vendor's instructions, and then eyeball the predrilled case mount holes against those in the PSU itself. Ninety-nine times out of 100, you'll have no trouble inserting the machine screws that hold the unit in place. To make sure the PSU is oriented properly, one of those screw holes is usually positioned off the corner so that lining up all holes forces proper positioning. When you've finished, remove the twist ties or cable holder from around the large bundle of cables that projects inside the case, to make ready to route power cables where they're needed. Of particular interest: the 24-pin (or perhaps 20-pin, for older motherboards/PSUs) motherboard power connector and the square 4-pin CPU power connector.

When it comes to tacking down the motherboard inside the case, you may have to begin by first installing standoffs to hold the motherboard a safe distance from the bottom or side panel on your case (bottom for horizontal cases, side for tower cases). Although you don't necessarily need to match every hole in your motherboard to a standoff and fasten it to the case, an average micro-ATX motherboard needs at least 4 to 6 screws to hold it securely, whereas an average full-size ATX motherboard requires 6 to 8 or more.

Check your cooler carefully. Some CPU coolers include backplates that mount under the motherboard, as well as clamps, heat sinks, fans, and other gear that mount above. If your cooler uses this kind of gear, you must mount the backplate under the motherboard before you can affix the cooler to its standoffs. Check instructions for your CPU cooler carefully!

Step 2: Installing the CPU (and Cooler)

Different CPUs require different installation maneuvers, but all require a gentle, deft touch to help avoid damage to delicate pins or contacts. In general here's how things work:

- AMD generally requires installers to raise a lever to enable the pins on the CPU chip carrier to slide into the socket, then to lower and lock the lever to hold the chip firmly in place.

- Pentium M CPUs generally mount into a socket that's opened and closed with a small screw. The socket usually comes with the screw loosened so it's ready to receive its chip. If you try to seat the chip and it won't go anywhere, back the screw out a half turn before trying again. Once seated, tighten the screw down to lock it into place.

- Pentium 4 CPUs using the LGA774 format have no pins; rather they use flat contacts on their undersides. You raise a lever to drop the chip into place, and then lower the lever to lock it into position just the same, much as with the AMD processors. Older Pentium 4s built for socket 478 use a lever lock, like those for AMD processors.

You'll find instruction manuals packaged along with CPUs when you buy them. Considering that the cheapest one in our three builds costs $225, it's not a part you can idly wreck and replace. Here, we expand the famous acronym as politely as possible to implore you to please "read the fabulous manual" (RTFM)! Also, remember to ground yourself before picking up a CPU, to avoid potential ESD damage.

Next comes the mounting hardware for your CPU cooler. This usually screws into four mount holes at the corners of the socket on the motherboard (unless you've already had to install it because of a bracket on the underside of the mobo). You might be inclined to slap the cooler down and declare victory at this point. Not a good idea! First, you'll want to spread a thin film of thermal paste onto the CPU's upper surface to improve heat transfer to the cooler while your HTPC is running. Only then is it safe to drop the cooler into position, and clamp or fasten it into place.

Caution

More is NOT better when it comes to thermal paste! Modern CPUs produce sufficient heat to require special help in transferring heat to their coolers. This takes the form of special chemical compounds called thermal pastes, designed to transfer heat with utmost efficiency. Because a little thermal paste is good, novice PC builders may be inclined to believe that more thermal paste must be better. Not true! A thin film works best when installing thermal paste, to help heat migrate from the radiating surface at the top of the chip to the conducting surface at the bottom of the cooler. Basically, thermal paste fills in irregularities between those two surfaces to maximize contact between them. Put too much thermal paste down, and it acts more like an insulator than a conductor. Tests show that too much paste produces measurable increases in CPU temperatures. The best way to install thermal paste on a CPU is to put a little dab square in the middle of the chip package, and then to spread that paste out into an even but thin, barely visible film almost to the edges of the metal cap or silicon die. We find an old credit card does the job nicely, but have also used business cards on heavy paper stock with good results. For thermal paste, thin is in!

Step 3: Installing the Memory

If you take good notes during the eyeballing phase, this part is pretty easy. You already know which sockets to populate, so go ahead and populate them. Start by gently pushing the locking tabs down as far as they will go. Then, ground yourself before picking up each DIMM. Next, make sure the key slot in the middle of the DIMM matches the block in its intended socket so the DIMM can slide in properly. Gently place the left edge of the DIMM into the left-hand side of the memory socket and then ease the DIMM into position so its right edge also lines up with the right-hand side of the memory socket.

Double-check that DIMM slot and socket block match up. If they do, push your left thumb down on the upper left-hand corner of the DIMM and then follow by doing the same with your right thumb on its upper right-hand corner. The DIMM should settle into place and locking tabs on both sides should snap into their upright and locked positions. Repeat for any remaining DIMMs, and that's it: You're done with RAM!

Step 4: Installing Drives

In cases where clearance on both sides of drive cages or bays is possible (and this usually means some kind of tower or cube case where the sides can be removed easily to provide free and unfettered access), this is a pretty easy job, both in principle and in practice. In HTPC cases, where clearance is typically easy only on one side, removing cages or bays to mount drives is the norm. If you're lucky enough to be able to slide drives in, position them properly, and fasten them into position, you should revel in that activity, because it's seldom that easy when working inside most HTPC cases.

Leaving easy, straightforward installs aside for the moment, installing one or more hard disks usually involves removing the drive cage by unscrewing it from the bottom or side of the case. Next, you must slide a drive into a bay, position it between the two side rails, and then screw it into position (further toward the back is usually best for easy access to cable and power connectors, but consult your manual for advice if you think it's needed). Of course, if you're installing more than one drive, repeat as necessary.

Installing the optical drive into some HTPC cases adds further complications. First, you must ensure that front-to-back alignment allows a case front button to make proper contact with the eject button on the front of the drive so you can manually eject media as you need to. Second, on those cases that provide cut-outs for media drawers, you must make sure the drawer on your optical drive can slide in and out unimpeded.

Both of these complications mean you must test drive placement in its cage or bay before you can lock things into position permanently. The best way to do this is to slide the drive forward so that the faceplate lines up with the case-front edge of the cage or bay. Then insert the mounting screws into the side rails and fasten them down so that the drive will stay put, but can still be made to slide frontwards or backwards with firm finger pressure on the face plate or back of the drive. Next, position the cage or bay inside the case so it's also ready to fasten and try the eject button (visual inspection is usually good enough to see if it's working). Then using a paper clip or the wire tool that's included with most optical drives, force the drawer to eject and see if it slides out of the case front properly.

In most cases, these jobs require little or no fiddling to get things working properly (if the case manufacturer has done its job properly, mechanical alignment to the front of the drive cage or bay makes the button and the drawer line up properly). But fiddling for position is sometimes needed and shouldn't scare you when it happens. You may also notice that the plastic drawer front on the drive won't fit the case opening. As noted earlier in this chapter, this happened to us with a Sony DRU-720A DVD drive that we tested and also explained why the packaging mentioned a "replaceable front panel" so conspicuously. As soon as we swapped the cream colored front panel (which included a somewhat oversized drawer front that caused the clearance problems) for its smaller black replacement, everything worked fine.

Another kind of fiddling about that you may run into can occur when a drive cage or bay won't sit still while you're trying to test alignment and fit. If that happens to you, take a deep breath, and resign yourself to screwing it in for testing, unscrewing it to adjust alignment, and then repeating that process as many times as necessary to get things right. Remember to cultivate the virtues of a bottled ship builder, and everything will be okay!

Step 5: Installing Expansion Cards

Depending on what cards your build calls for this may involve installing anywhere from one to three expansion cards. Because so many HTPC cases are cramped, and so many HTPC motherboards are micro-ATX in form factor, installing more than three cards can be problematic anyway. In fact, that requirement is enough to dictate an ATX motherboard and an oversized HTPC or conventional mid-tower case for most builds.

For this book, we assume that if you choose to run three expansion cards plus a graphics card inside an HTPC case you probably need all the following elements:

- A PCI-E X16 graphics card, which is probably something like the narrow, fanless eVGA 6600 card, because it's the only one we know of that permits all three PCI slots on a micro-ATX motherboard to be used.

- A TV tuner card, like the Hauppauge PVR-150MCE single-tuner or the Hauppauge PVR-500MCE dual-tuner card (or reasonable facsimiles, as described in Chapter 9).

- An HDTV tuner card like the AVerMedia A180 or DVICO Fusion 5 (or reasonable facsimiles, as also described in Chapter 9).

- A sound card, such as Gigabyte's AV-710 or perhaps one of the more advanced Sound Blaster Audigy 2 Pro or Platinum Pro, if not Audigy 4 Pro or X-Fi cards from Creative Labs. Because some high-end sound cards include both front panel outputs that need a 5.25" drive bay and/or a separate break-out box, we can only speculate that somebody with high-end audio editing or capture needs would spring for such a card. If so, make sure to pick a case with adequate room, not just for the cards, but also for the extra 5.25" drive bay that's required to install and use them properly.

Though this represents the outside edge of what you can cram into even a large HTPC case, it's still not an incredible load for a modern power supply. That said, 350–400 W or more is indicated for a P4 system with all of these other components installed as well.

Except for cabling up to a sound card inside the case, all these items are easy to install. Simply line the card up with the slot into which you intend to insert it and then gently rock it back and forth until it's fully seated therein. For those expansion cards that do require additional cables (audio and front panel for sound cards, power cables for some high-end graphics cards) be sure to route those cables carefully around heat sinks and fans. Other than that, this part of the job usually takes less than 5 minutes, all told.

Step 6: Working with Cables and Connectors

By the time you get to this point, believe it or not, you've got all your major system components in place. Now comes the interesting job of hooking all those components together. In practice, this means connecting interface and sensor cables to the motherboard, and power cables to the devices they must drive.

A certain amount of "situational wisdom" is required to do this job right, because you have to look at the cables you must deal with and decide how best to route them. This also happens to be one time when personal preferences or style comes into heavy play in the PC build process.

Certain individuals with perfectionist or "case-modding" tendencies (this increasingly popular practice involves tricking out PC cases with windows, lights, and all kinds of interesting accoutrements, and also involves serious attention to cable routing, selection, and management) spend a lot of time and effort on cabling. To begin with, such folks start by obtaining, making, or modifying their cables to get things just right (to be fair, replacing ribbon cables with narrow-profile or round cables where possible is a great way to ensure the best possible airflow inside your case). Then, they spend even more time deciding how to route cables from point to point and surround them with cable ties, nylon sleeves, spiral plastic wraps, and so on to make the cable layout as neat and attractive as possible. Opening a case like this is a real pleasure, but working inside one can pose challenges should any cables need to be moved around or replaced.

At the other extreme, some builders just run the cables any which way they'll go, performing only cursory checks to make sure nothing's too close to a fan or a heat sink. This is a more spontaneous school of cable management (or lack thereof) and can pose its own challenges when it comes to disentangling individual cables from the spaghetti that can result. Our own tendencies fall somewhere between these two extremes; we like things orderly and well organized, but balk at spending countless hours routing and wrapping cables.

Wherever your preferred approach falls in this spectrum, you'll want to have some cable ties on hand as you finalize your system build to tack cables down and keep them straight. Don't do any of this until after you've installed MCE and made sure all your hardware works properly — initial build testing can catch only outright hardware failures or problems, or gross installation mistakes. Once you've installed MCE you'll be able to tell if all the devices and expansion cards in your HTPC are working properly. There's no point in finalizing anything until you're sure you've got a working configuration worth finalizing at all. Until then, arrange your cables to keep them out of harm's way and start thinking about what you want to do with them for real when you're ready to finalize things later on.

Cross-Reference In fact, the case modding contingent beat the HTPC contingent to the punch when it comes to writing a book for this series. You'll find Russ Caslis's *ExtremeTech* book *Going Mod: 9 Cool Case Mod Projects* (Wiley, 2005) an amazing and valuable source of PC build information, particularly when it comes to routing and wrapping cables inside the case. Check it out for pictures, diagrams, explanations, great advice, and pointers to many more vendors that specialize in this area than we had room to mention in this book!

Step 7: Addressing Ventilation

It may be premature to worry about adding fans to your case during the build process. In fact, many HTPC builders prefer to wait until they've got MCE installed, their systems up and running, and then monitor case and CPU temperatures as they run their systems under normal loads to decide if they need extra ventilation. There's nothing wrong with this approach, as long as you take it seriously, so feel free to suspend fan-related advice in this section until that point if you prefer. That said, if you're running a faster, hotter chip like a P4, it's easy to predict that in most cases adding more ventilation to such air circulation as a CPU cooler and PSU fan can deliver will be needed, so why not get it over with sooner, rather than later?

But certainly, before you close up your case for any kind of burn-in testing (which we cover in the next section of this chapter), you should make sure your cables aren't too snarled up inside your case and that cables are routed to allow air to flow from the case intake to the exhaust fan on the PSU (and to any other fans you may have installed and running in the system already). The more compact your case, or the more power your chosen CPU consumes, the more important this becomes.

Our own practice for Athlon- and P4-based systems is to install at least one quiet fan (such as a Nexus or a Panaflo, or perhaps an Acoustifan or an Antec TriCool) at the back of the case, blowing out to facilitate air intake and circulation inside the case. If it can be a 120 mm fan, so much the better: bigger fans move more air, so fan speed can be reduced to lower noise output. If fan ports accommodate only 80 or 92 mm fans, they must spin faster to move the same amount of air. That should be an important consideration when choosing the right case for any given CPU.

Tip Not all PC fans are equally quiet. When choosing fans for HTPC use, noise considerations are probably more important for most users than in desktop machines. Web sites like EndPCNoise.com can not only sell you such fans, but they also rate them in terms of their noise output (don't be surprised to observe that quieter fans cost more than noisier ones, either). You will also find great coverage of this topic at SilentPCReview.com under headings that include "Cooling," "Fans & Controls," but most important the "Fans" item among that site's excellent "Recommended" entries (which also includes tips and techniques to reduce fan voltage as a way of lowering noise output).

Step 8: Testing and Burn-In

As you build a PC, it's by no means a bad idea to stop and test occasionally to make sure you're not spending time and effort adding to a non-working system. In fact, we can identify several worthwhile stops along the building path you should make to ensure yourself that everything is going okay so far. We present each one as a subheading in this part of the chapter, starting with the mobo and PSU check next.

Step 1: Basic Core Component Check

Once your PSU is installed, your motherboard has been tacked down to the case, and the CPU and its cooler are installed, it's a good time to conduct a first quick test to see if these most basic components are working. Check your motherboard manual to understand how to hook up your case speaker and front-panel on/off switch, and then do so. You'll also need to insert the 24-pin mobo power connector (20-pin on older mobos) and the 4-pin CPU power connector, attach the AC power cord to the PSU, and plug it into a wall socket to conduct this test. You may also want to insert a single DIMM into memory slot 1 just to be on the safe side (careful reading of your mobo manual will tell you if the mobo can POST without memory present; we habitually insert a single DIMM when we perform this test ourselves to avoid that effort).

This test is absurdly easy to conduct. Here's how, once you've made all necessary connections:

1. Flip the power switch on the PSU from off to on (this is normally a rocker switch with a zero (0) on one side, and a 1 on the other. If the rocker side with the zero is down, the PSU is off; if the rocker side with the 1 is down, it's on. Make sure it's on.

2. Push the PC's front-panel power-on switch (bold and hardy souls may instead choose to short an insulated screwdriver across the motherboard pins to that switch instead, if they like).

3. Observe what happens. Take special note of the following: PSU fan, CPU cooler fan, onboard mobo power LED (if any), and sounds from the case speaker (if available).

If things are working properly, here's what you'll observe as you check your work:

1. The PSU fan and the CPU cooler fan will spin up and keep running indefinitely.

2. If the mobo has a power indicator LED, it will light up and stay that way indefinitely.

3. If the mobo will begin its POST (power-on self-test) routines with such a minimal configuration present — you're still far away from a fully functional PC right now — you'll also hear a sequence of beeps from the speaker.

If things aren't working properly, you may observe either that nothing happens, or that perhaps the fans start up and run for a short while, but then stop working. The LED may light up and then turn off, or may stay lit even after the fans stop turning. Because you've got only a handful of components to worry about, you've only got a handful to troubleshoot at this point. These include the PSU, the mobo, the CPU and cooler, and the case itself (but possibly also the DIMM you chose to insert).

Normally, if you unseat and reseat the PSU power cables to the motherboard, your problems will be solved. But if things still aren't working after that, it's time to perform some more serious troubleshooting. You can purchase a simple PSU tester from Antec for about $13. After plugging the power supply into an AC outlet, plug the tester into the mobo power connector and then turn both the PSU and the tester on (the tester has the same kind of rocker switch that the PSU does). If the LED glows green, the power supply tests good; if not, the PSU is bad and should be replaced.

By a process of elimination (we find that swapping questionable components for known good working ones is marvelously effective, although it may be beyond most HTPC builders' immediate ability or means) you should be able to figure out what's not working. Once the malfunctioning component is replaced with one that works, this test should complete successfully.

Caution

Troubleshooting serious PC problems takes time and may consume lots of effort and involve incurring expenses. If you try the basic PSU check and things still aren't working, you may want to consider asking for help. If you know somebody who's good at building PCs, enlist their aid. If all else fails, consider taking your parts to a local PC repair shop or a national chain with PC repair/troubleshooting services (like Best Buy's Geek Squad) and paying for some help! They can perform tests (and swap out components) that you can't normally do yourself anywhere near as quickly or as easily. Although it may cost you $100 to $200 to diagnose your PC's ills, that could turn out to be a pretty good deal, once you start putting some kind of value on the time you'd otherwise spend solving problems yourself or waiting for replacement parts to show up.

Steps 2 through . . .

You can repeat the same test you conducted in Step 1 after installing each additional system component to see if basic functionality remains intact. Because the test in Step 1 is just a basic go/no-go test, we normally don't repeat it ourselves until we've installed all remaining system components: the drives, the expansion cards, and wired up the case and fans. Cautious souls can test as often as they like; we have built enough PCs to feel reasonably capable at putting them together. Thus we wait until the initial build is complete to try the same test described in Step 1 again.

Initial Build Test

This is what we just described when we said that we wait until all components have been installed to test again. But because the PC is more or less fully assembled by this point, some additional connections are needed, and a great many more things should happen when you power on your HTPC.

To enable the POST to complete successfully — that's the outcome you want — you must hook the graphics card or motherboard graphics port to a display device (POST creates character outputs onscreen to report on its results, and any problems it finds, should they be encountered). You must also hook up a keyboard, so as to be able to provide input to your computer if the POST test completes successfully.

If you're lucky, you'll see a series of text messages onscreen that inform you about POST results and other BIOS checks (for the graphics card, primarily). Then you'll get a rundown of the various PCI devices sensed. After that, you'll get an error message saying that no operating system can be found on your boot drive — that's okay, because that's exactly what you should expect, considering the PC has just come to life and has no operating system installed just yet. That's the subject of our next chapter anyway.

Burn-In Test

Professional PC builders usually perform what's called a burn-in test before they sell a system to anybody. It's normally performed after the operating system and other software have been installed, but we mention it here because it remains primarily a hardware test rather than a software test, per se. The idea is to turn the computer on, start it up, and let it run for anywhere from 12 to 48 hours continuously. The underlying belief is that if anything is wrong with the hardware, or with the hardware configuration, it will manifest itself within that time either in the form of one or more errors that the operating system can report, or in some kind of out-right system crash or device failure. It's called a *burn-in test* because this period of continuous operation is supposed to shake out and expose any problems while the system is running over an extended period of time. We don't always do such tests on systems we build ourselves, but there's certainly nothing wrong with turning your HTPC on and letting it run overnight, then checking in the next day to make sure everything's still working okay.

Step 9: Cleaning Up and Closing Up

When the build is done and the POST completes okay, you're ready to move on to the next step in building your own HTPC — namely, installing the software that enables it to act as Media Center PC and work with all the devices and sources of media you want it to handle on your behalf. You'll get a chance to dig into that in the next chapter, but before you do that, it's probably a good idea to do a little clean-up and to make sure your case is all buttoned up and ready for networking, audio, TV, and other connections.

Now's a good time to rearrange cables inside the case to make sure you're not adding to any potential airflow problems. This is also the time to button up the case itself, which usually means replacing the cover, or one or more panels, and then fastening them into place as required.

This is also the right time to pick up any loose parts that may have gotten scattered during the installation process and to put them in your hardware Ziploc. You'll also want to pick up your mobo manual and any other documentation or software that might be laying around and put it (or them) into your software/documentation Ziploc as well. Although you may not need to root around in the hardware Ziploc again, you can count on rooting around in the software/documentation Ziploc in the fairly near future.

It's Never Too Early to Tweak Your HTPC!

Once your system gets up and running, you can check important hardware settings before you install Windows XP Media Center Edition 2005 on that hardware, if you like. As you boot your machine, you can instruct the motherboard to let you inspect existing CMOS settings during that process (for most motherboards, this requires pressing the Delete (del) key before POST runs to completion).

At this point, what you need to check is pretty limited. You'll normally worry about only a small number of settings at this point. You want to make sure the CPU is running at the desired speed (which may not be its rated speed, for those who choose to underclock hotter, faster CPUs). You also want to be sure that the front-side bus (FSB) is running at the desired speed, and that your memory is using the right multiplier vis-à-vis FSB speed (typically this will be something like 5:3, 4:3, or 2:1) and also that the right settings for CAS latency, RAS Precharge, RAS to CAS Delay, and Cycle time (see Chapter 6 for details) are in place.

It's not uncommon for default settings to apply when a PC boots up for the first time. These defaults tend to be conservative and may not give you all the performance your system can deliver. It's not at all a bad idea to page through your CMOS screens after you bring your PC up for the first time, not just to see where things are set, but also to see what kinds of controls your motherboard's BIOS gives you over CMOS settings. At the same time, you can check these basics to make sure you're not giving too much away in performance in exchange for whatever level of stability those defaults deliver.

We've built systems where FSB speeds were set by default to half their top speeds, and where memory defaults read from DIMMs themselves (memory vendors are also pretty conservative) didn't match their rated capabilities. Usually a few small adjustments are all that's required, but every little bit helps!

But if you clean up now, and put things where you can find them later, you'll be not just ready and willing to do what can (or may) come next, but you'll also be able to lay hands on the items that may be necessary to perform those tasks.

Vendor Information

For convenience, Table 16-1 lists all the vendors whose products are mentioned in this chapter. Although you can visit these sites for product information (and probably, news about newer products as well), please use the price comparison tools we mentioned earlier in Chapter 15 to find for the best deals. (In addition, please don't forget to check on eBay or to consult the appendixes at the end of the book, many of which also provide pointers to comparison and shopping information as well).

Table 16-1   Vendors Mentioned in Chapter 16

Vendor	Components Mentioned	URL
Acousti Products	Acoustifan case cooling fans	www.acoustiproducts.com
AMD	Athlon, Athlon 64 processors	www.amd.com
Antec	PSU tester, Tricool fans	www.antec.com
AVerMedia	A180 HDTV card	www.avermedia.com
Chaintech	VNF4/Ultra mobo	www.chaintech-usa.com
Creative Labs	Audigy 2 Platinum, Platinum Pro, Aduigy 4 Pro sound cards	www.creativelabs.com
DVICO	Fusion 5 HDTV card	www.dvico.com
eVGA	Fanless 6600 PCI-e graphics card	www.evga.com
Fry's	Source for all kinds of PC components & equipment	www.outpost.com
Gigabyte	Fanless GeForce 6600 graphics card, AV-710 sound card	www.giga-byte.com
Hauppauge	PVR-150MCE (single tuner), PVR-500MCE (dual tuner) TV cards	www.hauppauge.com
Intel	Pentium 4, Pentium M processors	www.intel.com
Nexus	Recommended PC case cooling fans	www.nexustek.nl
Papst	PC case cooling fans	www.papstplc.com
Panasonic	Recommended PC case cooling fans	www.panasonic.com
Silverstone	SST-FP52-B fan controller	www.silverstonetek.com
Sony Corporation	DRU-720 A DVD read/write device	www.sony.com
Zalman	PC case cooling fans & fan controllers	www.zalman.com

Wrapping Up

The beauty of careful planning and equally careful eyeballing is that it makes the build process pretty easy. If you follow our approach, and heed our advice, we hope you'll also experience a painless and trouble-free build as well. But no matter what your experience may be, we have to believe that reading and thinking through the process in advance will help prepare you for the real thing. That's what motivated this chapter, and what also makes Chapters 18, 19, and 20 so important to this book. We also invite you to send your build diaries to us so that we can post them to the book's Web site and share your build experiences with other readers. Send them to etittel@yahoo.com, but be sure to put **HTPC:** at the beginning of the subject line in your message, in order to get past our spam filters. You can visit this book's Web site at www.wiley.com/go/extremetech.

Installing Windows XP Media Center Edition 2005

Windows Media Center Edition 2005 is the latest version of Microsoft's software for Home Theater PCs. The 2005 edition generally does things right. It is one of the easiest interfaces to use and has every major function one expects built into an HTPC. Media Center Edition (henceforth called MCE) is a custom version of Windows XP Professional; as such, the MCE application integrates tightly with Windows XP itself. This allows scheduled recordings to occur whether or not the MCE interface is open.

In this chapter you get step-by-step instructions on how to install MCE onto your new HTPC. You also find tips to help you set up each MCE module quickly and correctly.

Pre-Installation Tips and Caveats

Before you start installing MCE, we recommend that you take some time to prepare your new system and that you collect any drivers you might need, so you'll be ready to supply them if and when Windows requests their access.

Gathering Drivers

We recommend that you gather up all the CDs, DVDs, and diskettes included with your various system components (if you followed our earlier advice in Chapter 16, you'll have them all in a software Ziploc ready to use). You should also belly up to another PC with a CD or DVD writer and download all the drivers you can find for your system before starting the MCE install on your HTPC. Common drivers you need include those for the motherboard chipset, the video card, networking, the TV card, the sound card, and certain Serial ATA controllers. You can find a list of common system component vendors in Table 17-1.

Taking our Athlon 64 test system as an example configuration, we must assemble the following drivers:

- nVidia nForce 4 chipset drivers (includes IDE, SATA, LAN, and chipset in one collection)
- nVidia "ForceWare" MCE-certified display drivers
- Realtek AC97 audio drivers
- AMD Athlon 64 CPU Cool 'n' Quiet Driver
- Driver for the Hauppauge PVR-150MCE

We recommend you put them into separate folders labeled by device or function. For example, you could create an "audio" folder and drag the Realtek installer file into that folder. Burn all of these files onto a CD and keep it handy for the final portion of the setup.

Tip

Here's a "gotcha!" to watch out for. If you use a RAID array, a motherboard that is based on VIA or SIS technology, or if you use a motherboard that employs an extra chip to provide Serial ATA support, you must create a special driver floppy disk for the Serial ATA Windows XP drivers. During the character mode install you must instruct Windows to include a special storage device driver. It then looks for a floppy drive with a diskette that contains those drivers. Without this input, Windows cannot recognize your SATA hard drive or RAID array.

Most HTPC cases don't include a floppy drive bay and that's OK. You need the floppy drive only while you install MCE. You can buy a floppy drive at any local computer shop for under $20. Attach the floppy to the motherboard. Leave the case open and the floppy sitting on top of (or next to) the computer while you install Windows. When that's finished you can remove the floppy and its cable, and then store it for possible future troubleshooting or reinstallation use.

Loading a SATA driver is covered in more detail in the "Character Mode Install" section later in the chapter.

Table 17-1   Common Chipset, LAN, Audio, Video, and Storage Vendors

Vendor	Products	URL/Remarks
Intel	Intel i800 and i900 series chipsets, Intel LAN controllers, and Intel motherboards	www.intel.com; The king of PC chipsets, they also make well-respected LAN chips and their own line of motherboards.
nVidia	GeForce series graphics processors and nForce series chipsets	www.nvidia.com; One of the leading manufacturers of PC graphics chips and motherboard chipsets for both the Athlon and Pentium platforms.
VIA	KT, K8T, and PT series chipsets, audio chips, and LAN controllers	www.viatech.com; A large vendor of motherboard chipsets for Athlon and Pentium CPUs. Also produces audio, 1394 (FireWire), and LAN chips.

Vendor	Products	URL/Remarks
ATI	Radeon graphics processors, and XPRESS chipsets	www.ati.com; One of the leading manufacturers of PC graphics chips. Also makes the Radeon XPRESS series of motherboard chipsets.
Creative	Sound Blaster Audigy series	www.creative.com; Creative is leading sound card peripheral manufacturer. Creative's products can be found in any retail computer store.
Realtek	ALC series of motherboard audio chips	www.realtek.com.tw; Perhaps the most popular provider of motherboard audio solutions.
C-Media	CMI series of motherboard and peripheral audio chips	www.cmedia.com.tw; C-Media's chips are the second most popular for use on motherboards.
Analog Devices	AD series of motherboard audio chips	www.analog.com; The AD series of audio chips are used on many motherboards.
3Com	LAN controllers	www.3com.com; Well-known vendor of networking-related products, 3Com controllers are found on various motherboards.
Silicon Image	Storage controllers	www.siliconimage.com; Popular Serial ATA and RAID controller vendor—found on many motherboards.
Promise	Storage controllers	www.promise.com; Well-known Serial ATA and RAID controller vendor—found on many motherboards.

Tip Power users, this tip is for you. If you are the owner of a motherboard that requires drivers from a floppy disk and would rather not deal with connecting a floppy drive, there is an advanced method whereby you make a customized version of the first MCE CD-ROM. In this custom version you integrate extra drivers and updates into a new copy of the Windows XP CD. This way when you use the new CD-ROM it will install the new drivers and updates automatically. No floppy is needed! For more please see the article "Unattended Windows 2000/XP Installations" from PCStats.com at www.pcstats.com/articleview.cfm?articleID=1703.

Preparing Your Motherboard BIOS

When you start your HTPC, you see the familiar boot screen, where it tots up how much memory is installed and tells you what kind of processor it detects. Sometimes this information may be hidden by a graphic and you must press a key—usually the Tab key—to see these details. Next, you must enter the BIOS setup; to do this, you normally must press the Del key. The BIOS lists boot devices and indicates which one is used first, second, and so forth. This information appears within various menus depending on the BIOS vendor. In many it appears in the Advanced BIOS Setup, but sometimes it may show up within a submenu called Boot Sequence. In other BIOSes it appears as a main menu entry simply labeled Boot. Wherever you find it (and you can use your motherboard manual to steer you to the right menus for your machine), change the first boot device to CD-ROM then set Hard Disk as the second device. This enables your HTPC to start the MCE setup automatically from the CD-ROM (or DVD player) the next time it reboots.

Note Motherboard BIOSes vary widely. If this cursory explanation doesn't turn up the right menu entry, consult your motherboard manual to dig out all the necessary details.

Put the first Windows XP MCE 2005 CD in the DVD drive and then perform a Save and Exit maneuver to leave the CMOS setup program and save your new BIOS settings (the F10 key will usually do this in a single keystroke). Your HTPC should reboot. Somewhere during that next reboot the PC informs you that if you wish to boot from the CD-ROM, you may press the spacebar (or some other key). Follow these instructions and then continue on to the next section.

Loading Installation Media

As described in the previous section, all versions of Windows XP, including MCE, install from the CD-ROM drive — no boot floppy is needed. Boot from the CD and Windows setup starts up shortly thereafter.

Unlike other versions, Windows XP MCE includes two CD-ROMs. The first one contains the system files and the second contains all files needed for Media Center. The setup program asks for Disc 2 somewhere in the middle of the graphical installation.

Character Mode Install

Windows first loads the core files it needs to access your hardware. It reports on progress in text form on the bottom line of your display.

Loading Special Drivers for SATA or RAID

During initial setup, Windows XP pauses briefly and states "Press F6 if you need to install a third party SCSI or RAID driver" (see sidebar figure). If your system meets the criteria specified in the "Gotcha!" tip in the preceding section, you must press the F6 key and insert the right floppy (for two of the three builds in this book, that meant inserting a SATA driver floppy). Windows setup reads the floppy and then asks you to specify additional devices by pressing "S" on your keyboard. It then shows you a list of drivers found on the floppy. Select the driver for Windows XP, and then press Enter to continue with the setup.

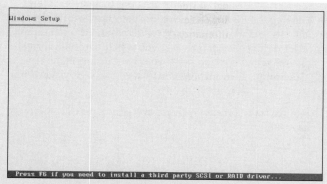

Windows Setup

Press F6 if you need to install a third party SCSI or RAID driver...

The F6 screen requests additional drivers if needed.

Advanced Hard Disk Setup

If you are comfortable with installing Windows, we recommend you partition your HTPC's hard disk into a system partition and a media partition. This way large files containing music, videos, and recorded TV remain separate from the Windows core. Here's how to split your HTPC's hard disk into two virtual drives (partitions). When the setup program displays your hard disk, rather than pressing Enter to proceed with a single monolithic partition, press "C" to create new partitions instead (see sidebar figure). Create a new partition of around 40GB for Windows by entering **40960**. Next create a second partition that uses all remaining space for your media files. Windows asks you to let it format the 40GB C: drive and then continues on with setup.

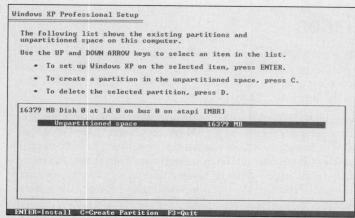

Windows XP Professional Setup

    The following list shows the existing partitions and
    unpartitioned space on this computer.

    Use the UP and DOWN ARROW keys to select an item in the list.

        • To set up Windows XP on the selected item, press ENTER.
        • To create a partition in the unpartitioned space, press C.
        • To delete the selected partition, press D.

    16379 MB Disk 0 at Id 0 on bus 0 on atapi [MBR]
            Unpartitioned space   16379 MB

ENTER=Install   C=Create Partition   F3=Quit

The partition screen lets you carve your hard disk up into multiple partitions.

Once Windows Setup finishes loading its core files and drivers it asks you to agree to its end user license agreement (EULA) by pressing the F8 key. Next, you are presented with a screen that shows you all hard disks(s) installed. If you aren't comfortable with advanced setup, simply hit Enter to install MCE to your first hard drive. Setup then asks you which hard disk format it should use; select NTFS (FAT is an antiquated file system). If your hard disk is brand new, we recommend not choosing the Quick option. That way, Windows also thoroughly checks the drive for errors as it formats.

A yellow progress bar appears as Windows Setup finishes copying everything it needs to proceed with the graphical portion of the install.

Graphics Mode Install

Your computer reboots after the character mode install completes. If you inserted a floppy with drivers, remove it now. Leave MCE disc 1 in your optical drive. When your PC restarts *do not* boot from the CD. Windows XP loads from the hard disk and continues setup instead. Windows gathers information about your PC and then copies files to your hard disk.

Near the middle of the graphical phase, the setup program asks for "Windows XP Professional Disc 2." Despite the odd identifier, this actually means the second MCE CD-ROM. Insert that CD-ROM and let setup continue; it copies files from that CD, ejects it, and then asks you to re-insert disc 1 to complete its activities.

When setup finishes copying files, a setup wizard appears. It prompts you to provide a product key, to specify geographical region and language, date and time, set an administrator password, and then sets up standard user(s) for your HTPC. This signals the end of the official setup process, but there's still more work to do before you can declare victory. That's covered in the next section.

Finishing Up Installation

You should now be able to access the Windows desktop on your fresh copy of Windows XP MCE 2005. Eject the Windows setup CD-ROM and insert the driver CD-ROM you made earlier. We recommend that you copy the contents of this CD-ROM to a folder on the C: drive (*drivers* is a good name for this folder, in fact).

Your first task is to enable your motherboard's core hardware properly. Carrying on with our Athlon 64 test system as an example, this means you should run the nVidia chipset setup program. Reboot when it asks you to do so. This allows your system to run at its fullest potential. Next, install the nVidia ForceWare display drivers. Here again, reboot when it asks you to do so. Install the Realtek sound driver package and reboot as directed. You may or may not install the AMD Cool 'n' Quiet driver as you choose. We recommend it highly because it helps keep things cooler by managing the Athlon 64's speed depending on processor demand.

Once your core Windows drivers are all updated, it's time to make sure you have all extra peripherals installed correctly. Open the Device Manager (it's located in the System control panel, accessible using Start → Control Panel → Performance and Maintenance → System. Then click the Hardware tab and click the Device Manager button).

Tip

A shortcut to open the Device Manager is to click the Start menu and then choose Run. In the Open: box type **devmgmt.msc** and then click OK. This sure beats menu hopping!

Look for any yellow exclamation points. The Hauppauge PVR-150MCE card should be listed as an unknown Multimedia Video Controller. Right-click this entry and choose Properties. Click the Driver tab on the top. After you click the Update Driver button you are prompted to search for a driver. Choose Install from a list or specific location (Advanced). Then point the wizard to the folder where you copied all the drivers from the CD you made earlier. Once the drivers are updated, your HTPC should be ready to roll.

You will need to install an MCE-certified DVD decoder to view TV and DVDs (see Table 17-2). If you are using nVidia graphics cards, as we do in our sample configurations, nVidia's own DVD Decoder comes highly recommended. That's because it exposes extra features not otherwise available in the GeForce 6 and GeForce 7 series.

Table 17-2 MCE-Compatible DVD Decoders

Name	Version	URL/Remarks
Cyberlink Power DVD	OEM 5.0.2027C, Retail 6.0 and up	www.gocyberlink.com; Retail available DVD decoder, a pack-in version is included in many DVD drives and is the foundation for ATI's DVD decoder.
InterVideo WinDVD	OEM 5.0 Build 11.670, Retail 6.0 and up	www.intervideo.com; Retail available DVD decoder, a version of this is often a pack-in with many DVD drives.
nVidia DVD Decoder	1.00.58 and newer	www.nvidia.com; The newest versions are now called PureVideo Decoder. The nVidia decoder is a unique decoder made by graphics chip designer nVidia rather than a third party, optimized for image quality and features. Despite its name it works on modern graphics cards from any mainstream vendor (including ATI).

Cross-Reference For more information about DVD decoders see Chapter 9.

Last, run Windows Update and download any critical updates, as well as MCE updates. Media Center updates aren't listed as critical, so you must add them manually to the download queue. A key item is Update Rollup 1 for Windows XP Media Center Edition 2005 with HDTV Support (KB873369). Another helpful item is Update for Conflict Management in Windows XP Media Center Edition 2005 (Q890760). Note: please install the Rollup first before installing the conflict management fix.

Starting Media Center for the First Time

To start Media Center you can press the Green Button on your MCE remote or select the Media Center icon from the Start menu. The first time you run MCE it asks you a series of questions to help you set up your HTPC. You are asked for your Zip code and about where your TV service originates: from an antenna, cable, digital cable, or satellite.

Once you are all set up, navigate to the Settings menu and choose General, then Startup and Window Behavior. Select the Start Media Center when Windows starts option to make sure Media Center loads automatically (see Figure 17-1), select Save, and then press the Green Button to return to the main menu.

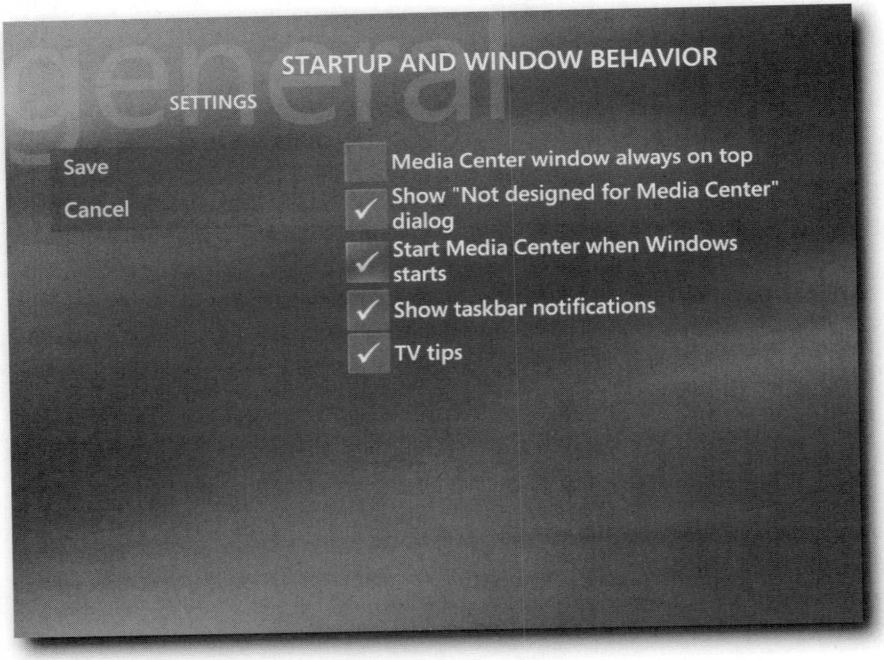

FIGURE 17-1: Setting Media Center to start when Windows starts.

Making Music, Videos, and Pictures Work

When you first enter My Music, My Videos, or My Pictures, MCE pops up a box that asks if you would like to add new media now (see Figure 17-2). If you choose Yes, MCE asks you questions about whether you want to add or remove folders. If you choose to add a folder, it asks where the files are stored: on the HTPC or on your home network. You are then shown a list of folders and drives from which you can choose. By selecting the + icon you can expand drives to show subfolders as in Windows Explorer. When you are done choosing folders, select Next and then Finish. Next, MCE imports the media you selected automatically.

FIGURE 17-2: MCE asks if you want to add new media now.

Making TV Work

Before you jump into recording all your favorite programs, remember that if you set up a second partition for media storage, you must first instruct MCE to use its drive letter rather than the main C: drive reserved for Windows MCE. To do this from the main menu, press the arrow key on your remote until you see the Settings menu. Then, select the TV option, then Recorder, and finally select Recorder Storage. Here you can see the drive MCE uses by default and how much space MCE allocates for recording. Change the Record on drive: value to match the drive letter assigned to your media partition (most probably, it's D:).

Even if you didn't split your hard disk, you may still want to expand the default drive space MCE allocates to recorded TV. By default. MCE allocates a conservative amount of drive space. You bought a big drive, so why not let MCE use more of it for TV recordings? In the Recorder Storage screen, all settings reflect estimates of how many hours of standard TV you can record in the space allotted (see Figure 17-3).

By default, it's set at 50GB of space. On a 160GB drive this should be increased to 90GB–100GB of space (leaving plenty of room for other things). Select the Save button on the top left and then hit the Green Button on your remote to jump back to the main menu.

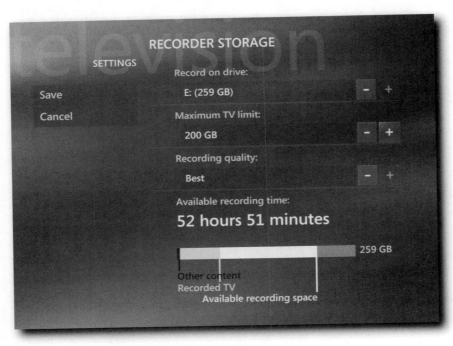

FIGURE 17-3: Setting Recorder Storage settings.

During the initial setup your guide listings were downloaded for you automatically. If you select My TV and then the Guide you can see TV listings waiting for your perusal. If you select a show from the guide that is currently airing, you are taken to a live TV view. If the show is set to air in the future, you are shown a recording screen instead. Here, you can choose to record a show once (see Figure 17-4) or set up recording for all pending airings of the show, called Record Series (see Figure 17-5). When you select Record, it uses defaults from global preferences in the Settings. You can change recording settings by selecting Record Settings. Here you can choose the recording quality level and when MCE should remove the recording. MCE can remove a recording for you when it gets low on space, or you can tell MCE to retain the show even if disk space runs low. If you choose to record a series, you have even more options to work with, such as which channels to record from and whether or not to include repeats.

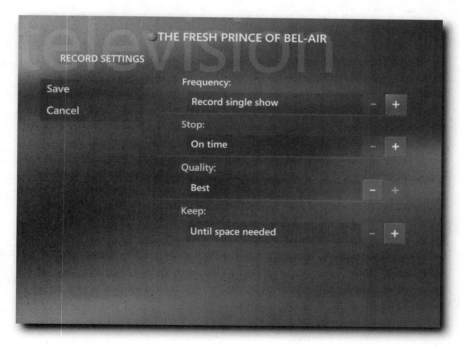

FIGURE 17-4: Recording a TV show options.

FIGURE 17-5: Recording a series options.

Making Radio Work

Radio in MCE is straightforward. If you have an antenna hooked up to your TV tuner card, MCE tunes in local radio stations for you (see Figure 17-6). Simply enter the frequency with your remote, for example, type in **1005**, and it will tune to 100.5. Then sit back and listen! MCE can also pause radio and let you return to it where you left off just as with live TV.

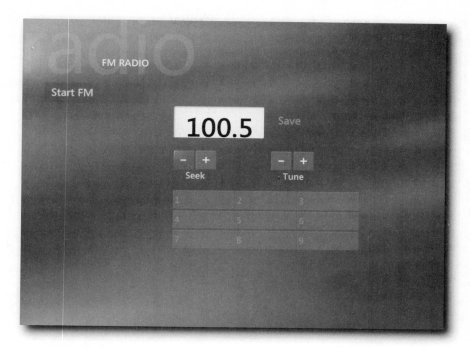

FM RADIO

Start FM

100.5   Save

− +   − +
Seek   Tune

1   2   3
4   5   6
7   8   9

FIGURE 17-6: MCE radio module.

Integrating Your PC with Home Entertainment Gear

Most modern surround sound receivers understand Dolby Digital and DTS streams directly from a DVD. Those receivers that can decode digital multichannel audio (Dolby and DTS) offer either coax or optical digital inputs (known as S/PDIF). Your HTPC is equipped with digital outputs just like a set-top DVD player. If you have such a port on your surround sound equipment, we recommend you use this all-digital connection to your home theater. You generally want to use the multichannel output (discrete six-channel analog cabling) only if you are connecting straight to a set of amplifiers or speakers, or if your receiver supports such inputs.

Beware that if you use the analog outputs, your HTPC must decode Dolby and DTS on its own rather than handing streams off to your home theater equipment for processing.

Unlike various analog audio connections, MCE's setup wizard does not include an explicit setting for S/PDIF mode. S/PDIF mode is enabled by a combination of your sound card's control panel settings and your DVD decoder's preferences. You will probably need to exit the Media Center interface and open your DVD software to set this up (see Figures 17-7 and 17-8 for examples of how to do this).

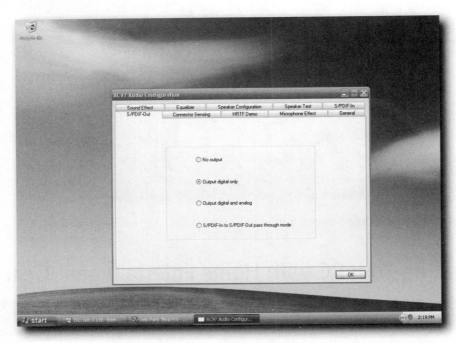

FIGURE 17-7: Example of checking whether S/PDIF mode is enabled with Realtek drivers.

FIGURE 17-8: Example of setting S/PDIF mode in the nVidia DVD Decoder.

Wrapping Up

Installing Windows can be daunting. But a little bit of preparation and following our tips from this chapter should help you on your way to Media Center bliss.

Installing the right drivers is key: if you forget your motherboard's drivers, you may end up with reduced functionality or non-functional components. Please do make use of a CD-R or use some other removable media like a USB Flash drive to gather up all the drivers you need before installing MCE.

Don't forget that Microsoft requires MCE-certified graphics and TV card drivers. Thus, you must look for Media Center Edition drivers from your component vendors. On a similar note, you also need an MCE-compatible DVD decoder to view DVDs and television.

Although most of Media Center's settings are available through some wizard, we've already provided information and guidance about more important settings that some wizard doesn't support. Finally, to complete your home theater experience, don't forget to connect your HTPC to the best possible audio connection you can afford. Enjoy!

Media Center PC Projects

part

IV

Building a P4 HTPC

In building a Home Theater PC around a Pentium 4 PC, we certainly stretched the notion that it's better to use slower, cooler CPUs rather than hotter, faster ones. The guiding notion in that case is to keep cooling requirements to a minimum and thus to avoid the need to use fans as much as possible, thereby also avoiding the most common sources of noise.

But in talking to friends, colleagues, and other interested parties, we kept coming up against a special kind of HTPC scenario. We could call this a "do-it-all" situation, in that plenty of people at home, in a dorm, or at the office find themselves in a situation where they have room for only one PC. Thus, however much they may want to exercise MCE's capabilities to capture, record, and display media for entertainment, learning, or business reasons, these people also want a computer they can use for more typical computing tasks as well. That's what prompted us to include this particular build in our book.

Because we'd been warned about heat output and definite needs for active and serious cooling with a P4-based HTPC, we also decided to choose a big, well-ventilated tower case instead of a more typical horizontal A/V component type case for this build. Cynics might argue that because author Mike Chin helped design the Antec P180 case we chose for this build, using that case was a foregone conclusion. But although Mike did recommend this case as particularly suitable for a hotter running PC, HTPC or otherwise, he otherwise had nothing to do with this build.

chapter 18

in this chapter

☑ Component choices

☑ Pre-build warm-up and initial build-out

☑ Installing expansion cards and drives

☑ Cabling up

☑ MCE and media attachments

☑ Testing, cleaning up, and closing up

In this chapter, we cover the following topics while walking through the build process for our Pentium 4 tower case build:

- **Component selection rationale:** We'll revisit the reasons why we picked our components, describe where and how we bought them, and how long it took all the parts to arrive.

- **Pre-build preparation:** We describe what we did with our parts before we actually started building and review some configuration changes from the planning stage to the actual implementation. We learned some interesting lessons along the way, and share them with you as well. As we eyeballed the case, the motherboard, the CPU, and the cooler, we realized quickly what we had to do to get the build started. Certain unique aspects of the Antec P180 case came into play here, as did the dimensions of our Antec Phantom 500 PSU, and we describe how we planned to deal with cabling issues as well.

- **Initial build-out:** This took us as far as installing the motherboard, the CPU and its cooler, the PSU, and the memory. A quick power-on test also convinced us that everything was going okay so far.

- **Installing the expansion cards:** We installed our graphics and TV cards at this point, with a single interesting concession to the graphics card's massive heat sinks and wider-than-average footprint.

- **Installing the drives:** Best practices dictate that we install the hard drive in the 3.5" bay at the bottom of the case across from the PSU, but clearance issues and fan placement argued otherwise. Thus, we installed both our optical and hard drives in the upper compartment.

- **Cabling up:** Once all the pieces were in place, we hooked everything up for a quick check to make sure all was well. When the system posted, we got serious about cable routing issues and arrived at a more or less final layout. Some interesting shenanigans were required.

- **OS install and finish work:** Installing MCE takes time, but was surprisingly easy — even more so because our motherboard didn't require a SATA driver disk during the install. We jumped through some interesting hoops in getting the BIOS updates and settings just right, and again, when adding drivers and a DVD decoder.

- **Installing the remote:** The MCE remote worked like a charm as soon as we plugged the IR receiver into a USB slot.

- **Making media connections:** Our Scientific Atlanta set-top box posed no problems for MCE, and a single IR blaster was all it took to get ready for recording. TV hookup and access worked like a charm, as did our radio link. DVD decoder already installed made TV and DVD playback a breeze.

- **Testing and burn-in:** We let the machine run overnight just to make sure everything was working okay. One of our monitoring programs gave us a scare, but a quick touch of the finger convinced us the measurements were wrong and everything was okay. We report on case and CPU temperatures and wonder why PSU readings seem so out of whack.

- **Clean-up and close-up:** We tweaked a few wires here, cable-tied a few others there, and produced a final layout we could close the case on without too much trepidation.

- **Concluding postscript:** We report on actual total costs and components, and ruminate on ways to save money to bring those costs down, or spend more money to get more system in return.

The Antec P180 case, although not without its challenges, proved to offer a truly inspiring building experience. We were very happy with the system that resulted from this particular collection of components and observed it to be surprisingly cost-effective as well. It probably wouldn't work in a typical entertainment center, but is a great choice for a do-it-all PC.

In addition to the photos in this chapter that illustrate this build, you'll also find five figures in the color signature in the center of this book related to this build as well (Figures 1–5). They show the motherboard and all parts related to installing the CPU and its cooler thereupon, with isometric (45 degree or profile view) shots of the build after expansion cards were emplaced, and after cabling and clean-up were completed. These provide different views of what you'll find here and should help illuminate the build process further.

In the sections that follow, we walk you through the process of building this Pentium 4 powerhouse, and intersperse the build with some pictures that show you what the whole thing looks like.

Component Selection Rationale

Though we picked a Pentium 4, we tried to limit our selection in that processor family to its slower and cooler members. Eventually, we settled on a Pentium 4 630 CPU: at 3.0 GHz it's certainly more than adequate for HTPC use and for light office duty and gaming as well. The 6*xx* P4s run somewhat cooler than the 5*xx* P4s, so we expected to lessen our heat burden to some extent through that selection. Subsequent case and CPU temperature measurements of 36 degrees C (about 97 degrees F) and 48 degrees C (about 118 degrees F) at idle, and of 40 degrees C (104 degrees F) and 52 degrees C (about 126 degrees F) under a typical load showed us later that our rationale was reasonably sound. That said, the case has four 120 mm fans (all running at slow speeds to minimize noise) and moves lots of air to keep things cool.

We picked a large power supply for this case to leave ample room for growth and expansion and because regular HTPC operation should seldom put much strain on the PSU or cause its fan to spin at very high rates. Even under heavy loads running synthetic benchmarks, we never saw the PSU fan spin as fast as 2000 RPM. But this PSU could support many more hard disks, if needed or wanted, and the motherboard still has room for one more conventional PCI card, plus two PCI-E X1 cards as well.

The ASUS P5AD2-E Deluxe motherboard offered lots of attractive capabilities for a mid-range price (we paid $207 for our board, but by the time we finished this chapter, prices as low as $171 were available). Its support for eight-channel (7.1) high-definition audio and both optical and coax SPDIF outputs made a sound card unnecessary. Gigabit Ethernet and DDR2 memory up to 711 MHz speeds gave us plenty of speed to draw on should it ever be needed. Likewise, the board also supports up to four SATA drives and three Ultra ATA drives with numerous RAID options, should those ever be needed (unlikely on an HTPC but not necessarily so on a desktop or gaming machine). We chose two Corsair 512MB DDR2 538 PC24300 DIMMs for this system because of their reliable operation and speedy memory timings.

We chose the Gigabyte nVidia 6600 Silentpipe graphics card because the case has ample room and cooling for its massive heat sinks and because it's a great choice for HTPC use with or without HDTV. We chose the Hauppauge WinTV PVR-150MCE single tuner TV card, though we were strongly tempted to go with the dual-tuner WinTV PVR-500MCE card instead. Both work like a charm with our local cable TV provider's offerings.

We decided to purchase an aftermarket CPU cooler with an extremely quiet fan to maximize cooling and limit heat output. We tried the fanless Scythe Ninja at first, but couldn't make the mounting bracket work with our motherboard, despite the vendor's claim of socket 775 compatibility. We chose the Thermalright XP-120 cooler instead, and mounted an ultra-quiet Nexus 120 mm fan on top. During all our testing, we never observed CPU temperatures higher than 65 degrees C (149 degrees F), nor case temperatures higher than 43 degrees C (about 110 degrees F). Because the case came equipped with three 120 mm adjustable-speed Antec fans, additional ventilation wasn't necessary, though we did power up all those fans.

We went with SATA for both the hard disk and the optical drive, using a Maxtor DiamondMax 300GB drive, and a Plextor DVD R±W drive. Both proved adequate and offered a decent compromise between noise and capability. 300GB probably isn't enough disk space for long run, but we plan to use external drives to keep heat and noise to a minimum. Given the Antec P180's astonishing eight 3.5" drive bays, others might simply choose to pop another drive or two into the case instead.

Once we ordered all our parts, most of them from general PC dealer Newegg and HTPC specialist PCAlchemy.com, it took about 10 days for everything to show up. Once we had case, mobo, CPU, cooler, and memory in hand, we felt like we had enough to start planning, and ultimately, to get going.

Pre-Build Preparation

When the P180 showed up at our door, we unpacked it to see if the real thing lived up to the various reviews we've read (you'll find good ones at numerous Web sites, including ExtremeTech.com and SilentPCReview.com). We quickly recognized that the case layout posed some atypical build considerations.

In many ways, in fact, the Antec P180 case made this the most interesting build of all. For one thing, the case is incredibly well-designed. Among features too numerous to recount completely, it offers the following characteristics significant for HTPC use despite its mid-tower format and formidable dimensions:

- Double-walled construction throughout for extra insulation from noise (and to lengthen sound paths more than any other case we've ever worked with).

- The interior is divided into two chambers, a lower chamber for the power supply and up to five 3.5" drives (perfect for a RAID array and a large power supply, like the Antec Phantom 500 we built into the case).

- Upper and lower drive bays include easy out hardware (the drives are bolted into slides, which offer mechanical isolation from the case using the same plastic slides that make it easy to slide drives in and out of their bays as needed).

- There's a special heat exhaust you can park over the expansion card area on most mobos, designed to channel heat away from the interior of the case straight to an exhaust on the back.

- The case includes three quiet 120 mm fans. One is at the back of the lower enclosure to pull air out of the case right in line with the PSU exhaust fan (great for cooling any drives down below); the other two fans are at the upper rear of the case, one blowing out from the back panel more or less in line with the CPU and its cooler, the other blowing up from the back rear of the top panel. Both combine to remove hot air from the case expeditiously (and Mike Chin, who helped design this case, also indicates that turning both fans on may not be necessary in cooler systems). Each Antec fan also includes a three-speed setting (low, medium, high) but is sufficiently quiet only at the low setting, so we engaged all three and set all on low.

Other than routing cables from the PSU to the motherboard, drives, and fans, and our decision to house the single hard disk in the upper chamber because of the size of the Antec Phantom 500 PSU, we didn't see any other situations in need of extra planning or attention. Thus, resolved to find creative ways to route cables around the CPU and its cooler, we decided to start our build. Figure 18-1 shows what things looked like inside the roomy P180 case before we added anything to its interior.

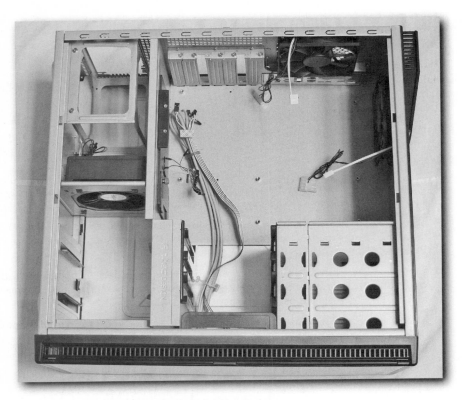

FIGURE 18-1: The Antec P180 case prior to installation.

Initial Build-Out

Figuring out how to route cables from the PSU into the main chamber posed some interesting problems. Because we used an oversized Antec Phantom 500 PSU (about 3 cm, or just a little over 1" longer than most PSUs), we had to move the lower compartment fan to the other side of the middle case rail (to the front half of the case, in other words). In turn, this created clearance issues that persuaded us to install our single 300MB drive in the upper case compartment.

Those seeking the absolute quietest configuration would be well-advised to stick to less bulky PSUs to leave room to mount their drives down below and route their cables to the upper compartment. It might also make sense either to substitute the 120 mm fan in the lower compartment with a slimmer replacement, or to remove the pre-supplied fan from its stand and mount it to the center partition instead (mounting holes are thoughtfully provided).

Installing the mobo was no problem at all, because we installed the CPU cooler bracket in advance. After that we simply dropped the motherboard into position and tacked it down to eight standoffs already installed in the case. The full-size ATX mobo was easy to position, and we encountered no significant clearance issues during its installation. CPU and cooler installation proceeded without difficulty, even though the Thermalright cooler we used was large and bulky. Once installed, the cooler tower and the 120 mm Nexus fan we installed on top became the primary landmark inside the case, and an obstacle around which we had to route power cables (see Figures 1 through 3 in the color section of the book for views of the parts involved and their assembly).

We installed our two RAM modules in their respective color-coordinated slots to support interleaved memory without any difficulty. As a quick check of the build so far, we attached the 24-pin motherboard power connector, the 4-pin CPU power connector, and hooked the on/off switch to the proper motherboard pins, so we could perform a quick interim build status check. When the fans spun up with only a single beep (the POST code that indicates proper operation), we heaved a sigh of relief before unhooking power cables and moving on to the next step. Figure 18-2 shows what the system looks like with motherboard, CPU, cooler, and memory installed.

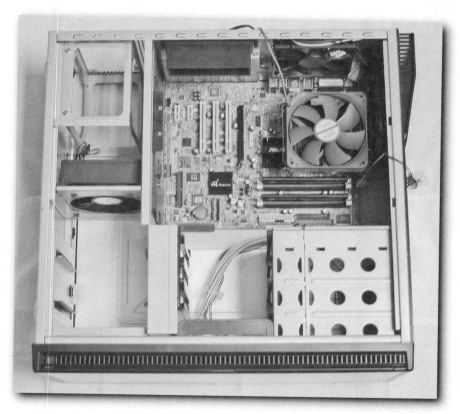

FIGURE 18-2: The P180 case with motherboard, CPU, cooler, and memory installed.

Installing Expansion Cards

Next into the case went our Gigabyte 6600 Silentpipe PCI-E X16 graphics card and the Hauppauge WinTV PVR-150MCE card. Both went in without incident. To maximize airflow around the graphics card, we installed the Hauppauge TV card as far away from the PCI-E slot as possible. You can see a sizable gap between the two cards in the upper-left portion of the motherboard compartment in Figure 18-3 (for a different view of this step along the way, check out Figure 4 in the color section of the book).

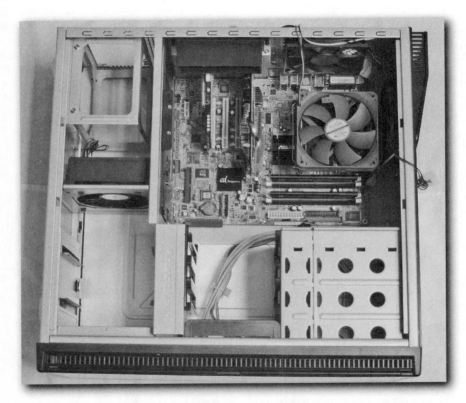

FIGURE 18-3: The Gigabyte nVidia 6600 graphics card shows off its hefty Zalman heat sinks, but there's not much to see on the Hauppauge TV card.

Installing Drives

The drives also went in extremely easily, thanks to the P180's totally friendly design. The mounting hardware and slides provided with the case made this part of the job far easier than usual. All we had to do was mount rails on the sides of the optical drive and the hard disk and then slide them into position. We decided to put the optical drive in the top 5.25" bay and the hard disk into the top slot in the upper 3.5" drive bay. Given the size and layout of this mid-tower case, it's also much easier to gain access to and work on drive bays than in the other, smaller cases we used in the two chapters that follow. These were by far the easiest drive installs we encountered in researching this book! There's really not much to see in Figure 18-4, which shows the optical drive at the top of the case (but the hard disk is completely hidden by its drive cage).

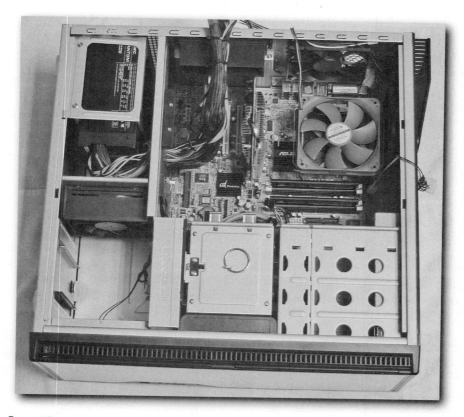

FIGURE 18-4: You can see the optical drive in the 5.25" bay at the top of the case, but you'll have to take our word for it that the Maxtor is ensconced in the 3.5" bay as well.

Cabling Up

The biggest challenge in the build came when trying to route power cables to their respective destinations. Accessing the 24-pin ATX mobo connector was easy because the big cable bundle came up from below and plugged right into the socket on the lower edge of the case. The 4-pin CPU power cable, however, had to stretch all the way to the far upper-left corner of the mobo (facing the board through the open panel on the left side of the case). We had to route it around the CPU cooler/fan stack. We found the switches connected to the Antec fans in the case (which are mounted on 3" lengths of stiff flat wire much like standard telephone wire) to be helpful as anchor points for this cable, which we cable-tied to the case top fan switch wire to keep it clear of the CPU cooler fan.

Other molex cable strands proved interesting as well, but by routing cables around the edge of the motherboard as much as possible, we were able to create a decent-looking configuration nevertheless. Cabling up front panel devices (2 USB, 1 FireWire, microphone/headphone audio outs) was also easy and straightforward, thanks to well-labeled cable ends and a well-designed motherboard manual.

Total time for the hardware portion of the build was about three hours, not including time out for shooting photographs. We did spend an hour or so talking through the process in advance and that really helped speed things up as soon as we picked up our screwdrivers and got going.

This was the only build that required no special tools. We did the whole thing with two screwdrivers, a couple of bags of cable ties, and a pair of flush cutters with which to trim the latter. Ventilation proved to be a snap, thanks to the four fans in the case (three included, the fourth snapped atop the Thermalright XP-120 Socket 775 CPU cooler) and our selection of SATA for both optical and hard disks. See the finished results in Figure 5 of the color section of this book.

Final Build Components and Costs

We made a few changes from our original budgeting plans for this build. The final and actual bill of materials appears in Table 18-1 and reflects some reduction in costs between the planning and purchasing phases. Please note also that we substituted the bigger and more expensive Antec Phantom 500 PSU for the Seasonic S12 380 we originally specified and a different optical drive (chosen because of its great price and SATA cabling).

Table 18-1   Final Build Components and Costs

Vendor	Item	Cost
Antec	P180 case	$110
Antec	Phantom 500 PSU	$162
ASUS	P5AD2-E Deluxe motherboard	$171
Intel	P4 630 CPU 3.0 GHz	$226
Gigabyte	NVIDIA 6600 Silentpipe	$120
Hauppauge	WinTV PVR-150MCE	$65
Maxtor	DiamondMax 300 GB SATA-I hard disk	$150
Plextor	712SA SATA R±W DVD Drive	$60
Corsair	DDR2 PC4300 538 MHz RAM, 2 x 512 MB	$181

Vendor	Item	Cost
Nexus	120 mm silent fan	$18
Thermalright	XP-120 CPU Cooler	$50
Microsoft	MCE 2005 software	$120
Microsoft	MCE remote	$35
Microsoft	Optical Elite desktop set (keyboard & mouse)	$75
TOTAL		$1,543

Saving More, Spending More

If you're seeking to cut these costs you could consider the following money-saving items:

- Refurbished P5AD2-E Deluxe boards are available at Newegg for as little as $130. Other motherboards with identical features are available from other well-known vendors such as DFI, Abit, MSI, Gigabyte, and AOpen for $90 and up. Savings of up to $80 are possible in this category.

- The Antec Phantom 500 could easily be replaced with our favorite, the Seasonic S12 380 for $50, for a savings of $112. Even the smaller Antec Phantom 350 costs $131.

- Cheaper DDR2 PC4300 512MB modules are available for as little as $35 from no-name vendors, to $65 each for value RAM from big name vendors like GEiL, Crucial, Kingston, and so forth. This saves between $50 and $110.

Total savings of up to $292 are possible without significant loss of functionality. That brings costs down to a very reasonable $1,351.

On the higher side of this budget, the following substitutions or additions could make sense if you have a little more to spend:

- Replacing the Hauppauge WinTV PVR-150MCE with a PVR-500MCE brings dual tuners into play and permits recording two programs at once, or watching one while recording another. The price tag for this nice increase in capability is about $60–$75 more than the single tuner card.

- Adding an HDTV card like the DVICO Fusion 5 or the AVerMedia AVerTV HD MCE A 180 costs from $80 up to $160.

- Doubling up on memory to 2GB for 512MB DIMMs or going as high as 4GB for 1GB DIMMs could cost anywhere from an additional $70 to as much as $800.

- Adding more SATA drives might make sense for some users. Figure on $150 for each additional 300GB SATA drive.

Total additional outlays up to $1,185 are easy to make — as long as you can afford them!

Installing MCE and Media Attachments

Next, we installed MCE 2005 on the Pentium 4 PC without a single snag or difficulty and followed that up with drivers from the motherboard update CD. Next, we visited Drivers Headquarters (www.drivershq.com) and used that site's free Driver Detective Scan to catch and bring all of our other drivers up to date. Next, we installed the nVidia DVD Decoder, to take best advantage of our Gigabyte 6600 graphics card's special capabilities. Total time required was a little over an hour and a half.

We had no difficulty attaching this HTPC to a speaker rig (the Logitech Z-5500 Digital rig we hooked up supported a single SPDIF coax cable from the back of the PC to the speaker controller). The speaker unit recognized the device outputs immediately and worked fine with DVDs, music, and TV playback. We also found a deal on these speakers online for $220.

We used S-Video cables to link our Hauppauge PVR 150 input to our Scientific Atlanta cable TV box output and then took a DVI output from our Gigabyte nVidia graphics card into a Syntax Olevia LCD HDTV set. Everything worked as soon as it was hooked up and Windows detected what was going on. We also used one of the two IR blaster lines on the MCE remote IR receiver to enable the PC to drive the cable box for unattended recording. With the FM antenna included with the PVR 150 in place, MCE had no trouble picking up local radio stations, either.

Testing and Burn-In

Once all the software was installed, and all the media gear hooked up, we left the PC up and running overnight to make sure everything was working okay. We used two programs to monitor the PC's temperatures:

- The ASUS PC Probe utility was included on the utility CD that shipped with the P5AD2-E Deluxe. We left it up and running to keep tabs on the system. It registered values of between 45 and 50 degrees C (113 and 122 degrees F) for CPU temperatures, and 33 and 48 degrees C (92 and 119 degrees F) for motherboard temperatures.

- PC Wizard 2005 is a tool first introduced in Chapter 6 of this book. It reports on processor and motherboard temperatures as well (and agreed with PC Probe's readings), plus PSU temperatures. Our scare came when the display showed PSU temperature at 126 degrees C (about 259 degrees F, or 47 degrees above the boiling point for water). A quick "touch test" on the PSU indicated no unusual warmth, so we guessed the temperature was reported in Fahrenheit, even though we requested a Celsius read-out. The next reboot of the system confirmed this, much to our great relief!

- The Seasonic Power Angel we used to monitor the unit's power consumption varied from a low of about 120 W to a high of 222 W for this configuration — well within the 500 W of power that our Antec power supply delivered for this unit. At idle, the unit consumed between 120 and 130 W; at heavy load (playing a DVD, handling music, or performing big file transfers) the maximum readings never topped 222 W, and seldom exceeded 200 W.

Everything about the system behaved nicely and worked just fine, so we would be comfortable putting it into production — or everyday use in a home entertainment center, if you prefer. We were incredibly pleased with the results of this build; the system managed to be powerful and quiet enough for living room use, if a bit too big for your average entertainment center.

Clean-Up and Close-Up

Convinced that our P4 system was ready for prime time, we cleaned up the cables inside the case for a final close-up. This involved a little fiddling with cable ties, as you can see in Figure 18-5. In particular, notice how we routed fan and control cables along the top edge of the case to keep them out of the way and how we tied the black and yellow 4-pin CPU power cable to the white switch wire for the back panel 120 mm fan to keep it off the graphics card and away from the CPU cooler fan. Overall there's plenty of room for air to circulate around the CPU cooler and the heat sinks on the graphics card, which were our primary ventilation concerns in routing cables inside the main case compartment.

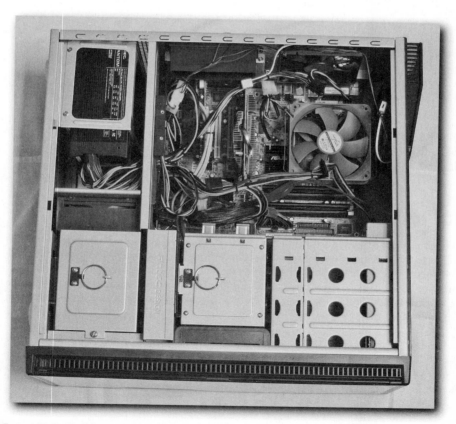

FIGURE 18-5: The cleaned-up final version of the build shows extensive use of cable ties to keep wires away from fans and heat sinks.

About the only thing we could have done better would have been to use some kind of spiral wrap or nylon mesh around the power cables. But all in all, we're quite pleased with the way the wiring lays out. There's still easy access to populated open PCI or PCI-E X1 slots, and low case temperatures indicate we have achieved good air circulation inside the case.

A quick look at Figure 18-6 shows the back of the Antec case. We used all three stock 120 mm Antec fans included with the case, but ran them on their slowest speeds to keep noise to a minimum. Including the Nexus 120 mm fan on the CPU cooler, and the 120 mm fan on the PSU, we had plenty of ventilation for this system. That's why we didn't take advantage of its mounts for two additional 60 mm fans above the expansion card slots that appear in the lower center of Figure 18-6.

FIGURE 18-6: The rear view of the Antec P180 case shows the motherboard's port block beneath the fan housing (left), the extra vent holes above the expansion card slots (center), and the PSU vent (right).

Vendor Information

For convenience, Table 18-2 lists all the vendors whose products are mentioned in this chapter. Though you can visit these sites for product information (and probably, news about newer products as well), please use the price comparison tools we mentioned earlier in Chapter 15 to find for the best deals. (In addition, please don't forget to check on eBay or to consult the appendixes at the end of the book, many of which also provide pointers to comparison and shopping information as well.)

Table 18-2 Vendors Mentioned in Chapter 18

Vendor	Component	URL
Antec	P180 case, Phantom 500 PSU	www.antec.com
ASUS	P5AD2-E Deluxe motherboard	www.asus.com
Corsair	XMS2 DDR2 TwinX PC4300 DIMMs	www.corsair.com
Crucial	DDR and DDR2 memory	www.crucial.com
GEiL	DDR and DDR2 memory	www.geilusa.com
Gigabyte	nVidia 6600 Silentpipe PCI-E X16 graphics card	www.giga-byte.com
Hauppauge	WinTV PVR-150MCE TV, WinTV PVR-500MCE TV cards	www.hauppauge.com
Intel	P4 640 CPU (3.0 GHz)	www.intel.com
Kingston	DDR and DDR2 memory	www.kingston.com
Logitech	Z-5500 Digital 5.1 Speakers	www.logitech.com
Maxtor	DiamondMax 300GB SATA hard disk	www.maxtor.com
Microsoft	MCE software, remotes, keyboards, and mice	www.microsoft.com
Nexus	120 mm silent case fan	www.nexus.com
Syntax	Olevia 34" LCD HDTV	www.syntaxgroups.com
Plextor	712SA SATA DVD R±W drive	www.plextor.com
Scientific Atlanta	CATV set-top box	www.sciatl.com
Scythe	Ninja LG775 cooler	www.scythe-usa.com
Thermalright	XP-120 LG775 cooler w/adapter	www.thermalright.com

Wrapping Up

If we could have some druthers for this build, they'd be pretty few. The P180 could benefit from a rail over the middle of the upper (motherboard) compartment on which to route cables. The cable opening between the upper and lower compartments could be 1 or 2 cm wider, to make for easier cable routing between the two chambers. The Pentium 4 could run a little slower and a little cooler without bothering us too much, either. But other than that, this system turned out great.

For a relatively modest price of about $1,500 it offers nice features and functions and very good performance. All we can say is that all builds should go so nicely and easily. This one was a real peach!

Building a Pentium M HTPC

O f all the builds for this book, we were most excited about putting the Pentium M to work. Originally designed for notebooks, this processor is well known for its low power consumption and relatively cool operation. If you look at any of the photos inside the case in the chapter (and in the color section in the center of this book), you need only compare the size and heft of the CPU cooler for the Pentium M to those we used for the Pentium 4 and Athlon 64 to see for yourself that the motherboard designers agreed with this notion wholeheartedly. In fact, the Pentium M motherboard looks relatively empty compared to the other two builds because the CPU cooler is so small.

Given the Pentium M's eminent suitability for HTPC use, we put ourselves to a bit of a challenge in designing this build. We deliberately chose a small case — the Ahanix D5 — that would strain our digital dexterity (and we mean the kind with your fingers in this case, not the kind with ones and zeros) and permit us to build relatively small and svelte.

Surprisingly, the Pentium M turns out to be a relatively expensive proposition for building HTPC systems. This CPU was pretty expensive, and the motherboard we chose cost nearly $100 more than any of our other choices. Despite the extra cost, however, we still believe it's smart to build an HTPC around the Pentium M because it's likely to live longer and work better in a home entertainment center setting. This also turned out to be the most interesting build of the three, for a variety of reasons that we recount as we work our way through this chapter. As you learn in detail, we had to deal with multiple hardware and troubleshooting issues while building this system, and also decided at the last minute to switch motherboards to take advantage of some new Intel technologies for the Pentium M.

chapter 1

In this chapter, we cover the following topics while walking through the build process for our Pentium M HTPC build:

- **Component selection rationale:** We'll revisit the reasons why we picked our components, describe where and how we bought them, and how long it took all the parts to arrive.

- **Pre-build preparation:** We describe what we did with our parts before we actually started building and review some configuration changes from the planning stage to the actual implementation. As we eyeballed the case, the motherboard, and particularly the drive cage arrangement vis-à-vis the motherboard's IDE and SATA connectors, we understood the special characteristics of this build. Connector clearance issues loom large in our story, which turned out to involve too many interesting contortions. We also discovered problems arising from assumptions the case designers made about what motherboards would make themselves at home therein.

- **Initial build-out:** This took us as far as installing the motherboard, the CPU and its cooler, and the memory. A quick power-on test convinced us everything was okay so far.

- **Installing the expansion cards:** We installed our graphics and TV cards at this point and found ourselves enmeshed in our first troubleshooting exercise.

- **Installing the drives:** This is where digital dexterity definitely comes into play. Given somewhat cramped quarters in the case, removing the drive cage to install the hard disk and the DVD burner proved both essential and vexing.

- **Cabling up:** After all the pieces were in place, we determined how to solve our cabling issues. We'll explain why those issues arose and how we solved them, in part through some sleight of hand and in part through judicious cable choices and arrangements.

- **OS install and finish work:** Installing MCE involves a second CD and takes about half an hour longer than installing plain vanilla Windows XP Professional. We sailed through this exercise, and then applied updates, installed drivers and a DVD decoder, and adjusted the BIOS to make sure we were getting the most out of our system.

- **Installing the remote:** We used the IR receiver and blaster from the MCE remote (absolutely necessary for HTPC use) and then installed the Logitech Harmony remote. It worked straightaway, but we had to use the USB link to download controls for our other AV components after performing the next step in this list.

- **Making media connections:** TV hookup and access worked like a charm, as did our radio link. DVD decoder already installed made TV and DVD playback a breeze. We spent another half hour identifying the other devices in our entertainment center and downloading the IR codes to operate them through the Harmony remote. This took a while, but was far easier than any other universal remote we've ever messed with.

- **Testing and burn-in:** We let the machine run overnight, just to make sure everything was working okay. Temperature readings proved to be a bit warmer than we'd guessed, but we quickly understood that a small case and rather less active cooling than we're used to contributed to warmer than average conditions. We also observed that the Ahanix case fails to provide the kinds of PSU or fan sensors we'd like to find in any HTPC, especially a small-case build.

- **Clean-up and close-up:** We had to solve our major cabling issues when hooking up the drives, so everything else was easy by comparison. The resulting final photos show a surprisingly open layout with rather less spaghetti than we've seen in other builds.

- **Concluding postscript:** We report on actual total costs and components, and ruminate on ways to save money to bring those costs down or to spend more money and get more system in return.

The Ahanix D5 case challenged us in several ways, particularly when it came to installing and cabling up to our drives. We have some issues with the manufacturer's PSU selection and its built-in case fans (more on these items in the concluding section of this chapter). We also found ourselves laughably frustrated and subject to crazy improvisation in linking the case VFD to the motherboard (more on this in the concluding section as well). But all in all, we were pleased with the results of our build and judged it a good value for the money.

In addition to the photos in this chapter that illustrate this build, you'll also find five figures in the color signature in the center of this book related to this build (see Figures 6–10). They show the motherboard and all parts related to installing the CPU and its cooler, with isometric (45 degree or profile view) shots of the build after expansion cards were in place, and after cabling and clean-up were complete. These provide different views of what you'll find here and should illuminate the build process further.

In the sections that follow, we walk you through the process of building this Pentium M HTPC, and include some pictures to show you how the build process unfolded.

Component Selection Rationale

Between the time we started writing this book and the time we finished our first draft, Pentium M motherboards went into a new generation. Our initial choice was the AOpen i855GMEm-LFS, and indeed we built a complete system around that motherboard, which included the Intel 855GME Northbridge and the ICH4-M Southbridge chipsets. But because this motherboard didn't support eight-channel sound, we included a sound card in that build (which meant that system had no open slot for an HDTV expansion card).

When we heard that AOpen had released a new Pentium M motherboard built around the next generation 915GM Northbridge and the ICH6-M Southbridge, we immediately decided to abandon our older motherboard for the newer one. Here's what we gained by making that switch:

- The graphics card slot changed from an AGP 4X to a PCI-E X16. Because this let us include a slim-profile nVidia 6600 graphics card in our build, it was a compelling reason to upgrade. Narrow profile is good in this case because of clearance issues on heat pipe graphics cards. That kept us from using all three PCI slots on the motherboard at a minimum, and also eliminated AGP cards with front and back heat sinks with wrap-over heat pipes, such as the Gigabyte nVidia 6600 Silentpipe AGP card and other similar models.

- The newer Southbridge provided support for eight-channel sound with coax or optical SPDIF input and output. Because this let us drop the add-in sound card from our original build, it also made a compelling case for a switch to the newer motherboard.

- The newer motherboard offered more and better temperature monitoring and improved fan controls, also important in an HTPC build (we weren't able to take full advantage of the latter, however, much to our frustration as we explain later in this chapter).

This switch came with about a $100 increase in the price, but we judged the AOpen 915GMm-HFS worthwhile because of its extra flexibility and the additional build-out options it enabled. To save money on the overall build-out, we chose a Pentium M 745 processor: its 1.8 GHz speed is adequate for HTPC use, and at prices ranging from $210 to $300, it's cheaper than faster models that cost significantly more (we used a midrange price of $270 in our budget at the end of the chapter). We also used two Kingston DDR 333 512MB DIMMs in the build-out (though the motherboard includes two DDR2 533/PC4300 memory slots as well, we chose the slower, cheaper variety to save money).

The Ahanix D5 case includes a 300 W proprietary power supply and two small case fans. In fact, all three are the same size: 60 mm (2.36"). All fans are also noisier than we like, so we'd be inclined to replace them with something quieter, perhaps the Papst 612FL (at $17 each, this means added expense).

We chose the eVGA nVidia 6600 fanless graphics card because its narrow profile leaves room to use both other PCI slots on the AOPen motherboard, and because it's a great choice for HTPC use with or without HDTV. We chose the Hauppauge WinTV PVR-150MCE single-tuner TV card, which works like a charm with our local cable TV provider's offerings.

AOpen bundles a CPU cooler with the motherboard, though apparently it switched from a smaller model to a larger one during the initial production run. The company was kind enough to send us the larger fan to replace the unit included in the original packaging. These two fans are easy to distinguish by inspection. The smaller fan has cooling fins only about 7 mm tall and has a metal plate on top of the plastic fan housing; the larger fan has cooling fins about 35 mm tall with no plate on top of the plastic fan housing. Because "cooler is better" when it comes to HTPC, we tested only with the bigger fan and cooler. During testing, we never observed CPU temperatures higher than 53 degrees C (128 degrees F) or motherboard temperatures higher than 40 degrees C (104 degrees F). These were higher than expected, but well within safe tolerances for the hardware.

We went with SATA for the hard disk, using a Maxtor DiamondMax 300GB drive. We also used an IDE-based NEC ND-3520A DVD R±W drive because it's relatively quiet as optical drives go. Both proved adequate and offered a decent compromise between noise and capability. 300GB probably isn't enough disk space for the long run, but we don't think it's a good idea to put another drive inside such a small case (we observed drive temperatures ranging from 35 degrees C (95 degrees F) to 45 degrees C (113 degrees F) for the Maxtor drive, depending on activity levels). Those who need more storage for this computer could opt for a bigger drive inside the case (more heat), access more storage through USB or FireWire to an external drive (better), or access a networked drive (best).

Once we ordered all our parts, most of them from general PC dealer Newegg and HTPC specialist PCAlchemy.com, it took about 14 days for everything to show up. Because of drive cable clearance issues that seemed likely to (and did) present themselves, we waited for the drives as well as case, motherboard, CPU and cooler, and memory to get started.

Pre-Build Preparation

When the Ahanix D5 showed up at our door, we unpacked it to see what it looked like, both inside and out. Like the cases used in our other builds, the D5 has been the subject of numerous reviews (you'll find good ones at several Web sites, including HTPCnews.com and ViperLair.com). We quickly recognized that the drive cage position vis-à-vis the motherboard's IDE and 20-pin PSU connector would pose some interesting issues — and indeed, those posed the biggest challenges in this build.

The D5 also offers no front-panel ports of any kind, though it does have a two-line Vacuum Fluorescent Display (VFD). Though the side, top, and bottom panels are relatively light gauge aluminum, the front panel is massive. Because the case is fastened together well, and s ide panels are reinforced along top and bottom edges, the case is sturdier than its light weight suggests. The case is shown in Figure 19-1 (and in Figures 9 and 10 in the color section of this book).

We also noticed immediately when examining the case and the motherboard that we had a small problem: the VFD's wiring block terminates in a 25-pin parallel port connector. The AOpen i915 motherboard has no parallel connector on its port block. For the short term, we cobbled a multistage adapter together to plug into a USB port instead: from the male 25-pin connector coming out of the case, we went to a female 25-pin to male 9-pin adapter, then to a female 9-pin to female 9-pin gender changer, then to a male 9-pin to male USB connector, and finally into a USB port on the motherboard's port block. Then we switched to a PCI parallel port adapter (shown in Figures 9 and 10 in the color section of the book). Fortunately for future buyers, Ahanix is switching over to a cable with USB headers, so that you can connect to a USB pin block on the motherboard instead. Right now, a cable has to exit the case to hook the VFD up to the motherboard's port block — a real kludge, if we ever saw one!

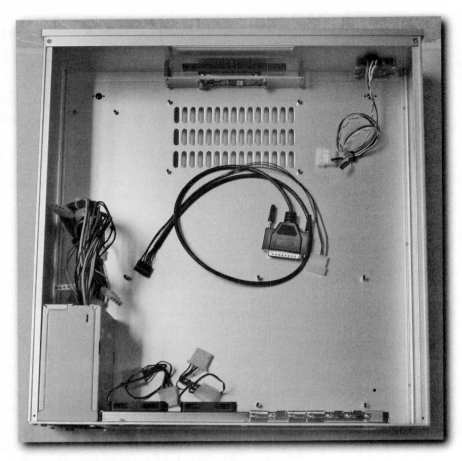

FIGURE 19-1: The Ahanix D5 case prior to installation.

Initial Build-Out

Installing the mobo was no problem at all, because we installed the CPU and its cooler in advance. The cooler screws right into the motherboard, using spring-tensioned Phillips-head screws on top. After that, we simply dropped the motherboard into position, and tacked it down to the four lone standoffs already installed in the case (the motherboard was a little wobbly, but we didn't have trouble installing memory or expansion cards, with a single exception — more on that in the next section). The full-size ATX mobo was easy to position, and we encountered no significant clearance issues during its installation.

We installed our two RAM modules in the two blue 180-pin slots without difficulty. As a quick check of our build so far, we attached the 20-pin motherboard power connector, the 4-pin CPU power connector, and hooked the on/off switch to the proper motherboard pins, so we could perform a quick interim status check. When the fans spun up and the motherboard LED lit up, we were good to go. Then, we unhooked the power and switch cables before moving on to the next step. Figure 19-2 shows what the system looks like with motherboard, CPU, cooler, and memory installed (but without power or switch cables connected).

FIGURE 19-2: The Ahanix D5 case with motherboard, CPU, cooler, and memory installed.

Installing Expansion Cards

Next into the case went our eVGA fanless 6600 nVidia graphics card and the Hauppauge WinTV PVR-150MCE card (see Figure 19-3). We tried an interim status check, with a monitor and keyboard attached, but nothing happened. Thus, we knew we had a problem with the video. We swapped in a different video card (which we were lucky enough to have at our disposal), and everything went fine. This made it very easy to pinpoint the video card itself as the source of our problems, so we took steps to procure a replacement. But we proceeded with the rest of the build using a different video card, just to keep moving that process forward. When the replacement card showed up later, it was easy to install the necessary drivers and such.

FIGURE 19-3: The fanless eVGA nVidia 6600 graphics card sports a narrow heat sink and leaves room for the neighboring PCI slot to be occupied, as the Hauppauge TV card therein demonstrates.

Troubleshooting Advice: Isolating Culprits

Whenever you're building a PC and things don't work the way they're supposed to, it's time to put on your thinking cap. Because the monitor we attached to the system for testing didn't switch from standby (yellow LED) to active (green LED) mode when we turned the system on and it began to start up, we knew the video card had to be the culprit. By replacing that card with a known, good working card we were immediately able to verify that the graphics card was indeed the culprit. This is the best reason to keep checking your work in small steps as you build: because the number of items you add at any given step is small (two in this case, and we weren't even using the TV card at this point) the potential causes for trouble are easy to run down.

Further investigation showed that the card wasn't seating properly in the PCI-E X16 slot. Even with the PCI bracket screwed tightly to the case, the card would still wiggle in the slot. And although the card's heat sink and onboard capacitors warmed up—which indicates some power was getting to the card—no video output convinced us that the card was somehow defective. Later on, we took out a micrometer and measured the thickness of the PCI board and observed that it was 4/1000ths of an inch narrower than the other, working card. This might have been enough to prevent all pins on the card from making contact with the matching leads inside the slot. We'll probably never know for sure, though we did send the defective card back to eVGA for testing. When the replacement showed up, it worked on our first try, and we also noticed that this card seated itself much more tightly into the motherboard's PCI-E slot as well.

The real reason we chose the eVGA fanless 6600 is because it poses no vertical clearance issues, as do other cards of this type. This is in sharp contrast to other fanless PCI-E cards, such as the Gigabyte Silentpipe 6600. It routes a heat pipe from a heat sink on the front to another on the back of the card across the top edge of the card. That heat pipe projects between 1 and 2 cm above the top of the card, in fact, making it impossible to replace the top of the D5 case. And of course, that's why we chose this smaller, more petite (but also more expensive) model.

Installing Drives

After removing the drive cage, the drives themselves were easy to install. But once the time came to replace the drive cage itself, we found our manual dexterity severely taxed. Not only was it difficult to insert the four small machine screws that hold the cage in position, it was also hard to bring a screwdriver to bear on their heads. A certain amount of fumbling and grumbling ensued, after which we made good use of a grabbing tool to insert the screws into position to get them started, and even better use of a brand-new, long-shafted Excelite screwdriver to fasten the cage into position.

Once the job was finished, we found ourselves questioning whether we should have indeed installed the hard disk underneath the optical drive, instead of between the two mounting rails on top of the optical drive enclosure. It turned out to be a no-win situation later on, as we realized we would have struggle with cable position and access either way. The results of this activity are depicted in Figure 19-4.

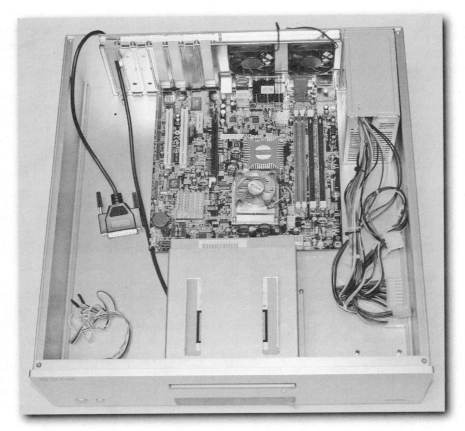

FIGURE 19-4: The optical drive in the 5.25" bay at the top of the cage is easy to see, and the Maxtor sits beneath it obscured from easy view.

Cabling Up

The biggest challenge in the build came when trying to route drive interface and power cables into position. The basic problem stems from the drive cage's location: because the AOpen motherboard situates both IDE interface and 20-pin ATX power connectors roughly in the middle at the rear of the board, we had issues cabling up to the optical and hard disks, which occupied roughly the same area looking down from the top.

We inserted the drive interface cables into the motherboard first and then maneuvered them into their respective slots on the back of each drive. Next, we stretched out two molex power cables. We used one to deliver power to the SATA drive (which also involved plugging an adapter cable into a standard 4-pin molex connector with a SATA power connector on the other end) and also to deliver power to the two fans at the rear of the case. We used the other cable to drop power off at the optical drive and extended it to the front of the case to deliver power to the VFD and the case front switches. Because there weren't enough molex connectors to go around, we had to buy a molex splitter (one in, two out) to plug both the VFD and the switch block into the molex connector at the end of that cable.

The real challenges came from the interface cables. Because both ends of the IDE cable were almost on top of each other, we strung a big cable tie across the drive mounts on the top of the optical drive enclosure, to pull the IDE cable up out of the way. AOPen furnished us with narrow-profile IDE cables and thereby prevented extra expense for round replacement cables as is our usual practice. We also replaced the standard SATA cable included with the motherboard (and another with the hard drive) with a 6" model with a right-angle connector on one end. This proved perfect for plugging into the drive interface and was short enough to bend up and out of the way of other cables.

Total time for the hardware portion of the build was about $2\frac{1}{2}$ hours, not including time out for shooting photographs, or the half hour or so we spent troubleshooting our graphics card problem. Again, we spent more than half an hour talking through the build process in advance, which probably helped keep actual build time under control.

This build caused us to go out and buy a new set of Excelite Phillips-head screwdrivers with hardened steel tips. The medium-sized long-shafted model and the smallest model both proved invaluable in taking things apart and putting them back together. We also made good use of our grabbing tool to retrieve screws dropped repeatedly while trying to reinstall the drive cage. Clearance down there at the bottom was tight!

Tip Optical SATA drives are worth considering. Given that Plextor offers several DVD burners that use SATA rather than IDE interface cables, another way to solve the problems this build posed would have been to replace the IDE optical drive we used with a SATA-based replacement. If we'd used the Plextor 712 SATA model, it wouldn't have even added much to the cost, and routing the cables would have been much easier (especially if we'd used another right angle connector as we did for the hard disk).

Final Build Components and Costs

We made a few changes from our original budgeting plans for this build. The final and actual bill of materials appears in Table 19-1. It reflects some component changes as well as some cost reductions that occurred between the planning and purchasing phases.

Table 19-1 Final Build Components and Costs

Vendor	Item	Cost
Ahanix	D-Vine Home Theater System D5 case	$195
AOpen	i915GMm-HFS motherboard	$281
Kingston	2 x 512MB DDR333 PC2700 RAM	$100
Intel	Pentium M 745 1.8 GHz	$270
eVGA	nVidia 6600 fanless graphics card	$168
Hauppauge	WinTV PVR-150MCE	$65
Maxtor	DiamondMax 300 GB SATA-I hard disk	$150
NEC	ND-3520A DVD-R±W IDE	$60
SATAcable.com	8" straight to left SATA cable	$5
Microsoft	MCE 2005 software	$120
Microsoft	MCE remote (needed for IR xcvr/blasters)	$35
Microsoft	Optical Elite desktop set (keyboard and mouse)	$75
Logitech	Harmony remote	$120
TOTAL		$1,644

Saving More, Spending More

If you're seeking to cut these costs you could consider the following money-saving items:

- By shopping around on price search sites you'll find you can beat our prices by anywhere from $10 to $50 for some items. We chose prices from well-known dealers in order to consolidate shipping charges and avoid special deals that may no longer be available by the time you read this.

- Drop the Harmony remote altogether and stick with the MCE remote. Though it won't drive your other home entertainment devices, it will save you $120 to do without.

- As long as you can access external or network storage outside the D5 case, dropping drive size not only saves money but lowers case temperatures. A 160GB SATA drive costs as little as $85, a 200GB as little as $94, for savings of $65 and $46, respectively.

Total savings of $200 or more are possible without significant loss of functionality. That brings costs down to a more reasonable $1,444.

On the higher side of this budget, the following substitutions or additions could make sense if you have a little more to spend:

- Replacing the Hauppauge WinTV PVR-150MCE with a PVR-500MCE brings dual tuners into play and permits recording two programs at once, or watching one while recording another. The price tag for this nice increase in capability is about $60–$75 more than the single tuner card.

- Adding an HDTV card like the DVICO Fusion 5 or the AVerMedia AVerTV HD MCE A 180 costs from $80 up to $160.

- Switching from DDR 333/PC 2700 memory to DDR2 PC2 4300 memory adds $200 or more to costs, depending on how fast (and how much) memory is involved.

- Bumping the CPU from a Pentium M 745 to a 755 (2.0 GHz) increases the price an astonishing $150 or so. The 780 is the fastest Pentium M currently available at 2.26 GHz. It goes for a whopping $780 or so without a cooler, and figuring $50 for a good cooler, that means spending $560 more.

Total additional outlays of $900 or more are easy to make — if you can afford them!

Installing MCE and Media Attachments

Next, we installed MCE 2005 on the Pentium M without a single snag or difficulty and followed that up with drivers from the motherboard update CD. As in the previous chapter, we visited Drivers Headquarters (`www.drivershq.com`) and used that site's free Driver Detective Scan to catch and bring all of our other drivers up to date. Next, we installed the nVidia DVD Decoder to take best advantage of our Gigabyte 6600 graphics card's special capabilities. Total time required was a little over two hours.

We had no difficulty attaching this HTPC to our Outlaw Audio 950 pre-amplifier and processor — the brains and switching center of our home entertainment system — using the optical adapter that plugs into the coax SPDIF output from the motherboard and then running an optical cable into an optical input on the pre-amp. The unit was able to recognize and decode conventional stereo CD audio, as well as THX, Dolby Digital, and DTS audio from various DVDs we tested. We also like its ability to simulate 5.1 sound from stereo inputs (purists will blanch, but we think if you've got the speakers, you should use them).

As in the last chapter, we used S-Video cables to link our Hauppauge PVR 150 input to our Scientific Atlanta cable TV box output and then took a DVI output from our Gigabyte nVidia graphics card into a Syntax Olevia LCD HDTV set. Everything worked as soon as it was hooked up and Windows detected what was going on. We also used one of the two IR blaster lines on the MCE remote IR receiver to enable the PC to drive the cable box for unattended recording. With the FM antenna included with the PVR 150 in place, MCE had no trouble picking up local radio stations, either.

Testing and Burn-In

Once all the software was installed, and all the media gear hooked up, we left the PC up and running overnight to make sure everything was working okay. We used two programs to monitor the PC's temperatures:

- An AOpen utility was included on the CD that shipped with the motherboard. We left it up and running to keep tabs on the system. It registered values of between 45 and 50 degrees C (113 and 122 degrees F) for CPU temperatures, and 33 and 40 degrees C (92 and 104 degrees F) for motherboard temperatures.

- PC Wizard 2005 is a tool first introduced in Chapter 6 of this book. It reports on processor and motherboard temperatures and also showed drive temperatures in this installation. Readings were as follows: 47–53 degrees C (117–128 degrees F) for the CPU, 33–37 degrees C (92 and 99 degrees F) for the motherboard, and likewise for the hard drive. We're not sure where the discrepancies between the two programs came from, but we're equally happy with either set of measurements.

On the power consumption side, the Pentium M really showed its true abilities. We used a Seasonic Power Angel to measure power draw during software installation, burn-in, and casual use, and observed power draws in a range from 72 to 90 W, with typical usage in a surprisingly narrow range from 75 to 78 W (not much above the minimum). Those struck by the high cost of this unit may take solace from long-term savings on electricity. This is less than either the Athlon 64 or the Pentium 4 (somewhat less in the former case, much less in the latter case: 93 to 120 W, and 120 to a whopping 222 W, respectively).

Other than minor troubleshooting and access issues during the build, we were happy with the results. The D5 is a good-looking case that could fit into most entertainment centers without attracting much attention. We didn't notice much difference between this system and its P4 counterpart in terms of everyday use and overall performance, either.

Clean-Up and Close-Up

By the time we were finished with burn-in, we didn't even really need to do much clean-up on the cabling — just a few cable ties here and there and we were ready to close. We did have some issues with the case fan cables. For one thing, there is no provision to connect to a motherboard (like the AOpen i915GMm-HFS, in fact, which offers great fan speed sensing and management capabilities). We were frustrated that not only were we unable to manage fan speed because there were no sensor outputs from either the PSU or the case fans, but we couldn't even monitor them.

Had we been able to purchase extremely short round or flat IDE cables — 12 inches long was the shortest we could find for sale anywhere — we'd have opted for something in the 6-inch range to keep excess cable out of the way. But we pulled the excess cable up above the optical drive by stringing two large cable ties through the upper 3.5" drive rails, and routing the IDE cable around that loop to keep it out of the way down below, where congestion was a problem. This is shown clearly in Figure 19-5.

We also took a rear view shot of the finishing build to show what the final design looked like from that perspective, as shown in Figure 19-6. All three 60 mm fans (PSU on the left, both case fans to its right) line up on the top-left quadrant of the case, and all three were of identical make — unfortunately, they were also noisier than those we'd have chosen if they hadn't been included with the case. Note also the VFD cable at the far right, and the video and TV cards on the left side of the expansion card slots (in slots 1 and 3, respectively).

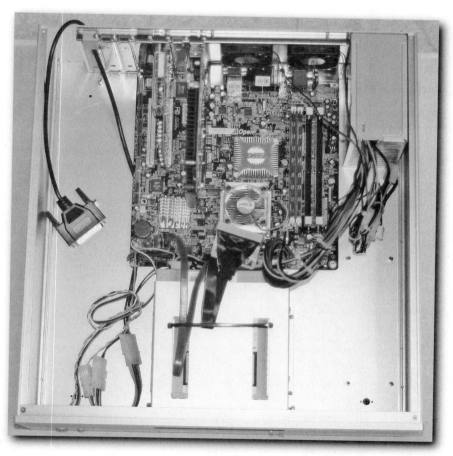

FIGURE 19-5: The close proximity of the optical and hard drive power and interface connectors to the back edge of the motherboard (and to PSU and IDE connectors) made plugging things in a challenge.

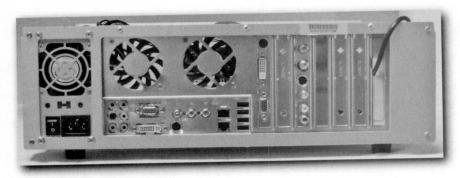

FIGURE 19-6: Rear view of the finished unit.

Vendor Information

For convenience, Table 19-2 lists all the vendors whose products are mentioned in this chapter. Although you can visit these sites for product information (and probably, news about newer products), please use the price comparison tools we mentioned in Chapter 15 to find the best deals. (Also, please don't forget to check on eBay, Froogle, or to consult the appendixes at the end of the book, many of which provide pointers to comparison and shopping information as well.)

Table 19-2	Vendors Mentioned in Chapter 19	
Vendor	*Component*	*URL*
Ahanix	D5 D-Vine Home Theater System case	www.ahanix.com
AOpen	i915GMm-HFS motherboard	www.aopen.com
AVerMedia	AVerTV HD MCE A180	www.avermedia.com
DVICO	Fusion 5 HDTV card family	www.fusionhdtv.co.kr/Eng/
eVGA	nVidia 6600 fanless PCI-E X16 graphics card	www.evga.com
Gigabyte	nVidia 6600 Silentpipe PCI-E X16 graphics card	www.giga-byte.com
Hauppauge	WinTV PVR-150MCE TV, WinTV PVR-500MCE TV cards	www.hauppauge.com
Intel	Pentium M 745 CPU (1.8 GHz)	www.intel.com
Kingston	DDR and DDR2 memory	www.kingston.com
Logitech	Harmony remote control	www.logitech.com

Vendor	Component	URL
Maxtor	DiamondMax 300GB SATA hard disk	www.maxtor.com
Microsoft	MCE software, remotes, keyboards, and mice	www.microsoft.com
NEC	IDE DVD R±W drive	www.nec.com
Outlaw Audio	Pre-amps/processors, amplifiers, subwoofers, and so on	www.outlawaudio.com
Papst	Quiet case fans	www.papst.de/english/
SATAcable.com	All kinds and sizes of SATA and other cables	www.satacable.com
Scientific Atlanta	CATV set-top box	www.sciatl.com
Syntax	Olevia 34" LCD HDTV	www.syntaxgroups.com

Wrapping Up

We've got a pretty long list of druthers for this build. First and foremost, given that there's ample room inside the case, we wish Ahanix had provided left, center, and right mount points for the drive cage. If we'd been able to move either right or left of center, we'd have had a much easier time with this build.

We'd also like to see them improve the human factors on the drive case. Why, for example, couldn't they have welded small sleeves on the cage underside to go around the standoffs and hold the case in place for easy re-installation? We also think it's interesting to pay nearly $200 for a case that while it has a very nice VFD doesn't have any front-panel ports at all — no USB, FireWire, or audio of any kind.

Finally, we'd urge Ahanix to spring for quieter case and PSU fans, and upgrade its PSU to include 24-pin ATX and SATA power connectors in its cable bundle. On the nice-to-have side of things, we'll be very glad when Ahanix sends us a VFD to USB header cable, so that we don't have to run a cable outside the case to hook up and use the VFD.

For a price of about $1,650 this build offers nice features and functions and a convincing overall HTPC package. Of all the systems we built, this is the one we'd be most likely to keep!

Building an Athlon 64 HTPC

Though we've worked with AMD processors since the mid-1990s, this was our first build of an Athlon 64 system (and we were lucky enough to try out both single- and dual-core models). We also chose a motherboard that incorporated the new nVidia nForce4 chipset, which offers interesting functionality of its own. Combined, we figured the power and capability of an Athlon 64 and its relatively modest power requirements (it draws somewhat over half as much power as the Pentium 4, but twice as much as the Pentium M or more) would make for a good HTPC combination.

That said, we went through two major troubleshooting exercises in completing this build, both of which improbably involved case problems. After a decade's worth of experience building PCs without encountering a single faulty case, we apparently made up for this deficit by dealing with two different defective cases on a single project (albeit one each from two different vendors).

To some extent, we have to confess falling prey to equipment lust for this build. Our original design called for it to include the Origen x15e HTPC case. It's a beautiful case with an external touch panel and VGA display, but an expensive proposition at a retail price of $600. Unfortunately, as we got into building with that case, we discovered the manufacturer had omitted the on/off switch wires that run from the front panel to its built-in IR block and then to the motherboard. Because it would void the warranty to remove the touch panel and insert the correct wires — an option we elected not to take — we switched to a different case instead.

That's where the Silverstone LC14-B/M came into play. We'd requested more cases than we could document in builds to try to find those that would serve our readers best. Far from a "second-best" selection, the LC14 has many virtues: it's affordable, good-looking, and its horizontal profile fits an entertainment center well. It also offers enough vertical clearance to make a slim profile eVGA nVidia 6600 card unnecessary, with ample room for heat pipes on other, less expensive designs. Unfortunately, when we started the initial build with this case, we couldn't get the on/off switch in the case to work properly (more information on that later in this chapter). A phone call to Silverstone and a replacement was on its way — which, fortunately for us worked just fine!

chapter 2

In this chapter, we'll cover these familiar topics while walking through the build process for our Athlon 64 HTPC case build:

- **Component selection rationale:** We revisit the reasons why we picked our components, describe where and how we bought them, and how long it took for the parts to arrive.

- **Pre-build preparation:** We describe what we did with those parts before we started building, and review configuration changes from planning to implementation. As HTPC cases go, this one's a peach, with thoughtfully designed drive bays and case components designed for easy access. The case also provides a rail across from front to back that makes routing wires across the case (mostly, power cables from the PSU to the motherboard and to the case fans) a real pleasure.

- **Initial build-out:** This took us through installing the mobo, the CPU and its cooler, and the memory. The obligatory quick power-on test started our troubleshooting off with the first case and revealed nothing amiss when we did the same with the second case.

- **Installing the expansion cards:** We installed graphics and TV cards and found nothing wrong.

- **Installing the drives:** Though the quarters are a little cramped, drive cage placement made this build much easier than we originally thought it would be. Fearing clearance or routing issues, we sailed through this part of the build.

- **Cabling up:** Once all pieces were in place, we completed case cabling. This was where the value of the center rail showed itself, and where we successfully (and creatively) recycled the reusable cable tie that Seasonic wrapped around its PSU cable bundle.

- **OS install and finish work:** We plowed through both CDs in about an hour, after realizing that the Chaintech motherboard required us to copy drivers from the CD to a floppy and install a (temporary) floppy drive to supply them to Windows MCE during the character mode portion of the install. Figuring this out took about 15 minutes to flip through the motherboard manual to the right pages (very near the end, of course), but took only 2 minutes to handle once we had marching orders. After that, things got really interesting as we recount later in this chapter.

- **Installing the remote:** We used the IR receiver and blaster from the MCE remote (absolutely necessary for HTPC use) and then installed the Logitech Harmony remote. It worked straightaway, and we were able to leverage the downloads we'd already made for that remote for the previous Pentium M build. Repetition does have an occasional virtue.

- **Making media connections:** TV hookup and access worked as before, as did our radio link. Pre-installation of the nVidia DVD Decoder made TV and DVD playback a breeze.

- **Testing and burn-in:** Here again, we let the machine run overnight, just to make sure everything was working okay. It was, and it did!

- **Clean-up and close-up:** Though there is some effort involved in securing power and interface cables (many to the center rail, a nice design feature), this goes quickly and produces good results. After we got past our case and motherboard problems, this turned out to be an easy and straightforward build.

- **Concluding postscript:** We report total costs and final components used, and describe ways to save money to bring those costs down, or to spend more money and get more system in exchange. We also talk about single- versus dual-core Athlon 64 CPUs.

The Silverstone case proved to enable a much easier build than the Ahanix D5. Less than an inch of vertical clearance difference between the two cages accounts for some of this difference. But an open left side (facing the front of the case) and intelligently designed and well-placed drive cages made a bigger difference. The 3.5" cage detached easily from the case interior (it mounted onto the rail on the left-hand side of the 5.25" bay for easy on/off access) to provide open access to both sides of the 5.25" drive bay. Neither grumbling nor grabbers proved necessary while performing this build!

In addition to the photos in this chapter that illustrate this build, you'll also find five figures in the color signature in the center of this book related to this build as well. Figures 11 through 15 show the motherboard and all parts related to installing the CPU and its cooler thereupon, with isometric (45 degree or profile view) shots of the build after expansion cards were emplaced, and after cabling and clean-up were completed. These provide different views of what you'll find here and help illuminate the build process further.

In the sections that follow, we talk you through the process of building this Athlon 64 HTPC, with strategic photos to depict various steps along the way.

Component Selection Rationale

With a new generation of nVidia nForce4 chips available to motherboard designers, we decided it would be informative and instructive to try one built for 64-bit AMD CPUs. We chose the Athlon 64 because it's the most affordable 64-bit CPU family from AMD (dual-core and Athlon 64 FX processors are more costly).

That led us to the Chaintech VNF4 Ultra motherboard, a modestly-priced motherboard with lots of interesting functionality, much of which is relevant to HTPC use:

- PCI-E X16 slot for graphics card, plus two PCI-E X1 slots for other expansion cards and three conventional PCI slots: lots of room for typical HTPC add-ins. So far, PCI-E X1 is not terribly useful, because card offerings for such slots appear limited to serial I/O, modest graphics, and network interfaces at present. But hopefully, USB and FireWire won't be too far behind.

- Support for eight-channel audio, including an optical adapter for optical SPDIF output (the best way to connect to a suitably equipped AV receiver or pre-amplifier).

- The motherboard supports four SATA-II ports (backward compatible with SATA-I). For an HTPC machine this is more of a nice-to-have than a must-have feature.

- Onboard temperature monitoring and fan controls, also important in an HTPC. The VNF4 Ultra has four pin blocks for fans — as many as we've ever seen on a mobo. Related BIOS and reporting tools are also pretty nice (even so, we couldn't take full advantage of fan monitoring, as we explain later in this chapter).

About the only thing that's missing from this motherboard is FireWire, but given the numerous open slots available, those who need it can easily add it — and without major expense, as PCI FireWire expansion cards are readily available for under $30 nowadays (expect to spend more for FireWire 800 capability, however). A PCI-E X1 FireWire card would be ideal, but we are unable to find any currently available for sale.

We used a Seasonic S12 380W power supply as part of this build and were impressed to observe its typically low fan speeds — the fan seldom spun faster than 800 RPM. This is only one of a few PSUs with separate fan wiring that we've worked with; it matched up well with onboard support for three additional fans (CPU, Northbridge, system fan, and case fan — though that's not exactly how we used them).

We chose a Gigabyte 6600 Silentpipe graphics card for this build because the LC14 case leaves plenty of clearance for the heat pipes and because it's a great choice for HTPC use (with or without HDTV). We stuck with the tried-and-true Hauppauge WinTV PVR-150MCE single-tuner TV card because it's a great value and works well with our local cable TV provider's offerings.

AMD sent us a cooler along with the Athlon 64 3500+ CPU they loaned to us. It's an AVC Z7UB301001 cooler with a copper base and aluminum fins on the heat sink, and a thermostatically controlled 80 mm TUV fan. It shares the honors of being the noisiest component inside the case with the Silverstone 92 mm front case fan, both of which we'd replace if we wanted to quiet this build down as much as possible. Reasonably quiet coolers from vendors like Zalman, Thermaltake, Thermalright, and so forth are available for socket 939 CPUs at prices from $30 to $50, and a quiet 92 mm replacement fan like the Nexus costs around $15.

As in our other builds, we used a SATA hard disk: a Maxtor DiamondMax 300GB drive. We also used an IDE-based NEC ND-3520A DVD R±W drive because it's relatively quiet as optical drives go. Both proved adequate and offered a decent compromise between noise and capability. 300GB probably isn't enough disk space for the long run, and there's room in the case for another disk drive along with adequate cooling to support it. We observed consistent drive temperatures from 35 degrees C (95 degrees F) to 45 degrees C (113 degrees F) for the Maxtor drive, depending on drive activity levels. In general for HTPCs, we recommend instead that users access additional storage using USB or FireWire to an external drive (better) or access a drive elsewhere on the network (best).

After we ordered all our parts, most of them from general PC dealer Newegg and HTPC specialist PCAlchemy.com, it took 10 days for everything to arrive (we opted for regular ground shipping and didn't expedite order fulfillment to save money). Because we didn't anticipate (nor did we experience) any significant clearance or access issues, we started our build as soon as we had case, motherboard, CPU and cooler, and memory in hand.

Pre-Build Preparation

When the Silverstone LC14 showed up at our door, we liberated it from its sturdy box to check it out, inside and out. Like the two cases used in our other builds, the LC14 has been the subject of numerous reviews (you'll find good ones at several Web sites, including `hardCOREware.net`, and `forums.moditory.com`). We immediately noticed that because there is no side panel on the left-hand side of the case (as you face its front), sliding in the motherboard would be easy and that placement of and access to drive cages would make for an easy install overall. As we found out later, we weren't wrong. We also wondered about the bar that separates the 5.25" bays from the 3.5" cage and crosses the case from front to back (that became clear later on during the build).

The LC14 also includes front panel access to four USB ports, one FireWire port, and microphone and headphone outputs, cleverly tucked around the left-hand side of the front cover. All the case wiring is well-organized and terminates in clearly labeled connectors, which made it easy to cable up to the motherboard when the time came for that task.

We had no trouble deciding to mount the CPU and cooler on the motherboard before attaching it to the standoffs that came pre-installed in the case. We also quickly realized we would have to remove the 3.5" drive cage to get unfettered access to both sides of the 5.25" bay, so that made it clear the optical drive would be installed first, followed by the hard disk (after we replaced the drive cage, of course). Nor did installing the PSU pose any special difficulties or concerns, either. For a look at the case prior to any installation, take a gander at Figure 20-1.

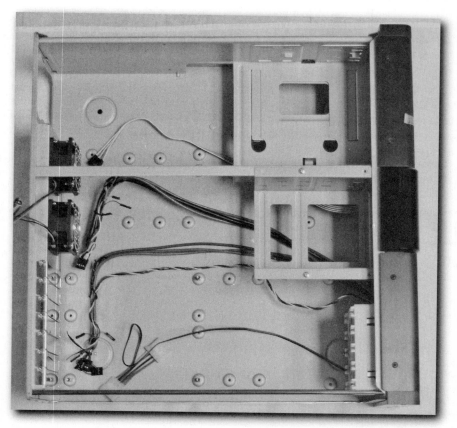

FIGURE 20-1: The Silverstone LC14 case prior to installation.

Initial Build-Out

Installing the mobo was no problem, because we installed the CPU and cooler in advance. The cooler included a backplate to mount beneath the motherboard, which bolted to the cooler stand on the other side. Next, we mounted the CPU into its lever-operated socket, applied a small dab of thermal paste, locked the cooler and fan assembly into place, and then attached the cooler fan connector to the Fan1 pin block as per the motherboard manual's instructions (check out Figures 11 through 13 in the color section of the book for more photos).

After that, we simply slid the motherboard into position and tacked it down to all six standoffs that were pre-installed in the case. Next, we popped our two DIMMs into memory bank 1, color-coded in black (note: unlike other motherboards we've worked with both slots for bank 1 sit next to one another, instead of being interleaved with the slots for bank 2, which were blue in this case). The full-size ATX mobo was easy to position, and we encountered no significant clearance issues during installation.

Next, we installed the Seasonic S12 380W PSU. Interestingly, we weren't able to use the Antec PSU Noisekiller PSU gasket that normally sits between the PSU and its case attachments. That's because clearance was so tight at the top of the back panel that there simply wasn't enough room for the gasket to fit. We did, however, apply the self-adhesive gaskets around the screw holes on the PSU and also used the replacement screws that Antec provided, which included silicon grommets to dampen PSU vibrations.

To check the build to this point, we attached the 24-pin motherboard power connector, the 4-pin CPU power connector, and hooked up the case control header block to the motherboard (for access to the on/off switch) so we could perform a quick interim status check. With our first case, this produced no action though we were able to start up the fans by shorting the switch pins on the motherboard with a screwdriver. This prompted us to try the remaining system components in a known good working case. When this worked perfectly, we knew the case had a problem and initiated the phone call to Silverstone that led to its replacement two days later by air freight.

With the second case, we encountered no difficulties at all. When the fans spun up, we were ready to proceed to our next step (after removing the power cables and making sure the PSU was turned off). Figure 20-2 shows what the system looks like with motherboard, CPU, cooler, and memory installed (but without power or switch cables connected).

FIGURE 20-2: The Silverstone LC14 case with motherboard, CPU, cooler, and memory installed.

Installing Expansion Cards

Our next task was to install the Gigabyte 6600 nVidia Silentpipe graphics card and the Hauppauge WinTV PVR-150MCE card. We made another interim status check, and the system posted without error, so we felt comfortable proceeding to the next step. Figure 20-3 shows the case with both cards in place, ready for us to move on to installing the drives.

As is typical, the Gigabyte Silentpipe 6600 card poses potential interference with neighboring slots. Our build calls for no PCI-E X1 cards (though another such slot remains available anyway), and we don't really need all three conventional PCI slots, either, even if we decide to add an HDTV card to our base configuration. Only if a third PCI card were necessary should you reconsider the choice of graphics card (the eVGA fanless 6600 makes a great, but more expensive, alternative in that situation).

FIGURE 20-3: The large profile on the Gigabyte Silentpipe 6600 butts right up against the neighboring PCI slot on one side, and blocks the PCI-E X1 slot on the other side.

Installing Drives

After removing the 3.5" drive cage, both drives were a snap to install — we encountered no needs for digital dexterity here, unlike our experience with the Ahanix case. It was just as easy to put things back together as it was to take them apart. We mounted the hard drive into the drive cage while it was detached from the case. Then, when we had the optical drive in place, we had to fasten two screws to reattach the 3.5" drive cage with drive inside, ready for power and interface cables hook-ups. You can see the results of this minimal effort in Figure 20-4.

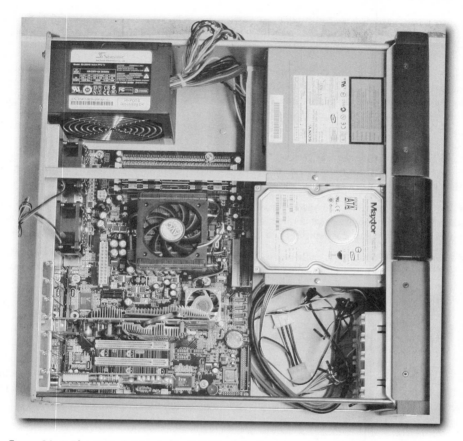

FIGURE 20-4: The optical drive in the 5.25" bay sits between the right-hand side of the case and the mid-case rail, and the 3.5" cage to the left of that rail, making both drives easy to see.

Cabling Up

The biggest challenge in this build came from the sheer number of wires we had to deal with. This was where we began to appreciate the mid-case rail (the same one to which the 3.5" drive cage is attached at the front of the case). This rail made an ideal cableway for PSU and fan cables, and provided a convenient anchor point to pull cables up and away from the CPU cooler. Because we used an IDE optical drive for this build, we purchased a 12" round IDE cable to replace the ribbon cables furnished with the drive and the motherboard to ensure good air circulation inside the case. This also made it easy to route all other cables around the back of the motherboard. We also slid two molex power cable bundles under the drive cages to route power to the hard disk and the case front fan and controls. We also coiled up the 12" SATA interface cable (again, we got one each with the drive and the motherboard, both a bit too long for the local layout) to keep things neat.

None of the cables proved difficult to route, and only one access issue popped up, one that was easily resolved. The Fan 3 pin block sits immediately to one side of the secondary IDE connector on the motherboard. By the time we realized we had to insert one of the case fan connectors into that block, we'd already seated the IDE cable. But the pull tab on that particular cable made it easy to remove, which we did to make room for our fingers to steer that fan connector into position. After that, we replaced the IDE connector without incident. We also had to route the PSU fan cable all the way over to the other side of the motherboard to plug it into the Fan 2 pin block (which also took a while to find, as we scanned the motherboard's pin-out diagram). But because Seasonic's cable was more than long enough to reach, this was no big deal.

Clear labeling on case cable headers made installing them a snap. We didn't even have to consult a manual for the interface connections, only for the on/off and reset buttons. Our final power-on test produced a healthy POST, so we were done with the initial build at this point.

Other than the round IDE cable we used to connect the optical drive to the motherboard, we didn't have to buy any additional cables or other items for this build, nor did it require any special tools (or cause us to break much of a sweat, either).

Final Build Components and Costs

As in the other builds, we saw some changes from our original plans. The final and actual bill of materials appears in Table 20-1. It reflects some component changes, including abandoning the expensive Origen x15e case in favor of the cheaper Silverstone LC14, as well as some cost reductions that occurred between planning and purchasing phases.

Table 20-1   Final Build Components and Costs

Vendor	Item	Cost
Silverstone	LaScala LC14B HTPC case (no VFD)	$149
Chaintech	VNF4 Ultra Zenith VE motherboard	$87
Crucial	2 × 512MB Ballistix DDR400 PC3200 RAM	$182
AMD	Athlon 64 3500+ 2.2 GHz	$273
Gigabyte	NVIDIA 6600 Silentpipe graphics card	$121
Hauppauge	WinTV PVR-150MCE	$65
Maxtor	DiamondMax 300 GB SATA-I hard disk	$150
NEC	ND-3520A DVD-R±W IDE	$60
Fry's	12" round IDE cable	$5

Vendor	Item	Cost
Microsoft	MCE 2005 software	$120
Microsoft	MCE remote (needed for IR xcvr/blasters)	$35
Microsoft	Optical Elite desktop set (keyboard and mouse)	$75
Logitech	Harmony remote	$120
TOTAL		$1,442

Saving More, Spending More

If you're seeking to cut these costs you could consider the following money-saving items:

- A slower AMD 64 can save some money. For example, the 3200+ (2.0 GHz) costs $190 or so, for a savings of $83.

- Drop the Harmony remote altogether and stick with the MCE remote. Though it won't drive your other home entertainment devices, it will save you $120 to do without.

- Replace the Crucial Ballistix with cheaper memory, and you can cut those costs in half, for savings of about $90.

- As long as you have access to external or network storage outside the LC14 case, dropping drive size not only saves money but also lowers case temperatures. A 160GB SATA drive costs as little as $85, a 200GB $94, for savings between $46 and $65.

Total savings of $350 or more are possible without significant loss of functionality. That brings costs down to a very nice $1,092.

On the higher side of this budget, the following substitutions or additions could make sense if you have a little more to spend:

- Replacing the Hauppauge WinTV PVR-150MCE with a PVR-500MCE puts two tuners to work, so you can record two programs at once or watch one while recording another. The price tag for this bump up in capability is about $60–$75.

- Adding an HDTV card like the DVICO Fusion 5 or the AVerMedia AVerTV HD MCE A 180 brings costs up from $80 to $160.

- Switching to 1GB DIMMs adds about $200 to the cost, doubling up to 4GB of memory adds about $600.

- Bumping the CPU to a dual-core Athlon 64 X2 adds anywhere from $77 (3800+ 2.0 GHz) to $826 (4800+ 2.4 GHz). We were able to try out a 3800+ just as we were finishing up this book, and we comment on price-performance issues later in this chapter.

Total additional outlays of $1,000 or more are easy to make — as long as you feel like shelling out the extra cash!

Installing MCE and Media Attachments

Installing MCE on this system proved interesting, in the sense of the Chinese curse. We couldn't make the SATA drivers included with the motherboard work with MCE at all, though they worked fine with a plain-vanilla install of Windows XP Professional. Despite repeated tries, multiple sets of media, and various ingenious (or desperate) techniques, we couldn't get MCE 2005 to install. Finally, after about 3.5 hours of experimentation and analysis, we noticed the USB 2.0 drivers hadn't loaded and determined the motherboard itself was defective, but in a very subtle away. Next, we substituted a Gigabyte K8NF-9 motherboard very like the Chaintech VNF4, and realized the motherboard was our problem: a test build with the different motherboard sailed all the way to completion without problem one (our thanks to contributor Matt Wright for his sage advice of "enough already" that led us to stop trying to make the Chaintech work, and try other alternatives).

Once again, a phone call to Chaintech produced a replacement in two days, and we were off and running after its delivery. This time, not only did all previous steps complete successfully, but MCE installed without a hiccup or hitch. Of all the builds we performed for this book, our experience with the first Chaintech motherboard proved most vexing from an MCE perspective.

Once we got MCE 2005 running on the machine, the rest of the install went well. As in the previous chapter, we visited Drivers Headquarters (www.drivershq.com) and used that site's free Driver Detective Scan to catch and bring all of our other drivers up to date. Next, we installed the nVidia DVD Decoder, to take best advantage of our Gigabyte 6600 graphics card's special capabilities. Total time required was a little over six hours, but four hours involved repeated trial-and-error attempts to get MCE running. Once this phase was over, we heaved a vast sigh of relief!

We had no difficulty attaching this HTPC to our Outlaw Audio 950 pre-amplifier and processor — the brains and switching center of our home entertainment system — using the optical adapter that plugs into the coax SPDIF output from the motherboard and then running an optical cable into an optical input on the pre-amp. We continue to believe that the Outlaw 950 (now discontinued, so those not interested in buying used equipment will have to turn to the more expensive Outlaw 990 instead) represents the best value in the multichannel audio pre-amplifier/processor marketplace today.

As in the other builds, we used S-Video cables to link our Hauppauge PVR 150 input to our Scientific Atlanta cable TV box output, then took a DVI output from our Gigabyte nVidia graphics card into our Syntax Olevia LCD HDTV set. Everything worked as soon as it was hooked up and Windows detected what was going on. We also used one of the two IR blaster lines on the MCE remote IR receiver to enable the PC to drive the cable box for unattended recording. With the FM antenna included with the PVR 150 in place, MCE had no trouble picking up local radio stations, either.

Testing and Burn-In

After all the software was installed, and all the media gear hooked up, we left the PC up and running overnight to make sure everything was working okay. We used two programs to monitor the PC's temperatures:

- The nVidia chipset comes with its own set of tuning and monitoring capabilities, collectively known as nTune. This includes a utility called nVidia monitor that reports temperature readings from the onboard BIOS. Necessarily, this number agreed with the BIOS itself, so check the next bullet for some astonishing temperature readings.

- We couldn't get PC Wizard 2005 (a tool first introduced in Chapter 6 of this book) to work with the Chaintech motherboard, so we checked the hardware monitor (PC Health) in the BIOS each time we rebooted the system. It reports on processor and system (motherboard) temperatures. Readings were consistently in narrow ranges as follows: 33–38 degrees C (92–101 degrees F) for the CPU, and 36–41 degrees C (about 97–106 degrees F) for the motherboard. Frankly, these measurements seemed too good to be true (and are cooler than the Pentium M), but the case itself never even got warm to the touch, so they can't be that far off, either!

Other than the snafu in getting MCE up and running on this machine, we were quite pleased with the results. The Silverstone proved to be our favorite HTPC case among all those we tried out for this book. And certainly, the Athlon 64 processor offers more than adequate performance for its HTPC role.

Power consumption figures for this machine proved pretty interesting as well. For the Athlon 64 3500+ we installed for our initial build, we observed power consumption over a range of 80 to 106 W, with normal operation between 90 and 93 W. Of course this ties in nicely with low case temperatures, given the good ventilation and excellent airflow in the Silverstone LC14 case.

An Affordable Dual-Core Alternative?

As we were finishing this book, we learned that AMD had released a new dual-core processor at the bottom of its product line—namely, the Athlon 64x2 3800+. It's built around the Manchester core, which features two 512K L2 caches, one per core. Because pricing was attractive ($350–$400 depending on where you shop) and Manchester cores have reputations for drawing modest power and consequent cooler operation, we decided to try one out in this build. We observed a modest 10–20 percent improvement in performance, but were blown away by its power consumption and temperature readings.

With a 3800+ running in place of the 3500+ we saw temperatures stay about the same: 35–40 degrees C (95–104 degrees F) for the CPU, and 38–43 degrees C (100–109 degrees F) for the motherboard. In other words, the increase in performance isn't matched by equal temperature gains. Also, power consumption occurs in a range from 90 to 120 W, with normal operation between 93 and 98 W—which explains why temperatures didn't rise to match performance, because power consumption didn't either. This suggests that the 3800+ is a great HTPC choice, if its $350–$400 price tag isn't too much to swallow. Because other dual-core Athlon 64s cost more, the 3800+ is the only one we considered or fooled around with for this book.

Clean-Up and Close-Up

After burn in, we let proximity of multiple cables dictate how we tied them up. The best part of this exercise came when we used the center rail to route fan and power cables across the top of the case. Other than that, this exercise simply involved bundling up cables in close proximity to one another and tying them up. As Figure 20-5 illustrates, we again made good use of the reusable cable tie that came with the PSU — this time to secure case header and power cables to the rail on the right-hand side of the case.

This was another case where we'd liked to have been able to purchase 6" or 8" long SATA cables instead of looping a 12" cable around itself. But without waiting for mail-order delivery, these weren't readily available to us.

FIGURE 20-5: The cleaned-up cables inside D5 are arranged to both sides of the drive cage up front — not much spaghetti in here!

Figure 20-6 shows the back panel of the built-out unit, PSU and port block to the left and expansion cards to the right.

FIGURE 20-6: Rear view of the finished unit.

Vendor Information

For convenience, Table 20-2 lists all the vendors whose products are mentioned in this chapter. Though you can visit these sites for product information (and news about newer products), please use the price comparison tools we mention in Chapter 15 to find best deals. (Also, please don't forget to check on eBay, Froogle, or to consult the appendixes at the end of the book, many of which provide pointers to comparison and shopping information as well.)

Table 20-2   Vendors Mentioned in Chapter 20

Vendor	Component	URL
AMD	Athlon 64, Athlon 64 X2 processors	www.amd.com
Antec	Noisekiller sound dampening products	www.antec.com
AVerMedia	AVerTV HD MCE A180	www.avermedia.com
Chaintech	VNF4 Ultra Zenith VE motherboard	www.chaintechusa.com
DVICO	Fusion 5 HDTV card family	www.fusionhdtv.co.kr/Eng/
eVGA	nVidia 6600 fanless PCI-E x16 graphics card	www.evga.com
Fry's	General computing/electronics/appliance superstore	www.outpost.com

Continued

Table 20-2 *(continued)*

Vendor	Component	URL
Gigabyte	nVidia 6600 Silentpipe PCI-E X16 graphics card	www.giga-byte.com
Hauppauge	WinTV PVR-150MCE TV, WinTV PVR-500MCE TV cards	www.hauppauge.com
Logitech	Harmony remote control	www.logitech.com
Maxtor	DiamondMax 300GB SATA hard disk	www.maxtor.com
Microsoft	MCE software, remotes, keyboards, and mice	www.microsoft.com
NEC	IDE DVD R±W drive	www.nec.com
Nexus	Silent fans	www.nexustek.nl
Origen	x15e HTPC case with touch panel/screen	www.origenae.com
Outlaw Audio	Pre-amps/processors, amplifiers, subwoofers, and so on	www.outlawaudio.com
Seasonic	S12 380W Silent Power Supply	www.seasonic.com
Silverstone Technology	LC14B HTPC case	www.silverstonetek.com
Scientific Atlanta	CATV set-top box	www.sciatl.com
Syntax	Olevia 34" LCD HDTV	www.syntaxgroups.com
Thermalright	CPU coolers	www.thermalright.com
Thermaltake	CPU coolers	www.thermaltake.com
Zalman	CPU coolers	www.zalmanusa.com

Wrapping Up

We don't really have too many things to complain about regarding the hardware portion of this build. We could wish for a world without hardware defects, but that isn't terribly likely to do any good. The only real changes we'd make to this case would be to replace existing fans with quieter ones, and perhaps to add another center rail orthogonal to the center rail to extend its great cableway capabilities between the backs of the drives and the front of the motherboard — a natural path for cable routing if ever there was one.

We'd also prefer to see all fans in the case equipped with 3-pin connectors suitable for attachment to a fan monitor (the LC14 actually has two 5.25" bays, and a fan monitor/VFD would make a good candidate for the unoccupied bay in this build). The front case fan sports only a molex power connector, and despite various attempts to bring sensor readings to the motherboard, we were unable to monitor or control that fan's speed (of course, replacing that fan would probably take care of that problem, too).

For a price of about $1,450 this build offers great features and functions and a convincing overall HTPC package. Of all the systems we built, this one ran fastest for us at the keyboard or remote control, performing normal everyday activities. And of course, the dual-core 3800+ version ran just a bit faster than that!

Appendixes

part

V

More about Media Center PCs and MCE

appendix

A

in this appendix

- ☑ Media Center PC manufacturers

- ☑ Official MS MCE resources

- ☑ Unofficial third-party MCE resources

Since Microsoft introduced Windows Media Center Edition in 2003, not only has that operating system gone through two revisions, but also numerous manufacturers have partnered up with Microsoft to produce branded Media Center PCs. The original intent of this program was to make MCE available only through such partnerships, so that only by buying a properly equipped and configured PC could users take advantage of what MCE had to offer.

This program was designed to create more opportunities for hardware vendors while also minimizing Microsoft's support burden. Presumably, because partner vendors would know how to work with the many kinds of add-in hardware for radio, television, DVDs, music, audio, and so forth that MCE can support, this would offload the hardware side of the equation. And because Microsoft could require those same partners to train their staff in building, installing, and configuring MCE on their own systems, this would lower Microsoft's support requirements on the software side.

What happened is a little different as this book attests: MCE has escaped from the original equipment manufacturer (OEM) channel and is now available to hobbyists or enthusiasts willing to climb the learning curve, who want to build their own HTPCs. That said, there are still plenty of vendors who build Media Center PCs and who will gladly sell you a turnkey system.

In this appendix, you'll find pointers to Media Center PC vendors, along with pointers to official Microsoft MCE resources and information, as well as to unofficial MCE resources and information from third parties. The idea is to equip you to learn what you must about the hardware and software that go into a Media Center PC — even if you do build one yourself!

If you have special sites or resources you find to be extremely or unusually helpful or informative, please share that information with us. We can't promise that we'll include everything that hits our inboxes, but we will respond to all suggestions and include those in online updates that we agree will benefit the book's general readership. You can e-mail Ed at etittel@yahoo.com and Mike at mikec@silentpcreview.com, but be sure to put **HTPC:** at the head of the subject line in your message, in order to get past our spam filters. Thanks!

Media Center PC Manufacturers

Interestingly, Media Center PC manufacturers differ region by region around the world. The U.S. site currently lists 17 Media Center PC companies, but European sites list 19 such companies. And there is less than 50 percent overlap in the composition of both groups. It turns out that, particularly where TV technology and regulation are concerned, regions of the world differ enough to cause some vendors to limit themselves only to certain markets, whereas others decide to compete wherever Media Center PCs are sold. If you live outside North America, be warned that only some of the information in Table A-1 will apply to your region, and consult your country's Microsoft Web site for the most up-to-date and relevant lists. When you visit manufacturer sites, search on Media Center to find the specific product pages (they were omitted from the URL listings to keep the links viable and to make them as short as possible).

Table A-1 North American Media Center PC Manufacturers

Company	URL	Description
ABS	www.abspc.com	Several Media Center PCs, all in horizontal component-type cases.
Alienware	www.alienware.com	Several Media Center PCs, including fanless options, all in horizontal component-type cases.
CyberPower	www.cyberpowersystem.com	Several Media Center PCs, including traditional tower cases as well as a horizontal component-type case.
Dell	www.dell.com/mediacenter	Several Media Center PCs, including notebooks, traditional tower cases, and a slimline tower case.
Gateway	www.gateway.com	Three different Media Center PCs, all in traditional towers.
Howard Computers	www.howardcomputers.com	Tower unit depicted, Media Center PC info not readily available.

Company	URL	Description
HP	www.hp.com	Two families of Media Center PCs available: one in a standard tower (Media Center PC), the other in a horizontal component-type case (Digital Entertainment Center).
Hush Technologies	www.hushtechnologies.com	Multiple fanless Media Center PCs, in small form factor horizontal component-type cases.
iBUYPOWER	www.ibuypower.com	Large horizontal case, two models (one Intel, the other AMD).
Niveus Media	www.niveusmedia.com	Two summit series Media Center product families, both in fanless horizontal cases: the slim Ranier (based on Hush technology) and the larger Denali (with HDTV support).
Ricavision	www.ricavision.com	Two product families, both in horizontal component-type cases: PLIX HD (supports HDTV) and Silverlake EMC.
Sony	www.sonystyle.com	Three product families, all in conventional tower cases.
Systemax	www.systemaxpc.com	Three product families, all in horizontal component-type cases.
Toshiba	www.qosmio.com	Qosmio laptop includes all the same features and functions as desktop Media Center PC products.
ViewSonic	www.viewsonic.com	Single product family, with slimline tower case.
Voodoo	www.voodoopc.com	ARIA product family uses Ahanix D5 touchscreen horizontal component-type case, with tricked-out finishes.

Of the preceding manufacturers mentioned, we've had the opportunity to work with units from Hush Technologies, Niveus Media, HP, and Dell. It's really quite educational to crack open their cases and see what's inside, how components are laid out and wired, and which cards go where.

Official Microsoft MCE Resources

Throughout this book, we've mentioned countless details about installing, configuring, and using Windows Media Center Edition 2005 (abbreviated here and elsewhere as MCE). As is usually the case with Microsoft products, there's a ton of information available on the company

Web site, most of which is readily accessible through the Media Center home page at
`www.microsoft.com/mediacenter`. (Note: although it translates into a different URL
once you reach the Microsoft Web site, it's the fastest way to get there and should continue to
work for some time, despite Microsoft's fondness for reorganizing its Web site regularly.)

You'll find all kinds of useful MCE resources on and through this page (more than you may
have time or inclination to visit, in fact). That's why we summarize key items in Table A-2.

Table A-2   Official MS MCE Resources

Page	URL	Description
MCE 2005 home page	`www.microsoft.com/mediacenter/`	Launching point for MCE news and information of all kinds
Using Windows XP	`www.microsoft.com/windowsxp/using`	How-tos and guides to all the primary features of MCE.
Product Information	`www.microsoft.com/windowsxp/mediacenter/evaluation/`	General information, documentation, how-tos, tutorials, and more. Information about Media Center Extenders plus supported components and peripherals is especially helpful
Expert Zone	`www.microsoft.com/windowsxp/expertzone/`	Microsoft's community center, which features input and info from Microsoft representatives. See especially the Media Center Community at `www.microsoft.com/windowsxp/expertzone/communities/mediacenter.mspx`

Other parts of the Microsoft Web site are also worth consulting about MCE, particularly when
solving problems or shooting trouble. In particular, Tech Net (Microsoft's massive collection of
technical and knowledge base articles at `www.microsoft.com/technet/`) can be a source
of help and information when it's needed.

Unofficial Third-Party MCE Resources

Anybody who has dealt with Microsoft for any length of time knows that the company's official materials don't always tell the whole story about its products, about related problems and
gotchas, and about the workarounds that permit users to keep using before official updates
become available. That's where third-party resources become incredibly valuable and that's why
we mention our favorites here (all of them have helped us figure things out, or bailed us out of
trouble, from time to time).

Table A-3   Unofficial MCE-Related Web Sites

Site	URL	Description
AnandTech	www.anandtech.com	Ruminations on Windows hardware and OS topics, including some great thoughts and analysis of MCE.
ExtremeTech	www.extremetech.com	Advice and sample configurations for building MCE-based PCs.
Ed Bott's MCE archives	www.edbott.com	Information from a well-known Windows wizard, see especially weblog/archives/cat_windows_media_center_edition.html (append to his root URL).
Mark Salloway's MCE Resources	mvps.org/marksxp/MediaCenter/2004/harmony.php	Great general compendium of MCE resources listings.
MCE 2005 Resources	www.dotnet-online.de/web/mce	Pointers to official and unofficial MCE resources of all kinds (blogs and newsgroups especially interesting therein).
MCE Development	blog.retrosight.com	Insights, news, and information from MCE developer Charlie Owen; often includes information anybody could (and should) use.
Paul Thurrot's SuperSite for Windows	www.winsupersite.com	Thurrot tells it like it is, has a lot of useful stuff to say and report, and has written and reported extensively on MCE (search his site on Media Center Edition to see what we mean).

(HT)PC Hardware Information and Resources

The World Wide Web is literally bursting with potential information about PCs, and the same is no less true for shopping outlets for PC parts and supplies. Out of this myriad of virtual locations, quite a few also cover (or focus more directly on) Home Theater PCs. The sites mentioned in this appendix represent only a miniscule fraction of what's out there, but they are also sites that your authors (and many other experts and aficionados) hold in special or high regard. The sites are listed in alphabetical order in each of the tables that presents them later in this appendix; this order is purely for convenience and says nothing about their respective rankings.

Of course, another good way to start looking for information or outlets is to visit the companion Web site for this book. Not only will you find live links to everything mentioned here (and elsewhere in this book), you'll also find new and updated information there, too. Because the HTPC world is one that keeps changing all the time (not to mention Microsoft Windows Media Center Edition, itself the subject of Appendix A), keeping up with new products, tools, and technologies requires both dedication and effort. Fortunately for gadget freaks and hardware lovers like us, this tends to be more a labor of love and interest than a chore.

If you have special sites or resources that you find to be extremely or unusually helpful or informative, please share that information with us. We can't promise that we'll include everything that hits our inboxes, but we will respond to all suggestions and include those in online updates that we agree will benefit the book's general readership. You can e-mail Ed at etittel@yahoo.com and Mike at mikec@silentpcreview.com, but be sure to put **HTPC:** at the head of the subject line in your message, in order to get past our spam filters. Thanks!

General PC Hardware Info

General PC hardware informational sites (see Table B-1) specialize in describing and explaining how PCs and their constituent components work, but they also often review these things as well. In addition, you'll find how-tos galore, including coverage of do-it-yourself PC construction as well as occasional coverage of do-it-yourself HTPC construction. Thus, you can turn to these sites to help you understand what you're doing, what to do it with, and how to build your PC projects. And because these sites are always reviewing the latest and greatest of what's available to the PC world, their value as a supplement to this book increases with time.

Table B-1   General PC Hardware Info Sites

Site	URL	Description
ExtremeTech	www.extremetech.com	Covers leading/bleeding edge PC technology and hardware.
PC Guide	www.pcguide.com	Provides copious PC hardware and do-it-yourselfer coverage.
PC Magazine	www.pcmag.com	Has been a long-time source of PC information in print and online.
PC Perspective	www.pcper.com	Specializes in general, thorough, and unbiased info for PC enthusiasts.
PCSTaTS	www.pcstats.com	Has great PC hardware coverage; "Beginner's Guides" have some of the best do-it-yourself coverage around.
SysOpt.com	sysopt.earthweb.com	Provides community sponsored/staffed collection of info, ratings, and more.

As the patron site, if not saint, for this book, the ExtremeTech Web site is worthy of special emphasis in considering the various sites mentioned in Table B-1. The pages at ExtremeTech often include reviews of high-end components (especially motherboards, CPUs, and memory) likely to show up in HTPCs, as well as all kinds of other technologies relevant to HTPC owners and users. Be sure to bookmark this site, and to visit whenever you need current, accurate PC technology news, reviews, or information.

HTPC Resources

Throughout this book, we've argued that building a Home Theater PC takes more careful selection of components than building a more conventional desktop or general-purpose computer. Much of the content we present in this book, including key criteria involved in choosing components and the arguments we offer to support such selections, reflects what we've learned from the sites presented in Table B-2. This is particularly true for the components we recommend (and those we use in the sample projects that put this information to work) throughout the book.

All of these HTPC sites are operated by individuals who are passionately interested and heavily invested in Home Theater PC technology. Though some are commercial enterprises and others are group or individual efforts that don't seek to generate income from their sites, all contain lots of useful information, explanations, and rationales about how and why you might prefer certain components over others when assembling an HTPC.

When pondering the information you'll find on these sites, remember that the ultimate test of what works or doesn't work for you is your own perception and your own experience. Don't forget to take this information with a grain of salt and be prepared to separate opinions and prejudices from statements of fact. Table B-2 presents a short but potent list of such resources

Table B-2   HTPC-Focused Web Sites

Site	URL	Description
HTPC News	www.htpcnews.com	Commercial Web site devoted to news, reviews, how-tos, and other information specific to HTPC.
Secrets of Home Theater and High Fidelity	www.hometheaterhifi.com	News, reviews, and interviews with key industry players dominate their coverage, but they also have a nice set of primers.
Silent PC Review	www.silentpcreview.com	Focuses on quiet PC technology, and related thermal issues; strong technical content and obsessive attention to detail make this site very valuable.

Outside the aforementioned sites (all of which have their own active user communities), there's an extremely vocal Home Theater PC user community active on other sites as well, including various user forums. What ultimately makes such forums valuable is that they reflect somebody else's experience and understanding of HTPC topics and activities. They give the rest of us a chance to learn from their mistakes and misapprehensions, rather than having to repeat all that experience for ourselves. They are also much more opinionated and idiosyncratic, and often less objective, than the more general HTPC sites mentioned in the preceding table. That's why we present them separately in Table B-3.

Table B-3   HTPC User Forum Web Sites

Site	URL	Description
AVS Forums	www.avsforum.com	Look in Video Components → Home Theater Computers for the right forum; active, ongoing, and highly technical traffic.
HTPC Forums	www.htpcforums.com	More exclusive coverage on HTPC topics for entire site.
The Green Button	www.thegreenbutton.com	Look for HTPC and related video, TV, HDTV topics.
Home theater discussion	www.hometheaterdiscussion.com	Plenty of HTPC and related coverage, including Windows MCE-specific discussions.

Online Computer Parts Outlets

The outlets in Table B-4 provide computer components and parts of all kinds for PCs of all types. The recent upsurge of interest in HTPC has increased the range of relevant parts and components they carry, but what makes these outfits attractive is lower prices, ready availability, and quick delivery. You may still need to turn to the category covered in the next section — namely, HTPC Specialist Outlets — to meet specific or additional needs.

When you know what you need to buy, don't forget you can use online comparative shopping services to shop on price as well. Though these stores are likely to offer the lowest prices or best deals on certain items, none of them seems able to beat all the others on all prices. So do yourself a favor, and shop around (try the "Shop for gear" link at ExtremeTech, extremetech. shopping.com, to find and compare prices very easily). Table B-4 lists some of the best-known outlets in the computer business.

Table B-4   PC Parts and Components Supplier Web Sites

Site	URL	Description
Computer Geeks	www.compgeeks.com	Generally good prices, with the occasional fantastic deal here and there.
eBay	www.ebay.com	Although not really a computer parts outlet per se, if you know what you want and aren't afraid to buy it at auction, the best deals come here to those who are both patient and persistent.

Site	URL	Description
Fry's Outpost	www.outpost.com	Mega-computer-superstore Fry's also has an online arm, but if you can cruise their stores, the experience is hard to beat.
Newegg	www.newegg.com	Great selection, good service, and generally low prices explain why so many PC builders shop at Newegg.

HTPC Specialist Outlets

For certain specific components likely to show up in an HTPC, but unlikely to show up elsewhere — HTPC cases and remote controls are great examples — it may be necessary to turn to retailers who specialize in serving the HTPC marketplace. Though some of the vendors mentioned in Table B-5 do venture beyond HTPC market coverage, all cover that particular niche well (or provide pointers to other specific vendors who meet HTPC needs, as with the Shopper's Guide mentioned below).

Table B-5   HTPC Component Supplier Web Sites

Site	URL	Description
Addict PC	www.addictpc.com	Offers complete MCE systems, plus virtually all HTPC components.
EndPCNoise	www.endpcnoise.com	Great source of quiet PC components (good for HTPC use).
pcalchemy, The HTPC Store	www.pcalchemy.com	Best provider of HTPC components around, also good source of information and community.
Digital Connection	www.digitalconnection.com/shopper_htpc.asp	A source for both home theater and HTPC gear, including hard-to-find products such as PC HD tuners.

Don't forget that when it comes to looking for information online, a search engine can be your best tool. The more you know about what you're looking for, the better your results will usually be. In addition to Google and Yahoo! (some personal favorites) we also make heavy use of Ask Jeeves (www.ask.com) because it takes loosely worded queries and often produces very good results. When we really don't know exactly what we're after, Ask Jeeves often helps us find our way to where we want to be.

DVD and Movie Information and Resources

The World Wide Web is a paradise for movie fans. Movies are available both as DVDs and in other forms such as video-on-demand. Out of this cornucopia of virtual outlets, some stand out because of their depth and breadth of coverage, or by virtue of low prices. The sites mentioned in this appendix represent only a smattering of what's out there, but they are sites that your authors (as well as other movie buffs and entertainment aficionados) judge to be among the best of this particular breed. We list all sites in alphabetical order in each of the tables later in this appendix; this order is purely for convenience and says nothing about their ranking in our (or anybody else's) view of this world.

Of course, another good way to start looking for information or outlets is to visit the companion Web site for this book. Not only will you find live links to everything mentioned here (and elsewhere in this book), but you'll also find new and updated information there. Because new movies and sites that cater to movie fans come and go with astonishing frequency, keeping up with this world requires both dedication and effort. Fortunately for most movie fans, this tends to be a welcome task rather than a chore.

If you have special movie or DVD sites or resources that are extremely or unusually helpful or informative, please share them with us. We can't promise we'll include everything that hits our inboxes, but we will respond to all suggestions and include those sites in online updates that we also find beneficial to the book's readership. You can e-mail Ed at etittel@yahoo.com and Mike at mikec@silentpcreview.com, but be sure to put **HTPC:** at the head of the subject line in your message, to get past our spam filters. Thanks!

Video-on-Demand Info and Sites

Given that viewing video-on-demand (VOD) requires a player, and that Windows Media Player 10 is built right into MCE 2005, you should already be equipped to watch most forms of VOD on a Media Center PC. Should you run into some format you can't play back, try one of the free Cliprex players available for download at www.cliprex.com—either the Cliprex DVD Player Professional or the Cliprex DS DVD Player should be up to the task. If you're still stumped, try searching on the file extension to get more information about the type of player you'll need to play back the file or stream (if you're paying for VOD, chances are extremely good that the seller will happily provide all necessary information and probably a link to the necessary player).

Video-on-demand is a market that's really just getting started, and one that promises to explode with more vendors and many more offerings in the years ahead. The proliferation of personal video recorders such as TiVo got this movement underway, but the availability and growing popularity of Media Center PCs, network entertainment servers, and other computer-based alternatives is causing it to accelerate beyond belief. Although what you'll find here in Table C-1 represents some of the best-known names in this business, search the Web for "video-on-demand service" if you want to get a sense of how many thousands of players could be involved.

Table C-1　Video-on-Demand Sites

Site	URL	Description
CinemaNow	www.cinemanow.com	Rent, buy, or subscribe: integrates with MCE, large movie library.
LikeTelevision	tesla.liketelevision.com	Monthly or annual subscription fee: cartoons, classic TV, movies, sci-fi, vintage commercials.
MovieFlix	www.movieflix.com	Some content is free, monthly subscription: $6.95; large library of shows & movies, active community, nearly 900 MCE-format movies.
Unitedstreaming	www.unitedstreaming.com	Annual subscription $199 for home schoolers; Discovery Education's library of 4000-plus educational programs.
Vod.com	www.vod.com	No membership or subscription, pay by the minute or the movie, downloads also available; large movie library.

As we were writing this book, Microsoft was holding its annual Tech-Ed conference in Orlando. They use the conference as a platform to talk about new tools and technologies, among other things. High on that list in Orlando was the company's announcements of major partnerships for IPTV (a suite of tools for creating, storing, and delivering television programming over IP networks, including the Internet) with Tandberg Television, Motorola, Scientific Atlanta, and Harmonic (it already had numerous other IPTV agreements with other major market players). It's not presuming too much to predict a much greater media presence on the Internet, nor is it pure "crystal balling" to guess that MCE will be able to accommodate IPTV data streams.

DVD Rental Services

For those who travel and like to carry movies along, or those who can't (or don't want to) tie up their Internet links with streaming media, DVDs remain a good source of entertainment content. They're also a terrific medium on which to acquire and store old or offbeat movies or programs not likely to be rebroadcast any time soon.

Though the movie rental business today is a far different animal than it was in the last century, DVD rental services remain a good option for viewing movies that you don't necessarily want to buy. Many of these services support Internet access for selecting DVDs and managing account status, even if they do use the mail to move DVD rentals in and out of your household.

Here again, what's shown in Table C-2 is just a smattering of a great many possible providers. Use your favorite search engine to add to this list (and do share your favorites for inclusion in a later edition in this book and on the book's companion Web site).

Table C-2   DVD Rental Sites

Site	URL	Description
Blockbuster Online	www.blockbuster.com	Monthly subscription $14.99, new orders accepted when returns received by mail.
Cafedvd	www.cafedvd.com	Subscription or a la carte rentals, great catalog, lots of foreign films; standard term: 8-day rental, $3 per extra week per DVD.
DVD Avenue	www.dvdavenue.com	Monthly subscription plans starting at $19.95, pre-paid return postage; great catalog; also includes Playstation games.
CleanFilms	www.cleanfilms.com	Supplies DVD rentals and sales from which profanity, sexual situations, and violence have been removed; $19.95 monthly.
Netflix	www.netflix.com	Monthly subscription plans starting at about $9.99; large library, good terms.

Readers outside North America will please forgive us for not mentioning sites that cater to other parts of the world. But a visit to any good search engine, especially one that can help find sites by geographical proximity or language, will help you quickly find as many as listed in Table C-2, if not more.

Movie Information Sites

Sure, MCE will use its built-in tools to look up movie metadata on your behalf. But for real movie buffs, those kinds of brief listings just whet their appetites and make them beg for more. Don't beg! Visit one or more of the sites listed in Table C-3 instead (and don't forget the many great movie almanacs and guides also available in print, either).

Table C-3   Movie Databases and Information Sites

Site	URL	Description
As Open Database	www.asopen.org	Open editor-managed filmography and movie database.
The Digital Bits	www.thedigitalbits.com	Latest gossip, rumors, and info on upcoming DVD releases.
Hollywood Movies	movies.about.com	News, reviews, and movie information, listings, and so on.
Internet Movie Database	www.imdb.com	The "mother of all movie databases," with information about more than 200,000 movies available.
littleman.com	www.littleman.com	Movie listings and additional information.
Miscellaneous movie Info	Movies.about.com/ od/miscellaneous	Movie information about actors, directors, soundtracks, and so on.
Rasp New Movie Database	rasp.nexenservices.com	Information about movies made since 1950; some spotty earlier coverage; great links to partner sites.
Your Movie Database	www.ymdb.com	Community supplied and managed movie information, lists, discussions, and polls.

Don't forget that when it comes to looking for information online, a search engine can be your best friend. The more you know about what you're looking for, the better your results will usually be. In addition to Google and Yahoo! (our two personal favorites) we also make heavy use of Ask Jeeves (www.ask.com) because it takes loosely worded queries and often produces good results. When we really don't know exactly what we're after, Ask Jeeves often helps us grope our way to where we want to be.

Digital Music Information and Resources

The World Wide Web is an incredible playground for digital music fans. There are more ways to acquire digital music now than ever before, and the number of models supported continues to grow. The sites mentioned in this appendix represent only the smallest fraction of what's available, but all are sites that your authors (and other digital music fanciers and gurus) find particularly noteworthy. All sites appear in alphabetical order in each of the tables in this appendix; this is purely for convenience and says nothing about their rankings or relative importance.

As always, another good way to start looking for information or outlets is to visit the companion Web site for this book. Not only will you find live links to everything mentioned here (and elsewhere in this book), but you'll also find new and updated information there. Because new music and sites that cater to music fans come and go all the time, keeping up with changes requires regular effort. Fortunately for most music lovers, including your authors, this is a worthwhile endeavor.

If you know about special music information, playlist or purchase/subscription sites or resources that really should be included in these listings, please share them with us. We can't promise we'll include everything that hits our inboxes, but we will respond to all suggestions and include those sites in online updates that appear beneficial to the book's readership. You can e-mail Ed at etittel@yahoo.com and Mike at mikec@silentpcreview.com, but be sure to put **HTPC:** at the head of the subject line in your message, to get past our spam filters. Thanks!

Music Download/Access Sites

Though some pundits are predicting that buying music could become totally passé (see the next section here for an explanation of why this might indeed be true), there are still plenty of outlets where listeners can purchase music, either by the album or by the song. Table D-1 lists numerous well-known examples where you must pay for your listening pleasure.

Table D-1 Fee-Based Digital Music Downloads

Site	URL	Description
Artist Direct	www.artistdirect.com	Buy music by the song ($0.99) or the album ($9.99 and up) for download.
Buy.com	www.buy.com	Click Music Downloads to buy by the song ($0.79) or the album (prices vary).
MP3.com	www.mp3.com	Find songs and albums, and where to buy them (prices vary).
MSN Music	music.msn.com	Access to music downloads, news, videos, radio, and more.
Musicmatch Music Store	www.musicmatch.com	Click Music Store to buy songs ($0.99) or albums ($9.99 and up) for download.
MusicNow	www.musicnow.com	Buy music downloads by the song ($0.99) or the album ($9.99 and up).

There are also sites where music is available mostly for free (all of the sites mentioned in Table D-1 offer some free content, but it's limited). These sites (see some of them in Table D-2) all adhere to the doctrine of *copyleft*, which is often explained as the opposite of copyright. Copyleft basically means that the music is free because artists have agreed to surrender royalties in exchange for wider distribution but retain other licensing rights and ultimate ownership. In fact, you must agree to a free art license to download and play copyleft works legally. You can find other free music sites outside this community, but beware of potential copyright infringement issues and proceed at your own risk (that's why we don't mention them here).

Table D-2 Free (Copyleft) Digital Music Downloads

Site	URL	Description
easyMusic.com	www.easymusic.com	Offers both copyright and copyleft music downloads.
Internet Archive	www.archive.org	Click Live Music Archive for legal access to 20,000 live concert recordings, and "Netlabels" for access to lots of indie tracks.
Opsound	www.opsound.org	Open Sound Resource offers sounds, music, radio, and more.
Prison Soup Records	www.prisonsoup.com	Experimental electro netlabel offers all kinds of genres and artists.
Purevolume	www.purevolume.com	Promos, freebies; good search engine, great selection.

Site	URL	Description
SoundClick	www.soundclick.com	Large, well-organized collection of copyleft music.
The Weed Files	www.weed-files.com	Sizable collection of indies, with 70,000 song "CD Baby" catalog also available there soon.
Uberlabel.com	www.uberlabel.com	Look for "creative commons free music downloads" on the site.

Music Subscription Services

For those who like to listen to lots of different kinds of music, renting access to a large library of tunes may be a better deal than buying (but be sure to read the "Music: Rent or Buy?" sidebar at the end of this section before plunking down any of your hard-earned cash). Music subscription services usually charge modest fees of less than $15 a month for access to their music collections, and indeed many people feel like this offers an unbeatable deal. It seems to be tailor-made for a Media Center PC, where you're hooked up to the Internet as well as to a quality listening environment.

In fact, music subscription is turning into a big business and is attracting all kinds of interest and activity. As we write this appendix, rumors are flying thick and fast that Apple's iTunes and MSN Music are both pondering subscription deals and seem likely to launch their own offerings—perhaps even before this book makes it off the presses.

As elsewhere, what's shown in Table D-3 is just a sampling of numerous possible music subscription providers. Use your favorite search engine to add to this list (and do share your favorites for inclusion in a later edition in this book and on the book's companion Web site).

Table D-3   Music Subscription Services

Site	URL	Description
eMusic	www.emusic.com	Access to over half a million songs for about $10 a month.
Napster To Go	www.napster.com	Access to over a million songs for $9.95 a month; requires XP and Windows Media Player 10 (slam dunk for MCE).
Yahoo! Music Unlimited	music.yahoo.com/unlimited	Yahoo's 1,000,000 songs are available for $4.99 per month (billed annually) or $6.99 per month (billed monthly).
Rhapsody	www.rhapsody.com	RealAudio's e-music service offers access to over a million songs for $14.99 per month.

Music: Rent or Buy?

When you sign up for a music subscription, be sure to read the terms of use carefully. Some subscription services are good only on the machine to which downloads are made (in other words, you can't copy them to another machine and play them there; in some cases, you may not be able to download them to an MP3 player, either). And although you can download songs to your machine, you can play them back only as long as your subscription stays current (if your account expires, so does your ability to play back songs from the service). That explains why many people use subscription services to listen to lots of stuff, but then buy the songs or albums that they really, really like—so they can listen in perpetuity, and copy those songs to other PCs or players as they see fit. By itself, rental alone doesn't seem to cover all the bases for many music lovers.

Though there are some gotchas covered in the following sidebar, music subscription services are a great fit with Media Center PCs. They just might be worth joining as a great way to gain access to a huge music collection for a small (but ever-present) monthly cost.

Music Information Sites

Digital music is very much a world unto itself. Those who dig into its depths will find themselves learning lots about music file formats, format conversions, and music encoding, decoding, ripping, and burning. If you find yourself wanting to explore this vast and mellifluous realm, you'll probably find the digital music resources at the sites mentioned in Table D-4 interesting, if not downright useful and informative. There are plenty of books and articles on this topic, too, not to mention reams and reams of articles and how-tos also available online. Use the sites in Table D-4 purely as a point of departure, and let your fancy take you where it will.

Table D-4 Music Info Sites

Site	URL	Description
AudioForums.com	`www.audioforums.com`	Resources, forums, plus some great Windows XP audio optimization tips.
CNET Music Center	`www.cnet.com`	Articles, how-tos, software, devices, and anything else related to digital music you might want to find or know.
Digital Music	`mp3.about.com`	News, articles, tools, and reviews on digital music.

Site	URL	Description
Digital Music Overview	`www.intel.com/personal/do_more/music/`	How intel processors, chipsets, and technology help make digital music sound better, along with lots of info and other pointers.
Hydrogen Audio	`www.hydrogenaudio.org`	Dedicated to scientific evaluation and development of codecs; everything you need to know about codecs.
MP3Machine	`www.mp3machine.com`	Poke around in the Windows directory for information about all kinds of digital music tools, technologies, and sound library tips and techniques.

Don't forget either that when it comes to looking for information online, a search engine can be your best friend. The more you know about what you're looking for, the better your results will usually be. In addition to Google and Yahoo! (two personal favorites) we also make heavy use of Ask Jeeves (`www.ask.com`) because it takes loosely worded queries and often produces good results. When we really don't know exactly what we're after, Ask Jeeves often helps us grope our way to where we want to be.

Windows Radio: Finding Stations and Recording

With the right kind of TV tuner card in a Media Center PC, tuning into FM radio stations on the machine is easy. But it's also the case that many radio stations broadcast right onto the Internet so that any audio-equipped PC with loudspeakers can tune in online rather than through the radio.

One of MCE 2005's more vexing limitations is its inability to record broadcast FM radio. But there are other ways to capture radio outside the MCE umbrella. Later in this appendix, you'll find pointers to various software tools that will permit you to use your PC to record radio broadcasts in much the same way you use the EPG to record TV broadcasts in MCE or with a third-party alternative like TiVo. And this software can save broadcasts in any number of listenable audio formats, including MP3, Real Audio, or Windows Media (WMA).

If you have special sites or resources you find to be extremely or unusually helpful or informative, please share that information with us. We can't promise that we'll include everything that hits our inbox, but we will respond to all suggestions and include in online updates those that we agree will benefit the book's general readership. You can e-mail Ed at etittel@yahoo.com, and Mike at mikec@silentpcreview.com, but be sure to put **HTPC:** at the head of the subject line in your message, in order to get past our spam filters. Thanks!

Internet Radio

Except perhaps for local stations that don't stream audio onto the Internet, one can't help but be amazed by the number, range, and variety of stations that are available to any PC with a working Internet connection, a Web browser, and the ability to play back one or more music/audio formats (the most common include Windows Media or WMA, MP3, and Real Audio or RA and RAM).

Thus, although MCE may not be able to record broadcast FM radio, it's relatively trivial to augment MCE with Web-based applications that are happy to play Internet radio stations using Windows Media Player 10 (installed as a key element of the MCE runtime environment). After that's done, it's surprisingly easy to capture radio broadcasts in forms that Media Player can handle (and that MCE can manage as part of the digital recordings under My Music's purview and control).

Because there are so many thousands of Internet radio stations around, Table E-1 provides pointers to directories to such stations rather than listing individual station URLs themselves. Most of these sites include tools to help you browse what's available by category or location, so you should be able to find plenty of listening material. And because the most effective use of MCE requires a broadband or faster Internet connection, it's no big stretch to observe that (like most forms of streaming data) Internet radio also works best on such Internet links as well.

Table E-1   Internet Radio Station Directory Web Sites

Site	URL	Description
Launchcast	`launch.yahoo.com/launchcast`	Customizable virtual radio stations by selection, genre, theme, and so on
Live 365	`www.live365.com`	Searchable listings of thousands of free Internet radio stations
My Radio	`Windowsmedia.com/radiotuner`	Microsoft's searchable, genre-oriented Windows Media radio tuner
Nullsoft SHOUTcast	`www.shoutcast.com`	Winamp-based streaming audio, with 1,000s of worldwide broadcasts on the SHOUTcast directory
Radio Free World	`www.radiofreeworld.com`	Guide to free Internet radio and TV stations on the Web
Radio Locator	`www.radio-locator.com`	Worldwide directory of Internet radio stations, formerly known as the MIT List of Radio Stations on the Internet
Radio Tower	`www.radiotower.com`	Radio and music listings in a comprehensive, searchable Internet radio station guide

This is just the tip of the veritable iceberg, as a quick hop to your favorite search engine for a look at "Internet radio stations" or "Internet radio station directory" will quickly confirm.

Windows Radio Capture

One of the most glaring oversights in MCE is its inability to record the radio stations it will so readily and cheerfully allow its readers to tune in. Though a workaround to record those input streams isn't yet available, given the huge number of radio stations that broadcast on the Internet and the wide variety of software tools that can record those input streams, if you're willing to shell out of MCE you can indeed record plenty of radio if you so choose.

As is the case with so much other Windows software, you have your choice of more capable, full-featured commercial software that costs money, versus somewhat less friendly and capable free software. Whether or not you choose to invest your own funds into this activity, you'll find there's no shortage of options for recording the Internet radio stations to which you might choose to listen.

These tools generally tend to support the most popular audio file formats, whether free or for a fee, including Windows Media (WMA), Real Audio (RA or RAM), MP3, wave (WAV) files (another native Windows audio format), and so forth. Table E-2 lists some of the more popular commercial and freeware radio recording tools (please note that any prices listed are the prices at the time of writing and may be subject to change).

Table E-2   Internet Radio Recording Tools

Tool	URL	Description
AudioStreamer	www.rmbsoft.com	Receive, record, and play Internet radio ($39.95, free eval)
Audiolib MP3 Recorder	www.audiolib.com	Shareware for capturing PC audio into WAV or MPC ($19.95)
Easy Hi-Q Recorder	www.roemersoftware.com	Easy, visual VCR-like PC audio recording tool supports all major formats ($29.95, free eval)
FairStars Recorder	www.fairstars.com	Recording all PC audio in multiple formats ($24.95, free eval)
My MP3 Recorder	www.softpedia.com	Record Internet radio, save to MP3 or WAV formats (freeware)
OpD2d	www.opcode.co.uk/opd2d/	Direct-to-disk audio recording in MP3 and WAV formats (freeware)
Replay Radio	www.replay-radio.com	Record Internet radio broadcasts in multiple formats ($29.95, free eval)
RipCast	www.xoteck.com/ripcast/	Shareware for capturing SHOUTcast streams into WAV and MP3 formats ($17.95)

If you spend some time with these tools, you'll quickly realize they fall into two broad categories: those designed as general-purpose audio capture tools, which you'd use with some other tool or Web site to select the radio station you want to record, and those designed for radio capture, which include station searching and selection tools as well as recording and capture tools. The biggest trade-off between free and commercial tools is convenience versus cost, so that to get the kinds of program guide scanning and selection tools you find in MCE for recording TV, you'll want to investigate the commercial programs. If you have more time than money, you may be inclined to stick with freeware offerings instead.

Beyond the tools mentioned in the preceding table, inexperienced users may find the About.com article "How to Record Streaming Audio from Internet Radio Stations and Sources" useful. It explains how to use a number of tools and utilities to tune into, select, and record Internet radio stations, and includes pointers to general radio information, articles and tutorials, and more. You can check out this great article and its pointers at `radio.about.com/cs/recordingstreams/ht/RecordStreams.htm`.

PC TV and Related Hardware Info

Some of the most interesting — and vexing — problems come from trying to integrate TV hardware with Windows Media Center Edition. Sure, hooking up a conventional TV set is pretty easy. But start adding one or more set-top boxes, satellite receivers, and so forth, and things get interesting in a hurry. Add the emerging standards and technologies for High Definition Television, or HDTV, and they can soon become overwhelming. As we write this book, the current official line on MCE and HDTV is "broadcast only," which means that while you can grab broadcast HDTV signals through properly equipped MCE-compatible tuner cards, there's no easy or officially supported way to integrate an HDTV digital set-top cable box or satellite receiver into this mix.

That said, there are plenty of rumors that the next version of MCE will include such support (but rumors that preceded the launch of MCE 2005 made the same claims). The real issues are not technological, but rather legal and regulatory. Although the Washington, D.C. District Court of Appeals struck down the FCC's "broadcast flag" requirement in May 2005, none of the vendors we asked point blank would say if they would take this ruling to mean they could incorporate direct attachments for cable or satellite boxes into their HDTV cards or not. We guess nobody still knows for sure if North American video/tuner card manufacturers will take this plunge or not. All we can say is that you can already integrate both cable and satellite HDTV feeds into Media Center PCs built for the European market, using hardware and services available in Europe (but not, alas, in North America).

The coverage in this appendix perforce deals with three sets of pointers to resources and information:

- A set of information that relates to conventional and 480i TV signals, whether broadcast, cable, or satellite based. This is by far the easiest and most straightforward TV capability in MCE 2005 and works pretty much straight out of the box. This is covered in Table F-1 and surrounding text.

- A set of information that relates to HDTV (and by extension to EDTV) also known as 480p, plus 720p and 1080i signaling (the smaller number is for EDTV, the higher numbers are for HDTV; all numbers reflect the scan lines in each digital format, where *p* is for progressive, and *i* for interlaced). This includes pointers to sources of equipment, information, troubleshooting, and news. This is covered in Table F-2 and surrounding text.

- A set of information about legal and regulatory issues surrounding HDTV, including news and information sources to let you know if and when the legal situation clears up enough to make manufacturers feel comfortable building for North American what European users already have, and service providers feel comfortable delivering what European users already consume. This is covered in Table F-3 and surrounding text.

If you have special TV or HDTV sites or resources you find to be extremely or unusually helpful or informative, please share that information with us. We can't promise that we'll include everything that hits our inboxes, but we will respond to all suggestions and include those in online updates that we agree will benefit the book's general readership. You can e-mail Ed at etittel@yahoo.com and Mike at mikec@silentpcreview.com, but be sure to put **HTPC:** at the head of the subject line in your message, in order to get past our spam filters. Thanks!

Conventional TV Information and Resources

Although working with conventional TV and MCE 2005 is about as close to "plug and play" as anything gets in this environment, that doesn't mean access to additional resources and information won't be handy from time to time. Generally, as the hardware or connections involved get more complex, the more helpful it is to lean on the experience of those who've gone before you into the deepest details of installation, configuration, and setup to get things working, or working as best they can be made to work.

We'll illustrate with an example. As part of the preparatory research for this book Ed ordered a Hush Technologies Media Center PC from Logic Supply, a reputable and competent system integrator based in Waterbury, Vermont. Because he wanted to put the coolest possible CPU into a fanless system, he requested that they build a system around an Athlon 64 processor rather than the other option, a Pentium P4. He also ordered a dual-tuner TV card (a Hauppauge WinTV-PVR-500) as well. To make a long, difficult story short, because of interrupt problems caused by the second TV tuner on that card, neither Logic Supply nor Hush Technologies could put together a system around the Athlon 64 and their chosen motherboard that would work with the dual-tuner TV card. To take delivery of a working system, Ed had to switch his CPU selection to

P4 and take the matching motherboard (a Gigabyte P4-Titan GA-8IG1000 Pro-G). The moral of the story is that component compatibility is sometimes discovered the hard way — that is, by trial and error — and that not all theoretically workable configurations turn out to be workable in practice or implementation. (A note to those with near-pathological technical tendencies: The best minds in our team later decided that timing issues related to the riser card required to insert two PCI interfaces parallel to the motherboard in the Hush case also played a role in the problems encountered with the Athlon 64 configuration.)

Because there are so many conventional TV and TV for the PC resources available online, Table F-1 is smaller than it could be, but includes sites that we found helpful in making Media Center PCs work with conventional TV, whether using single- or dual-tuner TV cards.

Table F-1   Conventional PC TV Info and Resource Sites

Site	URL	Description
Capturing TV	`dvr.about.com/od/capturetvwithacomputer/`	Covers compression, TV capture cards, DVD recording software, and basic technology articles
Digit-Life	`www.digit-life.com`	Digital lifestyle and information site, loaded with technical info and device reviews; great PC TV, video, sound, and other coverage
External PC TV Tuners	`www.digit-life.com/articles2/external-pc-tv-theor/`	Nice discussion of signals and conversions necessary to get PCs to display TV on various types of monitors (great background info)
Ruel.Net	`ruel.net`	PC-TV intro, comprehensive PC TV card listing, plus lots of other equipment, news, and hook-up info
TV-Cards	`www.tv-cards.com`	TV-card news, reviews, drivers, FAQs, links and community, plus great list of free and commercial video/TV applications

Those interested enough in TV technology and operations might also be interested in the following books:

- Robert L. Hartwig's *Basic TV Technology: Digital and Analog* (Focal Press 2005) builds up from basic electronics and signals to complex tools and technologies. Covers conventional TV and HDTV, with lots of diagrams and schematics.

- Connie Ledoux Book's *Digital Television: DTV and the Consumer* (Blackwell Professional Publishing Professional 2004) reviews the history of digital TV, including discussion of SDTV (Standard Definition TV, or 480i), EDTV (Enhanced Definition TV, or 780i), and HDTV (High Definition TV, or 1080i) including discussion of technical terms, broadcast and delivery technologies, and public policy issues.

HDTV Info and Resources

This is one of the most interesting and difficult topics in this book, not least because Microsoft's current official position on MCE 2005 and HDTV may be succinctly summarized as "broadcast only." Although it's just a matter of time before that situation changes, nobody really knows right now exactly how long it will take for MCE to add support for cable and satellite HDTV (which are already the most comprehensive, viewable, and widely available sources for HDTV programming). In fact, this will primarily depend on when the right kind of hardware becomes available to bring the same kind of support for cable and satellite HDTV into PCs that's already available for conventional TV.

HDTV is an exploding technology area and involves all kinds of issues beyond the PC connection. That's why you'll find something of a hodge-podge of equipment and service coverage, technology topics, and good troubleshooting forums in Table F-2. Keeping an eye on PC TV card vendors (like Adaptec, ATI, AVerMedia, Creative Video, Diamond, Hauppauge, Kworld, Leadtek, Pinnacle, and so forth) product announcements is probably the best way to stay tuned to when more HDTV support might be forthcoming in MCE.

Table F-2   HDTV Info and Resources

Name	URL	Description
Addicted to Digital Media	`blog.seanalexander.com`	Sean Alexander's 10/22/2004 blog lists key MS and third-party MCE-HDTV info; other blogs on MCE and HDTV also good
Engadget	`www.engadget.com`	Covers gadgets and e-toys of every description, including a great section on HDTV
HD Library	`www.hdlibrary.com`	Forums on nearly any HDTV topics you can imagine . . . and then some
HD Nut	`www.hdnut.com`	HDTV news and reviews from enthusiasts; includes complete list of HDTV broadcasters
HDTV and Digital TV Basics	`hdtvinfoport.com`	Basic technology primers, buyers guide, glossary, and more
HDTV Introduction	`www.ee.washington.edu/conselec/CE/kuhn/hdtv/95x5.htm`	Two-part engineering lecture from Prof. Kelin J. Kuhn, University of Washington on HDTV history and technology
HDTV Magazine	`www.hdtvmagazine.com`	HDTV print and e-zine offer news, reviews, and opinions

Name	URL	Description
Hidef Magazine	`www.hidef.org`	Free print and e-zine coverage of HDTV news, reviews, info, glossary forums, FAQs, and more
Home Theater Spot	`www.hometheaterspot.com`	A general home theater site with heavy emphasis on HDTV, plus lots of stats and measurements to back up reviews
How HDTV Works	`electronics.howstuffworks.com./hdtv.htm`	Good basic description of HDTV terms, technology, and equipment (also covers many other topics related to HTPC)
MCE Usenet Group	`www.msusenet.com/forumdisplay.php?f=98`	Microsoft's MCE Usenet group includes constant detailed Q & A on HDTV topics, mostly troubleshooting and configuration details
The HDTV Tuner	`www.the-hdtv-tuner.com`	HDTV information, explanations, and equipment reviews
Ultimate AV	`ultimateavmag.com`	Magazine with news, reviews, and technical information on audio and video, with heavy HDTV coverage

HDTV Regulatory Issues and Info

The key historical issue in regard to HDTV recording has been what's called the *broadcast flag*, a sequence of bits that identifies digital HDTV signals and copyright status. The FCC had mandated that by mid 2005 all digital video recorders be capable of recognizing this flag and configured not to record bitstreams with the flag turned on. On May 6, 2005, the Washington, D.C. U.S. Court of Appeals struck down this ruling, in part because cable and satellite transmissions were deemed not to be broadcast media and therefore not subject to FCC control. Although the ruling no longer stands as we write this summary, music, motion picture, and TV studios are lobbying Congress to seek legislation to enforce as law what the FCC couldn't enforce as regulation. This probably explains why none of the PC TV card manufacturers is yet willing to commit to more capable HDTV hardware that would also support links to cable boxes and satellite receivers. Only time will tell how this situation will work out, but we believe it's pretty likely that we'll see hardware support for cable and satellite HDTV before the end of this decade.

The pointers in Table F-3 are something of a mixed bag and involve advocacy groups, technology news outlets, and plaintiffs in the suit against the FCC that brought this matter to a May 2005 ruling from a Federal Court of Appeals.

Table F-3   HDTV Regulatory News and Info Sites

Site	URL	Description
Boing Boing	`boingboing.net`	Eclectic news and opinion feed that has covered HDTV issues and debate closely.
Electronic Frontier Foundation	`www.eff.org`	One of the parties to the broadcast flag suit against the FCC; you'll find coverage and technical information galore on their site.
HDTV Advocate	`www.interfacers.com/CurrentEvents/HDTV`	HDTV advocacy and information group.
News.com	`news.com.com`	Source for breaking news online has covered HDTV issues closely.
Public Knowledge	`www.publicknowledge.org`	Another party to the suit; site offers detailed summary, explanation, and consumer-friendly views of the issues involved.
Wired	`www.wired.com`	Well-known technology and gadget news, reviews, and trend analysis; has covered HDTV issues since day one.

Home Video Hardware and Media Info

Media Center PCs not only deal with commercial video, but they also support numerous digital home video formats as well. This creates all kinds of opportunities to download and work on digital home movies and then make them part of the multimedia collection that MCE manages on your behalf.

But as with other aspects of MCE, a little bit of information and guidance can go a long way when it comes to migrating movies into your Media Center PC. In this appendix, you'll find information about copying home videos to your PC, format conversion and editing tools, and recommended camcorders and connections you might consider using if you don't have a camcorder already, or are considering a new one.

One of the unsung heroes of MCE 2005 is Windows Movie Maker. Although it's available as a free download for Windows XP in general, it's included with MCE. The program allows you to create, edit, and share your home movies with others (you can share them via the Web, e-mail, or on CD). The addition of the right third-party software makes it possible to burn DVDs of your home movies. These are the tools (and related resources) covered in Table G-1.

If you have special home video or camcorder sites or resources you find to be extremely or unusually helpful or informative, please share that information with us. We can't promise that we'll include everything that hits our inboxes, but we will respond to all suggestions and include those in online updates that we agree will benefit the book's general readership. You can e-mail Ed at etittel@yahoo.com and Mike at mikec@silentpcreview.com, but be sure to put **HTPC:** at the head of the subject line in your message, in order to get past our spam filters. Thanks!

Home Video Info, Tools, and Resources

Theoretically, working with home videos on Windows Media Center Edition is as easy as attaching an IEEE 1394 (FireWire) cable from your camera to your HTPC. But if your camera doesn't support FireWire, you'll have to acquire an analog capture card—and hope you've got a remaining slot free to make the connection work. On the other hand, if your HTPC doesn't support FireWire (and some of the motherboards we checked out for this book didn't, nor do all of the cases include front-panel FireWire access—highly desirable for camcorder hook-ups), you may also want to acquire a FireWire/IEEE 1394 PCI or PCI-E X1 expansion card.

But once the physical hook-up is accomplished, it's really not that bad. Once movies hit the MCE desktop, Windows Movie Maker becomes your (free) tool of choice for editing and managing home video content.

There's a whole world of information emerging around Windows Movie Maker (as we write this, the most current version available is 2.1). You'll find pointers to downloads, documentation, and discussions in Table G-1, as well to tools you can use to turn Microsoft Movie Maker home movies into DVDs.

Because there are so many home video resources available online, Table G-1 is shorter than it probably should be, and includes sites that we've found particularly useful in dealing with our own PC home video situations and learning requirements. Therefore, we're especially open to your suggestions and ideas on other items that could or should be added to this category. For brevity, we also abbreviate Windows Movie Maker as WMM in the name column in Table G-1.

Table G-1   Home Video Info, Tools, and Resource Sites

Name	URL	Description
Connecting to Your Home Video Camera	www.microsoft.com/windowsxp/using/mce/getstarted/connectvideo.mspx	Step-by-step instructions on how to hook up FireWire and analog connections, including photos of cables and connectors; Very helpful.
Learning WMM	movielibrary.lynda.com/html/modPage.asp?ID=127	Movie-based tutorial with David Rivers on CD-ROM.
WMM for Beginners	www.microsoft.com/windowsxp/using/moviemaker/getstarted/default.mspx	Microsoft's introduction includes overview, tutorial, download, how-tos, and lots more.
WMM Release Notes	www.microsoft.com/windowsxp/using/moviemaker/releasenotes.mspx	Windows Movie Maker release notes for most current version.
Using WMM	www.dummies.com/WileyCDA/DummiesArticle/id-359.html	Quick and easy Windows Movie Maker tour and tutorial.

Name	URL	Description
VideoHelp	`www.videohelp.com`	Search article and guide listings for WMM coverage; also check "capture" listings: they cover most common digital video capture situations.
WMM 2 Review	`www.winsupersite.com/reviews/wmm2.asp`	Paul Thurrot's SuperSite for Windows coverage of Movie Maker 2 is definitely worth a read-through.
WMM Manual	`www.underwaterphotography.com/Video-Editing/Windows-Movie-Maker/Software/windowsmoviemaker.asp`	Reasonably complete, third-party, "tell it like it is" user manual for Windows Movie Maker.
Windows Movie Makers	`www.windowsmoviemakers.net`	Great independent site with tips, tutorials, add-on, forums and hardware recommendations, all related to Windows Movie Maker.

Those readers interested enough in Windows Movie Maker to want to do more reading might be interested in the following books:

- Jan Ozer's *Microsoft Windows Movie Maker 2: Visual Quickstart Guide* (Peachpit 2004) brings friendly and approachable Visual Quickstart Guide coverage to Windows Movie Maker. Clear, well-written, and chock-full of examples.

- John Buechler's *Microsoft Windows Movie Maker 2: Do Amazing Things* (MS Press 2004) provides a great overview of the tool and how best to use it, and also includes lots of step-by-step instructions and copious examples.

Home Video Hardware Info and Resources

This is another tangential topic for this book, but those seeking compatible camcorders and other video gear that works with a Media Center PC (or perhaps that should be the other way around) should find these resources informative and hopefully useful. We've tried to steer clear of retailers because those who want to sell you their products are not always the most objective or reliable sources of information (you will find one such listing, but only because it points to a free handbook that's well researched and written).

This is another busy market niche, as the number of publications you'll see mentioned in Table G-2 readily attests. Between these and purely online enthusiast and review sites, there's no shortage of resources upon which to draw—though you will find only very scarce mention of MCE at this point. Over the next year or two as more home movie buffs get to know more about MCE, we expect this to change.

Table G-2   Home Video Hardware Info and Resources

Name	URL	Description
AVguide	www.avguide.com	Print and online magazine that specializes in audio and video reviews, with regular coverage of home movie video equipment
Desktop Video Handbook	www.videoguys.com/dtvhome.html	A reasonably comprehensive and approachable guide to home video creation, editing, and sharing (free, but from a video vendor)
DisplayMate's Best Video Hardware Guide	www.displaymate.com/best.html	The leading vendor of digital display output test and measurement tools rates computer video and output devices yearly; definitely worth a visit
DV doctor	www.dvdoctor.net	News, reviews, articles, and advice on editing digital video and creating DVDs
Internet Video Magazine	www.internetvideomag.com	Covers topics related to creating, sharing, and recording video from the Internet; lots of useful news and information
REwind Video	www.rewindvideo.com	E-zine for independent and amateur filmmakers, mostly video oriented
Sound and Vision Magazine	www.soundandvisionmag.com	Premier audio and video product news, reviews, and opinions
Videomaker Magazine	www.videomaker.com	News, reviews, how-tos and information for home video buffs

PC Audio Hardware and Playback Info

Media Center PCs must include a sound card so they can deliver audio output for digital music, plus television and movie sound from various sources. There's a lot of technology at work involved in pumping sound out of a PC, and depending on how much work, time, and money you want to spend on making the most of audio output, there are myriad ways to actually produce the sounds to which you'll ultimately listen.

Listening to a Media Center PC can be as simple as hooking up a set of speakers directly to that PC's sound card, or as complex as linking sound card output into a receiver or pre-amp to integrate the PC into an existing home entertainment or theater system. To make things yet more interesting (and sometimes frustrating for those in search of quick, simple answers) audio is a world where at least as many aficionados and fanatics are active as you'll find in the various PC communities around the world.

Thus, the intersection between the PC and high-end audio is one where considerable interest, an embarrassment of rich options and choices, and an almost unlimited opportunity to spend time and money all come together. We urge readers to seek alternatives that fit their budgets and their entertainment center racks or furniture as the most practical ways to resist inevitable urges to go overboard on audio equipment. When researching a replacement for our own pre-amp that could integrate with an MCE-compatible remote control, for example, we could only laugh when the initial results from online searches for compatible gear turned up units priced from $5,000 to $8,000. Although we could indeed fit such enclosures into our audio equipment racks, there was no way we could fit that expense into our annual equipment budgets (that's more than any of us normally spends on audio and PC equipment in any given year).

If you have special sites or resources you find to be extremely or unusually helpful or informative, please share that information with us. We can't promise to include everything that hits our inboxes, but we will respond to all suggestions and include those in online updates that we agree will benefit the book's general readership. You can e-mail Ed at etittel@yahoo.com and Mike at mikec@silentpcreview.com, but be sure to put **HTPC:** at the head of the subject line in your message, in order to get past our spam filters. Thanks!

PC Audio Info and Resources

There's a strong but understandable tendency to lump the categories of PC and digital audio together. Thus, though some of the resources and references you find here may seem a bit off the PC track, they can (and will) still provide plenty of information about and insight into the digital audio technologies and tools that PCs use.

We've tried to collect resources and references that provide technical information about PC (and digital) audio, file formats, conversion tools and techniques, and sound cards or add-on equipment that allows PCs to store, create, record, and play back high-quality audio of many different kinds from innumerable sources. To us, one of the biggest attractions for MCE is its ability to gather up, organize, and manage vast collections of sound. That's why at least one of your authors plans to digitize his sizable analog music collection on tape and on vinyl and bring them under MCE's umbrella. We have to suspect this same impetus will move a lot of other baby boomers (like some of your authors) who would like to dig into their sound archives with greater ease than current technology and playback equipment permits.

Because there are so many thousands of PC audio resources available online, Table H-1 is far shorter than it probably should be, but it includes sites that we've found particularly useful in dealing with our own PC audio situation and learning requirements. Still, we're especially open to your suggestions and ideas on other items that could or should be added to this category.

Table H-1 PC Audio Info and Resource Sites

Site	URL	Description
Audio Engineering Society	www.aes.org/resources/www-links/	Audio- and music-related links cover conventional and PC equipment, publications, and more. Good search tools, too
Audioholics	www.audioholics.com	Online A/V magazine, with great buying advice and info
Audio World	www.audioworld.com	News, info, reviews, and community for anybody interested in audio, with lots of home theater and PC audio coverage
Audio Forums	www.audioforums.com	Expert and user dialog on digital audio hardware, software, setup, tools, and techniques
Creating Digital Audio Resources	ahds.ac.uk/creating/guides/audio-resources/GGP_Audio_Overview.htm	AHDS Guide to Good Practice covers digital audio hardware, analog to digital conversion, and use of computers
Educypedia	users.pandora.be/educypedia/electronics/digitalaudio.htm	Covers digital audio, file formats, all kinds of audio topics, and hardware, including PC topics

Site	URL	Description
PC AV Tech	www.pcavtech.com	Sound card and PC video gear tests, device reports, advice, and analysis (somewhat dated, but still good)
PC Recording	www.pcrecording.com	Covers hardware options, software, setups, tips, and reviews
Primer on PC Audio	www.highcriteria.com	Follow primer link for info on PC audio technology, file formats, CDs, and more
Sound on Sound	www.soundonsound.com	Bills itself as "world's best music recording magazine" and includes coverage of PC and conventional audio tools and hardware
Surround Associates	www.surroundassociates.com/fqmain.html	Great surround sound FAQ from a commercial but nevertheless excellent source

Inevitably, some readers will visit one of more of the sites in Table H-1 and note a strong emphasis on audio hardware as well as coverage of PC audio (and related sound cards and other gear). Many of these sites do indeed cover all these topics and more, but because they turned up as we were searching for especially informative or useful PC audio sites, they show up here. If apologies appear necessary, consider them proffered! And remember that these listings represent just the smallest fraction of the possibilities available, as a quick hop to your favorite search engine for a look at "PC audio information" or "PC audio resources" will quickly confirm.

Audio Hardware Info and Resources

This truly is a tangential topic for this book, but those seeking compatible high-end audio equipment to support a Media Center PC (or perhaps that should be the other way around) should find these resources informative and hopefully useful. We've tried to steer clear of out-and-out retailers because those who want to sell you their products may not always be the most objective or reliable sources of information.

This is also a very well-served market niche, as the number of publications you'll see mentioned in Table H-2 readily attests. Between these and purely online enthusiast and review sites, there's no shortage of resources upon which to draw — though you will find only very scarce mention of MCE at this point. Over the next year or two as more audiophiles wake up to HTPC in general and get to know more about MCE in particular, we expect this to change dramatically.

Table H-2   Audio Hardware Info and Resources

Name	URL	Description
AVguide.com	`www.avguide.com`	Reviews, news on home theater and stereo gear, plus music and movies (reviews from Absolute Sound and The Perfect Vision)
Electronic House	`www.electronichouse.com`	Magazine covers all kinds of e-home topics, including home theater and digital issues
Enjoy the Music	`www.enjoythemusic.com`	High-end hobbyist audiophile site with lots of interesting, opinionated hardware reviews
Home Theater Magazine	`www.hometheatermag.com`	Online articles, reviews, news, and opinions, plus an active online user community
Sound and Vision	`www.soundandvisionmag.com`	Magazine devoted to high-end home AV equipment, news, and reviews
Stereophile	`www.stereophile.com`	Magazine provides news and reviews of high-end audio equipment and recordings
The Absolute Sound	`www.theabsolutesound.com`	Popular, informative high-end audio magazine provides news and reviews; has been around for more than 20 years
The Perfect Vision	`www.theperfectvision.com`	High-performance home theater magazine reviews equipment, technology, and tools
WOList: Audio	`wolist.com/wo/recreation/audio-21021/`	Community listings of audiophile resources, including pubs, e-zines, tips and tweaks, equipment reviews, and more

Index

Index

Continued

Continued

Continued